Echoes from Dharamsala

Echoes from Dharamsala

*Music in the Life of a Tibetan
Refugee Community*

KEILA DIEHL

University of California Press

BERKELEY   LOS ANGELES   LONDON

"Knockin' on Heaven's Door" © 1973, 1974 Ram's Horn Music.
All rights reserved. International copyright secured. Reprinted by
permission.

All photographs by the author

University of California Press
Berkeley and Los Angeles, California

University of California Press, Ltd.
London, England

Library of Congress Cataloging-in-Publication Data

Diehl, Keila.
   Echoes from Dharamsala : music in the life of a Tibetan refugee
community / Keila Diehl.
     p.   cm.
   Includes bibliographical references (p.) and index.
   ISBN 0-520-23043-4 (cloth : alk. paper).—ISBN 0-520-23044-2
(paper : alk. paper)
     1. Tibetans—India—Dharamsala—Music—History and criticism.
I. Title.

ML338.8.D53 D54   2002
7809.899954054—dc21   2001005934

Manufactured in Canada

10 09 08 07 06 05 04 03 02
10 9 8 7 6 5 4 3 2 1

The paper used in this publication is both acid-free and totally
chlorine-free (TCF). It meets the minimum requirements of
ANSI/NISO Z39.48–1992 (R 1997) (Permanence of Paper). ⊗

In memory of Ida Mechan Mackie (1899–1990)
Memsahib, theosophist, grandmother

Contents

Illustrations

Acknowledgments

These acknowledgments are meant to underscore the remarkable degree to which the process of transforming experiences into narratives is both rational and fortuitous. Attempting to unearth the *sön tsa* (seeds and roots) of this project has revealed the paradoxical ways in which one is always both entangled in and supported by multiple webs of influence and yet often simply winging it. This book is the product of my own interests and inclinations, anthropological training in a particular program at a particular theoretical moment with particular professors, the specific conditions of my fieldwork, the people who brought it to life, and various twists of fate.

Curiosity about the colonial branch of my family tree—a long, sturdy limb with branches in India, Malaysia, Palestine, and Nigeria—led me to graduate study in anthropology. Thanks are due to all the far-flung great aunts and uncles who shared their stories and to an Indian college professor who kindly scolded me out of feeling guilty for enjoying those colonial tales. She put everything in a compassionate historical perspective and convinced me that one could, in fact, be of British descent and have something to contribute to postcolonial studies.

Since its founding more than three decades ago, the Folklore and Ethnomusicology Program at the University of Texas at Austin (now the Américo Paredes Center for Cultural Studies) has been philosophically and methodologically grounded in the folksy assertion that "expressive culture"—music, art, dance, poetry, and so forth—is not "fluff." To sum it up, culture is not only reflected in but is also actively created by expressive performances. In general, the serious study of aesthetics and performance in the social sciences has, until relatively recently, been obstructed by a general tendency to consider the arts as mere reflections of culture or "reality" or as cathartic exercises that facilitate the maintenance of social order, the expression of fantasies, and the venting of emotions. While such frameworks restrict the possibility of artistic expression to those ideas and styles a group already knows are possible or relegate the gift of artistic genius to a handful of specialists, I found myself as a graduate student at University of Texas, Austin, among faculty and students who were all convinced intellectually and experientially of the salience of artistic expression as a site for examining wider social and political issues. "Be multisensory!" were my advisor Steven Feld's parting words when I left for India in 1994.

In addition to his extraordinary ethnographic attention to emotions and senses, an extension of Feld's influence on this project has been his commitment to accepting responsibility for the inherently political nature of anthropological research and working hard to maintain an honest balance between scholarship and advocacy. I have been deeply inspired and encouraged by his handling of the production and marketing of his commercial recordings of Kaluli sounds and by his continuing dedication to supporting the indigenous people of New Guinea and Irian Jaya.

Other anthropology professors and students opened intellectual and creative spaces that are explored in this book, particularly James Brow, Andrew Causey, Aaron Fox, Edmund Gordon, Calla Jacobson, Deborah Kapchan, Ward Keeler, P. Christiaan Klieger, Frank Korom, Meg McLagen, Kirin Narayan, Dawa Norbu, and David Samuels.

As I expected, doing fieldwork in a place that is a focal point of Western interest presents its own challenges. Unlike the researcher of yore, who was a strange object of curiosity to the natives, in Dharamsala I found myself nearly doing back flips in offices, shops, and homes trying to differentiate myself from the droves of Western tourists in the area. Once this was accomplished—primarily by virtue of the length of my stay—I then had to negotiate around and cooperate with the continual flow of film crews, journalists, college study-abroad programs, and other doctoral students researching various aspects of Tibetan culture. All this energy aimed at documenting a small town's life has a huge impact on the community, particularly on those individuals who are well informed and articulate in English. Furthermore, a widespread cynicism about *Injis* had developed among many who had had previous contact with foreign researchers, owing to the number of promises that had remained unfulfilled. In those circumstances, I felt great respect, gratitude, and responsibility for those refugees who chose to engage in professional and personal relationships with me.

I am particularly grateful to members of the older generation of Tibetans in exile who have demonstrated genuine interest in my work and who are, or were, remarkably open-minded, creative, and intellectually and politically active. Sadly, several of the most generous, knowledgeable, and caring of these elders I had the privilege to learn from and befriend passed away soon after I returned home. Kongoe Maya, Professor Jampa Gyaltsen Dakton, and Phuntsok Namgyal.la all contributed enormously to my understanding of the spirit, as well as the sounds, of old Tibet and the ways these can and cannot be successfully brought to life today. Other elderly Tibetans who were important to this study and who remain in my thoughts include Ama Palmo in Dharamsala and Professor Ngawang Jinpa in Darjeeling. I must also mention Geshe Sopa, in Wisconsin, who breathed life into my initial relationship with Tibetan culture with the same energy and enthusiasm that he put into teaching aspirated Tibetan consonants.

Thanks are also offered here to the many young Tibetans in India, Nepal, and North America who have shared their music and their alternately radical and ultraconservative ideas and dreams with me. I am further indebted to those musicians, composers, and friends in Tibet who were of great help, sometimes putting themselves at risk, and must remain nameless here. Most of all, unlimited thanks to the Yak Band, especially to Tsering Paljor Phupatsang, for accepting a *dri* (female yak) into their herd.

Other friends, such as Ani Dawa, Ama Chog, and the Singhs, offered the easy companionship and unfailing hospitality without which fieldwork would be something akin to hell on earth. The impeccable, inexhaustible generosity, friendship, and professional assistance provided by Tsering Lhanzom held me, and this project, together.

I am also hugely indebted to all the *Inji* gals who found themselves for one reason or another in Dharamsala during the course of the research that led to this book—Jo Shaw, Vyvyan Cayley, Liz Fabel, Jeanne Herbert, Nuala Carney, Lisa Tracy, Robin Greenberg, Allyson West, Judi Lukas, Liz Fukushima, Betsy Hibbitts, Betsy Napper, Philippa Russell, Claire Isitt, and Tenzin Dechen—for tea and sympathy, imported foods, and local rumors. It was from these friends that I learned for certain that culture runs deep.

I offer respect and thanks to my mother, Sheila, for her willingness return to India, her birthplace, after sixty years. Most of all, thanks to Fred for getting me started on this project and for seeing me through it, to Nicholas for interrupting it, and to Annika for making sure it got finished.

For financial support, I am grateful to the University of Texas Anthropology Department for teaching assistantships, the Department of Asian Studies for four F.L.A.S. fellowships, the American Institute of Indian Studies (A.I.I.S.) for funding my year of fieldwork in India as a Junior Fellow, and to the university's graduate school for a Continuing Fellowship that allowed me to write full time when I most needed to. Finally, thanks to the faculty and staff, and my fellow Fellows, at Stanford University's Introduction to the Humanities program; to copyeditor Mimi Kusch; and to everyone at the University of California Press who helped make this book a reality.

Note to the Reader

For the reader's convenience, all Tibetan and Hindi words that appear in this book have been transcribed phonetically into English. With the exception of place-names, personal names, and words such as *bazaar* that are commonly used in English, all Tibetan and Hindi words appear in italics. All translations from Tibetan and Hindi are the author's.

Preface

It was my first Monday morning in India, and I was not where I was supposed to be. According to the grant proposal tucked in among my papers, I was at the Tibetan Homes Foundation in Mussoorie teaching elementary school children dressed in crisp green uniforms and neckties. In the afternoons, when English classes were finished for the day, I was to be found in the school's music rooms, dance classes, and art studios, easing into what was to be a nomadic year traveling from one refugee camp to another throughout India researching the ways traditional Tibetan arts were being taught to the youngest generation in exile. However, according to my senses—if they were to be trusted at this point—I was at the bus stop in Dharamsala, home of the Dalai Lama and busy hub of the Tibetan diaspora, wondering what to do with myself in a strange place at dawn and feeling very disappointed.

The original plan I had devised deliberately deemphasized Dharamsala because of the tendency of most researchers, journalists, and others interested in Tibetan refugees to focus their efforts entirely on this worldly capital-in-exile and to generalize their findings to Tibetans everywhere. Very little substantial documentary or ethnographic work had yet to be conducted outside Dharamsala, and I was uncomfortable with this trend. There are many logistical reasons for the stubborn centripetal force that attracts everyone to Dharamsala—permits to stay in remote settlements are, for example, difficult to obtain from the Indian authorities for security reasons—and there are other reasons involving the desires and expectations of Western visitors.

My own efforts to spend the majority of my fieldwork time away from Dharamsala were dashed within twenty-four hours of arriving in India because of political instability in the region where I was headed. My husband,

Fred, opened a newspaper over breakfast on our first morning in Delhi to learn that the state of Madhya Pradesh was in chaos over affirmative action legislation and that its government was on the brink of collapse. After reading that peaceful demonstrators in the quiet hill station of Mussoorie had been shot in the street by riot police, I quickly phoned the general secretary of the Tibetan Homes Foundation, who explained that she had arranged to have as many children as possible sent away from the area. I should, she insisted, put off my long-awaited arrival for at least a month. That afternoon, my Tibetan friend and advisor Dawa Norbu, a professor at Jawaharlal Nehru University in Delhi, advised me to go with the flow, jump on a bus to Dharamsala, and spend my first month in India making contacts in the various government offices and organizations there. "It can't hurt," he added, by way of encouragement. The next evening I boarded Mr. Bedi's Bus, the infamous and somewhat treacherous transportation lifeline between Delhi and Dharamsala, and fidgeted all night as we lurched our way up into mountains.

We found a room in a guest house full of German and Israeli backpackers, and I began making inquiries in Tibetan shops and offices here and there. "Know any musicians? Anyone who plays the guitar? Anyone who writes songs?" That afternoon at the Tibetan Youth Congress office, a group of young men understood that I wasn't interested only in the institutionalized arts scene at the Tibetan Institute of Performing Arts (TIPA), that I wanted to meet nonprofessional musicians among their own peers and neighbors as well. Happy to take a break from typing forms in triplicate, they initiated a brainstorming session that generated the names of ten Tibetans of all ages who would turn out to be the heart and soul of my year's research in India. The young office workers were particularly enthusiastic about one guitarist, their friend Paljor.la, [1] who worked as a translator over at the Reception Center. He had produced two cassettes and was now the lead singer and songwriter for a local rock group called the Yak Band. They led me out onto the TYC's rooftop balcony and pointed out a room built on the roof of a large yellow building with green railings on the next ridge. That's where he works. *Kong yakshö ray.* He's the best.

Days later, I climbed the dark cement stairs for the third time past the cavernous dorm rooms for recent arrivals from Tibet and was lucky. I found Paljor at his desk in a beige zippered jacket and blue jeans. He was about my age, with a kind face, short hair, and a thin mustache. Typewriter pushed aside, he was studying English vocabulary from a paperback called *Increase Your Word Power!* Thank God, I thought. He knows English. I really had no idea how to talk about the blues in Tibetan. "*Tashi delek.*

Hello. Excuse me. I heard that you play the guitar." This was before I learned something about how Tibetans make conversation, that you are supposed to talk about the weather for half an hour, drinking tea you have pretended to refuse, and then, as you are rising to go, casually let slip what you had come to say. But Paljor was used to dealing with inquisitive *Injis*, and he was clearly interested. [2]

He got a chair for me and a cup and saucer. I eagerly accepted the sweet milk *chai* he poured from the office thermos and launched forth. "I'm writing a book about Tibetan music and I'm going to be here for a long time and I heard that you play the guitar and I think it's great young people here are writing songs and I heard that you play the blues and I thought maybe is it possible that it was you playing on that purple tape I have at home?" I don't know who was more amazed. Paljor couldn't believe that this hyperactive American tourist owned a copy of his obscure purple tape, and I couldn't believe that out of all the Tibetans living in India, the first young musician I'd met had turned out to be the composer and performer of the "Tashi Delek Blues," the recording that had planted the seed for my research topic. We just stared at each other for a while with funny looks on our faces, registering this connection until it became embarrassing. At last Paljor poured more tea.

I had been intrigued by this person named Tsering Paljor Phupatsang before I ever met him. Maybe it's a funny way of backing into one's anthropological fieldwork on the other side of the world: to be amazed by the ability of the "other" to play the blues. But our love of the blues quickly turned out to be the common ground, the doorway that led to everything else. On a preliminary trip to India in 1993, I had bought a few cassettes of "modern" Tibetan music out of curiosity. Paljor's cassette had a striking image of barbed wire drawn at an angle over a photo of nomad children with wild tangled hair. It was a long time, though, before I ever listened to the tape all the way through. The tunes had a certain sameness—a kind of languid Simon and Garfunkel effect—and I couldn't understand the words. When the unmistakable lead into a solid Mississippi Delta blues number came on one afternoon when I'd let the cassette roll through to the end, I assumed it was a case of crummy Indian overdubbing. They must have slapped the Tibetan songs over a tourist's cast-off tape, I thought. But then the singing started: *Yay nay shön pa tso! Yö nay men shar tso!* ("Young men from the right side! Young women from the left side!") I really could not believe I was listening to a Tibetan performing the blues until a friend in Madison later helped me translate the liner notes printed in tiny, blurry *khyug* script. Having been away from India for many years, my friend didn't recognize the name of the musician, but he was pretty sure that the lyricist credited was the elderly Tibetan state astrologer who worked at the Medical and Astrological Institute in Dharamsala. That added a new twist that made the song even more intriguing to me.

Without knowing much more than that, I anchored the prospectus for my dissertation and a conference paper on the "Tashi Delek Blues," using it as an example of the kinds of complex contemporary forms of expression by refugee youth about which I wanted to learn more. I must have heard in this song the seeds of answers to many of the questions that had grown out of my graduate training in anthropology and ethnomusicology: Do Tibetans like this new music? Does it sound and feel "Tibetan" to them? Is it an aberration, this musician's own quirky idea, or part of a larger trend? Are such examples of musical borrowing by Tibetan youth living in the diaspora efforts to explore artistically, and even to create, their multicultural identities as individuals who are proud of their heritage and yet who have succeeded in developing deep relationships with other traditions as well? Or are these songs an indication that the "children of Tibet," the generations that are growing up entirely outside the homeland, are truly losing their parents' culture and being swept into the increasingly homogeneous cultural soup created by global flow? Either way, does it matter? If so, to whom?

To break the awkwardness of the moment, I changed the topic and asked across the desk in an offhand way, "Paljor.la, do you know anyone with a keyboard? I'd like to play while I'm here and use it to transcribe songs." It was a clumsy way to let him know that I am a musician too. "My band owns a keyboard," Paljor offered. "But . . ." Paljor slowed down, eyeing me, like he wasn't sure he wanted to deal with the implications of what he, as a kind and generous person, was already in the process of saying, ". . . we don't have a keyboard player." I burst out laughing. He did too. Fiddling with my teacup, I managed to say, "I'll just have to think about that, OK?" My mind was already racing ahead to images of us on stage somewhere under red and blue lights, reeling around cranking out "Smoke on the Water" or "Brick in the Wall," images laced with memories of high school dances under basketball hoops. Was that really how I wanted to spend my precious time in India? I have no memory of how this first conversation eight years ago ended—maybe the phone rang—but I do remember having to restrain myself from dancing up the dirt street past the vegetable sellers on my way back to town.

Two weeks passed. Then at last, after several rounds of notes left on doors, delays, and missed connections, I met Paljor.la at the taxi stand, and

Figure 1. The village of Naddi and the snow-covered Dauladar Range.

we hired a ride up to the yellow cement house where all the members of the Yak Band were living (except Paljor, who is married with three sons). It is also where the band rehearsed, far from the ears of neighbors and relatives. The rented house was up in Naddi Gau, a village six kilometers further still above McLeod Ganj, which commands a truly awesome view. The snow-covered Dauladar Range rises to 17,000 feet on one side of the ridge-top village, while, on the opposite side of the community's only road, all of India rolls out forever on the hazy plains far below. The hillside property where the Yaks lived belonged to a Gaddi family (local Indian shepherds) whose cluster of slate-roofed, mud-washed houses and animal pens sat just below the Yaks' front yard. *Namaste-ji*. We greeted the grandfather smoking a brass hookah on his porch. He nodded back at us, and his wife spinning wool nearby smiled. It seemed an unlikely setting for rock and roll.

Paljor and I sidestepped tentatively past the enormous black water buffalo tethered near the pathway and settled down on the front steps of the "Yak Shack" to wait for the others to show up, as we would do dozens of times. Paljor slipped a cushion under me as I bent over to sit on the cold cement. "You shouldn't sit on that. You'll get sick." After a minute or two, he said he thought I might find his family's history interesting. To pass the time, he started with the story about his father. His *pala* was a Khampa chieftain who was airlifted with other members of his resistance group back into Tibet by the C.I.A. in the late 1950s after being trained in guerilla warfare to fight the Chinese incursion from the East. But they were dropped in the wrong place and quickly found themselves captured by the Chinese. Paljor's father and his friends, now Tibetan folk heroes, all took cyanide pills and died. Paljor was born in Darjeeling (in West Bengal, India) a few months later. As a refugee and semiorphan, he was schooled by Irish Christian missionaries, thanks to financial support from Western sponsors alarmed by the 1959 flight of the Dalai Lama from Tibet.

Two other Yaks had arrived during this story and were squatting around the yard now too, listening to Paljor. Phuntsok had made ginger milk tea and handed it round in the small glasses used in *chai* stalls all over India. I'd met Phuntsok and Ngodup briefly once before when they stopped by my guest house to leave a message, but no one ever gets introduced in Dharamsala anyway. You just figure out who's who. Over time I realized that musically inclined *Inji* tourists were regularly scooped up in town by the Yaks and brought to Naddi to jam with the band and teach them something new. The band's leader, Thubten, was apparently "out of station," but we ended up having a spontaneous rehearsal without him. Phuntsok hot-wired the cracked and dusty Yamaha keyboard, and we jammed for three happy hours. Periodically, the Gaddi kids from next door would half-appear in the doorway and linger wide-eyed with their hands over their ears until they caught someone's eye and ran away.

I was completely amazed by Paljor's skill on the guitar that first day, especially since I knew he had learned everything by ear from well-worn tapes. First the band worked on a new song called "Rangzen" (Freedom or Self-rule), which the Yak Band was preparing to use as the title song on their first cassette. Then, to my delight, Paljor launched into the "Tashi Delek Blues." Despite, or because of, the unbelievable din created by a full rock band in a small cement room, the song sounded fantastic. Actually, I could hardly even play along—I just listened with my hands hovering over the keyboard and smiled and smiled and smiled. Partly because it just felt so great to hear the blues again, but mostly because it was so amazing to be standing in a house in a Gaddi village in the Himalayas in north India improvising the missing keyboard part for the very song that had gotten me there. After a few more numbers, including Bob Marley's ubiquitous "Buffalo Soldier," Phuntsok started experimenting with ways to incorporate an amplified dranyen (six-stringed Tibetan lute) into some pieces, and the Yaks had a great time contorting a traditional Tibetan folk song into contemporary "dance music."

The light outside was incredible when we finished playing for the day. The mountains were lit up pink, with October's terraced fields of drying cornstalks glowing warm in front of them. Paljor said they were hoping to film a music video at this spectacular site after they returned from a planned concert tour in January. I got a ride back down to town through the deodar forest with Phuntsok on the band's red motorcycle—it was a beautiful ride, nice and slow—and found myself thinking that maybe things were on track after all, even if I had little idea of where the track would lead.

As it turned out, I made great headway that first month in Dharamsala and became so immediately and intensely involved with a number of both young and old musicians that by the end of it I felt it would be counterproductive to start over again so soon in a new location. It would, in fact, be six months before I got to Mussoorie and the Tibetan Homes Foundation, and then only for a short visit. Despite this significant change in plans, I did spend a lot of time in many other Tibetan settlements in India and Nepal and, unexpectedly, was able to visit Lhasa at the end of my year, trips that helped me maintain a perspective on Dharamsala's uniqueness. I do retain to this day some remorse that I have yet to contribute more to the ever-important cause of decentering Dharamsala in the ongoing effort to represent the experiences of late-twentieth-century (and early-twenty-first-century) Tibetans, but the seeds for future projects to be conducted out of Dharamsala's limelight were sown during my year in the Indian Himalayas, and I now find it difficult to imagine how things might have unfolded otherwise.

I have sought to write this book in a voice that is neither overly directive nor transparent, reflecting the personal-professional nature of the experience of being a participant-observer in a foreign community. As a result, my perspective naturally shifts, depending on whether I am writing about theories of globalization learned sitting at a desk in graduate school or about audience feedback learned while playing the keyboards in a Tibetan rock band. Both voices have their advantages. My hope is that the resonances between them, and the varied reverberations and echoes between the musical sounds that provide the score for Tibetan refugees' lives, will fill in some gaps for the reader familiar with Tibetan culture and pique the curiosity of the reader who is new to this field of study.

Paljor is lost. Or he's lost us. Hips forward, leaning way back, eyes

hidden by his baseball cap but focused on the neck of his "Givson"

(Indian rip-off of Gibson) guitar. His blues improvisations wail and

moan. Thubten and I shoot somewhat desperate looks at each other, find

no solace, then cast our eyes instinctively on Phuntsok's left hand.

Luckily, as the bass player, Phuntsok always knows where we are in the

twelve-bar pattern, even if Paljor's solo offers us no clues. Ah, there's the

E. We're back on track. I know I'll be ribbed again later over tea.

"Keila.la," Paljor will complain, "it's your music. I mean, how come you

get so confused?" I've made excuses all along, but it's not until I'm about

to leave Dharamsala, when we've been through enough together that

talking about things that make us emotional isn't so embarrassing, that I

can tell Paljor why I so often messed up the blues. It's because I know it

so well, because it's mine. It hurts so much, and feels so good, to play the

blues when I'm far from home that I lose my place. I tell him I think that

sometimes it makes him lose his place too. He knows what I mean.

That's what his music, and this book, is all about. Sounds and places and

pleasure and loss. Movement and being moved.

Introduction

Theory at Home and in the Field

> But what of the ethnographic ear?
> James Clifford

This book is concerned with the performance and reception of popular music and song by Tibetan refugees living in north India. It strives to convey how Tibetans hear the complex array of sounds that make up the musical life of their community-in-exile and explores the relationship they have with these sounds. The musical "soundscape"[1] (Schafer 1977) most Tibetan refugees live in includes traditional or revitalized Tibetan folk music, Tibetan songs and music perceived to be "Chinese" or "sinicized," Hindi film songs, Western rock, reggae and blues, modern Tibetan music made in exile, and Nepali folk and pop songs.[2] The ways in which different musics resonate with and against one another for Tibetan refugees—the ways these various song traditions are loved, debated, rejected, tolerated, or ignored—are themselves embodiments or performances of the challenges of building and maintaining an ethnically based community in diaspora. More specifically, the complexity of Tibetan refugees' relationships with various song traditions indicates the diversity and unevenness of their relationships with the places and people associated with those songs. These cultural changes and exchanges continually evolve, despite this exiled group's politically informed investment in, and often adamant rhetorical delineation of, cultural boundaries that discourage such ambiguity.

To explore the ways in which cultural boundaries are understood, negotiated, and enacted by Tibetan refugees, this book largely focuses on nontraditional musics that have found a receptive audience in this diasporic community. I emphasize popular foreign genres, such as Hindi film music and Western rock and roll as well as the "modern"[3] Tibetan song genre that has emerged in exile. Modern Tibetan songs, which have not been documented elsewhere, are given special consideration because they bring together in a particularly salient way the foreign and the familiar, the modern and the traditional; further, they effectively challenge the usefulness of those categories. Most Tibetan refugees genuinely enjoy this new locally produced, Western-influenced Tibetan music, but a close look reveals that tolerance of these modern songs is, in fact, quite qualified. While the formidable social and financial constraints on any Tibetan aspiring to be a musician today are readily apparent, the conservative artistic constraints on the actual music and lyrics of modern Tibetan songs (and on opportunities for and styles of performing them) only become evident when this new genre is considered or "placed" in conversation with all the other musics heard in the Tibetan diaspora in South Asia. Until recently, each of these local sounds—Tibetan, Indian, Nepali, Western, Chinese—have been compartmentalized into specific aural and social contexts, muting the ways in which they in fact constantly echo off one another and inform local notions of the appropriate content and use of each genre. With the advent of live rock concerts and dance parties in Dharamsala and elsewhere in the Tibetan diaspora, events where young Tibetan musicians juxtapose diverse musics in a single place and time, assumed musical and cultural boundaries are being challenged.

One sociologist has likened rock concerts to anthropologist Victor Turner's liminal ritual stage, in the sense that they are "crucibles for social experimentation" that generate both *communitas* and antistructure (Martin 1979: 98).[4] As social events, rock concerts do provide an unprecedented forum for Tibetan refugees to enact their relationships to one another as *punda-tso* (kin) and to the several cultures that inform their daily lives as refugees, often generating moments of deeply felt solidarity. However, these events have also revealed that maintaining the oppositional stance to "otherness" institutionalized by the dominant Tibetan refugee paradigm of cultural preservation and residential isolation in exile now can involve opposing one another, as various "foreign" practices and ideas—such as delight in Hindi film songs and American rap music—have inevitably become incorporated into the lives of many refugees. With these issues in mind, ingroup criticism of Tibetan refugee pop-rock musicians and concerts may be understood to be less about an intolerance for "modern" music itself than it is about discomfort with the creation of a venue where Tibetan refugees can and do publicly enact positive aspects of their relationships with other cultures (understood, by some, as their failure to stay Tibetan in exile).

CONVERSATIONS THIS BOOK IS JOINING

Despite the particular idiosyncracies of the Tibetan refugee case—such as having had a stable leader and relatively stable communities for more than four decades in exile as well as having received a great deal of international interest in and support for their cause—the experiences of Tibetans living in exile represent an important human resource that variously supports, qualifies, and sometimes contradicts a number of current academic assumptions and desires. Right off, I should briefly state two basic theoretical assumptions of this project that are perhaps by now anthropological truisms. First, I am operating from a belief that "culture" is not only reflected in, but also created by, expressive performances. I consider artful expression to be a domain where the known may potentially be (though certainly is not always) exceeded, a starting point that grants the arts "both the powers and responsibilities of a genuinely political medium" (Leppert and McClary 1987: xvii) and recognizes that "aesthetic perception is necessarily historical" (Bourdieu 1984: 4). The accompanying expansion of interest from product to process and from text to creative and performative contexts parallels a general recognition of culture as continually emergent (R. Williams 1977) in the daily practice of historically positioned individuals and of the meaning of the arts as arising from their use (Geertz 1983: 118).

Second, traditions are selected and ever changing. A number of important publications have problematized the notion of "tradition" by revealing it to be selective, invented, and/or symbolically constructed, articulating a position that has become a given among folklorists and anthropologists. More than twenty years ago, Raymond Williams coined the term *selective tradition* (1977: 115) to refer to an "intentionally selective version of a shaping past and a pre-shaped present, which is then powerfully operative in the process of social and cultural definition and identification" (1977: 116). Further, this selective tradition, which offers "a sense of *predisposed continuity*," is always tied, though often in complex and hidden ways, to explicit contemporary pressures and limits (1977: 116–17). In *The Invention of Culture* (1981), Roy Wagner suggested that because of the innovative and expressive force of tropes, or metaphors, through which we perceive the world, the world is constantly reconstructed. And Hobsbawm and Ranger's *The Invention of Tradition* (1983) drew attention to those practices "which seek to inculcate certain values and norms of behavior by repetition, which automatically implies continuity with the past" (1983: 1). Handler and Linnekin's 1984 article titled "Tradition, Genuine or Spurious" elaborated on the earlier work of Edward Shils (1971, 1981) to suggest that tradition refers to an interpretive process embodying both continuity and discontinuity, rendering it symbolically constituted rather than natural. These works, bolstered by advances in practice theory (especially Bourdieu 1977 and Giddens 1979, 1984) and other efforts to expose the historicity of interpretation

(Jameson 1981) opened the way for a general acceptance that "tradition," rather than being a finished object, is created through the decisions of historically situated individuals in a dialectic with inherited structures.

As I have said, these two positions are well established. The challenge remains, however, to move to the margins of these claims and to examine *how* they work (or don't work) in the field. Wholeheartedly embracing these now-mundane positions poses some risks, including the possible assumption that *all* expressive performances are creative and/or political and that any understanding of "tradition" or "heritage" as nameable or sacred is misguided. In the spirit of exploring the ways in which these fundamental intellectual assertions can both help and hinder attempts to articulate how "culture" is experienced, created, and articulated by participants, I have included below a discussion of the main theoretical conversations that this book is joining.

The general theoretical orientation of this project arose from a dilemma. Throughout my graduate coursework during the early 1990s, I was exposed to mountains of contemporary anthropological theory and ethnographic writing that celebrated transgression, displacement, innovation, resistance, and hybridity (and, significantly, often assumed the co-occurrence of these phenomena). With the theoretical cutting edge slicing its way across borders, genres, bounded entities, and assumed identities and "world beat" music tuning the ears of the planet to every possible combination of sounds, my proposed study of the rock-and-roll music being made by Tibetan refugee youth in India seemed inter*everything* enough to contribute to the conversation in a number of meaningful and timely ways. After I spent a few months living with Tibetan refugees, however, it became clear that many of the displaced people I had chosen to live among and work with were, in fact, striving heartily for emplacement, cultural preservation, and ethnic purity, even though keeping these dreams alive also meant consciously keeping alive the pain and loss inherent in the exile experience rather than letting or helping these wounds heal. While the lives of Tibetan refugees could certainly be *described* in terms of hybridity and pastiche, these characteristics were often regarded as the very unfortunate consequences of refugee life, as embarrassing failures rather than as sources of pride. These natives were proving themselves to be far more conservative than I had been led to expect to find in a study of "culture on the road." At this point, the ethnographer is faced with a clear choice: either dismiss the natives as mystified and carry on or back up and critique the theories that refuse a home to their experiences. Or do a bit of both. This project's aim was quickly altered, and a fruitful dialogue between theory and practice, home and the field, began.

As a result of this dialogue, I have become aware of the distance between much scholarship on displacement and the people whose experiences actually inspired and generated the current trends. My own prioritization of ethnographic detail is in itself a statement of concern regarding the overwhelmingly theoretical nature of the attention being paid to displacement in the social sciences and humanities. This study of echoes between cultures foregrounds a muffled dialogue between anthropology and cultural studies by examining the current interest in, even fetishization of, displacement, marginality, and multiculturalism; the normalization of expectations about how those conditions will be experienced; and the colonization of the spaces of exile and diaspora by theories that are, it sometimes seems, losing touch with the histories and conditions of existence of displaced people in today's world.

Further, many studies that do include ethnographic case studies tend to emphasize the richness, multivocality, dialogism, and creativity of their subjects rather than their deep conservatism, xenophobia, and dreams of emplacement. The current academic suspicion and censure of closure, which has certainly corrected many unfortunate aspects of rigid paradigms of the past, demands that culture be kept open, transient, in flux, and malleable. In many ways this shift is certainly appropriate and realistic today, but one still must examine the local significance of and reactions to the flux and impermanence described. Rather than simply finding a reflection of the celebration taking place in the halls of academia, one may, as I did, bump into deep desires and expectations that cycles of change will and must be completed, that boundaries will protect as well as devastate, and that firm grips will, ultimately, reclaim stability.

To address these issues, I will now consider four basic questions that any reader of this book is entitled, if not bound, to ask: Why study refugees? Why refugee music? Why refugee youth? Why Tibetans? The first three of these questions effectively get at the key issues of displacement and global flow, exilic creativity, the transmission of culture, and cultural hybridity, all of which are central to this project. The last question—Why Tibetans?—will be addressed throughout this discussion and in the brief literature review that follows.

Why Study Refugees?

But there is a big difference between "matter out of place" in the
classification of plants and animals and "matter out of place" when
people are in question. For people categorize back.

Liisa Malkki

Why study refugees? Or, considered in a more general framework, what do
analyses of transnational and global phenomena add to the cultural critique? Discussions of global and transnational "flow" are flowing so freely
themselves in academic and nonacademic discourse that it is important to
step back and consider this phenomenon, as anthropologists would consider any other cultural trend.

We generally accept that neither a totally global nor a myopically local
perspective is satisfactory, that the ideal perspective lies somewhere between these extremes. On the one hand, the concept of global flow was
provoked by the observable reality that unprecedented amounts of people,
ideas, and goods are moving across borders owing to improvements in
communications and transportation and the intense interdependence of
nations. This process has resulted in what anthropologist Arjun Appadurai calls an "altogether new condition of neighborliness" (1990: 2). By
drawing on images of interconnectedness and communalism, such as the
notion of the "global village," transnational or global paradigms have the
potential to contribute to a discourse of universal responsibility for a
shared planet and, especially, for those issues that can be said to affect everyone or are apparently "no one's in particular," such as environmental
concerns, arms buildup, hunger, and disease. From an anthropological perspective, global discourses have an appealing potential to challenge those
stubborn notions of bounded, pure, authentic cultures that have so naturalized the links between people and places and that persist, despite the development of a rhetoric of permeability and transformation that might
seem to suggest otherwise. A long-overdue and healthy challenge to the
naturalized idea of "cultures" as discrete entities—an assumption that has
long allowed the "power of topography to conceal successfully the topography of power" (Gupta and Ferguson 1992: 8)—is underway, though perhaps to an extreme.

There is the risk that the concept of global flow can transform local actors into passive victims of a homogenizing cultural whitewash with little
regard for the ways in which foreign practices and products (like, for example, rock and roll) are chosen, used, and made meaningful locally. Riding
the free currents of global flow, it can seem that everything is available to

everyone to patch together in a parodic or resistant manner. Going into the field, one of my main concerns was to challenge the discourse of global flow that emphasized cultural homogenization and overliteral understandings of the "local" that seemed to wipe out the ways "foreign" practices are thoughtfully and selectively incorporated into daily life. At the same time, I was wary of interpretations that seemed to overcompensate for these concerns by reading every local act as romantically unaffected by, or actively resistant to, the sweeping global forces that are clearly at work.

Studying the expressive culture of contemporary refugees complicates easy explanations of culture change provided by the popular idea of global flow, because individuals cut loose from their roots are not necessarily free to borrow cultural elements from here and there and arrange them as they please. As people living on the wrong side of borders, refugees are actually likely to be *less* free to innovate than others (a fact that further problematizes the celebratory view of multiculturalism and hybridity held by many outsiders and some innovative community members). Even though refugees are on the move, they still live in communities that largely strive to keep their members in place; they are not, in Gupta and Ferguson's words, "free-floating monads" (1992: 19). The current debate about tensions between homogenization and heterogenization (Appadurai 1990: 5) is not, after all, limited to the pages of scholarly journals. From a critical local perspective, it can be seen how many of the cultural constraints and opportunities operating in a community are still generated from within the community itself and cannot be simply explained as the indiscriminate results of sweeping international forces.

Displacement is another, albeit related, concept being actively considered in the field. In the 1990s, it became, along with its doppelgänger, *emplacement*, an intellectual metaphor with tremendous momentum. Uprootedness, transgression, transculturalism, genre blurring, boundary crossing, hybridity, and life lived in the interstices are all being celebrated in large part because they are, like the notion of global flow, important vehicles for challenging and complicating earlier, tenacious disciplinary assumptions about boundedness, typicality, and the maintenance of social order. Given this theoretical orientation, it is therefore surprising how few ethnographic studies of refugees have been undertaken, since their lives so profoundly embody the issues filling today's academic conferences and journals.

Refugee lives are inherently experimental and thoroughly modern. As informants, refugees are perhaps uniquely able to discuss the ways in which the cold, hard issues of politics and economics inform their personal and communal experiences, explicitly tied as these are to global forces. It would seem that these characteristics make refugee populations particularly well poised to receive attention from anthropologists seeking to meet the challenge of moving beyond symbol-and-meaning ethnography and figuring out how to "represent the embedding of richly described local cultural worlds in larger impersonal systems of political economy" (Marcus and Fischer 1986: 77). Marcus and Fischer go on to explain that

> this would not be such a problematic task if the local cultural unit was portrayed, as it usually has been in ethnography, as an isolate with outside forces of market and state impinging upon it. What makes representation challenging and a focus of experimentation is the perception that the "outside forces" in fact are an integral part of the construction and constitution of the "inside," the cultural unit itself, and must be so registered, even at the most intimate levels of cultural process. (1986: 77)

As evidenced by the few fine anthropological studies of refugees that do exist, one is immediately obligated when working with displaced populations to put aside presumed inside/outside or traditional/modern distinctions and focus instead on the often surprising ways in which the local and the global are experienced and described by participants in these communities.[5] Any study of refugee culture also necessarily problematizes the culture concept by exploring the processes of cultural maintenance and reconstruction required when a group of people (and their practices and beliefs) are unhooked from the reinforcing context of "their" place.

Given these interesting and timely advantages, I am concerned that the apparent neglect of refugees shows that the polemical motives generating the new paradigm focused on displacement and global flow indicate that scholars and scholarship remain the focus. It seems that focusing on the degree to which any given research subject appears theoretically useful often overrides understanding and documenting the *experience* of displacement for that person or group.[6] Liisa Malkki, a scholar with similar concerns, claims that, despite all the rhetoric, displacement has in fact been pathologized as an aberration in our persistent "national order of things," causing refugees in turn to be regarded as an abomination (in Mary Douglas's sense) that has been "produced and made meaningful by the categorical order itself, even as they are excluded from it" (1995: 6). She explains further:

> The construction of a national past is a construction of history of a particular kind; it is one that claims moral attachments to specific territories, motherlands or homelands, and posits time-honored links between people, polity and territory. . . . It is precisely the interstitial position of refugees in the system of nation-states that makes their lives uniquely clarifying and enabling for the anthropological rethinking of nation-

ness, of statelessness, and of the interconnections between historical memory and national consciousness. (1995: 1)

Likening the "structural invisibility" of displaced populations to that of Victor Turner's liminal personae, Malkki makes the observation that refugees are

> no longer unproblematically citizens or native informants. They can no longer satisfy as "representatives" of a particular local culture. One might say they have lost a kind of imagined cultural authority to stand for "their kind" or for the imagined "whole" of which they are or were a part. (1995: 6)[7]

There are many ways in which refugees challenge preexisting understandings of culture as well as traditional anthropological expectations and methodological assumptions. For example, their communities lack the real or imagined social and cultural integrity of stable communities, often harboring together individuals of shared ethnic backgrounds but great linguistic and cultural diversity; their populations can ebb and flow daily; and they expect visitors to become active advocates for their cause. Rather than being drawbacks, these characteristics are, it seems to me, precisely what make refugees intriguing and fruitful subjects of anthropological attention. The challenge is to investigate and honor the experiences of displaced people without making them into heroes. At times it seems the interest in theorizing space and place has provided an allegorical language for postmodern souls who seek to nourish their own feelings of alienation and, in turn, to express their suspicion of those who are still somehow, or desire to be, "in place." Anticipating this kind of appropriation of misfortune, Caren Kaplan cautions against a form of theoretical tourism on the part of the first-world critic, where the margin becomes a linguistic or critical vacation, a new poetics of the exotic (1987: 191). Similarly, Edward Said warns that to dwell on exile, "as beneficial, as a spur to humanism or to creativity, is to belittle its mutilations" (1984: 50). Importantly, it is not only Western scholars who valorize the marginal position of their research subjects. Complicating the picture is the fact that postcolonial "others" themselves (including many Tibetan refugees) often objectify their own marginal cultures for specific, often strategic, ends.

Navigating the rapids between the smoothie swirl of the New Age and the jarring discourse of posteverything academics is tricky and may only get trickier. Steven Feld, writing about the relationship between "world beat" and "world music," predicts that this dialectic between extremes will intensify:

> As the discourse of authenticity becomes more militant and nativistic,
> more complicated, and more particularized to suit specific interest and
> taste groups, the activities of appropriation get more overt and outra-
> geous, as well as more subtle, legally sanctioned, accepted, and taken-
> for-granted. (1995: 110)

Some tactics have been suggested. Writing about the maintenance of ethnic identity some thirty years ago, Fredrik Barth realized that we could no
longer justify simply studying the cultural stuff enclosed within boundaries, so he recommended shifting the focus of investigation onto the
boundary itself (1969: 90). His observation that boundaries persist "despite
a flow of personnel across them" (1969: 90) still rings true in a world in
which "as actual places and localities become ever more blurred and inde-
terminate, *ideas* of culturally and ethnically distinct places become perhaps
even more salient" (Gupta and Ferguson 1992: 10). Ulf Hannerz (1987)
suggests the concept of "creole culture" as a root metaphor for understanding the international interpenetration of practices, and Gupta and
Ferguson insist that we need to "give up naive ideas of communities as literal entities, but remain sensitive to the profound 'bifocality' that characterizes locally lived lives in a globally interconnected world" (1992: 12).

There is, certainly, still a lot to study locally, without denying the
influence of "outside" forces; even if you are "out of place" or very vulner-
ably "in place" you are still, after all, *somewhere*. Keith Basso, for example,
has chosen to study at the microlevel of linguistics the affective nature of
the relationships Apaches have with "their" landscapes—places that are
"always available to their seasoned inhabitants in other than material
terms" (1988: 102)—through the poetic use of place-names. Further, Feld
(1996) refuses easy interpretations of a New Guinea highlander who sings
out to Australian and American audiences:

> However the song satisfies a postmodern narcissism that can see only a
> world of fragmentary reflections off mirrors of its own shattering,
> there is something exquisitely local and deeply rooted here. . . . Rather,
> like all Kaluli songs, this one animates a dialectic of emplacement and
> displacement and resolves it in a poetics of replacement. (1996: 130)

It is my hope that this study of Tibetan refugees will contribute to the
work of those who are asking what this vast process of globalization looks
like from different and particular vantage points other than the space shut-
tle, since the global is, ultimately, experienced locally. Perhaps we should attend to Renato Rosaldo's general observation that anthropologists "have
given little thought to how members of other cultures conceive the transla-

tion of cultures" (1988: 83). The tension between homogenization and heterogenization, blur and splatter, proves that countless micronegotiations are going on all the time and suggests that the local-global binary may in fact be unproductive and reductive. Appadurai writes that "at least as fast as forces from metropolises are brought into new societies they tend to become indigenized in one or another way" (1990: 5). Yet, the flow is, as I have said, not a free-for-all. What gets grabbed out of the torrent by whom, what is done with it, and what this *means* to the grabber and his or her family and friends: this is where the global and the local come together and seem to preserve a place for ethnography for a while longer. The whole of the "grabber's" life is not in complete synchrony, after all, with the referential world that first gave birth to the foreign song or blue jeans or posture or religious doctrine they now call their own. People who are "out of place" or whose place has been sucked out from under them or hollowed out by tourists still have local frameworks that enable and constrain them and through which they make sense of their lives. Also important, they also have "alternate fears" (Appadurai 1990: 5) to the Americanization we prioritize.

These theoretical musings are not inert. There are real repercussions, for example, for refugees like the approximately 140,000 Tibetans in limbo in India and elsewhere who are living a life that, through its rupture and mobility, jibes well with the postmodern rhetoric of alienation, amorphousness, and indeterminacy. Between the extremes in Western scholarship of constructing exile as a "literary, entirely bourgeois state" (Said 1986: 121) on the one hand and dismissing it as a space inhabited by "people without culture" on the other (Rosaldo 1988: 79), displaced people are often used theoretically, without engagement with the often not-so-good-to-*live* realities of mass politics. The romanticization of Tibetans in particular is further exacerbated by the long-standing representation of their homeland as "Shangri-La." While this mystical aura has certainly brought unprecedented material and rhetorical support to Tibetan refugees, they have to walk a fine line to keep their sponsors and themselves satisfied that they are succeeding in staying the same, maintaining the purity of their unique culture until they can reclaim their proper place.[8] At the same time, achieving the kind of accessibility necessary to attract aid and sympathy requires great acts of accommodation and change.[9] As Tibetans create communities across national boundaries with friends and family scattered throughout the diaspora and with other disenfranchised "first peoples," they are all the while seeking precisely the literal kind of ethnic community and literal return to a literal place that is in danger of being deluged by global flow.

Notions of the "global" can be, and surely are, as carefully prescribed and attended with interest as any "bounded culture" ever was.[10] Constructed by people situated somewhere, these notions are, it is important to remember, *placed*. Malkki reminds us:

> Observing that more and more of the world lives in a "generalized condition of homelessness"—or that there is truly an intellectual need for a new "sociology of displacement," and new "nomadology"—is not to deny the importance of place in the construction of identities. On the contrary, deterritorialization and identity are intimately linked. . . . To plot only "places of birth" and degrees of nativeness is to blind oneself to the multiplicity of attachments that people form to places through living in, remembering and imagining them. (1992: 37–38)

Studying refugee attachments, memories, and imaginings deeply enriches Yi-Fu Tuan's poignant and political claim that *home* is a meaningless word apart from *journey* and *foreign country* (1977: 102).

Why Refugee Music?

Different people use different music to experience (or fantasize)
different sorts of community.

                                                        Simon Frith

Even before the fascination with global flow took hold, the "liminal" and "marginal" enjoyed a privileged status in anthropology. Earlier structuralist efforts in ethnography celebrated and sought to decode the systemic unity of cultures and were, therefore, focused on the "typical" or the "normal," while, today, culture making is generally understood in terms of a dialectic between creativity and constraints. Many anthropologists—as well as literary critics, historians, linguists, psychologists, and others—seek to reveal local or in-group taxonomies and thought processes by studying marginalized peoples (ethnic minorities, migrants, slaves, exiles, illegal aliens, colonials, missionaries, prisoners, the mentally ill, and so on). This approach is largely based on the belief that because these people have been removed from or denied the reinforcing context of the familiar—because they have experienced a social displacement that has rendered their "taken-for-granteds" into highly negotiable (if not impossible or illegal) practices in their new environments—they have been forced to acknowledge, at some level, that culture is constructed rather than "natural." That is, because they feel at odds with the status quo, they are better able to tell us what it is.[11] In Homi Bhabha's words, the "truest eye may now belong to the migrant's double vision" (1994: 5). Barbara Kirshenblatt-Gimblett has described the "cultural foregrounding effect" of the immigrant experience (1983: 44) in her work with Jewish immigrants in Canada. And Victor Turner articulated the seminal position on this notion of the special vantage point offered by marginality in his classic study of Ndembu ritual when he noted that the "phenomena and processes of mid-transition . . . expose the basic building blocks of culture just when we pass out of and before we re-enter the structural realm" (1967: 110).

Turner also drew attention to the liminal, and later the limin*oid,* as an important space/time for creative work. The editors of a collection of essays published in honor of Turner claim that his use of the three-stage model (separation, limen, and aggregation) has "set the agenda for the study of creativity in culture" in its movement from accepted configurations, through their dissolution into constituent elements to their subsequent reformulation (Lavie et al. 1993: 3).[12] A study of the role of music in the lives of refugees, particularly the kinds of music being invented by displaced people, explores this presumed connection between creativity and marginalization, in particular the connection between artful expression and place.

Gradually, for the past twenty years or so, greater importance has been granted to artistic expression, performance, style, and aesthetics in ethnographic and ethnomusicological studies. Due mainly, I assume, to a similar tendency in the social sciences generally, most of these studies have been conducted in communities that are firmly "in place," resulting in a number of thorough and evocative publications that focus on the connections between creativity and the natural and/or culturally constructed environments in which people live and have lived "forever."[13] Thanks to an extension of disciplinary boundaries from using a single culture as the framework for describing or analyzing an aesthetic tradition to embracing a multicultural frame that takes diversity as the norm (cf. Schramm 1989), other studies have investigated performances involving artistic practices or performers that are themselves "out of place."[14]

By recognizing and focusing on the importance of *place*—opened up to include emplacement, displacement, and the reclaiming of place—in the production and received meanings of artistic performances, researchers interested in aesthetics can take further steps to locate their work in, and make important contributions to, current interdisciplinary discussions concerning the fate of received notions of "culture" and the unprecedented movement of people and ideas in today's world. Whether looking at tribal healing songs in the Malaysian rainforest, the incorporation of Western classical music in Caribbean steel bands, or the persistence of Indian songs among the descendants of indentured laborers in Fiji, most studies of performance explore the tensions between tradition and innovation, exclusion and inclusion, and the interaction between certain aesthetic principles or "essentials" that over time have become iconic with a particular style and newly invented or borrowed practices. This scholarship foregrounds the intertextuality between history/convention and creativity/emergence and helps theorize the conversation between the synchronic and diachronic dimensions of cultural practice.

I chose to focus my work on the musical life of a group of displaced refugees to further explore these tensions—tensions that are simultaneously a source of deep cultural anxiety and of vitality—in a situation in which *both* the performers and the practices themselves are involuntarily and indefinitely "out of place." Under such social, political, and historical conditions, issues of style and aesthetics are highly charged emotionally and politically, granting artistic performances particular importance. In the Tibetan case, the arts play a central role in officially choreographed and privately initiated efforts to entertain and "place" Tibetan refugees, to negotiate an essential or shared Tibetan identity in exile, to celebrate and preserve the diversity of Tibetan culture, and to publicize the Tibetan cause internationally.[15]

In exile, for example, Tibetan performances such as public stagings of traditional folk operas (*lhamo*) entertain their audiences, as they always have done, but they are now highly marked events, less frequent, produced with great difficulty, and inevitably altered by the physical, financial, and other constraints of exile. Further, these events index "how things were," evoking happiness by means of their similarity with past performances in the homeland but also evoking loss, due to the performance's inevitable shortcomings. In this way, expressive performances can geographically "place" exiled Tibetan performers and audiences precisely by reminding them that they are *not* at home (which is both true and politically important to reiterate). At the same time, however, these individuals are participating in a moment in which sounds, images, and feelings fleetingly coalesce to create a place that feels like home, so that, potentially, "the expression of the desire for home becomes a substitute for home [and] embodies the emotion attendant upon the image" (Seidel 1986: 11). Simon Frith suggests that it is this "interplay between personal absorption into music and the sense that it is, nevertheless, something out there, something public [that] makes music so important in the cultural placing of the individual in the social" (1987: 137). Hamid Naficy understands the importance of reconnecting with familiar styles and traditions as a way of "reassuring the self that it will not disappear or dissolve in exile" (1993: 118).

Many exilic performances comprise a continual ritual reenactment of the memories of displacement, violence, and loss that are central to the shared experience of exile, memories that bond the Tibetan diasporic community together. These performances are emergent social constructions through which, in Edward Schieffelin's words, "each participant creates the meaning that the ritual has for him or her" (1993: 293). I am, then, thinking about exile as a performance space, which, like the ritual space described by Schieffelin,

> must be continually re-created during the course of the performance
> [which] means that the medium must commit the audience to the task
> of participating in its construction, and this is accomplished in large
> part through the spirit's songs. (1993: 277)

Naficy has argued that rituals gain additional prominence when the actual social boundaries of the community are undermined, blurred, or weakened (1993: 91). I suggest that the same importance is accorded to both traditional and modern artful performances in the Tibetan refugee community, events that are both painful and deeply gratifying through their embodiment and confirmation of a recognizable Tibetan style and whose purpose is to establish a "hegemony of feelings" (Keil 1985: 126). This attention to what is and is not "Tibetan" is exaggerated in the multicultural context of exile and speaks directly to the political nature of "taste" (cf. Bourdieu 1984). It also underscores the complexity of the process of innovation, appropriation, and naturalization by which particular sounds, grooves, and timbres—the musical version of which R. Murray Schafer calls a community's "soundmarks" (1977: 10)—come to be associated with a particular political-geographical-ideological entity.

It is surprising that artistic expression, performance, aesthetics, and/or style are only infrequently mentioned in studies of exiles, refugees, and diasporic populations.[16] Only a few studies I know of specifically address and ethnographically situate and theorize the aesthetic practices of displaced peoples. These include Naficy's work on the mediated art (primarily television) being produced and consumed by wealthy Iranian exiles in Los Angeles (1993) and Adelaida Schramm's brief articles on the musical tastes and practices of Vietnamese refugees in a Philippines refugee camp (1989) and in New Jersey (1986). To be fair, this dearth may have more to do with the relatively few anthropological or cultural studies of refugees and exiles at all, compared with the vast literature on, for example, migration and development, which draws largely on modernization and dependency theories. There is, however, a large and relevant literature that has well described and theorized the centrality of artistic cultural practice in other situations in which the identity of a person or an entire group is somehow vulnerable or threatened. These studies have addressed the salient role of artistic expression and performance among, for example, migrants to cities (de Gerdes 1995, Turino 1984, 1987), groups seeking political independence (Handler 1988), and ailing governments seeking to project desired images and maintain the appearance of national coherence (Buchanan 1991).

The issue here is most basically expressed, perhaps, as that of the effectiveness of the arts—and, for the purposes of this study, the effectiveness of music in particular—in contributing to and making believable the placement of the individual in the social, and the placement of the social in the world. In an observation that can be extended to artistic performances generally, I believe, Frith has noted that "music can stand for, symbolize *and* offer the immediate experience of collective identity" (1987: 140). Feld proposes the term *acoustemology* to argue the importance of "acoustic knowing" for understanding the "interplay of sound and felt balance in the sense and sensuality of emplacement, of making place" (1996: 97). Performances and aesthetic choices can, it is argued here, place individuals and groups in relation to others, based on their views of themselves, their views of the other, and the other's views of them. For refugees, this affective placement can meaningfully contribute to, confirm, or challenge the relationships they have with the various cultures and countries that feature prominently on the maps of their lives.

Why Refugee Youth?

Perhaps, like many other adults, anthropologists view youth as not
to be taken very seriously: occasionally amusing, yet potentially
dangerous and disturbing, in a liminal phase.

                                                        Helena Wulff

Socialization has been described by Bambi Schieffelin as an "interactive process between knowledgeable members and novices (children) who are themselves active contributors to the meanings and outcomes of interactions with others" (1990: 17). The interactive nature of the approach described in general terms by Schieffelin is exaggerated in a refugee situation, in which individuals of all ages are learning how, or are being (re)socialized, to live in a new way.[17] Narratives, habits, and songs explaining, facilitating, and reflecting on this experience of (re)socialization are being performed and responded to by Tibetan refugees at every stage of life, and the transmission of the knowledge and morals these expressions encode and engender is flowing in all possible directions between generations. For this reason, this study, which emphasizes the musical tastes and creativity of Tibetan refugee youth, poses a challenge to the generally accepted notion that "culture" (however traditionally or radically this concept is defined) is transmitted unidirectionally from older members of a society to the younger generation in "Indian file" (Connerton 1989: 39), a paradigm that effectively denies children and youth agency as cultural innovators. This book, then, is at once a study of youth culture and of youth-in-culture.

Although this multidirectional socialization process may be exaggerated in displaced groups, I believe that this dynamic is not unique to them. It has, however, been largely ignored in anthropological literature. Logotheti and Trevarthen point out that in anthropological writings it has generally been assumed that as soon as children acquire a separate self, they simply imitate adults, giving rise to metaphors such as "copycat," "primitive human," "personality trainee," or "monkey," which portray the growing child as an imperfect person (1989: 180). Indeed, a remarkable lack of attention is paid to young people in anthropological research, a void difficult to justify in a discipline concerned with the transmission, and transformation, of culture across generations.[18]

The challenge is to recognize the creativity of youths—for example, the metacommunicative power of play to comment on and transform everyday experience (Logotheti and Trevarthen 1989: 80)—without denying the degree to which youth are, in fact, formed during their "formative" years by the people and institutions in whose care they find themselves. I have found the theoretical efforts of Anthony Giddens (1979, 1984), Marshall Sahlins (1985, 1990), and, to a lesser degree, Pierre Bourdieu (1977) to reconcile the relationship between determining structures and individual agency extremely helpful in thinking about the simultaneously constraining and enabling dynamic that accounts for both structural continuity and change. These scholars recognize that structures and cultural categories themselves only exist in everyday practice, where they are necessarily modified by "unintended consequences" (Giddens 1979: 27) or are submitted to "empirical risks" (Sahlins 1985: ix) generated by the uniqueness of each interaction. Bambi Schieffelin provides an example of this dynamic in a study of language socialization in which she convincingly presents the child as an "active learner" (and, therefore, as a socialization modifier) by emphasizing the degree to which addressee identity affects the form and content of all utterances, as the ethnography of speaking and conversational analysis literatures have well established (1990: 19).

Extending this idea of active agency even further, it has been generally assumed in recent writings on youth culture that what youth do with the information and resources they formally and informally receive tends to be resistant or deviant (Wulff 1995: 1). Within this focus lie different interpretations, with some writers deploring the state of today's youth and others, notably those intellectuals adhering to the subcultural theory that emerged in Britain in the early 1970s, celebrating youth culture as bravely eclectic and antiestablishment. Stanley Cohen criticizes the latter position by noting that the "assumption of a monolithic drift to repression" (1980: xxv) has resulted in a "*too respectful* enterprise of picking up on the subcultural detritus of musical notes, hair styles, safety pins, zips and boots," which often strikes false and condescending notes (1980: xxviii). "We cannot," he concludes, "expect average kids to deviate with genius" (1980: xxix).

The Tibetan refugee case complicates this debate because the idealized path of resistance in this community involves pursuing (*as* a community) emplacement, stability, cultural preservation, and ethnic purity. Children and youth are those for whom the Tibetan government-in-exile's policies, the refugee community's concern about the future of Tibetan culture, and the identity-challenging realities of life in exile come together most complexly. A tension between the self-conscious honor/burden of being the bearers of their heritage and the seemingly unlimited opportunities for innovation in exile informs the socialization of Tibetan refugee children from the moment they are born and has been institutionalized in the structure of their schools. Despite a well-articulated academic curriculum and general commitment to cultural preservation, what is taught is not passed on unchanged, since Tibetan refugee youth are living undeniably displaced, fragile, and culturally hybrid lives. As Margaret Nowak, like many others, found in her fieldwork with young Tibetan refugees,

> In the modern context . . . life styles are much more a matter of individual choosing, for here social consensus and homogeneity increasingly give way to the pluralism that marks this more complex and specialized mode of existence. In brief, without moral or philosophical comment, for those living in the situation of greater complexity, the increased differentiation means more options. (1980: 219)

Differentiation is generally played down and even considered regrettable in the Tibetan refugee community. The key for the ethnographer in this situation is to move beyond a fascination with *formal* hybridity—the prayer beads entwined with digital watches, the country and rock music blaring at Himalayan dance parties—and pay attention instead to the ways in which the elements of this particular youth culture are chosen, reproduced, and even standardized. This attention to the motivations behind and feelings about the consumption of cultural elements from here and there reveals a generation of young people who are, for the most part, remarkably conservative and conventional in their beliefs and morals. In this community, after all, the typical kind of resistance framed in generational terms (youth versus parents or youth versus establishment) is greatly overshadowed by another kind of resistance framed in political terms (Tibetans versus Chinese).

Drawing largely on Mikhail Bakhtin's articulation of the political and aesthetic dynamics of the carnivalesque (1984) and his distinction between conscious and unconscious (organic or deliberate) hybridizations (1981: 358), scholars working on the issue of "fuzzy boundary problems" (Briggs 1988: 17) by analyzing "hybrid genres" are committed to moving away from the received "brand-name system" (Jameson 1981: 107) of genres and toward an understanding of genres as being continually transformed, combined, confronted and reimagined, a process Dell Hymes has called "metaphrasis" (1981: 87). This move from pure to hybrid genres clearly parallels the theoretical moves described in earlier parts of this introduction, which call for a shift of attention from notions of bounded, placed "cultures" to the creation of communities that are multiple, mixed, performed, scattered, and emergent.

To bring these observations to bear on the musical tastes of Tibetan refugee youth, the sounds they listen to and make are diverse and often hybrid. However, this hybridity of *form* does not necessarily indicate a tolerance for transgression. Rather, as will be discussed, I have found that the hybridity of modern Tibetan music, for example, is often predictable and repetitive to the extent that it may be better described as comprising a new definable genre. The composition and performance of new Tibetan songs by young refugees are certainly creative processes, but they are not as radical as one might expect within a paradigm that pairs newness and eclecticism with deviance. I suggest, therefore, that the acknowledgment, even encouragement, of artistic creativity and innovation in this community need not be at odds with the goal of maintaining and replicating traditional Tibetan genres of artistic expression in exile.[19] In fact, this book will show that persistent community constraints on the elaboration of Tibetan artistic genres—for example, limitations on the creative development of modern Tibetan music—may actually be increasing the appeal of foreign options for refugee youth, despite their commitment to tradition.

ZONES OF INVISIBILITY

My anthropological training, research findings, and concern for the future of Tibetans have all compelled me to attempt partially to fill in some of the gaps left by the many idealized accounts of Tibetans. Through its generally uncomplicated celebration of political solidarity and cultural preservation in exile, much of the available information on Tibetan refugees exhibits a troubling collusion with the community's own idealized self-image. However understandable this bipartisan process of romanticization may be (and it is a process with a long and well-documented history in the case of Tibetan-Western relations), its positive effects do not come without a price. An extended stay with Tibetan refugees taught me that public representations of Tibetan-ness and the lives of Tibetans have tended to smooth grossly over the striking unevenness of experience encompassed in refugee lives.

My concern is with the "zones of invisibility" (Rosaldo 1988: 79)—and, in the case of music, zones of inaudibility—created in large part by the well-intended selectivity at work in the Tibetan community and among scholar-advocates, however compassionate the motivations for such partial representations may be. After living and working closely with Tibetan refugees of diverse ages and backgrounds and documenting their conflicted lives, I am convinced that exploring the "not-saids" in this exiled community is crucial. My aim is not to dwell expressly on the negative aspects of the Tibetan refugee community (this ethnography is, indeed, full of moments of intense caring, solidarity, and celebration); rather, it is to make more believable the accomplishments of this group by complementing those accounts with the tales of disillusionment, in-group tensions, and change that make those accomplishments meaningful. I do not intend to present myself as an objective observer who simply tells all without an interested perspective. Because I am concerned about Tibetan refugees, I care about the long-term effects of idealistic representations and expectations, however positive and practical these may seem at the present moment.

Western and Tibetan accounts have together played an important role in the development of an ideal Tibet and, by transference, of an ideal Tibetan refugee. The following overview of representations is meant primarily to define important trends in research and publishing on Tibetans, to lay the groundwork for understanding the ways in which these trends inform the multiple and interwoven contemporary discourses about identity and representation that are both brought to bear on and produced by Tibetan refugees. Because public interest in Tibet in the "West" is quite keen, there is a large body of popular literature on Tibetans that I have summarized in chapter 4, in the context of a discussion of Western-Tibetan relations. The brief survey here focuses on the ways this book engages in conversation with well-established lines of historical and academic interest in Tibetan Studies, even as I am attempting to create new spaces of inquiry in that field.

A survey of representations of Tibet must be anchored to a discussion of "Shangri-La," a term that can refer to a place, to no place, to a psychological desire, or to a heavenly realm, among other possibilities. Whether the concept is embraced uncritically or battled against, it is a literary, cultural, and experiential legacy with which anyone writing about Tibetans today must grapple. This trope has become deeply implicated in descriptions and studies of Tibet, and in the self-conscious construction of personal and national identity by Tibetans themselves, a native perspective regrettably excluded from Bishop's seminal book on the topic (1989) but wrestled with directly by Lopez (1998) and Schell (2000), among others.

Rather like the life-sustaining atmosphere of the particular Shangri-La described in James Hilton's 1933 novel *Lost Horizon* (an atmosphere that enables its residents to enjoy full lives for centuries), the very notion of "Shangri-La" seems itself continually to fuel interest in Tibet and, in turn, to be rejuvenated by this attention. It is only quite recently, and for the most part only in academic circles, that the use and usefulness of the Shangri-La paradigm—for both non-Tibetans and Tibetans—has come under critical scrutiny, as scholars, like Hilton's protagonist Conway, "hanker after some more definite reason for envying the centenarian" (1933: 127).[20] Is it really wonderful for an individual (or a root metaphor) to live on and on? It is precisely the relationship between Shangri-La and time (or timelessness) that provides a useful metaphor and foil for the ways "Tibetan culture" has been conceived in the various popular, religious, political, and anthropological trajectories that together comprise the literature on Tibet:

> When he sat reading in the library, or playing Mozart in the music room, [Conway] often felt the invasion of a deep spiritual emotion, as if Shangri-La were indeed a living essence, distilled from the magic of the ages and miraculously preserved against time and death. (Hilton 1990: 138)

The romantic image of Tibet as an unchanging, medieval sanctuary of natural and spiritual mystery has its roots in nineteenth- and early-twentieth-century travel literature produced by missionaries and adventurers and has been perpetuated ever since by authors, photographers, and filmmakers fascinated by the "roof of the world." It was, for many, a "forbidden" land, by virtue of its vague political status nestled among three great empires, its naturally enclosing topography, and the conscious efforts by Tibetans to remain uncontaminated by the outside world.[21] In fact, of course, Tibetans were actively involved with a large number of other countries over the centuries, particularly in their roles as traders. Yet the enduring image of Tibet is of a "forbidden" land:

> In the heart of ageless Asia, brooding darkly in the shadow of the un-
> known, is to be found a veritable explorers' paradise—Tibet, the strange
> and fascinating, forbidden land of magic and mystery . . . where the op-
> posites are kin and the extremes go hand in hand. (Forman 1936: vii)

Although a "desire to assault this 'forbidden Acropolis' " (Forman 1936:
ix) may have been the initial inspiration for many of the expeditions to
Tibet that resulted in the numerous travel accounts published between 1900
and 1950, few adventurers seem to have had their fantasies of Shangri-La
confirmed. Most accounts focus on the hardships of travel and on appalling
and gruesome local customs and serve to glorify the author now safely back
at home after being imprisoned and tortured by Tibetan authorities or having nearly drowned in a glacial river. Elliot Sperling (1992) has pointed out
the tendency of late-twentieth-century Tibetophiles to read the early literature narrowly and to downplay the bad experiences and feelings of individual travelers. He accuses Bishop, for example, of "overlooking [Alexan-
dra] David-Neel's lack of reticence in pointing out instances of what she did
not hesitate to label Tibetan cruelty or, in regard to sham magic, gullibility"
(1992: 350). In so doing, Sperling claims, Bishop is "actually creating his
own imaginative construction of 'Tibetan Travel Writing,' much as he pic-
tures his subjects constructing an imaginative 'Tibet' (and much as those
who reproach Western scholars for their construction of 'The Orient' have
in many respects constructed 'Orientalism')" (1992: 350).

Part of the enduring romance with a particular idea of Tibet is the clear
disciplinary bias within Tibetan Studies toward the monastic culture of
pre-1950 Tibet, particularly since the Dalai Lama fled into exile. Soon after
1959, the materials that had been successfully smuggled into exile by fleeing
monks and laypeople were collected together and assessed, and translation
efforts were immediately undertaken in an effort to educate the world
about Tibetan Buddhism (for spiritual and political reasons). This religious
work has remained a priority for both Western and Tibetan scholars. The
results of this trend are manifold. Keen attention has been paid to the
preservation of texts and monastic practices in exile, but there is a
significant lack of information about Tibet's historical and modern lay populations. Notably, and perhaps signaling an expansion of interest, in the
past decade or so a number of studies and publications retaining a Buddhist
focus have approached the subject matter from an anthropological, rather
than primarily religious, perspective.[22]

The prioritization of religious practices over lay life is reflected in the
area of Tibetan music as well. A number of fine studies of Buddhist musi-

cal theory and practice exist, but very little substantial work on Tibetan lay music and song.[23] "Tibetan music" remains virtually synonymous with "Buddhist ritual music" in the minds of both musicologists and Tibetans themselves. Often when I told Tibetans that I was interested in Tibetan folk music, they would respond, "We don't really have music as such" and suggest that my efforts would be much better spent learning about the rich instrumental traditions of India. In 1979 the editors of a special issue of *Asian Music* devoted to (mostly sacred) Tibetan music introduced their collection with this observation:

> Western studies of Tibetan music have only recently begun to shift
> from a kind of missionary-in-the-cannibal-pot cartoon stereotype of
> simple nomad folksongs and chaotic ritual noises towards an apprecia-
> tion of the special forms and functions of music in a unique civilization.
> (Ellingson and Slobin 1979: 1)

In fact, apart from collections of folk song texts, very little has ever been written about "simple nomad folksongs" or other Tibetan lay traditions.[24]

With few exceptions, the efforts of many native and foreign commentators and scholars to document Tibetan culture in exile are descriptive evaluations based on time- and space-bounded notions of the "rich culture heritage of Tibet" that are dependent on a reductive binary of "preservation" and "loss." Until very recently, the myth of Shangri-La seems to have been uncritically extended to incorporate equally powerful expectations and desires for Tibetan refugees to survive the experience of exile unchanged as well. This hopeful rhetoric is eerily anticipated in *Lost Horizons* in the High Lama's dying words to the Westerner he has recognized as his successor:

> "I believe that you will live through the storm. And after, through the
> long age of desolation, you may still live, growing older and wiser and
> more patient. You will conserve the fragrance of our history and add to
> it the touch of your own mind. You will welcome the stranger, and
> teach him the rule of age and wisdom; and one of these strangers, it
> may be, will succeed you when you are yourself very old. Beyond that,
> my vision weakens, but I see, at a great distance, a new world stirring in
> the ruins, stirring clumsily but in hopefulness, seeking its lost and leg-
> endary treasures. And they will all be here, my son, hidden behind the
> mountains in the valley of the Blue Moon, preserved as by miracle for
> a new Renaissance." (1990: 158)

Although the preoccupation with pre-Occupation Tibet, and with a miracle that will preserve its "lost and legendary treasures," still dominates the field of Tibetology, anthropological and sociological interest in Tibetan culture in exile has, in fact, grown since the mid-1970s. By that time, it had become clear that the refugees were not likely to return to Tibet any time soon, and the settlements or "camps" in India and Nepal had taken on a certain feeling of permanence. Also, after a decade of closed borders during the Cultural Revolution, the death of Mao Tse-tung in 1976 opened the way for handfuls of Westerners to visit Tibet. However, rather than being replaced by the increase in accounts of Tibet published during this opening-up period, the prevalent nostalgia for a pristine and timeless Tibet was given new life, since the image of Shangri-La contrasted so dramatically and appealingly with the disruption and chaos of the Chinese invasion, the Cultural Revolution, and the squalor of the refugee camps in India and Nepal. Along these same lines, many recent publications about Tibetans are primarily interested in "pure survivals"—native cultural elements that have not been "torn away by the roughness of modern society" (Forbes 1989: 159). As Calla Jacobson has noted,

> Material and environmental conditions are, anywhere that refugees set-
> tle, vastly different from those of pre-invasion Tibet. Yet there is little
> discussion of how Tibetan cultural practices, and the everyday lives of
> Tibetan people, are changing in response to such conditions. (1994: 13)

There are, of course, exceptions to this romantic trend.[25] In particular, new scholarship on Tibetans being produced by graduate students and young professors, much of it unpublished as yet, indicates a hopeful shift in interests that may well finally establish anthropological, artistic, literary, and sociological concern with the lives of laypeople as valuable fields of inquiry in Tibetan Studies. These studies are honest, sometimes jarring, accounts that consider refugee life holistically and include critiques of the field's historically selective vision in their design. Much of this new work, including this book, sympathetically but critically examines not only the effects of scholarly biases but also the particular effects of the dominant paradigm of "cultural preservation" espoused by the Tibetan government-in-exile in Dharamsala on the everyday lives of refugees. "Shangri-La" is now being examined from the inside out as a rhetorical trope employed as frequently and perhaps more fervently by Tibetans themselves than by Westerners. After four decades in exile, many Tibetans realize not only that the utopian dream is still an important source of hope but also that it can be a source of disappointment and frustration that has very real effects on individuals and communities who are raised to feel responsible for its actual, though unlikely, realization.

A glance at the kinds of topics being addressed and at the approaches being applied by this new generation of scholars reveals a general concern for the long-term effects of exile on Tibetan refugees, greater attention to the influences of Chinese socialization and culture on the refugee population, and a generally more global perspective that examines the intersections of international discourses and practices (academic, human rights, New Age, "fourth world") with local traditional and hegemonic discourses in refugees' daily lives. Even among young scholars of Tibetan Buddhism there is evidence of increasing interest in change, rather than only in preservation, and greater attention to contextualized religious practice than to isolated texts. Two recent collections of articles edited by Frank Korom address these issues and provide a substantial indication of the direction Tibetan Studies is heading (1997a, 1997b).

Yet a crucial gap in Tibetan Studies remains. Very little anthropological work has been conducted in Tibet itself in the last thirty years.[26] Tibet remains "forbidden" for many today owing to the expense of traveling there, the erratic visa and travel policies of the Chinese government, and fear of censorship and even imprisonment. Further complicating the situation is the fact that most Tibetans and many Westerners have tended to be suspicious of scholars who do manage to conduct fieldwork in Tibet, assuming that because they were allowed to do research they must have had to cooperate with the Chinese authorities and compromise the integrity of their findings. Even publications that attempt to balance misrepresentations made by parties on both sides of the Tibet Question (cf. Grunfeld 1987) are often dismissed as pro-Chinese by Tibetans and their Western sympathizers. As a result of these various constraints, much of the best anthropological documentation of Tibetan culture *in Tibet* is arguably still contained in the literature produced fifty or one hundred years ago.[27] Although a certain amount of cultural scholarship is being undertaken by Chinese and Tibetan academics in Tibet, the publications that reach foreign audiences are generally limited to the unabashedly propagandistic material issued, often in the English language, by the Chinese government. It seems, however, that scholarship and history itself are refusing to collude with essentialist discourses from inside and outside Tibet that attempt to authoritatively narrate the stories of Tibet and Tibetans from narrow and highly politicized perspectives.[28]

This raises the complicated question of advocacy, in particular the need for each scholar or individual working with or documenting Tibetans to negotiate a balance between sympathy and scholarship that has integrity and is sustainable. The American Anthropological Association's ethics statement has as its summum bonum the "welfare of subjects," a position that is wide open to interpretation. The issue of advocacy gets sticky, of course, when two ethnic groups are in conflict or when there is in-group discord. In the case of Tibetan refugees, the "subjects" generally assume and expect that foreigners working in their community are supportive of the Tibetan Cause and will maintain a proactive role in "getting China out of Tibet." This perception is generally confirmed as accurate by the content and tone of most of the documentary work being produced by Westerners. The effect this tacit agreement has had on anthropological scholarship, particularly its role in creating the "zones of invisibility" referred to earlier, is a thematic concern that underlies this project.

THE ORGANIZATIONAL DESIGN OF THIS BOOK

Both the content and design of this book are informed by the theme of echoes, as both a theoretical notion and as experience. Places, musical sounds and rhythms, languages, generations, individuals, and groups echo off one another in ways that are particularly complex and multiple for refugees. Intellectual theories echo off one another as well and this dynamic is another thread that winds throughout this text. In keeping with this theme, the chapters are meant to echo off one another, too, as do the sounds and places they discuss. I have chosen a narrative structure and voice that favor and depend on allowing the chapters to build on and ricochet off of one another as the layers of experience they articulate do for Tibetan refugees. It is the reader's task, then, to keep the stories and issues presented in each chapter in mind as they unfold, in order to experience the confusion, dissonance, and cultural richness that are revealed through the cumulative realization that these aspects of Tibetan refugee life are all happening continually and simultaneously.

To allow for in-depth discussion of each of the musics (and, in turn, the places and people) that contribute to the multilayered culture of Tibetan refugees in Dharamsala, and to highlight the physical, historical, and personal interfaces between this particular community and its wider context, I have constructed this book around a circular representation of places and sounds imagined from the generalized perspective of a Tibetan refugee living in exile in north India. This geographical and conceptual mandala places Dharamsala, as most Tibetan refugees would, at the intersection of perpendicular axes, a space located somewhere between Tibet (north) and India (south), China (east) and the "West." These spatial coordinates are, further, widely imbued with general qualities that are informed by both experience and hearsay. The common oppositional pairing of homeland

(Tibet) and exile (India), friend (the "West") and foe (China) by Tibetan refugees further substantiates this design:

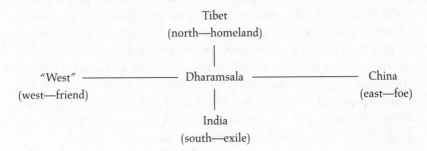

This simple diagram is, in turn, the foundation for an analogous mandala of musics that may be overlaid onto it. This move is meant to convey that, despite current academic discomfort with cultural boundedness and with the attribution of discrete origins to people and their practices, particular musical genres are, in fact, perceived by most Tibetans as aural icons of particular places and cultures and therefore can and should be analyzed from this local vantage point. As they do with the geographical places that anchor this mandala, most Tibetans also attribute the musics that make up Dharamsala's soundscape with specific qualities based again on a combination of historical information, personal experience, and desires. The common contrasting perceptions of traditional Tibetan music (meaningful and authentic) and Indian pop music (superficial and entertaining), Chinese music (colonial and oppressive) and Western rock (liberating and risky) both grow out of and inform how each of these sounds, their geopolitical origins, and the people who make them are understood locally. These perceptions also deeply inform the place that has been created in Dharamsala—the literal yet liminal intersection of the places and musics mentioned—for the new genre of "modern Tibetan songs" being made in exile:

In subsequent chapters, each of these song categories will be discussed from the perspectives of Dharamsala's Tibetan refugees, as will the links and echoes between Dharamsala and each of the places the songs index. I emphasize here and throughout this book that what complicates this apparently cut-and-dry native point of view is the fact that, despite these tidy conceptual categories and the strong investments people have in their integrity, sounds and musical boundaries are, ultimately, immaterial and are therefore felt and experienced in personal and varied ways. Ethnomusicologist Mark Slobin nicely expresses the cognitive and experiential gaps between the discrete, freestanding cultural forms we often desire and consequently perceive and the fluidity of these "forms" when considered more objectively:

> Amid a set of personal landscapes we can identify formations, musical Stonehenges, that stand free and look communal. Like that ancient pile, such structures are cryptic, mutely posing puzzles of who shaped them and what they represent. Unlike those changeless megaliths, musical monuments are mobile, flexible, more like a mirage. The nearer you get, the more their rigid outlines shift in the shimmering air. Less poetically, what I mean is that we make temporary shelters of our musical materials, not only personally, but collectively. Up close, what's "Irish," "American," or "Irish-American" looks like the work of tent-dwellers, not stone-raisers after all. (1993: x)

In this book about Tibetan refugees and their relationships to music, the categories of "tent-dweller" and "stone-raiser" are complicated and shown to be useful but not exclusive. It is *not* my goal to reveal by means of formal musical analysis that these people's deep and often-articulated belief and investment in a monumental "Tibetan tradition"—a Himalayan Stonehenge, if you will—is a hollow construction. I am primarily concerned with how various genres are experienced and narrated by Tibetan refugees as individuals and as a community. At the same time, my fieldwork experience has compelled me to consider frankly and to include stories and events that point to the significant effects cultural "megaliths" or traditions have on a community's life and, in particular, on the creative efforts of its younger members. The wide variety of relationships to sounds that I encountered during my stay in Tibetan refugee communities, perceived more widely as a variety of relationships to cultures, is exciting to some Tibetans and troublesome to others. To the former, an openness to new, more nomadic ways of "being Tibetan" is healthy, modern, and creative; to the latter, such openness to the fruits of unintended mobility indicates a weakening of commitment to community, with the blurring of boundaries signaling the end of the struggle and the fading away of any hope of returning to the homeland.

Starting with the exilic center (Dharamsala) and working clockwise (the auspicious direction for Tibetans) from Tibet (considered as both the traditional homeland and as a territory under Chinese rule) to India and the "West," the chapters that follow document and analyze all the issues raised in this introduction, showing how various traditions influence Tibetan tastes and identities in exile in material and less tangible ways. Sound values—ideas and feelings about which sounds are beautiful, authentic, foreign, or ugly—are shown throughout the book to be a crucial component in the embodied processes of self- and boundary-making that contribute to feelings of both solidarity and anxiety in exile. Because musical expression is the focus of this book, all the chapters are grounded in live performances that I attended, recorded, and sometimes participated in over the course of my year in India. Memories, associations, and stories ricochet off particularly important songs and crystallize the issues being theoretically and ethnographically explored in each given chapter, reinforcing that my analysis always emerges from performed sounds and relationships.

Chapter 1 introduces Dharamsala, my primary field site, and many of the people and local places that are central to this book's story. My discussion of Dharamsala is grounded in the concept of pilgrimage because of this Himalayan town's dual character as a holy destination for many Tibetan refugees and as a place they all hope to eventually leave. I suggest that the resulting tension between simultaneously feeling at home and out of place informs the emotional power songs have as icons of places for Tibetan refugee listeners.

Chapter 2 presents some of the imagined and tangible ways in which the roots of the Tibetan homeland penetrate and are selectively cultivated in Indian soil, thereby highlighting the historicity of popular memory and what comes to be called "tradition." Through descriptive accounts of traditional opera performances, school plays, and other musical events, I discuss efforts by the Dalai Lama's government-in-exile to preserve what is commonly referred to as the "rich cultural heritage of Tibet." I also discuss the benefits and risks of these preservation attempts, including concerns about the long-term effects of an official cultural paradigm that authenticates the past and largely discredits the present.

Whereas chapter 2 complicates understandings of the "there and then" (pre-1950 Tibet) and of refugee efforts to preserve and/or re-create traditional Tibetan life in exile, chapter 3 is concerned with Tibetan refugee life in the "here and now" of contemporary India. In particular, I examine the place of Hindi film songs in Dharamsala's soundscape and the concerns their popularity among Tibetans has raised within a community dealing with volatile inter-ethnic relations and a fear of assimilation.

Tibetan refugee dreams of political independence or autonomy for the homeland are presented and analyzed in chapter 4 through a discussion of the often idealized romance with the "West" engaged in by young Tibetan refugees facing limited opportunities in their South Asian settlements. I argue that, as a style and as an ideology, Western rock-and-roll music is a powerful resource for young Tibetan refugees trying to imagine and pursue personal and political *rangzen* (independence) and seeking ways of being "modern" without deviating from the conservative core values of their community. Participating in an international pop culture is, I argue, a way for these refugees to express a solidarity with a wider human struggle through sounds that have a historical relationship with social change.

Chapter 5 describes how "modern Tibetan music," a new rock-influenced genre that has developed over the past ten years, fits into Dharamsala's soundscape. The story behind modern Tibetan music is largely a story about the social and artistic challenges young Tibetan refugee musicians face in their efforts to convince their community-in-exile that there is room for a new kind of music alongside, or even within, the politically charged concept of cultural preservation that presides in the Tibetan diaspora. As the emergence of modern Tibetan music has not been documented before, I narrate the brief but important history of this genre, focusing on the role of one particular songwriter/guitarist (Tsering Paljor Phupatsang) in its development and on the experiences of a rock group called the Yak Band, which "Paljor" eventually joined in Dharamsala.

Most of this book is devoted to discussions of how the musical sounds resonating in Dharamsala contribute to the making of Tibetan refugee identity, community, and culture. However, such an analysis would be incomplete without a discussion of the role song *lyrics* play in these processes. Chapter 6 is concerned, therefore, with what the lyrics of modern Tibetan songs communicate to Tibetan audiences and, further, *how* they communicate. I argue that as sacred sounds that index the holiness of the Tibetan language, as secular sounds associated with the political and cultural struggles of the community, as carriers of meaningful semantic information, and as reflections of the social forces that in part produced them, the lyrics of modern Tibetan songs contribute significantly and diversely to the ways Tibetan audiences listen to this music.

Finally, chapter 7 focuses on public music concerts, new phenomena in Dharamsala and elsewhere in the Tibetan diaspora that bring all the sounds discussed in this book together in a single place and time. By juxtaposing Hindi, English, Nepali, and Tibetan songs, these concerts are profoundly revealing cultural performances in which many of the social dynamics and communitywide challenges raised throughout this book are enacted. Rock concerts provide a new and controversial venue where refugees can express their appreciation for Tibetan *and* non-Tibetan musics, revealing a level of comfort with cultural ambiguity and a passion for foreign cultures that is worrisome to some in the community. While my observations are informed by all the concerts I attended and participated in during my year living with Tibetans in India, this last chapter primarily depends upon the experiences of Dharamsala's popular yet troubled Yak Band, including my own perspectives as the band's keyboard player.

In the book's brief conclusion, I reiterate that the fundamental belief of Tibetans in cyclicity and in its premise, impermanence, significantly shapes and orders their experiences as refugees. It is for this reason that I chose the trope of echoes to link the idea of cyclicity to the book's focus on music. Various genres of music echo off one another in the daily lives of Tibetan refugees, as do ideas, habits, and languages. These reverberations are not faithful to their sources, however, with each projection shaping and being shaped by its echo. This book supports its claim by showing that the ways different musics resonate with and against one another for Tibetan refugees reveal both subtle and remarkable changes that have generated tensions and ambiguities in the community-in-exile, despite its desire for clear boundaries. Striving for emplacement, cultural preservation, and ethnic purity, these refugees are unwittingly challenging attempts in academic and public policy to normalize expectations about how the conditions of marginality and multiculturalism will be experienced in today's world.

1 Dharamsala

A Resting Place to Pass Through

> Most people are principally aware of one culture, one setting, one home; exiles are aware of at least two, and this plurality of vision gives rise to an awareness of simultaneous dimensions, an awareness that—to borrow a phrase from music—is *contrapuntal.*
>
> Edward Said

Dharamsala is both a place of rest or refuge (the meaning of its Hindi name) and a place to pass through, both a destination and a place one must leave to fulfill the very promise of pilgrimage. Historically and today, this north Indian hill town has existed as both a center in the periphery and as the peripheral edge of the center for a variety of groups of people who have needed, for various reasons, to pause here. As both a center and a limen, Dharamsala is perhaps best considered as a crossroads, a focused but misplaced point through which most participants in the contemporary Tibetan refugee network pass.

While this book is focused specifically on the experiences of Tibetan refugees, the Tibetan segment of Dharamsala's ever-shifting population cannot be understood without placing it in the ebb and flow of British and Indian civil servants, nomadic shepherds, merchants, aid workers, scholars, dharma students, spies, tourists, and pilgrims of many nationalities, whose arrivals and passages onward have traced the well-worn, winding paths of this hillside town. Dharamsala, like the slabs of smooth slate set into the banks of the area's steep trails, allowing one to perch a heavy load, is a welcoming place marked by transience where few who arrive plan to stay. Although it is flourishing and growing, the town still has a cyclic life, due to the winter out-migration of tourists and Tibetan refugee traders and their return to the mountains to celebrate Tibetan New Year in February. These patterns serve as important reminders of the tentative relationships most Tibetan residents have with their home away from home and of the refugee community's continuing dependence on other groups of people.

This chapter complicates the notion of "home" considered from the perspective of exile, emphasizing the deep connections for Tibetans between the

Dalai Lama's presence in Dharamsala and being "in place," connections that extend more literal or geographically based understandings of displacement. Yet, at the same time, Dharamsala is not home to Tibetans. In many ways Dharamsala is physically and psychologically constructed by them as a liminal space, a temporary resting place in which many Tibetans refuse or are unable to make material or emotional investments. The result is a community formed and dwelling in liminality, increasingly intertwined with other communities. Although Dharamsala is in many ways liminal, it is, however, a community that has, over the course of several decades, developed deep structures of its own. This chapter closes with a discussion of the relationship between structure and *communitas*, drawing on my experiences as a participant in Dharamsala's significant community of Western visitors and residents and on Victor Turner's enduring insights regarding the marginal camaraderie generated by shared rites of passage and pilgrimage.

LAYERS OF HOMES

People who are part of a transnational diaspora community may, over the years, develop ties to several places, although each site may evoke sentiments of different kinds and degrees of intensity. James Clifford takes this observation further to note that even a specific longing for "home" may be focused on more than one place, particularly in the case of people living in a multiply centered diaspora network (1994: 305). Clifford has, however, been criticized for overemphasizing the multilocal or global nature of diasporas at the expense of people, like Tibetans, who remain sharply focused on a literal territorial center (Venturino 1997: 107). While there is no confusion among Tibetan refugees regarding the whereabouts of their homeland, after more than forty years in exile Tibetan refugees can be said to have layers of homes. Attending to the various relationships Tibetan refugees have with these multiple homes is important for understanding their relationships to the diversity of peoples and cultures that share them. While home lies without a doubt over the Himalayas, the north Indian town of Dharamsala has emerged as the community's home in exile and the center of the Tibetan diaspora. In addition, other settlements throughout South Asia, Europe, Australia, the United States, and Canada are regarded as homes by particular families who have been scattered here and there through a process of "rediasporization" (Clifford 1994: 305) or, in local parlance, "resettlement."

The primary reason for Dharamsala's prominence among Tibetan refugees is that it is the place of residence of the Fourteenth Dalai Lama

and his government-in-exile, along with a number of other important religious figures and their monastic communities. Tibetan residents of
Dharamsala often express their gratitude at being able to live close to their
leader during this extended period of displacement, and many have
sacrificed other opportunities in exile to live in the cramped environment
of Dharamsala for this very reason. Tibetans sent away from Dharamsala
to work in other refugee settlements or even abroad sometimes feel long-
ings for home that vacillate between longing for Dharamsala and longing
for Tibet. This trans-Himalayan emotional echo is also experienced by
many Tibetans still living in Tibet who have never been to India yet who
regard Dharamsala as the contemporary spiritual and political center of the
Tibetan world. It is a center to them precisely because, in addition to being
the Dalai Lama's place of residence, it is located outside the homeland (and,
therefore, outside China's reach). For these Tibetans, ironically, staying behind in Tibet has proven to be its own form of exile, an experience that has
provided the impetus for a steady out-migration from the homeland to
India.

The ways in which Tibetan residents of Dharamsala understand "where
they are" depends on the physical, historical, and personal resonances for
them between Dharamsala and other places and, more specifically, on what
their route to the Tibetan capital-in-exile has been. Members of the oldest
generation in exile came to India from Nepal, Bhutan, or India's North East
Frontier Area (now Arunachal Pradesh) after escaping from Tibet in 1959
on foot over the Himalayas, traveling in family groups under the cover of
darkness, following their leader into exile. Since then, for forty years, Tibetans have continued to escape from their homeland in a procession
whose flow varies with the seasonal weather, the attentiveness of Nepali
border patrols, the effects of specific Chinese policies in Tibet, and the varying intensity with which these policies are implemented in different regions of the country at different times.

Looking back, Tibetan refugees living in exile today settle into three
general waves of migration. The first escapees (between 1959 and the mid-
1960s) mostly came from Lhasa, Tingri, or other southern border areas of
the country. Few Tibetans escaped during the worst years of the Cultural
Revolution (1966–1976), but in the 1980s a second wave of refugees, a
number of whom had been imprisoned during the first decades of Tibet's
occupation, fled Tibet. Since the early 1990s, a third wave of refugees from
Amdo in the northeast, known as *sar jorpa* ("new arrivals"), have arrived
in exile, putting the greatest demands on the government-in-exile's resources and institutions since the first months spent establishing tent

camps, clinics, and schools in 1959. Virtually all refugees who make it safely to Kathmandu—even those who ultimately resettle somewhere other than India and especially those who must return to Tibet—make the journey to Dharamsala to receive the Dalai Lama's blessing. His presence has made this Indian hill station a sacred site, a destination for pilgrims, and a temporary spiritual and political home for his followers. The sacralizing effect that the Dalai Lama's presence has wherever he is recalls Arnold van Gennep's early conceptualization of the "pivoting of the sacred" (1908: 12), in which the "sacred" is variable, rather than absolute, and is "brought into play by the nature of particular situations" (1908: 12).

Tibetans in Dharamsala always know where the Dalai Lama is on any given day, even though he travels abroad so extensively and frequently. Without fail, every time he returns to town, Dharamsala's Tibetan population, alerted through the local grapevine to the leader's estimated time of arrival, lines the winding mountain road from Lower Dharamsala to his residence near the main temple to welcome him home. Banners are strung across the road, a colorful archway is erected at the entrance to the temple compound, and roadside *chorten* are stoked with juniper enveloping the waiting crowds with sweet smoke. These arrival scenes always took me by surprise, and happening on one by accident on my way home from an appointment or in the course of doing errands made any day a joyful one. I would linger with the excited crowd on the passenger side of the road (heading uphill), always moved by the intense anticipation and devotion of those around me and reminded of the Dalai Lama's centrality to the sense of community here. At some point the crowd would suddenly go stone quiet, alerted to the imminent approach of the Dalai Lama's motorcade by some apparently telepathic communication from those waiting further downhill. When the leader's vehicle rounded the bend a few moments later, the deep silence always grew impossibly deeper and heads would bow. Those who looked up, as I always did, were greeted by a direct gaze from a smiling face behind hands placed together in a gesture of warm greeting, blessing, and appreciation. He always appeared truly happy to be home from Germany, Japan, Harvard, Delhi.

Though the car whooshed by in a brief moment, it always seemed to me as if time slowed down whenever the Dalai Lama passed by. Unlike most great things that, when glimpsed, leave you wishing you had paid more attention, I always felt like I had had a full dose, had noticed everything—as had everyone else around me. I felt a rush of happiness roll like a wave through those present as the car passed, and that joy burst out of the deep silence into chatter and jostling as the crowd quickly scattered the moment the car was out of sight. Within seconds, only Western tourists would remain by the roadside, mindfully savoring the auspiciousness of the moment or, as I overheard more than once, asking, "That was *it?*" Just a glimpse is all Tibetans need to be assured that order, within disorder, has been temporarily restored in their exiled community.

PLACING DHARAMSALA

Dharamsala is located in the farthest northern reaches of India, in the middle of a narrow finger of land that squeezes between Pakistan and the snowy Himalaya mountains that create India's border with Tibet. It is in many ways an odd place of refuge, perched as it is in the middle of one of the world's political hot spots. On a given day, it is hard to believe, looking out from the town's ridges over the valleys below, that one is only a few hours' journey away from a number of violent and desperately drawn-out struggles. To the north of Dharamsala, in the Muslim-majority state of Jammu and Kashmir, Islamic fundamentalists are fighting to become either part of Pakistan or independent from India; on the northern border of this troubled state, Indian and Chinese military forces have battled for decades over the contested glacial borders of Ladakh. To the south of Dharamsala, in the agriculturally rich Punjab, a militant sect of Sikhs persists in its struggle for an independent religious homeland called "Kalistan," causing unrest that frequently interrupts railway service through the region. To the west, Pakistan wrestles with internal leadership struggles and continues to build up arms and resentments against neighboring India. And, most significant to this study, to the east, in Tibet, Tibetans carry on a subversive freedom campaign of their own, refusing to accept the Chinese claim that their vast homeland is an integral part of the Chinese "motherland."

"Dharamsala" is actually a general name used to refer to several distinct communities—Lower Dharamsala, Gangkyi, and McLeod Ganj—stacked on a common mountainside and linked by a continual flow of people, vehicles, and goods up and down the hill. The actual town of Dharamsala is a medium-sized commercial center at the bottom of the steep slope. As the administrative center of the Kangra District of Himachal Pradesh, Lower Dharamsala features a busy and well-stocked bazaar; a large judiciary complex; numerous public offices; and a wide range of transportation, banking, and commercial services. This small city can be reached in twelve hours by bus from Majnu-ka-Tilla, the large Tibetan refugee camp on the outskirts of Delhi, or by taking the overnight train to Pathankot, a dusty and chaotic transportation hub on the plains, and continuing by bus or taxi for another

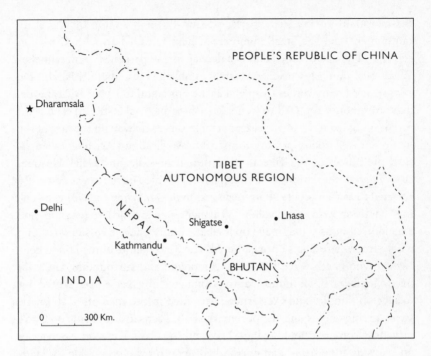

Map 1.   Dharamsala in its geopolitical context.

three hours up into the Himalayan foothills. The surrounding landscape is streaked with streams and rivers and dotted with lantana bushes and boulders scattered long ago by glaciers pushing through these valleys. Livestock grazes around packed mud houses roofed with local slate. Lower Dharamsala remains mostly Indian, although a cluster of Tibetan families live near the Lower Tibetan Children's Village school built, to their dismay, near the ghost-inhabited cremation grounds by the river. A few Tibetan merchants regularly set up roadside stalls and sell cheap ready-made clothing they have brought in from the larger Indian cities. Most of the Tibetans who live in the surrounding area buy all their staple foods, hardware supplies, household goods, and cloth from Indian merchants in Lower Dharamsala's extensive bazaar, one of many ways the Tibetan refugee presence has boosted the local economy. [1] The opening of a Phillips franchise, selling enormous boom boxes, televisions, and VCRs, as well as shops displaying formerly extravagant equipment such as washers and dryers for domestic use attest to this material boom.

The road splits at the top of Kotwali bazaar, dividing buses and lorries from taxis, scooters, and pedestrians. The left fork winds back and forth up the mountain in lazy switchbacks, passing through a large Indian Army cantonment and the small commercial hamlet called Forsyth Ganj that serves it. The narrow road enters a deodar forest, passes St. John's-in-the-Wilderness (an Episcopalian church established by the British in the 1850s), and finally comes to an end at the bus stand in Upper Dharamsala, most commonly referred to by its British name, McLeod Ganj. The right fork leaving from the lower bazaar steeply carves its way up the face of the mountain, eventually passing the Tibetan Medical and Astrological Institute, the offices of the Tibetan government-in-exile, and Delek Hospital clustered together midway up the hillside. This area of activity is generally referred to as Gangkyi (a shortened version of *Gangchen Kyishong*, meaning "happy snow-covered valley"). Farther along are the two tea shops and a handful of houses that make up Jogibara, a tiny enclave clustered around a holy tree where yogis once gathered. The descendants of the Hindu gentleman who once owned the entire compound and surrounding land still live in Jogibara, but a number of the stone dwellings have been rented out to Tibetan families and Westerners. Any turn in the road offers dramatic views, giving one, as one visitor remarked, the "sensation of being on God's private balcony, overlooking India" (Powell 1992: 36). The road, eaten away on one side by erosion and encroached upon on the other side by landslides, continues to wind uphill past the Dalai Lama's residence and the area's principal Tibetan temple (the *tsuglhakang*), finally entering McLeod Ganj, where most of the area's Tibetans live, via the "dry street" (parallel to the "muddy street," which is closed, in principle, to vehicles).

Although the regions around McLeod Ganj regularly boil with ethnic and political tension, for most Tibetan refugees living in Dharamsala, their capital-in-exile is an island, linked by grinding diesel buses across unfamiliar landscapes to specific and familiar destinations, including Delhi, Buddhist holy places such as Riwalsar and Bodh Gaya, and other Tibetan settlements scattered throughout India. The refugees harbor no great curiosity to explore their host country or eagerness to participate in its civil life; rather, most (except the youngest) interact as little as possible with its realities. The oldest are waiting to be told they can return home; others are unsure where to anchor their dreams. As I proposed in the introduction with simple spatial and musical mandalas, the ways in which many Tibetan refugees imagine the geography of their lives from this exiled perspective differ greatly from conventional geopolitical maps of the region. Rather, their maps of orientation, like most people's, are selective arrangements of particular people and places as these have been directly experienced or imagined.

Figure 2.   A quiet early morning in the streets of McLeod Ganj.

It is important to keep in mind that the first Tibetan refugees, like many who have followed, believed their stay in India would be brief, with most expecting to return to their homes in Tibet after one or two years at the most. Kongoe Jampa Phuntsok, a Tibetan language teacher at the Upper Tibetan Children's Village school who supervised the work conditions of Tibetan road crews during the early years in exile, told me: "If you had told me back then that I would still be in India after thirty-six years, I would have called you crazy." That a psychological and physical aura of temporariness has persisted in Tibetan settlements all over India and Nepal, despite the passage of so much time, reflects an often-conscious refusal by many refugees to accept their situation as permanent. The difficult decisions generated by this emotionally and politically informed temporariness—such as whether to apply for Indian citizenship or purchase immovable property—will be further discussed in chapter 3.

A HISTORICAL RESTING PLACE

Before the mid-nineteenth century, the area around Dharamsala was home only to Pahari-speaking Gaddi people, seminomadic goat herders who moved their flocks up and down the surrounding mountains as the seasons shifted. A good number of Gaddis still cling to their homes in the area, though many are entirely surrounded now by multistoried guest houses whose inhabitants can peer into once-private family courtyards paved with slate. The Gaddi men, dressed in bright pillbox caps and wool vests, defiantly drive their flocks right through busy McLeod Ganj, while their wives and daughters dressed in flowered *salwaar kameez* hack down the sparse foliage in the area to use as fodder (a practice that infuriates environmentally conscious visiting Westerners unfamiliar with local history). These Indians generally avoid much interaction with Tibetans and Westerners, but the tensions between the shepherds and the refugees are palpable, particularly since a Gaddi youth was fatally stabbed by a young Tibetan man in April 1994 during an argument over a cricket match. That incident, which will be further discussed in chapter 3, unleashed years of pent-up anger among the Gaddi and other local Indians, resulting in mob rioting and vandalism to Tibetan property.

The Gaddis were first encroached on in the early 1860s by the British, after Dharamsala had been established as the summer seat of the Jullundur Division. I quote John Avedon's description of McLeod Ganj during the Raj at length:

> Beginning with a military cantonment on the shoulder of the tallest crest, Mun Peak, [the British] had gone on to found a small town, McLeod Ganj, on a slender ridge facing the plains below. A colonnade was erected to house shops, fronted by a genteel park of cedar trees, a birdbath and stone benches. Down the hill rose the rusticated belfry of St. John's in the Wilderness, an Anglican church, while, scattered well apart over the slopes, more than a hundred bungalows sprang up, sporting turrets and gingerbread woodwork, vaulted ceilings and multiple wings, and dubbed with a bevy of romantic names such as Ivanhoe, Eagle's Net, Chestnut Villa, Wargrave and Retreat.
>
> By the turn of the century, McLeod Ganj supported one of the most vigorous societies, outside the cities, of any in the Raj. With the rail line put through to Pathankot, seven miles from the foothills, bureaucrats from both Delhi and Lahore flocked to the mountains. In the spring the woods were blanketed with primrose, mistletoe and red and mauve rhododendron, followed in June, after the onset of the monsoon, by an explosion of buttercups, violets and honeysuckle. Wildlife abounded: leopards, panthers, porcupines, foxes, jackals, hyenas, red-faced monkeys and huge white-maned langurs roamed the lower hills, joined in the colder months, when they descended to forage, by black and brown bears. Above McLeod Ganj hawks and white-bellied vultures wheeled in wide gyres on all sides. Partridges, pigeons, ravens and

snow pheasants flew tamely into town. Slated to become the summer capital of the Raj, Dharamsala's future seemed secure until an earthquake struck in 1905. The British picked Simla instead and those local officials who remained relocated their offices 1,500 feet down the hillside to the less exposed Lower Dharamsala. On August 15, 1947— India's independence day—they departed as well. (1986: 83–84)

Also in the late 1940s, resident Muslims left the area for Pakistan as the result of Partition, and the wealthy Hindus who had summered in the hills during the Raj returned to Delhi, reducing the town's population from four thousand to only seven hundred (Goodman 1986: 316). For more than a decade, McLeod Ganj was something of a ghost town, with the exception of a general store established in 1860 by a Parsi merchant and still run today by his descendants, who sell sweets, daily newspapers, and homemade sodas out of dusty Victorian display cases. As local lore has it, when Mr. Nowrojee, the latest patriarch of this merchant dynasty, who passed away in 1999, heard of the plight of the young Dalai Lama in 1959, he contacted the Indian government and proposed that the religious leader and his followers be allowed to stay as long as they needed in this remote mountain village, a proposal that some attribute to Nowrojee's great compassion and that others identify as economic foresight bordering on genius. Prime Minister Nehru approved the idea, and the Dalai Lama sent representatives from his temporary residence in Mussoorie to assess the site. In 1960 the Tibetan leader moved to McLeod Ganj, despite his concerns that this refuge was so far from Delhi, making travel and communication difficult. In an interview recounted by Avedon, the Dalai Lama recalled the warm welcome he received upon his arrival in the place that has now been his home-in-exile for four decades:

> Three thousand people, hill folk in their bright embroidered mountain caps, Sikhs in scarlet and blue turbans, bureaucrats and businessmen wearing black suits, their wives clad in diaphanous saris, and even Gurkhas, descended from the still-active army cantonment, lined the route showering their new neighbor with flowers, once of which carried a small caterpillar, which, as the Dalai Lama reminisced, rather ungraciously bit him on the leg. With the sun tinting the adjacent dome of Mun Peak violet, the column drove five miles more up steep switchbacks through the cantonment to McLeod Ganj, where at 5:00 P.M. it passed beneath a freshly hewn bamboo gate dressed in fir boughs and colored streamers, a big golden WELCOME written across its top. Behind it, 250 Tibetan refugees who had arrived a week before began performing full-length prostrations, while khaki-clad Indian police frantically urged them back. (1986: 85)

The older Tibetan women in Dharamsala whom I came to know as accomplished traditional singers and dancers recall that life in McLeod Ganj during the 1960s and 1970s was extremely hard. Many refugees lived in tents under trees or in the shelter of the Civil Dispensary's porch (one of the few British buildings in town that is still standing and in use) until temporary shelters built from flattened tin cooking oil containers and stones were built all over the surrounding hillsides. A good number of the refugees who were drawn to settle in Dharamsala because of the Dalai Lama's presence and the newly established Tibetan schools worked as "coolies" for many years, both for Indian government-sponsored road improvement projects all over northern India and for local building projects initiated by the new Tibetan government-in-exile (including the Dalai Lama's present residence and adjacent temple). As the population of McLeod Ganj swelled, the park that had been a median between two widely spaced rows of shops was replaced with a third row of two-story homes and businesses, thus creating the two narrow lanes one still stumbles along today.

A TEMPORARY HOME

In addition to being a center for Tibetan refugees, Dharamsala is simultaneously constructed and experienced as a liminal place, negatively defined as "not Tibet." Complaints about Dharamsala (and India more generally) flow freely among its refugee population, and efforts to sustain a sense of the place as a temporary camp are widely evident (though after four decades this impression must be nurtured in increasingly conscious ways). Some refugees in the diaspora avoid Dharamsala altogether, specifically because of the ambition, materialism, self-consciousness, and conservatism engendered by its status as an international hub of activism, tourism, and bureaucracy and because of its overcrowdedness and uncleanliness.

Little attention has been successfully paid to developing Dharamsala's infrastructure to keep up with the town's current building boom, initially (and still to some extent) due to the persistent optimism of local Tibetans that extensive planning was not needed, since they would not be staying there for long. Tom Grunfeld, who is openly critical of the Dalai Lama's administration[2] and is therefore often dismissed by Tibetans and their sympathizers as a Chinese apologist, notes that

> considerable sums of relief money have been sent to the refugees, but this money has not been managed adequately. Blame must be put with the Tibetan leaders in Dharamsala. Even in the Dalai Lama's own backyard, Dharamsala, where approximately 3,000 Tibetans live, the sani-

tary conditions remain deplorable—with an acute shortage of public la-
trines and no system for the disposal of garbage, as recently as 1979. . . .
It was not until 1981 that a Department of Health was established;
even, at that, only enough money was allocated to run the office in
Dharamsala. (1987: 194)

Indeed, even today the muddiness of the "muddy street" is primarily a
function of leaky water pipe connections and open sewage gutters bridged
haphazardly with doorsteps and grates. McLeod Ganj offers no reliable
system for garbage collection, with informally designated hillsides having
served for years as dumping grounds for household, shop, hotel, and
restaurant waste to the delight of wandering cows, crows, and monkeys
who carry plastic bags full of garbage all over the mountains. Each evening
merchants sweep trash out of their shop doorways into the street. Early the
next morning, low-caste Indian sweepers from nearby villages make their
way down the two streets with straw brooms, gathering the trash into bas-
kets at the end of town and tossing it over the hillside. Dumpsters installed
at the edges of town are of little use, since there is no system for collecting
the gathered waste and, ultimately, nowhere to take it. The contents of
dumpsters rejected by scavenging animals and birds are simply burned
when the containers overflow. Efforts by McLeod Ganj's "Green Office"
to educate town residents about recycling have effected some changes.
Tourists—who on average use and discard one or two plastic mineral water
bottles per day—are encouraged to refill their bottles with filtered water at
the Green Shop for half the cost of new bottles. In addition, at least for a
while, volunteers collected plastic shopping bags from households for re-
use by merchants.

Dharamsala's filthy state has drawn the attention of many Western visitors. The tangible nature of the town's garbage problem often makes it the
first of what will be many indicators to visitors that a gap exists between
the Dalai Lama's internationally broadcast statements on the importance
of protecting the planet and the daily practices of his own people living in
challenging circumstances in exile. As one tourist said to me: "But the
Dalai Lama has proposed making Tibet a huge environmental park. . . .
Does he plan on having Tibetans living there?!"[3] Tibetan residents generally attribute the mess to Indians personally or India generally, perceptions
of cleanliness and filth being an important aspect of intergroup relations
that Girija Saklani has addressed (1984), to be further discussed in chapter
3. The following theme song from a 1995 health-education video produced
by the local hospital is an interesting attempt to instill feelings of steward-
ship for Dharamsala in Tibetans:

SAVING THE ENVIRONMENT

by Ngawang Lhamo

To those who come here today and
To all Tibetan people together,
From all of us together
We wish you *"Tashi Delek!"*

About saving the environment,
Please consider this carefully.
Don't do things only for yourself.
You can also do good things to benefit everyone.

Please take care of your health and be clean,
To have a healthy body and happy mind.
You'll have less illness
And great mental happiness.

Please try to stop
Chang, liquor and cigarettes.
This helps your body.
When everyone sees you, it will look better.

This place is a pleasant landscape
Where His Holiness stays.
The way the palace turned out
Reminds me of the Potala.

Green forest and flowers
Surrounded by snowy mountains.
This place is a pleasant landscape.
It reminds me of my own country.

Drawing on religious notions of purifying the body and mind, local fears of being the target of chastising gossip, and geographic similarities between Dharamsala and Tibet, the song emphasizes the goodness of cleanliness. Beyond this rhetorical level, however, both Tibetans and Indians exhibit a general reluctance to improve the physical condition of Dharamsala. Local Indian officials are hesitant to allocate money for improving refugees' living conditions, especially when they are aware of the substantial foreign financial support the Tibetan community already receives. And Tibetans are not generally inclined to contribute to local improvement projects, since they assume that the money will only line the pockets of the Indian officials in charge. The result is a haphazard affair, layers of makeshift attempts by various people to make livable spaces for themselves over the course of 150 years.

A LAP OF MCLEOD GANJ

Contemporary McLeod Ganj has been described in many ways, most of which—starting with "Little Lhasa"—are extremely generous. On first impression, without the blindness to filth and overcrowding that can, it seems, come along with hard-earned affection for the life behind the walls of such a place, McLeod Ganj appears to be comprised of "tarpaper tacked to a mudslide," to borrow one Western visitor's words. Although there is no actual tarpaper to be seen in McLeod Ganj, the image conjures up an accurate sense of the jumble of hastily thrown-together and patched-up shacks and shops that fill the spaces between crumbling old stone buildings built during the Raj and new cement apartment blocks and hotels painted in pastel hues of yellow, green, and blue. The latter are almost as hastily constructed as the shacks, and the building by Tibetan and Indian speculators continues at a furious pace.

While the Gaddis and the Tibetans themselves are not pleased that Tibetan displacement has continued for forty years, others, such as Indian merchants and tourists of all nationalities, are making the most of the opportunities Dharamsala's unexpected reincarnation has created. Early each morning, Indian fruit and vegetable sellers heave huge canvas sacks of produce onto the roofs of diesel buses heading up the mountain and do brisk business all day on the sides of McLeod Ganj's streets. These merchants and meat sellers, in their elevated wire mesh shacks, are the remote town's only source of fresh food. Indians own most and run approximately half of the shops in McLeod Ganj (including all dry and canned food shops but two), perform all manual services such as tailoring and shoe repair, and provide all services that require permits from the Indian government, such as telecommunications businesses. When the Dalai Lama offered to move away from Dharamsala as a peace-making gesture after the intergroup violence of 1994, it was ultimately non-Gaddi Indian businessmen who held a formal meeting with the leader and urged him to stay, knowing full well that McLeod Ganj (and their bank accounts) would empty out soon after his departure.

During the winter months (December to February), when the tourists have left for the beaches of Goa and the majority of Tibetans have set out on pilgrimage or sweater-selling trips on the plains, it is easy to imagine what McLeod Ganj would look like should the local Tibetan population suddenly return to Tibet or seek a new home in exile. Because of the bitterly damp cold during this time, most of the town's population departs, leaving stores and homes shuttered and well padlocked, schools closed, and offices frigid and short staffed. Many of those who stay behind cherish the quiet of this season, despite the lack of services and the incessant cold. During the winter of 1994 to 1995, an even greater number of people than normal left town in January, myself included, because the Dalai Lama was offering the Kalachakra initiation ceremony (a high tantric Buddhist teaching) in the summery climate of south India. While many pilgrims continued on from the Kalachakra to other Buddhist holy places in India, including Bodh Gaya, I returned to the snow and peace of off-season McLeod Ganj and relished time with acquaintances who were so cold and bored in their empty restaurants and offices that they were more than willing to talk over tea for hours.

Day by day throughout February the population and energy of the town grows, as the place draws residents and tourists back like a magnet to welcome in the new year (*Losar*) at the end of the month. The night before the first moon of the new year, a ritual is held in which effigies of the bad spirits and evil things from the closing year are constructed by the Namgyal monks of the Dalai Lama's personal monastery. Serenaded by the explosive blasts of long ritual horns and skin drums, the *torma* (figures made of colored butter) are assembled onto an elaborate altar and carried by a procession of monks in their great arched yellow hats to the intersection by the main temple at nightfall. The entire Tibetan community gathers in anticipation around an enormous haystack erected in the middle of the crossroads. The haystack is laced throughout with armfuls of firecrackers, so when the monks hurl the altar away into an opening that has been left in the straw and light it on fire, the whole construction explodes, sending children screaming in all directions and flames thirty feet in the air. Having purged the public space, families then stream up the hill to town, through the traffic jam caused by the roadblock, to perform similar cleansing rituals in their homes. Scraps from everyone's special holiday soup, lumps of dough that have been pressed on aches and pains, humanoid effigies, and threads of old clothing are collected in cardboard boxes, and someone sweeps through each room of the house with a flaming torch, scaring away any stubborn evil spirits who remain. The box of scraps and lumps is then carried in a rush out of the building, as the woman of the house sweeps barley flour that has been scattered on the floor out the front door, followed by a bucket of water, hissing "Shoo!" before she slams the door tight. My assistant, Lhanzom, her then-husband, Tenzin Lodo, and I raced from their home above Friends Corner Restaurant through town to the edge of the forest with our box and dumped it on a boulder. Lodo.la lit two boxes of firecrackers by the box, and we ran away whooping, leaving it crackling and

Figure 3.   Community ritual bonfire the night before
the New Year (*Losar*).

smoldering with the torch. "Don't look back!" Lhanzom yelled to me, as we
dodged cars and everyone else's exploding spiritual refuse. As I walked
home late that night through the forest, piles of embers glowed here and
there along the path. In the morning, the world felt quiet and clean. Bright
green barley seedlings sprouted out of *ghee* (clarified butter) cans on win-
dowsills to symbolize new beginnings, and the avid annual house cleaning
and rug beating that had busied the town during the past weeks were completed.

The celebration of *Losar* lasts for several days, beginning with a community blessing by the Dalai Lama at the temple and continuing with
dancing, feasting, drinking, and visiting. The holiday marks the new year
and the reawakening of the town, providing friends and families separated

by the winter break with a chance to exchange stories of their travels, business developments, and other news. The floodgates of Tibetan hospitality are open on these days, and savings from the winter's work are quickly spent. I had dinner with Paljor's family and was touched and embarrassed that they had figured out how to roast a whole chicken—*Inji* food—on the gas stove just for me. Gompo's burly relatives from Kham waved me in and found room for another well-wisher around their small table covered with charred goat legs, small sharp daggers, and strings of dried cheese cubes. There was extra butter in the churned butter tea. During this time, the streets of McLeod Ganj are packed full with families dressed in their best *chuba* (Tibetan dress) and bright silk shirts, pilgrims in thick wool visiting from Tibet and Bhutan, wealthy Indian tourists shivering in their Delhi clothes, and Westerners tanned from their winter visits to the south. All the stores are open again, full of new merchandise acquired in Ludhiana, Delhi, Lucknow. Everyone buys new clothes and shoes at *Losar*, and bright new prayer flags replace those sun-bleached and tattered by the previous year's work carrying auspicious blessings on the wind to all sentient beings. Tibetan opera arias blare out from TIPA's speakers up the hill, acoustically uniting the spread-out community as they echo back and forth in the valley.

With schools and offices closed, there is plenty of time for doing laps through town past the guest houses, bookshops of recycled English novels and guidebooks, video halls, trinket stores, and cafés. The *momo*, steamed meat dumplings pinched plump into round balls or crescent moons, are fresh at the Yak Restaurant, a favorite place of mine because the heat of the kitchen fills the tiny blue dining room and makes it so cozy on cold days. The rooftop tables of the pink Tsongka Restaurant run by "new arrivals" from Amdo are set up again: chilly in March, hard work for the boys who carry orders up and down the narrow stairs, but worth the view and the profits. Friends Corner looks cheerful with its new red and white checked tablecloths and now offers "home fries" and chocolate chip cookies to its patrons. The traveling Sikh dentist in his turquoise turban is back in place at the top of the dry street, displaying old eyeglasses and rows and rows of single teeth and pliers (he will yank them out *or* glue them in). "As you like, Madam." The tall, blue-eyed Kashmiri *kuli* (coolies) in their drab beige wool capes hang out in the doorway of the abandoned British store by the taxi stand that has since been razed to make room for a three-story shopping complex. They are sad bearded men who will carry your full gas tank, duffel bags, or building materials across town, trotting on the downhill, desperate enough for work to leave their young families behind in their ruined homeland. The *taxiwalla* who normally lounge around together smoking *bidis* in their tiny booking office are busy, driving whole families up and down the mountain with their bundles. A long line winds out of the Security Office, where Paljor, the Yak Band's guitarist, used to work. Inside, Tibetan bureaucrats are taking down information from those who wish to attend the Dalai Lama's public audience, scheduled for later in the week.

The fuzzy pirated movies change daily now at the cramped "Om Vision" and "Shambala" video halls. The "Roamers"—romantic young Tibetan men disillusioned with their community's apparent complacency in exile, supported by welfare handouts and the profits from peddling hashish to Westerners—are back on the steps of the Shangri-La Café, smoking and watching the passing scenes. Captain Henry rum and extra-strength Thunderbolt beer are flowing at the dimly lit Hotel Tibet bar, where the local intelligentsia debate world politics and speculate about changes in a post-Deng China. Seemingly unaware of the changes around him, the man in the box by the empty lot on the muddy street has been in place all winter, hidden by the blankets and stray puppies that keep him warm and fed by Indian relatives who tend to him and remember him before he went mad. The streets are busy and full. While chatting on the steps of Friends Corner, Lhanzom and I are distracted by the sight of a huge cow happily eating imported mangos, one after the other, which had spilled out from under the burlap sack an absent *phalwalla* had tossed over the fruit he was selling. "Prakash! Oh, Prakash!" Lhanzom shouted to the seller who was enjoying *chai* with a friend across the way. Prakash dove at the cow, who turned and charged at me. I grabbed its horns, one in each hand, and playfully wobbled its head back and forth while scolding its brown eyes and slobbering mouth. There are enough people in town now that crowds form quickly. I have forgotten about the publicness of the streets, after a period of near-solitude, and am surprised by all the faces and laughter surrounding our semiserious charade.

I walk around town one evening, my tape recorder running in my jacket pocket. Listening later, I can make out the after-dinner sounds of the community over my footsteps on the uneven streets: an Air India Radio broadcast in Tibetan, the breathless dialogue of a Hindi film aired on Star TV, chanting from the windows of the tiny monastery just up from the post office, a Hollywood chase scene from behind the doors of the video hall, three boys chasing a metal hoop down the road, prayer wheels turning, clean-up sounds from the Friends Corner kitchen window, French backpackers telling transportation horror stories over apple pie in the smoke-filled vegetarian

Green Restaurant, and somewhere, always, the barking of pariah dogs echoing between hillsides.

LIVING IN A FISHBOWL

While Tibetan refugees represent a dependent, and therefore dependable, customer base for local Indian merchants, a significant proportion of the refugees depend, in turn, on tourists to make a living. Each fall and spring, hundreds of tourists fill McLeod Ganj's budget guest houses and restaurants to the point of bursting. While Indian merchants and service providers also benefit greatly from the semiannual influx of Israeli, British, German, and American backpackers and upper-middle-class Western students of Buddhism, it is no secret that these travelers have come to Dharamsala specifically to meet and support Tibetans. For many, time in McLeod Ganj or in the burgeoning nearby "hippie" colony at Bhagsu Nag is specifically intended as time *away* from the hassles many travelers typically associate with India and, by extension, with Indians. A number of Western tourists stay long enough to enroll in short courses in Buddhist philosophy at the Tibetan Library of Works and Archives or to participate in one of the ten-day introductory retreats offered at Tushita, a branch of the Kathmandu-based Foundation for the Preservation of the Mahayana Tradition. Increasingly, Westerners are renting apartments or small houses in the area for extended stays of several months or, in some cases, years. Taken together, *Injis* play a significant social, as well as economic, role in the life of the town.

Those travelers who fit the "dharma bum" cliché are numerous, but they do not stay long in McLeod Ganj, eager as they are for exposure to a smattering of new (to them) spiritual experiences from all over India. While the following excerpt from a *New York Times* article may be factually correct, the piece's cynicism about the local scene is based on common clichés and superficial impressions:

> With the Dalai Lama persuaded to stay [in Dharamsala], the real gainers, apart from the Tibetans themselves, were the foreigners from Europe, Japan and North America who flock here. Some come as committed Buddhists, and eventually become monks and nuns, with shaven heads and maroon-and-yellow robes, although the Dalai Lama discourages it. . . . For other foreigners, a sojourn in Dharmsala [sic] is an opportunity to "hang out, take drugs, and get mystical," as one longtime foreign resident put it. For the equivalent of $1.70 a day, a couple can get a room in down-market hotels with names like Tibetan Dreamland.

Hashish is plentiful, and for those with more sublime interests, a monk
will conduct tutorials in Buddhism, for a few dollars a week. (Burns
1996: A6)

Because of their transience, the "dharma bums" eat all their meals in cafés,
wander all day in and out of shops, have their clothes hand washed at the
tiny Laundry 2000, wear their long hair loose, block doorways with their
backpacks, and physically dominate local buses, all of which makes them the
most visible Westerners in town and the primary source of information
used by locals to draw their own ethnographically based conclusions about
Injis. Yet though they are the most visible Westerners, they are actually the
most marginally involved in the town's life. Those hippie types who do stay
for a while eventually find one another and cluster together at Bhagsu Nag
(the site of a Hindu temple and waterfall a few kilometers out of town) and
at all-night full moon parties high up near the snow line in Triund. These
parties are one way that young travelers seek to re-create the ritual conditions under which "spontaneous communitas may be . . . invoked" (Turner
1969: 138). Focused as they are on establishing intense shared experiences
with one another, their contact with Tibetans is limited to hanging out with
and, for some women, becoming romantically involved with, unemployed
Tibetan male youth who cultivate peripheral relationships with the Tibetan
refugee community for reasons of their own.

In contrast, a great number of Westerners come to Dharamsala with
specific charity, research, or self-improvement projects in mind. Dharamsala is their ultimate destination in India. Most stifle their senses upon
landing in Delhi, clutch their audio-visual equipment close to them on the
overnight train to Pathankot, and let out a sigh of relief when the first
prayer flags come into view upon rounding the last bend of Dharamsala's
Mall Road. Those Westerners who come to Dharamsala for spiritual reasons and choose to stay are, with a few exceptions of course, deeply committed students and practitioners who have contributed in many ways to
the welfare of the community as a whole: as English teachers, translators,
financial sponsors, business patrons, and friends. Other visitors are scholars, journalists, filmmakers, students on college year-abroad programs, and
representatives of aid organizations. Nearly all are very sympathetic to the
Tibetan Cause and hope to promote its success through their spiritual,
artistic, academic, or fund-raising activities. It is for them that restaurants
play cassettes of monks chanting, strive to make the best banana pancakes
in town, and resist their inclinations to rinse glasses clean with tap water
before bringing them to the table.

Almost any time of year, a quick check of the guest roster at the fanciest guest houses in town—Hotel Tibet, Chonor House, and Kashmir Cottage—will reveal the presence of at least one film crew, someone "writing a book about Tibetan refugees," two dozen college students conducting independent research projects for the Experiment in International Living or a college semester overseas, and maybe even celebrity devotee Richard Gere or Harrison Ford. The entire red apartment block down by the Library of Tibetan Works and Archives in Gangkyi is rented out to visiting scholars with established reputations and permission to handle the library's important collection of Buddhist texts.

Life in Dharamsala is lived in a fishbowl. Very little that is visually appealing or newsworthy happens in town without cameras flashing, videos whirring, and microphones probing. This attention is tolerated by most Tibetans, including the old *amala* and *pala* with wrinkled faces, gold and turquoise earrings, and long, ribboned braids whose images are constantly being captured as they round a corner of the temple or chat with their peers against a sunny wall. They are grateful to Westerners and are well aware that their people's cause is kept alive internationally by such attention. The Dalai Lama has made it clear that each Tibetan has a personal responsibility to educate the world about Tibet's situation. And the work of many *Injis* has significantly raised funds and consciousness.

The Tibetans' willingness to cooperate fits hand in glove, however, with a presumptuous streak in many uninvited Westerners who have come to "help" Tibetans, a sense that they deserve access and assistance from those who will benefit from their kind intentions. Many Western visitors with a project in mind commonly assume, for example, that they have a right to an audience with the Dalai Lama. As the leader's private secretary explained to writer Andrew Powell: "So many Westerners want to see the Dalai Lama nowadays that I get quite a few complaints from Tibetans. They ask me if they need a foreign passport to have an audience with His Holiness" (1992: 56). This assertiveness does not go unnoticed by Tibetans accustomed to more subtle arts of negotiation, causing considerable frustration in some cases (although the requests of Western "guests" are generally complied with). A good number of refugees in Dharamsala have been deeply disappointed by unfulfilled promises of books, videos, photos, letters, or money to be sent in return for their images, words, or time. And there are the scammers, both Tibetans and *Injis*, who seek out friends to establish relationships that will lead to material benefits, whether a coveted letter of invitation to the United States or a series of photographs that will be published or win a prize.

PRIVATE SPACES

Often I was embarrassed to join the other Westerners kneeling in the front row at the temple to get the best view, frustrated at being the tenth person to interview an old man, righteous *and* jealous when a new acquaintance boldly snapped a photograph in the face of an old toothless nun carrying a huge marigold in the evening light, confused by a growing awareness of this need to document everything, to write, record, preserve, possess. Yet in the course of the ten months I lived in McLeod Ganj—as I established relationships with Tibetans, focused my research topic, and found something of a routine and niche—the journalistic scramble faded into the crazy pattern and texture of the town, and I became grateful for the camaraderie and ideas provided by individuals in the long-term local *Inji* community whom I came to know. These were women working full-time on health-education videos; volunteering at the Tibetan Women's Association; engaging in medical practice at Delek Hospital; editing articles for the *Tibet Journal;* teaching English to "new arrivals" or to nuns; educating school children about flossing and brushing; encouraging village women to use solar ovens; supervising the construction of a new nunnery; donning nun's robes and enrolling at the Institute of Higher Buddhist Dialectics; or conducting doctoral research on tantric ritual, childcare practices, or, in my case, music. All deeply involved in the Tibetan community, a handful more oriented toward the Indian community, we also created an intense subgroup of our own, seeped in the deep cultural and linguistic connections that become so important when one is displaced. Halloween pumpkins purchased from a Sikh family's kitchen garden and carved with the Buddha's eyes from the stupa in Bodinath, Nepal. A Thanksgiving "turkey" made of three skinny chickens roasted in spicy *chaat masala* and placed close together on a platter, pomegranate seeds for cranberries. Huddling together drinking coffee in the vaulted stone space of St. John's-in-the-Wilderness after a Christmas Eve caroling service while a sleet storm blustered outside, the warm spirit and reluctance to leave belying deep cultural connections to familiar Judeo-Christian traditions, despite intellectual leanings toward agnosticism or newer commitments to Buddhism. These were our own formal ways, supplemented by many daily rituals (sharing food, letters, tea), in which we established our commonality while dwelling in voluntary displacement, while resting in this place most of us planned to pass through. Some of these friends will, it seems, stay in Dharamsala forever; others will remain for years, until a family situation or relationship calls them back to England or Australia. For the rest of us, Dharamsala had at some point come to feel, as I remember writing one day in my field notes, like "where I live . . . not home, but where I live."

Since Malinowski set the trend in anthropology of conducting extended fieldwork, isolation from one's own culture, family, and friends has been understood to be a fruitful condition for gaining scholarly and experiential insight into how the "natives" live and think. Aside from the fact that choreographing such isolation today is nearly impossible, I found that the process of building a familiar (and familial) community in exile increased my empathy for the refugees whom I had traveled to get to know. I am not referring to any shared experience of "liminality," since the situations of a well-funded American scholar with a passport and a return ticket home and a stateless refugee are completely different, but to a respect for the need for structure within the margin, community in liminality. As I valued my time with Vyvyan, Liz, Claire, Jo, and others and feel no need (and am unlikely to be asked) to articulate how and why we enjoyed ourselves, I became untroubled by and less hungry to ask about and document the private, unarticulated, unaccounted-for parts of my Tibetan friends' lives, the goings-on behind doors in McLeod Ganj I never entered. There were many times, of course, during the year, when these private spheres were voluntarily opened to me or involuntarily transgressed—walking in on a family argument, physically supporting a proud young Tibetan having a sudden epileptic fit in his shop, or steering a drunk friend home—but my respect for breathing room prevailed. Despite these spaces or gaps between Injis and Tibetans, or even because we each have, need, and protect such gaps, a close social bond exists between these two groups in Dharamsala, similar perhaps to a conviviality between two groups of pilgrims who converge by separate routes, for different reasons, at the same beautiful yet disquieting destination.

STRUCTURE IN COMMUNITAS

Victor Turner explains: "Communitas breaks in through the interstices of structure, in liminality; at the edges of structure, in marginality; and from beneath structure, in inferiority" (1969: 128). As new refugees, Tibetans found themselves far outside the rigid structure of Tibetan society, perched at the margins of Indian society, and inferior to all around them owing to their utter dependence. During this early period in exile (from 1959 through the 1970s), Tibetans of different regions, dialects, and social classes gathered in isolated settlements and developed intense comradeship based on shared adversity and dreams. Men now in their late forties and fifties tell me that during this time, distinctions of rank and status that mattered so greatly in Tibet were consciously deemphasized by many refugees. It was irrelevant, even laughable, to insist on special privileges or respect because one's father had been a regional chieftain in Tibet, when you had no more power to set foot in Tibet than your neighbor, the son of a petty trader from Lhasa. Because of the equally humbling experience of displacement and poverty, the use of third (family) names in exile was rare in Dharamsala for a long time, except in the most aristocratic families. The emphasis in the early years in exile, many nostalgically recall, was on everyone's shared plight as refugees separated from family, property, and homeland.

There is, however, a time dimension to the homogenizing effect on liminal personae. Turner explains that the spontaneity and immediacy of *communitas*—as opposed to the jural-political character of structure—can seldom be maintained for very long: "*Communitas* itself soon develops a structure, in which free relationships between individuals become converted into norm-governed relationships between social personae" (1969: 132). At this point, "existential" or "spontaneous" *communitas* transforms into "normative" *communitas*, where, "under the influence of time, the need to mobilize and organize resources, and the necessity for social control among members of the group in pursuance of these goals, the existential *communitas* is organised into a perduring social system" (1969: 132).[4] Ideally, according to Turner, the social mode of pilgrimage represents a "mutually energizing compromise between structure and *communitas*" (1974: 208). However, what happens to the "fruitful" nature of the darkness of Turner's pilgrim's marginal experience when this state lasts for decades, when the pilgrim is denied the aggregation phase that completes the ritual? That marginal stage is alternately imagined as a womb and as a grave, as a revitalizing space "in and out of time" and as a fearful space of anonymity. Dharamsala is such a liminal place, a social space, that despite its roughness and infrastructural chaos has developed deep structures of its own in the absence of aggregation (the opportunity to pass through India and continue on back to Tibet).

The self-consciousness and social awareness of Dharamsala's Tibetan residents have deepened as well. Increasingly, it seems, Tibetan refugees are asserting the differences among themselves and reenergizing the social, regional, and sectarian divisions that characterized life in "old Tibet." Obligations rival choices; family names matter more. Gossip in Dharamsala largely provides the infrastructure propped up in most communities by more formal legal or military mechanisms. Engendering "community" and the support it provides in exile necessarily creates structural and less tangible constraints on participants as well.[5]

MEDIATING CULTURES

James Clifford has described diasporas as "mediating cultures" (1994: 311), both in the sense of mediating between cultures and, perhaps to an even greater degree, mediating cultures within and for themselves. Dharamsala, as the center of the Tibetan diaspora, is a crossroads where a number of cultures and groups are, for a moment, exposed to and entangled with one another. More important for this study, it is also a space—at once central and marginal—where Tibetans mediate these cultures and groups for themselves as they become both more localized and more cosmopolitan over time. As it does for Turner's pilgrim, the route away from home has become for Tibetans "increasingly sacralized at one level and increasingly secularized at another" (1974: 182), as historically informed obligations and choices engage with contemporary responsibilities and opportunities. "The world [of the pilgrim] becomes a bigger place" (Turner 1974: 183), and, partially in response to this expansion of horizons, Dharamsala has become more rooted as a community. Clifford explains:

> [Diaspora] involves dwelling, maintaining communities, having collective homes away from home. . . . Diaspora discourse articulates, or bends together, both roots *and* routes to construct what [Paul] Gilroy describes as alternate public spheres (1987), forms of community consciousness and solidarity that maintain identifications outside the national time/space in order to live inside, with a difference. (1994: 308)

The next few chapters present some of the ways and reasons Tibetan refugees in Dharamsala and elsewhere in the diaspora live both inside and outside their ethnic community. For refugees living in Dharamsala, a home away from home, the inside/outside distinction is already ambiguous, especially with multiple cultures and groups echoing off one another as they cross paths. Foregrounding musical sounds and performances as rich examples of this dynamic, the next chapter focuses on Tibetan refugee roots, the homeland, while the following chapters explore more deeply the routes these people are taking from and into foreign lands.

2 "There Is a Tension in Our Hearts"

Constructing the Rich Cultural Heritage of Tibet

The fruitfulness of most outside wanderings ultimately does rest in return—whether it is to a state of health and harmony, a lineage blessed with sons and unafflicted by restless spirits of the dead, or a knowledge of divinity within that brings the human spirit closer to release from round-trip cycles.

Ann Gold

Attempted structural reproduction itself becomes the agency for change.

P. Christiaan Klieger

A polished white Ambassador sedan pulls up in front of one of the Indian tourist hotels in McLeod Ganj, and a young bride and groom step out of the car. Relatives help straighten their bright clothes and readjust their fur-lined brocade hats, while the British travelers having tea on the front lawn crane their necks around leggy rosebushes to see what is happening. The wedding guests are all inside the hotel's dining room listening to a new cassette of Tibetan rock songs and chatting over sweet tea as they wait for the ceremony to begin at 1:30 P.M., the auspicious time recommended by the astrologer. Outside the Hotel Bhagsu, an enterprise run by the tourism department of Himachal Pradesh, the couple is greeted by a line of older Tibetan women carrying elaborate silver vessels filled with *chang* (Tibetan barley beer) and rimmed with great smears of butter. As the empty taxi pulls away, the women burst into a full-throated song of welcome for the shy bride:

> We have called forth the serpent goddess
> From this place, the Norbu Ling.
> We offer happiness to her.

Figure 4. Dharamsala's *chang ma* greeting a wedding party with barley beer and song.

> Today, into this dwelling,
> We bring good luck and blessings.

This is followed by a song to greet and bless the groom's parents:

> Welcome! Welcome!
> The lords have gathered together.
> We offer them happiness!
> Today, come into this dwelling
> And dance to lively songs!

Women who sing such blessing songs and offer barley beer to the wedding party, the guests, and the gods during Tibetan marriages are widely known colloquially as *chang ma*. Such women played an important role in weddings in central Tibet before 1959, but it wasn't until the early 1980s that Dharamsala weddings began to incorporate these well-loved traditions. During the 1960s and 1970s, most young couples in Dharamsala and elsewhere in the new Tibetan diaspora had simple wedding ceremonies and celebrations, if any at all, mainly because of financial constraints and the fact that families were often scattered across several countries. Since Tibetan weddings are not legal or religious affairs, a small gathering of friends with good food, tea, a little *chang* just to be auspicious, and some *khata* (ceremonial offering scarves) sufficed to made the arrangement "official."

The combination of greater financial security and, more important, a strong desire on the part of some older Tibetans to resurrect a cultural activity nearly lost in exile motivated several families to undertake the research and work necessary to sponsor more elaborate and traditional weddings for their children. Gradually, the practice caught on, and today the *chang ma* are seen and heard at most public wedding celebrations in Dharamsala and, increasingly (though to a far lesser extent), elsewhere throughout the Tibetan diaspora. There are now two groups of *chang ma* in Dharamsala: an older group of a dozen women in their sixties and seventies and a smaller group in their forties and fifties.

Ama Tsering Palmo, considered the local expert female folk singer and dancer and now the leader and teacher of Dharamsala's *chang ma*, recalls the first time she was asked to sing at a local wedding, in 1982. She gathered together some friends she knew were particularly fond of singing and dancing, and they pooled their memories of weddings in Tibet to come up with an appropriate repertoire. None of the women, most of whom are from the Tingri region of Töd in south-central Tibet, had ever sung in any formal capacity at a wedding before, but they had often gathered to perform *khor shay* (circle song-dances) during community festivals and religious events, as they still do.

Ama Palmo had casually met Ama Dekyi and Ama Ming Chung in the early 1960s at Shar Kumbu, a camp set up for Tibetan refugees in Nepal. Ama Lobsang Dolkar, Ama Kyipa, Ama Tsering Tsomo, Ama Tsamchö Dolma, and some of the other modern-day *chang ma* spent extended time at Shar Khumbu as well. All the women had fled from Tibet with their families, acting on warnings that Chinese soldiers were coming, and were working as day laborers, petty traders, or wool spinners in difficult conditions in Nepal until, one by one, they decided to move to India to receive blessings from the Dalai Lama and to enroll their children in the new Tibetan-run boarding schools.

Eventually, they all made their way to Dharamsala and settled into lives generally patterned around seasonal work: first on road and building crews in northern India and later selling sweaters on the plains. In the early years, the women recall that there was "nothing" in McLeod Ganj. They camped under a big tree near His Holiness's old palace (now the Himalayan Mountaineering Institute) or on the veranda of the Civil Dispensary (now surrounded by cafés, shops, and guest houses). Some carried stones to be used in the construction of the Dalai Lama's new palace, which was completed in 1970. Others joined road crews with their husbands in the mountainous areas of Manali and Lahul-Spiti.

Ama Palmo, Ama Kyipa, and Ama Phurbu worked on the same road crew, earning about two rupees a day (or up to four rupees in Manali, where the conditions were particularly harsh), which was just barely enough to buy rice, oil, tea, and other essentials. They recall that although the working conditions were difficult, the workers were provided with good tents for their families and complete medical care from Red Cross doctors. Many of the Tibetan laborers were not happy in those days, having just left their homes and finding themselves in a strange place with an unfamiliar climate, language, and diet, so they worked hard in part to occupy their minds and to cover up their grief. However, there was not, I was told, the kind of despair one hears about and senses today among Tibetan refugees in India, because all the workers thought they would return to Tibet within a year or two.

Perhaps because of this general optimism despite immediate hardship, the *chang ma* remember their years working as laborers as *nawa kyipo* (happy-go-lucky) and *semgu yangpo* (carefree), as a time when they were healthy and young, despite the hard work breaking and hauling rocks eight hours a day, six days a week. They used to compete to see who could toss a shovelful of rocks the highest and to sing songs to pass the time and keep up the rhythm of their work:

> In this earth in the shovel
> There are various flowers of every kind.
> Flowers, the thoughts of youth
> Have been distracted by you

> Where is our fatherland?
> Please explain our lineage.
> Without our country,
> I hesitate to tell you our lineage.
> A pleasant homeland brings happiness.
> The country of another is determined by our fate.

> If the right hand is tired,
> Please join with the left hand.
> If the left and right hands are both tired,
> Partner, please join me.

The good humor and resilience of these women live on. The *chang ma* are perhaps most enjoyed and respected by Tibetans living in Dharamsala for their ability to take the legendary aggressive hospitality of their society to burlesque extremes. After the formal wedding ceremony has been completed and the guests have divided into small groups to play *bak* (mah-jongg), *sho* (dice), dominos, or card games, the *chang ma* fill up their pitchers with freshly made *chang* and methodically move from table to table, zeroing in on one guest at a time. Each person is handed an overflowing glass of liquor as the women begin to sing one of the many well-known Tibetan *chang shay* (beer songs). Only the most experienced wedding guests know exactly how to pace their drinking so the empty glass is slammed down on the table just when the song concludes with *"cheek, nyee, sum!"* ("one, two, three!") or the standard *"Gakyi dzompay kyi dzom!"* ("Let us all be happy together!"). If the guest drains the glass too quickly or too slowly, it is immediately refilled, and the song resumes. If the guest leaves even two drops in the bottom of the glass, his or her tormentors hoot with delight: *"O! Khyerang kom dook!"* ("Oh! You are thirsty!")—and splash another helping out of their bottomless vessels as they sing:

> Those seated at the head of the three rows on the right side!
> Our root lama is more valuable than one hundred ounces of gold.
> The one who liberates us from death is more valuable than one hundred
>   ounces of gold.
> I accept all that is said to be happy.
> I put aside all that is said to be bad.
> Please stay with good thoughts at this happy gathering.
>
> Those seated at the head of the three rows on the left side!
> Our head leader is more valuable than one hundred ounces of silver.
> The one who conquers the three realms is more valuable than one hun-
>   dred ounces of silver.
> I accept all that is said to be happy.
> I put aside all that is said to be bad.

And there is no point in protesting. Reluctant drinkers are mercilessly teased and, eventually, given *nyepa* (punishments). Rolling her eyes in dramatic exasperation, one *chang ma* will surely eventually unpin the brooch from her *chuba* and start pricking the troublemaker menacingly, while her cohorts cajole:

> Now, if you don't drink this, she's going to really prick you! You can't
> get angry. Getting angry is never allowed. This needle is not very thick;
> it's quite a thin one. It won't wound you. It's no problem at all.

If this incentive isn't enough, some *chang* is poured on the stubborn guest's head until . . . *"Da garab tung tsar shag!"* ("Ah, now he's finished drinking quite a lot!").

Teetotalers are not exempted either, although many try to be. These guests are offered bowls of scalding tea, which must be downed before the lump of butter at the bottom melts. "*Shab ta!*" (roughly, "Bottoms up!"), the women command. Even *chang ma* who take a seat to visit with friends or simply rest for a moment soon find themselves at the receiving end of their colleagues' jests.

When the *chang ma* are satisfied that all the guests have been individually welcomed (it is said that a really accomplished *chang ma* should be able to sing a different song to each and every guest), they put down their vessels and settle in for a few more hours of singing and dancing in the round, often accompanied by a man playing the *dranyen* (six-stringed Tibetan lute) in the middle of their circle. Their *pangden* (the colorful striped aprons worn by married women) of different lengths and brightnesses create a dazzling effect as the dancers move in synchrony. At this point any distinction between the roles of hostesses and guests, performers and participants, is completely blurred, as others join in the dance. The *chang ma* of Dharamsala are basically, one realizes, a group of dear old friends who feel *sem kyipo* (happy) when they sing and dance. "We sing to please the wedding guests and ourselves and to preserve Tibetan culture," Ama Lobsang Dolkar says. She hopes the tradition will continue now that it has been revived but isn't entirely confident that it will. She senses that many young people do not like the "old Tibetan style."

On the afternoon of the second day of the marriage festivities in the McLeod Ganj hotel, the circle dancing eventually subsides, and the *chang ma* are formally invited to sit down in folding chairs placed in the center of the room. The groom's relatives offer the women *chang*, which each one flicks into the air three times, and then hand them each envelopes containing an unfixed sum of rupees offered in thanks. The chairs and tables are pushed out of the way to clear the floor, some lights are dimmed and others start to flash, and the "Western dancing" begins. The *chang ma* settle down with the other guests to have a hard-earned drink, tap their feet, and enjoy the younger generation's antics. But underneath the teasing and the pleasure of celebration there is always, as Ama Lobsang Dolkar notes, a "tension in our hearts."[1]

■ ■ ■

A pilgrimage is usually a round trip. As was emphasized in the last chapter, however, the pilgrimage for Tibetan refugees to India—birthplace of the Buddha and temporary place of refuge from Chinese aggression—remains incomplete. One of the most common images employed in Tibetan poetry and song to express the exiled community's desire to return to Tibet is the white crane.[2] The poetic power of this bird, a symbol of longevity and happiness, is reinforced by the fact that it flies each autumn in small flocks from Siberia over the Himalayas (at thirty thousand feet) to India, where it stays until spring. Unlike Tibetan refugees who have made a similar journey once in their lives, the crane returns home every year. For now, the homeland must remain a vivid memory for the oldest Tibetans in exile and for the most recent to escape. For the majority of refugees, Tibet is an imagined and dreamed-of place, an idea of a land inconsistently informed by official efforts in exile to preserve and teach traditional culture, images from foreign-made documentary films and coffee-table books, political and economic information from newspaper clippings and the Voice of America, and firsthand stories from older relatives, tourists, and new arrivals.

This chapter is concerned with the resonances between Dharamsala and Tibet, with the imagined and tangible ways in which the roots of the homeland penetrate and are selectively cultivated in Indian soil. I discuss efforts at the official level to preserve in exile what is commonly referred to as the "rich cultural heritage of Tibet," focusing on the role of traditional music in government-sponsored community and school events. Establishing the power of the official paradigm of cultural preservation is essential to demonstrating that music of any kind in Dharamsala is made and experienced in conversation with this official (and widely shared) orientation toward, endorsement of, and emotional attachment to, the "there and then" (pre-1950 Tibet). Carefully crafted official performances, such as traditional opera and patriotic school pageants, are differentiated for this purpose from more spontaneous performances of Tibetan song and dance by untrained individuals and groups (for weddings, holidays, and so on), a split that can also be described in generational terms. I argue, drawing from Paul Connerton's work on "how societies remember" and from the Popular Memory Group's conceptualization of "popular memory," that these live performances of traditional music in exile contribute significantly to a shared sense of history and community in Dharamsala, underscoring the role of sound values in the embodied process of boundary making that is central to feelings of solidarity in exile.

In addition to strengthening the community as an inclusive social entity in an alienating situation, however, the paradigm of preservation has contributed (along with romantic Western accounts) to the development of essentialist notions of what and who is "really Tibetan" these days. Such notions can, in turn, be notably exclusive, circumscribing differentiated communities within the larger "Tibetan refugee community." That this idealized identity has evolved over the period of time during which Tibetans of all regions and sects have come in contact with one another for the first time and have had to learn about and confront the diversity of what the term "Tibetan" actually encompasses is an interesting and complex phenomenon. The general impression among Dharamsala's Tibetans is that long-term residents of the "capital-in-exile" are somehow "more Tibetan" than refugees resettled elsewhere in the diaspora and even culturally purer than Tibetans left behind in the homeland. Ultimately, such divisive impressions between Tibetans with different settlement histories threaten the very understanding of all Tibetans as *punda-tso* (kin) on which the rhetoric of cultural preservation and, ultimately, the struggle for independence, depend.[3]

To explore these issues, it is important to address the confused reception of *sar jorpa* (recent escapees born and raised under Chinese rule in Tibet) by Dharamsala Tibetans who are often embarrassed, scornful, and suspicious of the "Chinese" ways of their compatriots. Rather than being valued as fresh connections to the increasingly remote homeland, as might be expected, these Tibetans more frequently cause disappointment by failing to validate the hopeful dreams of those living in exile. Instead, their apparent foreignness only confirms dire thirdhand news of culture change (namely, sinicization) in Tibet. A close look at a particular performative moment, the ways "new" and "old" arrivals drew on their musical knowledge to celebrate Tibetan New Year at Dharamsala's main temple, reveals the chasm between segments of the refugee population defined by their relationships to temporal as well as geographical boundaries. This chapter closes by raising questions about the long-term effects of an official paradigm that authenticates the past and discredits the present, considering, in particular, the effect of this paradigm on young Tibetans.

CULTURAL PRESERVATION IN EXILE

Nearly all accounts of Tibetans living in exile acknowledge the remarkable extent to which they have been able to maintain their traditional culture against all odds, attributing their success to a lack of assimilation or, in positive terms, a "process of enclavement" (Klieger 1989: 55), to the continuity of the Dalai Lama's leadership in exile, and to remarkable amounts of untied support from international aid agencies and individual foreign sponsors.[4] Since 1959, the year the massive and continuing trans-Himalayan exodus of Tibetans from their homeland began, one of the primary concerns of the exiled Dalai Lama and the Tibetan refugee community has specifically been to preserve the "rich cultural heritage of Tibet." This attention to the preservation of linguistic, religious, and artistic knowledge—through both documentation and education—was prompted by two legitimate threats: the disappearance of Tibetan culture in the homeland under Chinese rule and the disappearance of exiled Tibetans into their host societies. Regarding the performing arts specifically, it was feared that traditional lay or "folk" dance, drama, and music practices would not survive the sweeping reforms and prohibitions of Chinese "liberation" policies in Tibet, and, further, that if they did survive, the indigenous performance genres would be influenced beyond recognition by the now-hegemonic classical and popular Chinese aesthetic styles (as is indeed happening). Particularly noticeable today are the influence of Peking Opera vocal techniques on *lhamo* (Tibetan opera) performers trained in Tibet and the influence of modern Chinese music on the popular Tibetan singing featured on cassettes and performed "live" every night in the numerous karaoke bars in modern-day Lhasa.[5] As the exile experience has extended into decades, the spheres of foreign influence on Tibetan culture have extended as well to include Indian, Western, and Nepali styles—influences that will be explored in other chapters—although local sensitivity to Chinese aesthetics remains the most politically charged and therefore the most censorial.

Of course, the adaptation of Tibetan refugees to their host societies has been inevitable. It has also been erratic, selective, difficult to explain or justify to outsiders, and increasingly difficult for refugees to explain to one another, given the growing pressure to "stay the same" as this challenge becomes more impossible to define or meet. What holds together groups of Tibetans who are culturally fractured at the level of day-to-day living may well be what Tibetan scholar Dawa Norbu has described to me as a "core of sacred things," which includes the Dalai Lama, Tibetan Buddhism, the Tibetan language, and a devotion to the physical landscape deemed to be the rightful home to them all. Ideally, Norbu adds, Tibetans borrow from their local situations, from surrounding cultures, to "enhance what is sacred." Exactly what should be borrowed and what can be enhanced are, however, hotly disputed issues.[6] There appears to be room in Norbu's conceptualization for practices that are hybrid, syncretic, even utterly non-Tibetan to become locally meaningful, valuable, and even "Tibetan" through this process of enhancement. And, although Norbu has long been considered an overly bold radical by elders in his community, many Tibetans articulated arguments similar to his over the course of my fieldwork.

A more conservative notion of preservation has informed innumerable official policy decisions by the Tibetan government-in-exile, as well as individual choices regarding every aspect of daily life, including language use, habits of dress, marriage ceremonies, and food preparation, often even when traditional practices are neither logistically practical nor cost effective. Yet a certain pragmatism does inform this conservatism. Keeping alive the possibility of returning to the homeland requires keeping alive the memory and lived experience[7] of Tibetan-ness to perpetuate the felt sense of loss and victimization required to fuel a long-term proactive stance against Chinese aggression. Children born in exile—second- and third-generation refugees who have never actually had to leave anywhere—must be taught to re-member the experiences of others. In Tibet, the memories of Tibetans strug-gle against the "forced forgetting" (Connerton 1989: 15) imposed by the Chinese; in exile, Tibetans are dealing with self-protective, opportunistic, or simply time-induced forgetting by developing what I call a "tutored mind-fulness" to ensure that if someday a window of opportunity opens for Ti-betans, someone will care enough to recognize and take advantage of it.

In exile, this sense of history, identity, and responsibility is conveyed to young Tibetans and is reinforced in others largely through narratives and performances in schools or other institutional settings, events akin to what Connerton describes as "acts of transfer that make remembering in com-mon possible" (1989: 39). While a great amount of traditional knowledge is still transmitted in refugee homes, it is in the public sphere that such casual tacit or explicit articulations of the "old ways" are confirmed and consoli-dated outside the homeland, part of an ongoing project of "making sense of the past as a kind of collective autobiography" (Connerton 1989: 70). In this way, the community strives to establish and emphasize continuities, to point out similarities in the midst of rapid change and extended displace-ment. Indeed, as time passes and the gaps in shared memory and experi-ence increase within this group, the self-conscious presentation of self in everyday life becomes more marked, more important. Nourishing connec-tions to the Tibetan homeland and performing the past to make it presently meaningful are ways of affirming one's identity (whether as an individual or as a community), of "reassuring the self that it will not dis-appear or dissolve in exile" (Naficy 1993: 118).

However, it is important to keep in mind historian Hayden White's ob-servation that "the extent to which the truth claims of the narrative and indeed the very *right* to narrate hinges upon a certain relationship to au-thority per se" (1980: 18). Because the relevance of certain traditional prac-tices or aspects of knowledge (that is, what should be preserved, told, per-formed) is not objectively determined, there is always the danger of a narrative becoming reified into a master narrative that is deemed relevant because of its efficacy in eliciting ideological and even financial support. In this way, Gil Bottomley notes, "'customs' can become strategies in the struggle for symbolic and material resources" (1992: 89).

As will be discussed, the religious and lay cultures of "old Lhasa" and its surroundings have gradually been canonized over the years in exile as every Tibetan's heritage, as a result of both the hegemony of the Tibetan capital's society and the demographic makeup of the earliest groups of Tibetans who fled into exile, with the result that refugees from Eastern Tibet, for example, have had their old folk songs scorned in Dharamsala for sounding "too Chinese" (that is, not Lhasan). The limited scope of the canonized tradition in exile has only recently been highlighted and challenged, owing in large part to the influx during the last fifteen years of so many refugees from far-flung areas of Tibet. As was described in the introduction, the efforts of many native and foreign commentators and scholars to document Tibetan culture in exile have been, with few exceptions, descriptive evaluations based on a time- and space-bounded notion of the "rich cultural heritage of Tibet" that is itself dependent on a reductive binary of "preservation" and "loss." This framework, which ignores or devalues nonhegemonic, hybrid, and popular foreign practices or points them out only as evidence of cultural decay, does little to account for (or respect) the complex mosaic of cultural practices that are continually being constructed in exile through the choices and circumstances of even the most "traditional" Tibetan refugees and that constitute their day-to-day realities.[8] Ironically, this popular framework with its interest in "pure survivals" does little to account for (or respect) the rich diversity of *pre*-1950 Tibetan culture either and is closely related to the attachment (by many non-Tibetans and Tibetans) to the image of Tibet as an unchanging, medieval "Shangri-La." It ignores the fact that appearing "unchanged" in keeping with dominant understandings of the "originary" or "traditional" often requires making significant and ongoing changes.

To illustrate how the paradigm of cultural preservation just described is played out in daily life, a discussion of some of the public and private representations of traditional Tibet performed in exile follows, with a particular emphasis on those secular genres within the *dögar rignay*[9] (performing arts) commonly presented in Dharamsala.

PUBLIC REPRESENTATIONS OF TRADITIONAL TIBET

Because liminal states are so potentially powerful, all societies
attempt to control or at least guide them through the authority of
the state, communal elders, and traditions.

Hamid Naficy

The Popular Memory Group (PMG) at the University of Birmingham's
Centre for Contemporary Cultural Studies has asserted that to study popular memory one must attend to two sets of relations: the relation between
"dominant" memory and "oppositional" forms (that together make up the
public field of representations) and the relations between these public discourses and the more privatized sense of the past generated within a lived
culture (and that may be personal or collectively shared) (1980: 211). Public representations involve "a public 'theater' of history" (1980: 207), a
sphere constructed by what the PMG calls the "historical apparatus," the
products of which are "dominant memory" (1980: 207). Like hegemonic
power, this "dominant memory" is produced in the course of struggles and
is always open to contestation and may not, therefore, in fact be "dominant" in the sense of being believed by a majority. These public representations are the narratives and performances that aim to minimize gaps in
the knowledge and experiences of members of this group over time. None
of these domains—public dominant, public oppositional, or private—is independent of the others, and together they make up the sedimentary "ge-
ology" of memory.[10] This image recalls Antonio Gramsci's admonition
about "'knowing thyself' as a product of the historical process to date
which has deposited in you an infinity of traces, without leaving an inven-
tory" (1971: 324). For Gramsci, it is by having a sense of history that we
may become self-conscious, a reflexive state without which our common
sense is condemned to a position of dependence and subordination.[11] Similar to advances in the reconceptualization of "tradition" as related to *present* responsibilities and needs,[12] the emphasis of the PMG's approach to
memory is not on the past but on the *past-present relation*. It is because of
the living, active existence of the past in the present that memory matters
so much politically (1980: 211). In Michel de Certeau's words, "Far from
being either the shrine or the ashcan of the past, [memory] thrives upon a
belief in possibilities and vigilantly lies in wait for them" (1980: 40).

In the Tibetan diaspora, as in most situations, the public representations
that confirm a group's dominant memory are most obvious when they are
linked to centralized state institutions—in this case to the Dalai Lama's
office—or to a specific department of the government-in-exile. In this cat-

egory I would include public statements and writings by the Dalai Lama, Tibetan school curricula, government-sponsored tourist activities, statements and performances by touring "choirs" of Tibetan monks, government publications, and so forth. The two public sources of representations of traditional Tibet with which this book is most concerned are the Tibetan Institute for Performing Arts (TIPA) in Dharamsala and the music, dance, and art curricula developed for Tibetan day and boarding schools in India and Nepal.[13]

Briefly, TIPA is a research, training, and performance center that was first established by the Dalai Lama in 1959 in Kalimpong (West Bengal) specifically to facilitate the preservation of traditional Tibetan music, dance, and drama. The responsibilities of this institution, which is now housed in a large complex on a hillside opposite McLeod Ganj, are threefold: to preserve the Tibetan performing arts for the Tibetan community by training professional performers; to present these traditions to others; and to train arts teachers for the Tibetan K–12 schools throughout the South Asian diaspora. The administrative, costuming, instrument-making, and archival work are handled by full-time staff, while master teachers train the troupe of senior "artistes" in preparation for local performances and international tours. They also provide teacher trainees with whatever rudimentary knowledge can be crammed into a one-year course designed to help them teach music and dance to refugee children in other settlements. Talented Tibetan students, many quite young, from remote and underdeveloped areas of India and Nepal are recruited annually to join TIPA's Cultural School. Some of these children are first trained to dance the ancient *gar* dances traditionally performed for the Dalai Lama and his close advisors during their tea break on the first afternoon of the New Year. Many of them stay on to live with foster parents and rehearse at TIPA for years and years, attending the Tibetan Children's Village school as day students and taking classes in Tibetan history, music, dance, and art at TIPA. Recently, arrangements were made for students to pursue university-level studies through correspondence courses without interrupting their training at TIPA. Other performers join TIPA later because of their interest in the arts or because their other career options are limited. The students in the teacher-training program are generally teenagers who did not pass their Class 10 exams and have little or no prior interest, developed talent, or background in the arts.

The number of performances TIPA presents to the Tibetan community in Dharamsala is actually very limited, owing primarily to the company's increasingly busy touring schedule. The group regularly visits Tibetan settlements in India and Nepal in addition to its more ambitious friendship tours to Japan, Europe, Australia, the United States, and elsewhere. As a result, the senior artistes are generally only "in station" when they are rehearsing intensely for their next tour. Aside from occasional evenings of traditional songs and dances staged for visiting dignitaries or foreign student groups, TIPA's local performances include the students' annual inter-house competition[14] and, most important, several days of Tibetan opera in April (an attempt to replicate the *sho tön* or "yogurt festival" traditionally held in Lhasa every summer). Marcia Calkowski has described *lhamo* or *achay lhamo* as they are performed in India as

> daylong spectacles of a demanding and haunting glottal-stop vocalizing, dancing, and clowning that unfold Buddhist Jataka stories (hagiographies) transported to Tibet and syncretized with Tibetan culture. While the opera libretto provides the text for the arias and for the narrator, who recites the plot in a fast-paced, syncopated chant, the musical score is transmitted orally from master to student. The opera performances themselves constitute a theater-in-the-round presented outdoors beneath the shelter of a canopy. These spectacles tend to be witnessed by well-provisioned audiences who make a picnic of the event. . . . Tibetans share a particular affection for their opera, which they view as an enduring symbol of their unique cultural identity. (1991: 646)

A huge storm had passed through Dharamsala the night before the opening day of the 1995 opera festival, and it was still cold and dripping when I left home early in the morning to hike up the hill to TIPA. On arriving at the institute only a short while before the performance was scheduled to begin, I found TIPA's huge paved basketball court and parking area completely covered with a patchwork of blankets and mats that enterprising people had put in place the night before. Despite the colorful round tent canopy that had been erected for the event, the blankets were sodden, and most of their owners were drinking tea and visiting under the eaves of the surrounding buildings. Luckily, I ran into "Uncle" (the video technician for the government-in-exile) who unexpectedly gave me a press pass and a last-minute space on a cushioned wooden bench near the front row. I was embarrassed that these prime seats were entirely filled with Western "guests of honor," but, ultimately, the rain did not play favorites. It began to pour, creating a truly miserable and cold spring morning in the mountains. The general consensus passed from under one umbrella to the next was that the performance would surely be cancelled, but suddenly horns blared and the Dalai Lama arrived through TIPA's gates, leaving no choice but for the show to go on. His Holiness climbed up to his viewing room (newly constructed and decorated in traditional Tibetan style for this performance), and there ensued an hour or so of chaotic ritual, as the male dancers sloshed around in the downpour in their brocade costumes and felt boots, purifying the performance space and prostrating in puddles, their fake black hairpieces plastered to their wet faces, making it difficult to see where they were going. They were joined by the demure female TIPA dancers who tried hard to hide their extreme displeasure at getting wet as they gingerly moved about singing in soggy headdresses. It seemed the day would be a disaster, but slowly, slowly the weather did clear, the audience reclaimed their blankets, and the well-known story of the classical opera *Gyasa Belsa* unfolded over the course of nine hours.

As a government-sponsored organization, and one of the only troupes in the world producing traditional Tibetan opera,[15] TIPA's performances enjoy a basic local authority challenged only by older refugees' memories of splendid *lhamo* performances in unoccupied Tibet. For other refugees, whatever TIPA produces *is* traditional Tibetan opera. In fact, the operas staged by TIPA are severely abridged versions of the original works, and while some of the singing is impressive, I was told, its quality is inconsistent. The success of the performances I saw in Dharamsala relied heavily on slapstick comic scenes, improvisations on the "vignettes of quotidian life" (Calkowski 1991: 646) that have always been included as sidelines to the main story line. In *Gyasa Belsa*, for example, the foreign ministers of India and Nepal[16] sent to woo the Princess of China had been reinvented as anachronistic (contemporary) stereotypes of their respective countrymen (from a Tibetan refugee point of view). The Nepali diplomats were shrewd businessmen, assessing the prospective bride with measuring tapes and calculators. The Indians were ludicrous hedonists in sunglasses, mostly intent on capturing the woman of their choice on their "wideo" cameras. The audience howled when during a competition proposed by the emperor all four ministers became completely drunk and began eating with their hands and rolling around on the floor. The Tibetan Minister remained, needless to say, cool and dignified throughout, eventually winning the princess through his displays of intelligence and bravery.

During the midday break of the rainy-day performance, the audience broke into small groups clustered around stacked Indian tins full of steaming dishes and flowered Chinese thermoses full of sweet or buttered tea. I joined my friend Tsomo's family for a picnic lunch, during which we talked about our faraway lives in Texas (where she had resettled), her children, and how soon we would both have to leave Dharamsala again. I excused myself to wander among the crowd of happy lunching families, picking my way between blankets, chatting with acquaintances. Certainly, I thought, this part of the opera—the *bar tsam* (intermission)—plays as important a role in generating strong community feeling and pride as the performance itself. Providing a space and a time in which to take the day off and *lingka tang* (picnic) is one of the many ways in which the abridged, sometimes amateurish *lhamo* performances staged in exile are still artful performances that are deeply gratifying (and perhaps also somewhat painful) through their embodiment and confirmation of a recognizable Tibetan "style," in Charles Keil's sense of the word: "a deeply satisfying distillation of the way a very well integrated group likes to do things" (1985: 122).

MARKETING TRADITIONAL TIBET

Despite the successes of TIPA's troupe, many in the local audience are attentive to its numerous shortcomings, and these are often attributed to a lack of resources. The Tibetan government-in-exile has faced criticism over the years from Tibetan performers, teachers, and supporters of the arts who feel that the interest of the Department of Religion and Cultural Affairs (which oversees TIPA) in the secular arts has largely been rhetorical, its primary concern clearly having been establishing monasteries in India to ensure the continuity of Tibetan Buddhist religious training and scholarship in exile. The government-in-exile's apparent prioritization of religious over lay traditions is a complex issue related to the issue of "canonization" mentioned earlier. Contributing factors include the centuries-old tendency in Tibetan society to regard musicians and actors as disreputable, the dismissal of the arts as a waste of time and resources in a refugee community plagued with more basic concerns, and the parallel prioritization of formal Buddhist practices to the near exclusion of nonmonastic traditions in Western scholarship in Tibetan Studies and among many Western supporters of Tibet (trends that deeply influence contemporary Tibetan self-representation). Critics note that although the importance of preserving the artistic heritage of Tibet is often mentioned in government publications and in public statements by officials, TIPA has never been allotted the financial or promotional support necessary to ensure that this heritage is, in fact, well learned, let alone *lived*, by young Tibetans born in exile.

In addition to their concern about the cultural education of Tibetan children and the quality of performances staged by TIPA's troupe, critics of Dharamsala's treatment of the arts have encouraged the government-in-exile to more aggressively exercise the power of the performing arts as a public relations tool, as the Chinese government has, and use the traditional folk arts to promote the Tibetan Cause internationally, as it has used the many groups of monks who have toured extensively to raise funds and awareness. One concerned individual in Canada wrote:

> At first glance the performances of the Zaxi Luge Tibetan Dance Group in Canada seemed to be yet another tedious attempt by the Chinese to undermine the successful Tibetan awareness programs of Tibetan exiles. But as the dancers proceeded from west to east, performing in six Canadian cities, protesters learned a serious lesson about the importance of performance art. The Zaxi Luge Dance Group thrilled Canadians with their professional presentation and left their audience with a lasting image of Tibetans cheerfully waving the Chinese flag. The Chinese government recognizes the potential of such images; the Dharamsala government does not. . . . The Tibetan community at large must support the promotion of their performing arts both financially and socially. Non-Tibetan supporters of the cause must recognize that the value of Tibet's lay culture parallels the religious and is just as crucial to the development of a future Tibet. (Samdup 1992)

As mentioned, during the past few years the Tibetan government-in-exile seems to have heeded the advice of those who recognize in the performing arts the potential for currying good relations with foreign audiences, despite the difficulties encountered by the first groups of refugee performers to tour abroad.[17] The effects of TIPA's full and successful touring schedule, however, are mixed. They are reaching wide audiences—providing an "unprecedented opportunity for Westerners and their governments to participate in Tibetan cultural politics" (Calkowski 1997: 53)—and becoming more self-sufficient financially, thanks to the revenues these tours generate through the sale of tickets and merchandise (cassettes, videos, T-shirts, postcards, and so on). TIPA artistes have gained some prestige locally in Dharamsala, as well, now that their profession, however humble traditionally, serves as a virtual passport to foreign lands and the souvenirs from these lands (including Doc Marten boots, bright ski jackets, and baggy jeans).

TIPA's new, more professional profile has come at some cost, however. The institute's most recent directors have been administrators and businessmen with little or no background in the performing arts, and the teachers and artistes/students themselves have little or no time left between rehearsals to learn new material. The result is a marked conservatism and refinement of a standard repertoire of set pieces, with performers (particularly the women) often appearing bored on stage. I was not surprised to learn that in 1994 TIPA came in last place in a friendly song and dance competition held among the staffs of various government departments in Dharamsala. According to one Western resident of Dharamsala who saw the competition, the Tibetan Children's Village schoolteachers "had a blast" (and won), while the TIPA representatives were "completely stiff, professional and over-invested" in their task. One TIPA artiste told me he was just generally "bored" from spending every day memorizing routines. Kelsang Yeshi, the Minister of Religion and Cultural Affairs, frankly agreed with me that TIPA's performances seem to lack vitality and noted the irony that an emphasis on preservation can, in fact, lead to "cultural death."[18] "It is better," he said, "to maintain a balance between creativity and preservation, as TIPA was doing in the 1960s and 1970s when a great deal of energy went into making new Tibetan songs as well."

TEACHING TRADITION

Yet composition and improvisation are not part of the curriculum offered to students in TIPA's teacher-training program. Unlike the performers who train at TIPA for ten to fifteen years, the teacher trainees have only one year to learn a core of traditional dances and songs by rote (with little or no background in the history, theory, or philosophy of the Tibetan performing arts) so they can in turn teach them, by rote, to Tibetan students in settlement schools. I interviewed a recent graduate of this program, now a young music teacher at the grade school at Dekyi Ling, a relatively new rural settlement outside Dehra Dun in Uttar Pradesh (an overnight train ride to the east from Dharamsala). Migmar Lhamo told me that she mostly teaches the old Tibetan songs she learned at TIPA but sometimes has the children perform new songs from cassettes like Ah-Ka-Ma Band's "Modern Tibetan Music" (to my dismay, she had never heard of Paljor or the Yak Band, although illegally dubbed versions of the band's new cassette were available in a kiosk by the village green). Migmar had never composed or written a new song, since composing was not part of her training, but she said that she supposed that if she ever ran out of songs to teach she might have to make some up. She emphasized that preserving traditional music in Dekyi Ling was solely her responsibility, since no other musicians were living in the settlement. Evidently some women have taken an interest in becoming *chang ma*, but at local weddings, unlike at weddings in Dharamsala, old people usually just sing along with Tibetan songs on cassettes.

Music teachers in the Tibetan schools in Dharamsala (all of whom, interestingly, have extensive training and experience) explain that their primary role is to design and produce traditional song and dance routines for the series of official competitions and holidays that punctuate the entire academic year. These routines—particularly those in honor of the TCV Anniversary, Nobel Peace Prize Day, Tibetan Uprising Day, and the Dalai Lama's birthday—are highly visible public events in Dharamsala attended by the local Tibetan community, foreign visitors with cameras and video equipment, and, several times a year, by the Dalai Lama himself. Aside from these major holidays, the main venue for staging routines inspired by traditional practices is the annual Inter-School Dance and School Competition held among Tibetan schools all over India. These competitions are second only to soccer matches in generating school pride. One music teacher at the Upper Tibetan Children's Village who was particularly stressed by the constant pressure she felt to produce spectacular routines that would determine which school is "on top," complained to me that, despite all her work, the students from Ladakh always take the prizes because they have such unique costumes and "really traditional" songs, whereas in Dharamsala they were limited to the "same old songs" learned from TIPA.[19]

Local music and dance teachers lay heavy emphasis on precision timing and group synchrony in the complex, impressive song-and-dance routines they choreograph, with the result that these qualities characterize most of the performances of traditional genres to which refugee children in Dharamsala are exposed today (primarily through their required participation in carefully choreographed cultural performances throughout their school years and their attendance at TIPA performances). As each holiday and competition rolled around, I was always distressed by the pedagogical emphasis on rote repetition and corporal punishment used during rehearsals, wondering how this kind of experience could possibly foster a sense of interest in the traditional arts. But I was also invariably impressed, even stunned, by the perfection of the routines in their final form and the obvious excitement and pride of the children in their accomplishments.

My favorite example of this transformation is the class of little drummer boys I came to know within a few weeks of arriving in Dharamsala. They were a particularly unruly pack of seven-year-olds who were supposed to perform a complicated traditional drum dance before the Dalai Lama during the TCV's thirty-fourth anniversary celebration, only a few weeks away. It took nearly the entire first class meeting for their teacher, Tashi Yangzom, and me to wrestle each of the boys down, tie the small painted drums over their shoulders, and line them up in descending order according to height. Once armed with their drumsticks, curved sticks with hard padded mallets at the end, they worked diligently at coordinating their hands and feet, while Tashi cried out again and again: "One two three! One two three! One two three four five six seven!" We often exchanged looks of despair and tried not to laugh as the grubby, barefooted boys tumbled over one another onto the cement floor or took to whopping each other instead of their drums (one boy got a bloody nose in the course of one battle and had to leave the room in a hurry). After each class, Tashi and I collapsed on a bench by the window watching the dust literally settle in the wake of the boys' clamorous departure outdoors.

I became involved in other things and did not attend drum-dance rehearsals after the first few meetings, perhaps assuming that Tashi would give up on the whole idea. A month later, on the day of the school anniversary, I arrived at the TCV football ground to set up my video equipment and was surprised to be greeted by a handful of the boys, dressed in bright costumes and heavy face makeup, their drums freshly painted and tied on with new ribbons. They were clearly nervous, particularly after the grand entry march featuring a brass band with bagpipes playing standards like "Yankee Doodle Dandy" and "Glory, Glory Hallelujah," during which the Dalai Lama arrived in a jeep. The leader walked to his seat between two rows of costumed students and stopped to chat with the drummer boys and pat the smallest in line. Several school administrators then gave speeches, followed by a few words from the Dalai Lama, giving the boys time to collect themselves before marching out like ants onto the enormous dirt arena. Tashi sat in a chair on the field beating on a huge drum to help the kids keep time, and they were brilliant: twirling and jumping and grinning, while the crowd went crazy. They ran off the field flushed with excitement, drums flopping at their sides, makeup smeared, and indulged every tourist who rushed over to photograph them.

Clearly, the job of music and dance teachers in Tibetan refugee schools involves much more than conveying a rudimentary knowledge of well-known folk songs or the ability to stomp out traditional dance rhythms. They are responsible not only for preserving culture per se but also for fostering in their students (and *then* preserving) a relationship with and investment in their homeland, Tibet, in the present tense. In this sense, the notion of "traditions" must be extended, as Liisa Malkki claims it is among Hutu refugees in Tanzania, to be "not culture or customs in any quaint or colorful sense, not crafts that could be peddled or museumized, but a raw and living history of struggle and loss" (1995: 227). The preservation of tradition and the conveyance of a sense of history and identity are, in this case, inseparable. The same observation applies, of course, to language and history teachers as well, but because of their performative, public format,

Figure 5.   Drummer boys performing for their school
mates at the Tibetan Children's Village anniversary
celebration.

the performing arts in particular have come to be closely scrutinized measuring sticks of the success of cultural preservation in exile. As colorful,
athletic, embodied activities, the competitive, celebratory, and didactic performances staged by students in refugee schools are powerfully evocative
for local audiences as well as for participants.[20]

PRESENTING HISTORY

I had been invited by a songwriter friend, Gadhen Paljor, to attend a student
drama being staged at the Lower Tibetan Children's Village as part of the
school's "Tibet Is My Country Day" celebrations. "Jippy" (his nickname

comes from his initials "G.P.") is a math teacher at the school, but as a hobby he writes and directs school dramas that often incorporate his original Tibetan songs. The few Westerners present, myself included, were quite upset by what we deemed to be the heavy-handed, manipulative, even propagandistic nature of the performance and were confused by its message to the children.

The play opened inside a house, where a mother and child finish their dinner and go to bed. During the night, the child has terrible nightmares in which a spirit is apparently trying to send him messages (the blankets are mysteriously pulled back on the bed, the bed rattles), and he wakes up screaming to the sound of a whip lashing. In the morning, the boy's drunk uncle staggers home for some comic relief. A *ngagpa*, or shaman, with dreadlocks tied up in a bun on top of his head is called in to do a *mo* (divination) to determine what is wrong with the child. It seems his father is trying to communicate with him from jail. The next scene takes place outside a Chinese prison. It is snowing, and stiff, evil-eyed Communist soldiers are marching around, while their chief in dark glasses barks orders here and there. A Tibetan prisoner is dragged onto the stage and mercilessly beaten and kicked and hit with gun butts, while the soldiers laugh and tease him. The prisoner is rolling on the ground moaning and sobbing and within an inch of losing his life, but the Chinese won't let him die. They throw water in his face to make him more alert and then beat him some more. Finally, the soldiers leave him in a heap and wander off. The boy and his uncle (no longer drunk) sneak into the prison, find the father in this terrible state, and weep and weep while hugging him. The uncle keeps a lookout, but the soldiers suddenly reappear and grab the boy. The police chief is brought in. Both the father and the child deny that they know each other, because they are both afraid of what will happen. So the chief hands a pistol to the boy and says, "Well, then, if this isn't your father, please shoot him." The soldiers shove the boy and force him to pull the trigger, and the father drops dead. The Chinese soldiers applaud and say "Well done!" to the boy and leave the child sobbing over his father's body. When one soldier suddenly returns, the uncle trips him up from behind and ties his hands and feet. The boy shoots the bound soldier before he and his uncle sneak off. They are gone when the other soldiers return and find their colleague murdered. The end.

During the play, the children in the audience (there were probably five hundred students aged eight to eighteen in the hall) thought the drunk uncle was hilarious. And when the Chinese attacked the prisoner and tackled him to the ground, they all burst out laughing, a reaction that was quickly followed by "Shhhhh." Was this from teachers? From students old enough to know that you are not supposed to laugh at Chinese soldiers torturing people? When the play ended, there was light applause, and the lights came on. The children started making restless moves for the doors, but a school administrator climbed up behind a podium on stage. Rather than dismissing the students row by row as expected, she made a speech in response to the drama. I was completely taken by surprise when she mopped her eyes with a handkerchief, and I realized she was crying. She went on talking and sobbing almost uncontrollably. And, within seconds, all the kids in the hall were sobbing too. Sitting cross-legged on the floor, they were suddenly all bent forward like wheat in a strong wind. She stressed that Tibetans should not become too happy in India and must never forget the suffering that their relatives have suffered, and are still suffering, in Tibet. When she finished, everyone stood and sang the Tibetan national anthem, and the actors on the stage raised their fists and shouted, *"Bö rangzen! Bö rangzen!"* ("Freedom for Tibet! Freedom for Tibet!"). There was more scattered applause, and the kids filed out of the hall across the dark playground to their dormitories.

Later, Jippy told me that he had intended for the drama to end with the following song, but the boy couldn't get it right so he had to cut it at the last moment. Rhetorically, the lyrics call for Tibetan children to extend their filial obligation to their parents and older relatives (living or dead) to include a political obligation to their homeland:

> My deceased father's words,
> I have written on my heart with blood.
> I shall follow in your path
> And abide by what His Holiness said.

> From now on, my life
> Will be devoted to *rangzen*.
> This is my promise to you, Father.

> Members of one family,
> Even if you don't work for the family,
> Don't harm the family.
> If you do, the parents will not be pleased.

A few weeks later in a café, I was talking about the drama to an Australian friend who had seen it the night after I had at a different school. We were commenting on the play's free use of violence and discussing its appropriateness in the context of Tibetan Buddhist schools, evoking, as it seemed to with the boy shooting the soldier at the end of the play, revenge and hatred for stereotyped images of the Chinese under the cloak of patriotism (none of which corresponds with the Dalai Lama's rhetoric of nonviolence and compassion for Chinese people, who are suffering as well). Suddenly, a young man sharing the table with us cut in:

> Excuse me, but I have been to those prisons and that's how the Chinese soldiers are. That's how violent it really is. And in situations like that, most people would react violently. You can't sit and rationalize when there's a gun to your head. If the boy hadn't shot the soldier, they would have surely killed the boy.

Rather than being upset with us for moralizing about an unimaginably horrible situation we are snugly removed from, a stance about which Jo and I were instantly embarrassed, the young man, who had come to India from Amdo in the 1980s, was genuinely interested in talking with us about the play. I emphasized that I was not questioning the historical accuracy of the soldiers' violence but rather expressing concern about the drama's message. Rather than trying to get children to think creatively and compassionately about the situation in Tibet and imagine their place in the struggle as refugees, the play seemed primarily to burden the children with guilt for being absent from the struggle. The young man agreed that the play had been oversimplified but defended its message—"You refugees are still responsible for what is happening at home!"—as crucial. Teachers and elders in the Tibetan diaspora who are involved in tutoring the historical memory or past of young refugees are also necessarily involved, then, in tutoring their understanding of multiple "presents," including a present that is actually taking place elsewhere but for which refugees are responsible. By making history present, the present (which in exile can seem depthless, foreign, and new) is made historical.

In her important ethnographic work with Hutu refugees in Tanzania and her theoretical reconsideration of the notion of "uprootedness," Malkki describes Mishamo, a refugee camp, as a "site that was enabling and nurturing an elaborate and self-conscious historicity among its refugee inhabitants" (1995: 52). She goes on to explain that the Hutu history represented in the camp (not unlike that generated through public performances in Dharamsala) was

> not only a description of the past, nor even merely an evaluation of the past, but a subversive recasting and reinterpretation of it in fundamentally moral terms. In this sense, it cannot be accurately described as either history or myth. It was what can be called a mythico-history. . . . The mythico-history was . . . a process of world making because it constructed categorical schemata and thematic configurations that were

relevant and meaningful in confronting both the past in Burundi and the pragmatics of everyday life in the refugee camp in Tanzania. In both cases, the mythico-historical world making was an oppositional process; it was constructed in opposition to other versions of what was ostensibly the same world, or the same past. (1995: 54–55)

It appears that the experience of displacement, of multiple physical, social, and emotional transformations, has fueled in Tibetan refugees a certain "consciousness of historicity," to use Gramsci's term. Gramsci maintained that such consciousness spurs self-knowledge, disallows passive acceptance of the status quo, and creates a resistance to processes of "naturalization." And, indeed, Tibetan refugees maintain pride in their ethnicity, continue to reject China's nationalist claims to Tibet, and persist in pushing against Chinese efforts to make their claims "natural." What, however, has been the effect of Tibetan refugee historical consciousness *within* the exile community? It seems that, owing to political pressure to maintain a unified force in the diaspora and/or out of desperation for community and continuity, the experience of extended displacement has, in fact, *increased* their acceptance of the status quo in Dharamsala and their dependence on official public representations, despite an increase in historical self-consciousness. Perhaps they have, in fact, gained historical consciousness *as a community*, rather than as individuals or smaller groups within a stable hegemonic society, as Gramsci had in mind. One result of this pressure to present a unified image and to *feel* unified—essentially, to articulate carefully the boundaries between self and others—has been the development of not only a shared master narrative about the events leading up to the Dalai Lama's flight from Tibet in 1959 and thereafter but also a widely shared aesthetic sensibility regarding the "authentic" and the "traditional." Together, these documentary and performative strands make up the body of knowledge considered worthy of preservation.

SOUND VALUES

At the beginning of this chapter, I suggested that live performances in exile of music deemed "traditional" or "authentic" contribute significantly to a shared sense of history and community in Dharamsala, thereby underscoring the role of sound values in the embodied process of boundary making central to feelings of solidarity in exile. It is also true that the dominant understanding of history and community contribute significantly to the content of exilic musical performances. A fundamental assertion of this book is that for Tibetan refugees certain sounds have come to be not only associated with, but also iconic of, particular ethnic identities, political affiliations, and moral stances, in addition to more obvious generational distinctions. For example, the unique sound of the *dranyen* is, for most Tibetans, the (musical) sound of traditional Tibet, along with certain vocal styles. The plunking timbre of the *dranyen* is literally *nyenpo* (sweet to hear) to Tibetan ears; its sound is also *nyingpa* (old) and *yakpo* (good). One Western anthropologist, prone to writing rather sentimental prose, takes the *ür*-Tibetan-ness of the *dranyen* even further:

> It's an harmonious blend of the primal basics: the yak-buttered, woolen homespun, long-haired nomadism at the root of their culture, in partnership with the exquisite silk and gold details of their art and the highly literate tradition behind their religious philosophy. Both aspects of Tibetan reality are embodied in the music of the damnyen [sic]. "Down-home" Tibet resides in the few lovely tones manifested by the left hand which, nevertheless, conveys the full range of human feelings in a simple and straightforward manner. Sophisticated Tibet is managed by the right hand, through its lightning fast motions that catalyze the emotive tones into a kaleidoscope of aural fireworks. Together, they pick up one's attention and transport it, like a Tibetan pony, along the great steppes and mountainous tracts of the Tibetan Plateau. How sweet the sound! (P. Gold 1988: 113)

Tibetans generally refer only to the "down-home" side of the *dranyen*, pointing out its status as the only instrument indigenous to Tibet and its simplicity, characteristics that make it a true voice of the folk, available to anyone. Indeed, the lute's seven-note scale can be learned in less than an hour, although the rhythmic plucking technique (like Buddhist philosophy, Gold would say) takes serious dedication to master.

The *dranyen* is heard in Dharamsala at TIPA, in school performances, at weddings, at large parties, and on holidays and is deeply associated, therefore, with community-level celebrations of friendship and ethnicity. If modern (post-1959) Tibetan music is music born of displacement, as I argue later in this book, traditional Tibetan music is for refugees the music of *em*placement.[21] Performances of regional folk songs (often accompanied by the *dranyen*), operas (*lhamo*), and formal instrumental ensemble genres (*nang ma* and *tö shay*) underscore continuity and companionship, which help heal the wounds of exile, rather than displacement and separation, which modern Tibetan songs tend to foreground and keep alive. Traditional sounds and dances thereby emphasize the ethnic and cultural identity of Tibetans as *Tibetans* over their political identity as refugees. Old, familiar sounds, images, and feelings fleetingly coalesce to create an acoustic "place" that feels like home, so that, as Michael Seidel has ob-

Figure 6.   Music teacher accompanying children's singing on the Tibetan lute (*dranyen*).

served in his work on the experience of exile, the "expression of the desire for home becomes a substitute for home [and] embodies the emotion attendant upon the image" (1986: 11). These are sounds that R. Murray Schafer describes as "soundmarks," which, like landmarks, are unique or possess qualities that make them specially regarded or noticed by a community and, therefore, worthy of preservation (1977: 10).

Affection for soundmarks, however somatically experienced or apparently natural, is gradually learned through exposure to linguistic and musical performances (and judgments) by others. The same process simultaneously serves to demarcate sounds that are untraditional and inauthentic, even threatening and worthy of eradication. In Dharamsala, these include specific nasal spoken registers, high sung vibrato notes held "too long," and a variety of other, often-subtle aural clues that many Tibetan refugees deem to be "Chinese" or the result of a slow but sure process of Sinicization in Tibet. Jamyang Norbu, an outspoken Tibetan intellectual and former director of TIPA, presented the current linguistic situation in Tibet in a lecture to a group of American college students in the following way:

> Television and radio announcers are trained, deliberately trained—this is told to me by a person who works in Lhasa television—they are trained

to sound Chinese. So they even add extraneous tones which mean nothing in Tibetan, you know, like "haw" at the end, but it sort of makes the whole language sound Chinese. And after a while they figure the people get used to the sound and begin to adopt it. It's gone to such an extent that a lot of Lhasa radio, a lot of Lhasa television broadcasting cannot be understood by the immediate neighboring sort of areas . . . But on the whole, the radio programs are not to make enlightened people. It's basically to gradually alter their appreciation of sound values. So you have all this—and it's very insidious. And it's been carrying on for a long time.

In an earlier publication, Norbu described a similar process at work in the performing arts in occupied Tibet:

It would not be an exaggeration to say that, for all practical purposes, the old performing traditions are now dead in Tibet. While the 'cham [monastic] dances have been absolutely proscribed, and its musical instruments, masks and costumes destroyed, there has, on the other hand, been a systematic and wholesale perversion of Tibetan folk songs, dances and operas to serve as vehicles for Communist propaganda and a buttress for racist and pseudo-historical claims. It would require many volumes to fully describe this, what I think can only be termed as, cultural "genocide"; though I am aware that the word itself is a much abused one, and I use it with reluctance. Painstaking efforts have been taken by the Chinese to remove, as far as possible, any vestige of Tibetan character in the performing arts. Even the very way that Tibetans sing has now changed. In the past, with the exception of opera singing, Tibetans sang in an easy natural way. Now female voices are invariably rendered in the hideous and shrill falsettoes of the Peking opera, while male voices reflect Russian operatic influences. This unfortunate trend is not just limited to professional singers, but seems widespread even among ordinary Tibetans especially in Lhasa and Eastern Tibet. (J. Norbu 1986: 5)

Norbu would be the first to agree that to contrast the "easy natural" singing of Tibetans with the "hideous" voices in Peking operas is a subjective observation informed by cultural, political, and moral positions, but the changes he notes are real. His statement reminded me of the time the chief of the Voice of America Tibetan broadcast leaned over to me from his seat in the radio show's control room in Washington, D.C., and whispered with some concern: "Listeners don't like her [the announcer's] voice. They say she sounds too Chinese, that she puts it all up here in her nose." Tibetan refugees have leveled similar criticisms at Dadon, a Chinese-trained Tibetan pop music singer who escaped from Tibet in 1992, now lives in the United States, and is often invited by Westerners to participate in high-profile fundraising events for the Tibetan Cause.

Although there is diversity within the core of the Tibetan refugee community in Dharamsala—diversity that is often downplayed or ignored—the combination of lived and remembered experiences in "old Tibet" and the official cultural preservation efforts in exile has helped coalesce and promote a certain body of knowledge (sounds, facts, movements, daily practices) that are widely shared and valued. In the case of the performing arts, the result is similar to what Roger Abrahams calls a "circuit of reciprocal relations," mutual patterns of expectation between performers with productive competence and audiences with receptive competence (1976: 16). Shared understandings of the "traditional" and the "authentic"—essentially, the "Tibetan"—lead to what Abrahams calls "schemes of significance" (1976: 16) or ways of getting to or sorting out what is meaningful or ideal for the community and, as important, what is not.

This sorting-out process can lead (and to some extent in Dharamsala and elsewhere in the Tibetan diaspora *has* led) to a notion of ethnicity imagined along a continuum between purity (ethnic integrity) and pollution (hybrid identity). The older generation in exile—those who escaped from central Tibet forty years ago and often embody the old ways in their language, dances, songs, religious practice, garments, and lifestyles—includes the majority of individuals for whom personal experience and lived knowledge are in synch with the dominant memory selected and promoted within the official paradigm of preservation. The *chang ma* singing at weddings, the goldsmith who drinks his everyday tea out of an elaborate silver and porcelain goblet worthy of the finest aristocrat in old Lhasa, the retired government official who plays formal Tibetan ensemble music with his friends once a month, the heavy felt boots and wool *chuba* worn right through Indian summers, the precious rupees spent on saffron water to offer at the temple: these are the ways that are revered (even by those who practice none of them and may even express frustration with "old-fashioned" relatives) as fundamental to the "continual distillation and disciplining of . . . categorical purity" (Malkki 1995: 223) or what I am calling "perceived ethnic integrity."

Most elderly Tibetan refugees are just doing things the way they have always done them; others have made conscious choices to keep traditional practices alive, in keeping with the Dalai Lama's call for cultural preservation in all domains of life. Because of their commitment, many in the latter group, including the *chang ma*, have created a niche for themselves in the community life of Dharamsala and have taken upon themselves the responsibility (and, in turn, have been granted the local authority) to perform "Tibetanness" in the public sphere. One such individual is Serso Dorje, a goldsmith who makes jewelry and precious objects on commission in his workshop in the Dharamsala guest house his family runs. Over the years, Serso Dorje has leveraged his knowledge of old *tö shay* (songs from the region of Tö) and *gya shay* (songs from the era of King Songten Gompo) into a community resource and a personal exilic identity and is never absent from public holiday celebrations. I met with this striking, huge, slightly effeminate man a number of times to record songs for the Tibetan songbook I was compiling in tandem with my research. Although clearly flattered to be included, Serso Dorje also enjoyed his status as an "expert" and frequently played hard to get, changing appointment times, continuing to hammer loudly on lumps of metal over my questions, acting extremely suspicious of my intents, yet finally granting songs to me one by one, as though each were a nugget of gold.

One morning, my assistant, Tsering Lhanzom, and I went to visit Serso Dorje again, hoping the goldsmith would put aside his white-hot tools as he had before and sing a few more old village songs for us. Serso Dorje's wife (a *chang ma*) brought us butter tea, and it was evident, despite the goldsmith's stern demeanor, that he was pleased we had returned. He sat, as usual, cross-legged beneath a huge framed photo of himself in full dance regalia and a small shelf supporting an old photo of His Holiness and a bottle of black Indian hair dye, traces of which were evident in a greasy spot on the turquoise wall against which the goldsmith often leaned back and rested his braided head. After chatting for a while, Serso Dorje sang a song for us, and then another. A few lines into the second song, Lhanzom and I made puzzled faces at each other. The goldsmith had assured us he was the only one in Dharamsala who knew any of these songs, yet just yesterday Ama Palmo (the elderly mother of the general secretary of the medical institute, widely recognized as *the* local folk song expert) had sung this same song for us in her sunny living room. Serso Dorje was extremely displeased to learn that we had been consulting others on matters of singing: "If you just go asking everyone you meet, it won't be right. I'm the only one here who knows the pure song, the original words. *Shing gi tsawa dee nga ray!* The root of this tree is me!"

Although in Serso Dorje's case, a healthy ego smattered with well-known sexist perspectives and a particularly hard-lined understanding of culture are involved, sources (*gyung khung*) and roots (*tsawa*), lineages and stories, matter in the process of authenticating "traditions." As the goldsmith further explained:

> Whether it is a song or religion, they all have their own sources. Where they go, where they don't go, it's all exactly in Tibetan history. Otherwise, just like that, these days we just guess or imagine that it might be like this, or it might be like that.

Vagueness is threatening to those who hold a literal view of tradition as a body of specific knowledge to be preserved. If the standards slip, the whole paradigm crumbles. If Tibetan newscasters say "haw" at the ends of sentences, youngsters emulate Dadon's polished singing style and gestures, and any person in the streets of Dharamsala is allowed to sing into the microphones of foreign researchers, the circuit is broken, the soundmarks teeter, the tree's roots are poisoned, and ethnic integrity is threatened.

As the years pass, many Tibetan refugees have difficulty acknowledging the variety of foreign habits and products that have inevitably become incorporated into their daily lives, while they may criticize others—whether their children, their neighbors, or relatives from other resettlement sites—for adopting the ways of *chin gyal gyi mi* (literally "people from a foreign kingdom" or "outsiders"). As mentioned earlier, adaptations to less-marked (Indian, Nepali, and Western) influences are more easily tolerated (though still marked as "other") than adaptations to ways perceived as being "Chinese." The most obvious and widespread evidence of this fact is the marginalization or ostracization of refugees and pilgrims in Dharamsala who are newly arrived from Tibet. The arrest by Indian authorities in 1995 and again in 1998 of several *sar jorpa* ("new arrivals") who were allegedly spying for the Chinese in Dharamsala bolstered festering ill feelings and resentment (often concerning the allocation of scarce welfare resources) toward newcomers in the community, despite these escapees' crucial role as eyewitness informants regarding current Chinese activities in Tibet.

In addition to fanning security concerns, these "new arrivals," having been raised and socialized under Chinese rule, offend many "old arrivals" and younger Tibetans raised in exile with their unfamiliar haircuts, mass-produced polyester clothes, *kacha* (literally "raw" in Hindi) manners, and variant sound values (particularly their enjoyment of Chinese-influenced Lhasan pop music).[22] Calkowski notes that the importation of "Sinicized versions of cannibalized Tibetan songs" has

> inspired some Tibetan performers [in exile] to refer to the infestation of a "Chinese virus" in Tibetan music and to express their fear that the popularity of this music may serve the function of "culturally assimilating" Tibetan children who would not be able to distinguish traditional from Sinicized Tibetan music. (1997: 56)

Trying to keep the airwaves in Dharamsala free of Chinese-influenced music is a way of teaching refugee children what to listen for, how to discriminate between authentic and bastardized Tibetan sounds. As new pop songs are sung by Lhasa Tibetans in Tibetan, the risk of confusion or naive "assimilation" of this music into youngsters' understandings of "Tibetan music" is presumed by many to be greater than the risk posed by other kinds of foreign musics (such as rock and roll, for example).

Despite this prevalent suspicion of "new arrivals" as "other" rather than "ours," as brothers and sisters who have been made strange by extended contact with the enemy, there are some who maintain that despite the undeniable influence of urban Chinese culture and aesthetics in Tibet, "traditional Tibetan culture," as such, will disappear in exile long before it does in the homeland. Indeed, Indian and Western practices, values, and aesthetics have become deeply ingrained even into private, everyday aspects of the lives of most refugees. Unfortunately, until more interest is taken in documenting the experiences and observations of "new arrivals," one can only guess at what they make of the fondness their predecessors in exile have for Indian candy, the songs and stars of Hindi films, bell-bottomed jeans, and hennaed hair. At a less superficial level, a number of well-educated Tibetans in Dharamsala, including the principal of the Upper Tibetan Children's Village, predicted in conversations with me that the Tibetan children escaping nowadays from Tibet (rather than those carefully schooled in exile) are the most likely to maintain a strong commitment to the "Tibetan Cause," since they have personally experienced the consequences of living under Chinese occupation. Easily picked out in exile classrooms by their ruddy cheeks and newly shaven heads, these new arrivals are deemed by some to be the real "hope of Tibet," fresh from the troubled homeland yet too young to have become enamored of counterespionage or karaoke-style singing.

NEW YEAR'S SONG OFFERINGS

On the third morning of *Losar*, most of the Tibetan community in Dharamsala gathered at the farthest point on the circumambulation path to make offerings and raise bright new prayer flags. At the end of the *puja*, firecrackers burst all around us and there was great rejoicing. *Lo jyenma ngatso Bö la thukpa sho!* May next year find us together in Tibet! Ama Palmo and the other *chang ma* found one another quickly after the ceremony ended and linked together arms-around-waists, getting the first song well underway before the circle was even complete. After several songs, the singers gathered up their bags, thermoses, and cushions and joined in the flow of the crowd, which had started making its way around the rest of the *lingkhor* to congregate in the temple plaza. The women kept singing as they moved along together, puffing between verses as they made their way up the hill. Their choice was a relatively new song, written by a

Tibetan refugee in Nepal for *Mangtso Duchen* (Democracy Day) in 1988. Because the Dalai Lama received the Nobel Peace Prize shortly thereafter, many consider the song auspicious.

> To the east, happy snowy landscape.
> To the east, happy snowy landscape.
> With the power of most-exalted Chenrezig, So-ah-la!
> The great one, Tenzin Gyatso. So-ah!

> The great one, Tenzin Gyatso.
> The great one, Tenzin Gyatso.
> Leader of world peace, So-ah-la!
> Leaders of Tibetans in Tibet and in exile. So-ah!

> To the south, Chomolungma.
> To the south, Chomolungma.
> Unchangeable Chomolungma, So-ah-la!
> Protector of the teachings. So-ah!

> To the west, Mt. Kailash.
> To the west, Mt. Kailash.
> Great blessings in that place, So-ah-la!
> There, sentient beings wash away their sins. So-ah!

I was surprised when the women abruptly paused in the pathway and put down their belongings in a heap. We were near the back entrance to the Dalai Lama's palace, with its high chain-link gate guarded as usual by a sleepy Indian soldier in khaki uniform. I assumed that the women were pausing because this spot was the nearest one could get to their beloved leader's home. Perhaps they hoped he would hear their song of praise. But the location was only a coincidence; they had simply reached the end of the fourth verse, and it was time to dance. They linked arms in the narrow pathway, stomped out the complex rhythms, gathered up their things, and continued on, singing as they went.

> To the north, Namtso Lake.
> To the north, Namtso Lake.
> High lake of Buddha's teachings, So-ah-la!
> Holy lake, source of oceans. So-ah!

> By the two red and black guardian deities,
> By the two red and black guardian deities,
> The foolish Chinese enemy of the teachings, So-ah-la!
> Will be completely destroyed. So-ah!

> To the soil of his own religious country.
> To the soil of his own religious country.

The great one, Tenzin Gyatso, So-ah-la!
Will surely quickly arrive. So-ah!

Having quickly arrived there,
Having quickly arrived there,
He will soon be seated on a golden throne, So-ah-la!
And blessing prayers will accumulate. So-ah!

At the temple plaza, the *chang ma* gathered in a corner between the palace gates and the Namgyal Monastery library. I settled down on the back of a park bench with my camera and tape recorder to watch these old women and their friends celebrate the day. *So-ah-la-so!* The goldsmith had joined the circle by now, full of energy and looking particularly smart in a cream-colored Tibetan shirt, turquoise sash, long black braids tucked up into a felt fedora, one huge gold earring, and polished leather shoes. Between songs one woman (who chose not to participate in the merrymaking because her husband had recently passed away) poured neon-colored punch out of a cooler and offered glasses round the circle.

Soon, however, I was distracted from this friendly scene by the intense sound of a woman singing *nam tar* (Tibetan opera arias) into a microphone. A crowd had gathered around the steps of the main temple about forty yards away, so I picked up my things, nodded somewhat apologetically to the *chang ma* and the goldsmith, and made my way across the plaza. A table with *Losar* decorations and a public-address system on it had been set up in front of the temple doors. I recognized the man who seemed to be acting as the master of ceremonies as the manager of Paljor's office at the Reception Center for new arrivals from Tibet. These were all newcomers and pilgrims from Tibet, those who had come to India by every means of transportation conceivable to receive the Kalachakra teachings the month before and to start the New Year in the presence of His Holiness in Dharamsala before, in the case of the majority, returning home to Tibet. Those without relatives in India had found one another, sleeping fifty to a room ever since arriving at the Reception Center in McLeod Ganj. Today, one by one, they were passing a microphone around and singing at a piercing volume, within earshot of the Dalai Lama himself, songs of praise and freedom that they had probably only hummed quietly in their homes or learned from notebooks filled with lyrics written at great risk.

The joyous crowd, packed onto the staircases and small platform, joined in, much as a chorus would in a traditional opera, holding the long notes of a performer's aria so the individual could catch a deep breath between the long phrases punctuated with intense glottal stops. Whether a performance

Figure 7.   Women enjoying traditional round dances in Dharamsala's temple plaza on New Year's Day.

was masterful or, as was more often the case, whether it dissolved into embarrassed laughter, off-pitch voice-cracking, or painful feedback from the amplifier, each singer received a resounding round of applause and cheering, as the next singer was prodded and cajoled to take the microphone. *Shay tang ro nang!* Please sing a song! The song offerings were brief, modest, incredibly loud, and nearly all sung by women, but with everyone joining in and clapping in rhythm when a particularly popular song was started. The perspective of the songs shifted quickly back and forth from one living in Lhasa gazing regularly and thoughtfully at the empty Potala to one having recently been forced to leave the homeland and wishing for a quick reunification with loved ones and landscapes.

> Lhasa has not been bought!
> India has not been sold!
> The Dalai Lama is not without a residence.
> His residence is the Happy Palace (Potala).
> His government is greater than before.
> On both the right and left of the palace,
> Lotus flowers have sprouted.
> *Ah! Ah!*
> In one or two years,

Ya so! Ya so!
A meeting time will come.

As the session carried on and on, I became completely absorbed in the scene, struck as I was, after nearly six months of listening to the *chang ma* and their peers and to modern Tibetan music made by youth in exile, at this completely different display of Tibetan musical expression and camaraderie. The high, wavering tones of many of the women and the carefully shaped melody lines, accentuated by unfamiliar sweeping arm gestures above heads carefully coiffed into complicated buns, resonated with nothing I had yet heard or seen performed by Tibetan refugees, though I recognized the style as "Chinese" from examples that had been played to me by dismayed informants in exile. The lyrics, though, were completely familiar, even interchangeable, with those of traditional-style and exilic song genres regularly performed in Dharamsala:

> Let's return to our beloved fatherland.
> Oh! Lhasa, Lhasa, so pleasant.
> Upon seeing the palace of the deities and serpent gods,
> I remembered seeing His Holiness's face.
> Upon seeing the palace of the deities and serpent gods,
> I remembered seeing His Holiness's face.
> Lhasa, beautiful fatherland,
> Upon seeing the palace of the deities and serpent gods,
> I remembered His Holiness's face.
> Great Tenzin Gyatso,
> May you live long!

Hoping to compare my impressions of the situation with those of a local acquaintance, I scanned the crowd again and again for a familiar Dharamsala face but found none. I repeatedly suppressed a strong feeling that "locals" were uninterested or actively avoiding the Chinese-influenced scene of religious devotion and patriotic celebration unfolding on the temple steps, until I exhausted every other explanation for their complete absence at this prominent place on a major holiday.

During a pause between songs, my attention was once again drawn back to the *chang ma* and Serso Dorje, who were still singing and dancing with full gusto (was it pure enthusiasm, I wondered, or studied oblivion to the offensive sounds coming from the amplifier?) across the empty plaza in a tidy circle, the complex rhythms of their foot stomping and strong, unamplified voices penetrating only during the brief moments between the presentations on the steps. I drew to the back of the crowd to position myself be-

Figure 8.   Pilgrim from Lhasa singing patriotic Tibetan songs on the steps of Dharamsala's main temple.

tween the two groups and let the sounds emanating from each mix together more evenly in a blur. In that liminal space between refugee cliques, both singing their hearts out for the same cause, expressing the same dreams, I wished I could somehow float up into the air and capture the whole scene on video. It seemed such a perfect illustration of the separate worlds refugee Tibetans and Tibetans raised in the homeland inhabit, even when living and dreaming in such close physical proximity. No Tibetan at the temple that morning wanted to be celebrating another new year where they were, and all knew exactly where they preferred to be, but the differences between their relationships to those reviled and desired places was being expressed in ways that exaggerated the temporal, spatial, and cultural experiences that had been their karmic destiny, seemingly muting their commonality.

Shortly after four women from Lhasa lined up behind the table with the P.A. system on it and performed a traditional dance in a very understated style to a recording of classical ensemble music, the singing party on the steps drew to a close with a brief speech by the master of ceremonies. The crowd scattered, so I wandered back over to the *chang ma* and joined in a dance, my arms linked around Ama Lobsang Dolkar and Ama Kyipa, whom I could always count on to haul me through the quick parts of the dance that always caught me by surprise. In the midst of a dance shortly thereafter, some sign—unavailable to my senses, as usual—brought the women to a sudden halt and triggered a rush for the nearby gates of the Dalai Lama's palace. While waiting for the leader to pass by on his way to bless the new Sakya College at Rajpur, the *chang ma* leaning on the gate amused one another by singing parodic imitations of the *nam tar* singing the Lhasans had been blaring into the now-silent plaza. The old ladies howled with laughter like schoolchildren, letting their voices crack high and wild, until the Dalai Lama's vehicle pulled into sight and passed by the now-deferent gathering at the gate. Within moments, the *chang ma* were back in their dance circle, picking up their village song lyrics right where they had left off shortly before.

THE BORDERS OF CULTURAL AUTHORITY

In an article comparing the performances and motivations of Tibetan drama troupes from Chinese-run Tibet and Tibetan-run Dharamsala, Calkowski articulates the grounds on which each group respectively bases its authority to represent Tibetan culture. Her framework of analysis is relevant and useful in attempting to understand what was going on in the temple plaza during Losar 1995. Calkowski writes:

> The respective dramatic troupes have drawn upon what Giddens (1984) terms the authoritative resources of competing social time-spaces. Tibetan refugees, who constitute a deterritorialized society, explicitly frame their performances as traditional, thereby advancing their authority by what Rutz (1992) would term "institutionalizing" the culturally dominant time of pre-1950 Tibet. The Chinese Tibetan musical troupes frequently describe their repertoires as both "folkloristic" and "traditional," but frame their representations to international audiences as emanating from the aboriginal land; that is, "China's Tibet." In so doing, the Chinese Tibetan musical troupes appeal to the audience's sense of spatial propriety. (1997: 52)

The performances and self-ascribed motivations of the *chang ma* and Serso Dorje fit well into Calkowski's understanding of a time-based authority, backed by the government-in-exile's institutionalized valorization of pre-1950 Tibetan practices as "traditional" and "authentic." In addition to this temporal factor, I would add that the very displacement of these individuals increases the cultural authority of their performances, as deterritorialization itself signifies freedom from the "Chinese virus." Malkki's observations concerning how displacement can become a "form of categorical purity" (1992: 35) are also helpful in understanding how and why many Tibetan refugees perceive themselves as "more Tibetan" than Tibetans in contemporary Tibet and, further, assume the authority to imagine what a modern, free Tibet should look (and sound) like in the future. In the Hutu case, Malkki observed that

> [b]eing a refugee, a person was no longer a citizen of Burundi, and not yet an immigrant in Tanzania. One's purity as a refugee had become a way of becoming purer and more powerful as a Hutu. The "true nation" was imagined as a "moral community" being formed centrally by the "natives" in exile. (1992: 35)

As for the pilgrims and "new arrivals" from Tibet (passport-holding citizens of China) who were singing on the temple steps, they were not, unlike the Chinese-trained professional troupe described by Calkowski, making explicit claims to "tradition." In fact, they were employing the range of their musical knowledge—a mixture of traditional and contemporary genres—to express conservative religious and political sentiments. As it turned out, because they had recently come from the physical homeland, their potential space-based authenticity was actually a liability in the context of Dharamsala rather than a resource for claims to cultural propriety. The motivations and heartfelt expressions of the Tibetans gathered on the steps that day were not simply disregarded by the wider refugee community, but actively disdained. This dynamic holds true beyond the scene described above, to the extent that recent and early arrivals patronize different restaurants in town and generally socialize within their distinct groups, a situation worthy of further study in itself.

Many people are "others" to Tibetan refugees. To explore, via musical sounds, the resonances between Tibetan refugees and their homeland and community boundaries less obvious than the Himalayas, this chapter has been concerned in part with those "others" who dwell in and, with increasing frequency, leak out of the homeland. The permeability of the mountainous border with Tibet—however difficult it remains to transgress—means, among other things, that the "traditional Tibetan culture" carefully being nurtured (both rhetorically and, to varying degrees, in practice) in official institutions and homes in exile must be continually and actively monitored.

As I have emphasized, the production and transformation of the mythico-history of Tibetan refugees—keeping in mind that a "mythico-history" is not, as Malkki explains, "mythical" in the sense of being false but in the sense of being concerned with order in a "fundamental, cosmological sense" (1995: 55)—involves judgments and a degree of consensus regarding how the "past" should be articulated within the present. Although some performers explicitly aspire to preserve the traditional Tibetan arts, formal and affective changes are inevitable, both in the occupied homeland and in exile. Based on his research with Tibetan refugees, P. Christiaan Klieger has concluded that "it is the context of interaction, not the content, which in appearing to remain traditional, provides a perceived continuity with the past" (1989: 366). Indeed, gathering with picnics for a folk opera performance, watching school children carry out flawless interpretations of traditional drum dances, moving a refugee audience to tears with a political drama, celebrating a marriage to the tunes of the *chang ma* and the rhythms of the *dranyen* engender for refugees a reassuring sense that their culture is alive and well. However, while an impression of continuity is certainly crucial, content undeniably matters. With its concern regarding which cultural practices are and are not acceptable to whom, this book aims to help clarify the limits of the remarkable adaptability Klieger and others have noted in this refugee community.

It was Pierre Bourdieu (1984) who so forcefully drew our attention in the social sciences to the "political nature of taste" and underscored the complexity of the process of innovation, appropriation, and naturalization by which particular styles/colors/timbres/grooves—again, in music, something akin to Schafer's "soundmarks"—come to be associated with particular political-geographical-historical-ideological entities and identities. Concerned by the "chilling traffic back and forth between the essentialist constructions of historians, anthropologists, and colonial administrators and those of Hutu and Tutsi ethnic nationalists," Malkki points out to her readers that it is "necessary to radically historicize our visions of culture and identity, and to cease digging down toward imagined sources of deep, originary essence" (1995: 13), an observation that brings to mind Clifford's definition of tradition as the "site of a thousand essentialisms" (1994: 321). Douglas Foley notes a similar parallel between the premises of the "salvage anthropology" conducted in Native American communities in the 1940s and the rhetoric of contemporary Native American "traditionalists" (1995: 119–20). In Stewart Hall's words, cultural identity

> is not a fixed origin to which we can make some final and absolute return. Of course, it is not mere phantom either. It is something—not a mere trick of the imagination. It has histories—and histories have their real, material and symbolic effects. The past continues to speak to us.

But this is no longer a simple, factual "past," since our relation to it is, like the child's relation to the mother, always-already "after the break." It is always constructed through memory, fantasy, narrative, and myth. (cited in Naficy 1993: 172)

Efforts by Tibetan refugees to "stay the same" may, then, actually be as innovative as they are conservative. The "preservation of culture" is not necessarily a battle against the acquisition of the Hindi language or a taste for rock and roll music, but against their *naturalization.* A language of maintenance and replication blurs here with a language of emergence, struggle, and desire. The Popular Memory Group has pointed out that when the influence of contemporary needs and responsibilities on memory is acknowledged, this effect is generally addressed as a "problem," as an obstacle to obtaining facts about the past, rather than as a "resource" for exploring the way popular memories are constructed as part of a *contemporary* consciousness (1980: 211). De Certeau captured the spirit of the PMG's rejection of the "past" as memory's sole domain when he likened memory to "those birds that always lay their eggs in the nest of other species," since it "does its work," as do refugees I would add, in a locus that is not its own (1980: 40). Memory is played by circumstances and, like a piano, it not only registers the touch of the player, it also replies (de Certeau 1980: 41).

CHOICE MAKING AND CULTURAL PRESERVATION

Hamid Naficy has noted that refugee narratives often have "dual and apparently contradictory roles: to communicate and celebrate continuity and to highlight discontinuities, to authenticate the past (and point to its legacy) and to discredit the present" (1993: 151). Without undermining the positive effects of cultural preservation efforts in Dharamsala, it is the effects of the accompanying "discrediting of the present" that concern me most in this book, since this aspect of Tibetan refugee life has not been addressed substantially elsewhere. At issue is the degree to which it is realistic, or even in the refugee community's long-term interest, to attempt to create and maintain a tidy, bounded notion of what is "traditional" and therefore worthy of preservation. While events like the annual spring opera festival in Dharamsala bring most members of the community together, the round dances and songs that always follow special religious events, mark holidays, bless weddings, and welcome in new years more often reveal and confirm the camaraderie of smaller communities within the larger "exile community": families, regional associations, even pre-1959 village ties. Although round dances at public occasions are ostensibly inclusive—those participating freely unlink their arms to let another dancer join in and the circle is never closed—they often take on the characteristics of formal performances in Dharamsala, with commonly recognized older "experts" dancing and other members of the community looking on and even clapping when each song concludes. Indeed, the hesitancy of most Tibetans in Dharamsala to jump spontaneously into a dance during a public celebration may point to a general professionalization of traditional Tibetan arts over time, due to a learned sense that these forms of expression are so important, even sacred, that ordinary folk cannot be trusted to do them correctly (at least in public). Calkowski voices a fear of unclear boundaries or undesirable influences typical of conservative preservation efforts:

> Contemporary tape recordings from Tibet, India, Switzerland and the United States offer conflicting examples of inscribed tradition, and various stage performances in the West mixing Tibetan artistes who embody tradition with those who pursue Eurasian pop, and with those reflecting their Chinese musical training, blur genres for uneducated Western and Tibetan audiences. (1997: 57, emphasis added)

I would argue that, while keeping traditional arts alive is crucial, genres are, in practice, typically more blurred than not. They may be best understood as the results of decisions made by historically situated individuals (both performers and audience members) rather than as canonized forms one can expect to be replicated and kept perfectly distinct. This assertion raises the interrelated issues of choice and of relevance in culture making, with which Arjun Appadurai is also concerned:

> As group pasts become increasingly parts of museums, exhibits, and collections, both in national and transnational spectacles, culture becomes less what Bourdieu would have called habitus (a tacit realm of reproducible practices and dispositions) and more an arena for conscious choice, justification and representation, the latter often to multiple, and spatially dislocated audiences. (1990: 18)

Similarly, regarding traditional performance genres, Dell Hymes maintains that

> [w]hat has survived for the telling now has largely been material that has continued to be relevant to the ethos of the community, to its moral and psychological concerns. . . . These are stories, anecdotes and the like that have continued to interest people, for which there has continued to

be some audience and so some nourishing of performance, some reward for style. (1981: 133)

Yet in Dharamsala, many musical genres that have deep relevance for contemporary refugees are being actively discouraged, with the potential effect that what survives may not after all entirely reflect the ethos and concerns of the community. However, keeping in mind some karmic wisdom that A. K. Ramanujan once offered—"Untold stories transform themselves and take revenge" (1991: 45)—a more likely scenario is that the whole array of sounds relevant to contemporary Tibetan refugees in India—traditional genres, Hindi film music, sinicized pop from Lhasa, Tibetan and Western rock and roll—will survive, proving Hymes's generalization true.

Young Tibetans in Tibet and in exile are not faced with a simple either-or choice between traditional or modern "styles." The good news for the *chang ma* and other older Tibetans who are concerned that Tibetan folk traditions are being forgotten in exile is that many young Tibetans in Dharamsala are increasingly aware of the uniqueness of their heritage and are actively seeking an understanding of traditional beliefs and practices. However, this is less of a "back-to-our-roots" movement, as Serso Dorje the goldsmith and others might hope, than an attempt to find meaningful ways of incorporating traditions like the *chang ma* into their already complex cultural palette of Tibetan, Indian, Western, Nepali, and Chinese styles. It is difficult, then, to assess most traditions as simply "preserved" or "lost." "Tradition," rather than being a finished object, is continually re-created through the decisions of historically situated individuals in conversation with inherited knowledge.

Young people are often portrayed as empty vessels waiting to be filled or, literally, enculturated. The youth of Dharamsala certainly learn from their elders and are, as a result, remarkably devoted to serving their community and ameliorating their country's plight. In this respect, the most important goal of cultural preservation seems to have been successfully achieved: nurturing a strong sense of Tibetan identity in refugee children. Young Tibetans living in exile are currently also adding to, and thereby helping to create, the "rich cultural heritage" of future generations of Tibetans. By drawing on their present and lived experiences as refugees, young Tibetan musicians, for example, are demonstrating that culture is the consequence, as well as the origin, of acts in time. This conceptual lacing by contemporary refugees of individual choice making, on the one hand, and culture making, on the other, conflicts with the temporally and spatially bounded understanding of "Tibetan culture" discussed in this chapter. This reorientation does, however, allow room for the expression of the "Tibetan-ness" that has been so carefully transmitted to Tibetan youth in ways that are most meaningful to them and will, over time, keep that spirit alive. It also allows for the possibility that these youth will "return" to a place where their elders have never been.

3 Taking Refuge in (and from) India

Film Songs, Angry Mobs, and
Other Exilic Pleasures and Fears

From its inception the experience of a refugee puts trust on
trial. The refugee mistrusts and is mistrusted.
                              Valentine Daniel and John Knudsen

Yet the craving for spectacle, for romance, for a funny turn or
two, for singing and dancing, remains and has somehow to be
met. If the film does not meet it, nothing will.
                                        Satyajit Ray

The sparkling lights and raucous firecrackers of the Indian holiday *Diwali*
filled the vast dark valleys below Naddi Gau during the Yak Band's final rehearsal before its long-awaited public concert in November 1994. As the
band's new keyboard player, I had spent all afternoon, right through twi-
light, on the flat cement roof of the Yak Shack waiting for the electricity to
come on and making posters to advertise the next day's show. "The Yaks
Come to Slow Rock You!" "Yaks Live in Concert!" Ngodup, the thin young
drummer, proved himself particularly gifted at drawing the band's logo, the
English word *yak* subtly incorporated into abstract, spreading horns, and
pointed hooves, with black ink and brushes. An American friend of the band
had recently paid for a huge black and orange banner with the same logo on
it to be used as a concert backdrop.

As we worked, Thubten, the band's rhythm guitarist and leader, helped
pass the time with stories about fighting on the Siachen glacier along the
disputed Pakistan border. I hadn't realized until that day that he, a young
man only a few years older than I, had spent seventeen years in the Tibetan
regiment of the Indian Army before quitting the military at age thirty-
three. His stories flickered, as usual, between gritty realism and the super-
natural, in this case between the cold and terror of mercenary military action and the reassuring protection of Tibetan amulets. Bundles of these
precious amulets hung around the necks of everyone present, even those

who shook their heads at Thubten's riveting tales of impossibly close calls and hand grenades that landed nearby and then mysteriously lay idle in the snow. I learned that afternoon that Tibetan soldiers carry around a kind of pill that they can take if they feel they are facing death. The pill is not poisonous, but if it is, in fact, the soldier's time to die, then he will expire instantly and peacefully on taking it. If it is not his time to die, the pill will have no effect and the solider can proceed without fear, even with extra confidence and enhanced bravery. This is big medicine in a dangerous world, but only if you believe in it. Thubten learned other tricks in the army, during the long hours waiting in tents or driving in convoys between camps: how to flick a cigarette in the air and catch it between his teeth, how to win any game (involving cards and dice, if not love), how to imitate any accent, mimic any film star, make any story last for hours, and pierce the heart and tickle the funny bone.

Phuntsok, the band's bass player, hooted from the kitchen downstairs that the power was up and running just as we were losing the evening's light. We gathered up our art supplies and empty tea mugs and climbed backward down the rickety ladder from the roof. While the Yaks set up the band's equipment, I sat out on the front porch watching some baby goats clamber onto the Gaddi neighbor's steep slate roof and slide off of it, out of control, into a haystack below. Laughing, I absentmindedly scratched the stomach of the anonymous and very pregnant black dog who was always hanging about the place, using a rock instead of my hands after being scolded by Paljor about fleas. A screeching sound check from the house soon drowned out the holiday firecrackers, scared away the animals, and drew me inside to the rehearsal.

For the first time, we ran through all the songs we planned to perform in concert. Several rehearsals had been cancelled this week out of respect to the surrounding Gaddi community, because the village headman's father had expired. The band members, who were the only Tibetans living in the immediate area, made continual efforts to maintain good relations with their Pahari-speaking neighbors, particularly since the interethnic trouble of April 1994. In fact, the Yaks seemed to have developed genuinely friendly relations with their landlord's family, although the two groups, divided by a tiny patch of mustard greens, maintained a certain distance from each other out of equal doses of respect and the natural suspicion most people have of others with unfamiliar ways. Because of this relationship, the Yak Band's yellow house on the hillside had been silent for days.

To my surprise, the concert set list Thubten had planned during our time off included a few Hindi film songs, a genre I had never heard the band play before. Despite their local popularity, I had not expected Indian

Figure 9.   Thubten, Yak Band leader, singer, and
rhythm guitarist.

songs to be included in a concert by the Yaks, a band whose self-image was
largely defined by its commitment to the Tibetan Cause, a cause itself
largely concerned with preserving traditional Tibetan culture. Paljor answered my queries in a dismissive manner: "Just to keep the audience entertained, we have to mix things up." He thought about it for a moment.
"Besides, the film songs will attract the *amala* to the concert." I puzzled
over that surprise—that these sexy songs with their coy lyrics were for the
benefit of the over-fifty set, not just for the kids—as I scrambled to figure
out the melodies being laid out by Thubten and a shy young schoolteacher
from the Tibetan Children's Village who I hadn't even noticed arrive. *"Jati
hung main!"* ("I am going!") the teacher warbled. As instructed by
Thubten, I echoed her riff on the synthesizer, high up on the keyboard on

Figure 10.   The Yak Band's Gaddi neighbor smoking a hookah on his porch.

the "oboe" setting. *"Jaldi hai kya?"* ("Why so fast?") he pleaded with her dramatically. And the playful song unfolded from there.

After weeks of intensely male time hanging out with the band, I was happy to meet Tenzin Dolma that night. I was entranced and intrigued by her near-perfect imitation of Lata Mangeshkar's high, swooning voice, the infamous three-octave voice of the "Nightingale of India" who recorded thirty thousand Indian film songs in twenty Indian languages (earning her a place in the *Guiness Book of World Records* until 1991, when the entry disappeared) and still fills Indian theaters through the mute, well-synched mouths of a new generation of stars.[1] Given Tenzin's deadpan stage presence, she may as well have been lip-synching too. Bundled in a thick down jacket with her eyes glued to lyrics written in a pocket-sized notebook, she seemed completely disembodied from the flirtatious meaning of the lines she sang so well. Thubten, meanwhile, was having fun, at once creating and playing off the delight on the faces of the other band members and the handful of friends sitting about on pillows on the room's cold floor. As a semiliterate speaker of four languages—all learned casually, colloquially, and partially—and a gifted singer, Thubten knows well how to imitate voices, play with words, and supplement grammar with gesture. He was hamming it up now, trying to break Tenzin's cool reserve and finally evoking a smile. Later that night, driving home in a friend's jeep, I was informed by the guys squeezed in around me that the demure Tenzin Dolma, with her moon-shaped face, fair skin, keen intelligence, and reserved nature, was surely the "most beautiful girl in Dharamsala."

The next night found us backstage in the TIPA auditorium, after a long day hauling equipment down the mountain. We nervously sipped whisky from coffee mugs to stay warm and to calm Paljor's stomachache, while a sold-out audience filled up the tightly packed rows of chairs. The crowd screamed and yelled with happiness as the red velvet curtains were drawn back and we struck up the first verse of "Rangzen," the Yak Band's most popular new song with its heavy, inspirational lyrics nested in a slow rock-and-roll beat and the sweet reassurance of a I-IV-V chord progression.

> The main responsibility of we, the Tibetan people
> Is to regain our national independence.
> All of us Tibetan people must do
> What we are required to do.

The room reverberated with Phuntsok's steady bass, Ngodup's sure drumming, Thubten's high harmonies, Paljor's gentle voice and guitar riffs, my keyboard noodlings, and the crowd's pleasure. New to this business, I was stunned by the crowd's enthusiasm, having forgotten to think about the fact that there would, in all likelihood, be an *audience* at this long-awaited concert. During Paljor's solo, my mind wandered from the keyboard to my *chuba*, full of premature mortification, in case I should I find that the left side of my Tibetan blouse was tucked under the right side, rather than the other way around, as it absolutely should be. I thought it ironic that Tenzin Dolma had elected to wear blue jeans instead, claiming it would seem too strange to sing Hindi songs in traditional Tibetan dress. I was brought back to the concert scene and my spot-lit place in it when someone, surely a fellow *Inji*, yelled "Yay, Keila!" from the audience. What on earth am I doing up here? I wondered, as Paljor moved from his heart-wrenching guitar solo into another verse and wrapped up the song, repeating the last word—"Independence!"—then letting it echo again and again, until we had faded away beneath applause.

> Independence! Independence! Independence!
> Independence! Independence! Independence!

After a few more Tibetan songs, Thubten waved Tenzin Dolma on stage from her hiding place behind stored TIPA props. Without ever glancing up to make eye contact with the audience or other band members, she took her place behind the microphone stand, notebook in hand, ignoring the whoops and whistles from boys in the back of the auditorium. Paljor laid out the first few notes of the melody line on his guitar before Ngodup joined in, and the band settled into the bubbly, loping groove of the Indian hit song "Churake Dil Mera" (Having stolen my heart) from the blockbuster film *Main Khiladi Tu Anari* (I'm the player, you're the fool). Had this song been performed in keeping with the original film scene, Tenzin Dolma—dressed in black, knee-high suede boots and a two-piece leopard-spotted Lycra outfit revealing plenty of skin—and Thubten—hair tousled and love struck— would have been absorbed in erotic dancing aboard a sailboat steered by no one on a sparkling sea. Instead, they stood about five feet apart encased in drab, neat winter wear, absorbed far more in the task at hand than in each other. Even so, the cat calls and whistles kept coming Tenzin Dolma's way—some flattering, some ("Hey, fatty!") less so, all for the benefit of the yeller's peers—and I instantly understood my new friend's firm refusal to slip for a moment and allow any parallels to be drawn between her person- ally and the loose "tamasha sirens" (Nadkarni 1984: 41) frolicking to the music in everyone's minds.[2] Tenzin Dolma, who later referred to herself in a letter to me as the "girl who did defy the audience's comments," loves to sing and hopes to record a cassette one day, but as a single woman and a schoolteacher she has a reputation to think about when giving a live per- formance in her hometown.

Since the crowd seemed happy, the good vibes were running high dur- ing intermission backstage in the mirrored dressing room amid traditional dance masks and TIPA travel trunks covered in Japanese and European air- port stickers. Young Tibetan women in bell-bottomed jeans, friends of the band, offered us trays of milk tea and biscuits and politely refused to share Phuntsok's whisky. Just as things were getting jolly, Thubten made a sud- den, terse remark, and the whisky disappeared. As leader of the band, he stepped forward, and the others righted their posture just in time for the most elegant Tibetan woman I had ever seen to appear in the room. The stately aristocrat was obviously well known to the band, but Thubten was nearly doubled over in respect as she complimented the musicians and in- vited them to give a concert on the final night of the government-in-exile's annual employee picnic in a few days' time. *Los, los, los,* Thubten intoned as the woman spoke, shyly and respectfully agreeing with her every word as it passed by. A short while later, I met Rinchen Khandro.la (Minister of Education, sister-in-law to the Dalai Lama, and, as it turned out, mother of the Yak Band's teenage sound man), when she returned to her seat next to my husband, Fred, who was videotaping the concert from the front row.

She explained to us in the King's English that she had been following the Yak Band's progress for quite some time, greatly admired what they were doing, and wanted to help them in any way she could. Our conversation was cut short when someone reached out through the curtains and hauled me up on stage for the second set.

A few days later, the whole concert scene was repeated a thousand feet down the mountain at the Tibetan government's staff picnic. For two solid days the office workers had been engrossed in eating, drinking, gossiping, and gambling, while their youngest kids ran in circles between the tables. I joined an elderly friend involved in a round of *bak* beneath a huge painting of the Dalai Lama but did not try to make conversation with him after I noticed that the equivalent of two weeks' salary was at stake. When it grew dark, the employees put aside their games and gathered outside around the building's raised terrace, where we had set up the band's equipment. After tuning up, the Yaks fractured the calmness of that winter Sunday night with the amplified refrains of "Rangzen." With the band playing out-of-doors and the audience free to move about, a completely different mood was cast on this event after the formality of TIPA's auditorium. Instead of teenagers hyperecstatic about having somewhere to party on a Friday night, the audience was made up of families—from babies to grandparents—far less savvy and far more intrigued by what we were doing than the cool, bandanna-wearing set up the hill had been. The dance floor we had optimistically kept clear in front of the stage was soon filled with small children jumping and rolling around to the music, while their more timid parents watched them and us with interested expressions, some looking quite stunned by the whole scene. Behind them, on the periphery, lurked a row of monks who had been drawn out of their nearby monasteries by the racket, and farther out still, beyond the edge of the canopy and just out of the light, a few drunk souls were staging a sideshow of their own. After a few songs, the Yaks were feeling quite miserable about the whole event, because the sound quality that night was truly awful, even worse than usual. I felt a bit guilty, too, subjecting the audience to the loud buzzes, squeals, and static we were producing between, under, and over our songs, but I didn't read any irritation on their faces. They registered only serious interest, as they grappled with the experience (novel to most) of hearing Tibetan rock and roll and tried to sort out the familiar rhetoric of the lyrics from the crazy sounds that carried them.

Things lightened up when Thubten, always sensitive to the moods of the band and the audience at any moment during a concert, cast a mischievous look at us, lit up with a grin, and told Paljor to pick out the sweet melody of a popular film song called "Jaadu Teri Nazar" (The magic of your glance) from the movie *Darr* (Fright). When Thubten joined in with the lyrics, the pack of little kids in front started wiggling their little hips, adults started giggling, and the young adults I recognized from office staffs gazed at Thubten with expressions of pleasure mixed with awe. Standing right up at the edge of the stage, Thubten crooned his love for the beautiful Kiran, a film character who spends most of the time during the original song space running through neon-colored azalea bushes searching for the source of the flattering music she hears. She hopes the source of the sung praises and expressive electric guitar licks is someone in particular, but the audience knows it is someone else, the lovesick heartthrob Shah Rukh Khan. When Thubten squatted down at the edge of the stage, the Tibetan children flocked to him. He held the microphone out for them to sing along with the chorus—a filling of "la, la, la's" arranged in the original version into counterpoint harmonies inspired by Bach, but flattened out tonight into a deafening univocal effort—and even let a few lucky ones sing the happy, drawn-out *"Jaaduuuuuuuuuuu"* that launches each refrain. Magic. Everyone was charmed—by the children, by the song, by memories of Shah Rukh Khan, by Thubten. After another hour of Tibetan music punctuated by Hindi songs and Western rock music, we called it a night. A government official in coat and tie joined us on stage, did a little speechifying, and presented us each with a *khata* in thanks. We responded to this show of gratitude, for some reason, with a raucous and extended encore of "Smoke on the Water" and "Brick in the Wall" and quickly packed up amid the chaos created by audience members dashing across the stage to get back to their card games and dice. After a simple dinner at the Staff Mess, Phuntsok gave Fred and me a ride on his motorcycle as far up the mountain as riding triple would allow. We walked the last steep, rocky stretch home from the isolated Open Sky Cafe, a *chai* stall run and frequented by Indians that was tucked in the elbow of a tight hairpin turn.

One afternoon shortly after the government picnic, I was hanging out drinking tea on the back porch of the Yak Shack overlooking the empty green hillside affectionately named the "rest room with the best view in Dharamsala" by the band. Suddenly, two Indian men rushed around the back of the house and urgently asked Thubten in Hindi: "Do you own a red motorcycle? There's been an accident!" My heart started pounding, and I feared the worst, since Ngodup had taken off down the curvy mountain road on the band's *pakpa* only a few minutes after I had arrived. But Thubten reacted very calmly. After asking a few questions, he and Paljor slowly got up and followed the agitated men to the accident site, leaving me behind to take care of Paljor's young son. My impulse had been to go along. In retrospect, Thubten must have been very grateful for little Jigme's presence, knowing that the accident scene, like nearly all exchanges between local Indians and Tibetan refugees these days, would be complicated enough without a Western woman hanging around trying to "help."

For two distressing and lonely hours, I tried to distract Jigme from playing with Thubten's army-issue rifle by building a house out of bricks and inventing a story about a family with yaks that insisted on sleeping indoors. I had run out of ideas (and Tibetan verbs) long before Phuntsok arrived and told me what had happened. Somewhere near Dal Lake, a Gaddi woman had apparently stepped out into the street without looking and Ngodup had bumped into her with the band's motorcycle. Ngodup was so terrified that the group of Gaddi witnesses would beat him up, and scared they would call the police since he didn't have a driver's license, that he stepped on the accelerator and fled into hiding up at the Tibetan Children's Village, where he stayed until well into the next day. The woman had only sprained her arm when she fell, but Ngodup had handled the situation poorly. As leader of the band, Thubten took full blame for what had happened, escorted the woman to Delek Hospital, paid her medical bills, and gave her an extra 1,500 rupees (more than two months' earnings for the woman, who gathered wood in the forest for a living and was supporting a daughter and elderly mother alone). The next afternoon, Thubten dragged Ngodup to the Gaddi village headman to apologize in person, as an individual and as a Tibetan. With that, the matter was closed, though surely not forgotten.

Months and months later, on the afternoon Thubten had chosen to come over and talk at length about the depression and disappointments that had led to his decision to leave Dharamsala and the Yak Band, I learned that he was descended from a *ngagpa*. I had no trouble believing that this kind-hearted and complex new friend of mine was the grandson of a lay shaman who had the power to exorcise evil spirits and curses. Remembering all the times I had seen Thubten turn bad feelings inside out and reshape travesties into tricks, I told Thubten in a half-jesting tone that he seemed like a late-twentieth-century version of the lay tantric, someone who had found modern ways of performing the ancient art of dissolving tensions through empathy, respect, humor, and music. As I expected he would, Thubten scoffed at my observation: "But I don't have any mantras! I don't have anything from my grandfather, so how could I do this job?"

■ ■ ■

Etymologically, *exile* means "to leap out of" (*ex salire*), which suggests more of an urgent *leaving* than an *arriving.* In the words of Jamaican-born scholar Stuart Hall, who ended up in London: "One is where one is to try and get away from somewhere else" (1987: 44). This backward orientation toward where one came from but can no longer be is the characteristic of exile that has received the most attention from scholars and, indeed, from most exiles themselves. "In exile," Naficy has written, "home colonizes the mind" (1991: 111). The Tibetan case is no exception to this tendency, as the last chapter aimed in part to document. Indeed, this orientation toward the homeland has dominated most scholarship and discourse about Tibetan refugees, to the extent that few voices in the conversation grapple with, or often even acknowledge, the Indian context in which the exile experience is actually taking place for the great majority of Tibetan refugees.

The shared disdain of many Westerners and Tibetan refugees for the day-to-day realities of India—hardship, corruption, poverty, and filth—is an important ingredient in the often-romantic collusion between these groups. Focused as Tibetans and their Western supporters are on preserving and gaining access to an ideal "Tibetan way of life," India must, it seems, be suppressed and reduced to a temporary and unfortunate backdrop for the struggle, with the result that a blind eye has been turned to the myriad ways in which India and Indians are in fact integral to any understanding of contemporary Tibetan culture or identity in exile. This attitude of stoic endurance corresponds well with Tibetan Buddhist and Western Christian (or, more broadly, humanistic) conceptualizations of exile as being, to borrow Lévi-Strauss's phrase, "good to think," as well as being a challenge that spurs spiritual growth. These paradigms are discussed below and contrasted with more common, secular experiences of exile as either simply polluting or, not surprisingly in the case of many youth, quite naturalized.

Whereas in the previous chapter I attempted to complicate understandings of the "there and then" (pre-1950 Tibet) and efforts to preserve and/or re-create traditional Tibetan life in exile, this chapter is about Tibetan refugee life in the "here and now" (contemporary India). Following along the lines of P. Christiaan Klieger's observation that "[it] is the oppositional process which has kept Tibetans Tibetan" (1989: 4), the last chapter focused on some of the ways Dharamsala refugees oppose themselves to "otherness" within the Tibetan population itself. This chapter is concerned with their oppositional stances to Indians as categorically "other" (thereby contributing to the reinforcement of a categorical "us"). I elaborate on what Indian sociologist Girija Saklani has characterized as the "aloofness" (1984: 347) of Tibetan refugees living in northern India, and the intergroup tensions resulting in part from this group strategy, and discuss the extent and nature of the social, cultural, and economic contacts many Tibetan refugees do, in fact, have with *Gyagar* (India) and its native inhabitants.

The separatist rhetoric and practices of Tibetan refugees in Dharamsala and elsewhere are complicated by their unabashed enthusiasm for many aspects of Indian popular culture, especially for blockbuster Hindi films. In keeping with the musical focus of this study, this chapter considers the "place" of Hindi film songs in Dharamsala's soundscape, the widespread affection and delight engendered in Tibetan refugees by the melodies, rhythms, and lyrics of India's *filmi geet*, an embracing genre described by one critic as being "more persistently noticeable than the proverbial Indian fly or even poverty . . . a musical tidal-wave . . . sparing no corner of the country" (Batia, quoted in Mohan 1980: 33).

Drawing on critical contemporary debates about the role of films in Indian culture, I compare and contrast the appeal these films hold for Indian and Tibetan viewers respectively, focusing in particular on their powerful role as agents of escapist fantasy, role modeling, and social catharsis. For many Tibetans, cinematic enthusiasm within the refugee community is understandably perceived as a significant threat to the paradigm of cultural preservation that is so central to their political work in exile. Tibetan fans of Hindi films, in turn, are well aware of this potential conflict and have developed ways of exploiting the slippery slopes between nonironic and parodic stances as they consume and, more recently, produce the film music that they enjoy so much. I suggest that, in this way, film songs are used by Tibetans both as an excuse or opportunity to participate in Indian life *and* to draw attention to the cultural differences that may deeply qualify the extent of or desire for that participation. A close look at a particular expressive site where Tibetan and Indian practices and interests overlap is useful for understanding the complexity of applying Tibetan exilic ideals and cultural paradigms to daily life in exile.

TIBETAN PARADIGMS OF EXILE

It is important to consider the paradigm of exile as it operates
within the exiles' native culture, because it is through that
paradigm that they think and experience their lives in exile, feel
nostalgia or desire to return.

Hamid Naficy

Naficy's methodological suggestion corresponds well with the current late-blooming commitment to put into practice a long-time concern of anthropologists: namely, to replace, or at least to supplement, our own analytical

categories and models with those already in use by the people whose lives
and expressive practices we are studying. For Iranian exiles, with whom
Naficy works, it is mystic Sufi poetry and the story of Karbala that provide
a paradigmatic worldview and language for the experience of exile. For Tibetan refugees, the dominant framework for thinking about and attempting to understand exile is the Buddhist doctrine of reincarnation and its
promise of eventual release through good action and compassion. The idea
of "taking refuge" is also, in addition to beliefs in reincarnation and karmic
law, an ancient cornerstone of Tibetan culture. Robert Lester explains that
the "Threefold Refuge" of the Buddha, the dharma, and the sangha[3] con-
tains two levels of meaning: (1) following the example of the Buddha by
practicing the dharma—giving gifts (*dana*), cultivating morality (*sila*), and
striving for wisdom (*prajna*) through meditation (*samadhi*)—and (2) rely-
ing on the power (merit) of the Buddha, dharma, and sangha, which is actualized by prayer, offerings, and ritual incantations (1987: 58). Since the
1950s, the idea of "taking refuge" has obviously taken on a third, highly
politicized, level of meaning for Tibetans as well.

The predominance of the cyclic theme of the "return," the journey
north, which suffuses so much of the art, music, literature, and conversation created in exile, was not, then, strictly born with the experience of living away from the Tibetan homeland. The paradigm of "returning" and of
patiently (but not passively) living out one's karmic destiny while attempting nonviolently to improve one's lot the next time around is familiar to all Tibetan Buddhists. Belief in karma (*lay*)—the notion that present
conditions are the *result* of what one has thought and/or done in the past—
can, however, be both a solace *and* a potent reminder of one's personal responsibility for the present and for the future. The Dalai Lama frequently
reminds his fellow Tibetans of their past role in creating their current situation and of their present opportunity to gain merit:

> Now a different fate has ripened for the Tibetan people. Due to our own
> bad karma, our country has fallen under the domination of a ruthless for-
> eign invader. Our mountainous land of peace and calm has become a place
> of terror and great suffering (1980: 3). . . . From the Chinese side, the
> cause is the presence of delusions such as greed and lust for power; and
> from the Tibetan side, the cause is the previously collected negative karma
> which in turn was created by delusion. If one's mind is spiritually evolved,
> one no longer creates this type of problem for oneself or others. (1980: 7)
>
> Our life here as refugees in India is not easy, but if we rely upon
> the practice of Buddhadharma it can be an excellent catalyst for spiri-
> tual development. And hopefully within a few years or decades we will
> be able to return to our country and to the loved ones we were forced

to leave behind. Let us pray for this end, and make every effort that it may be realized. (1980: 11)

Inspired by the Dalai Lama and other enlightened religious leaders of the exile community, many Tibetans therefore work hard, through focused spiritual practice, to regard the difficulty of exile as a source of inner strength, an approach reminiscent of a religious and intellectual stance Palestinian literary scholar Edward Said has called the "redemptive view of exile":[4]

Exile, then, is an experience to be endured so as to restore identity, or even life itself, to fuller, more meaningful status. This redemptive view of exile is primarily religious, although it has been claimed by many cultures, political ideologies, mythologies, and traditions. Exile becomes the necessary precondition to a better state. (1984: 53)

While in the Tibetan case religiocultural resources such as the belief in karma, reincarnation, and spiritual refuge may have mitigated the day-to-day difficulties of exile for Tibetan refugees to varying degrees, they have without doubt provided them with an interpretive model, pattern, and language for attempting to make sense of their displacement in a way that is, in moments of reflection, meaningful and reassuring to their community. In an effort to characterize how Tibetan refugees deal with the experience of exile, it is not sufficient, however, to stop here at the pinnacle of formal Buddhist belief and practice. Assuming a correspondence between the philosophical ideals of a culture's religious paradigm and the attitudes of the general population is neither ethnographically accurate nor fair to lay Tibetans, as such expectations are virtually impossible to meet. Such assumptions, which are not uncommon in contemporary accounts of Tibetans, may well be an act of transference that says more about the desires of Western Tibetophiles than about Tibetans themselves. As Lynelleyn Long has noted, "When survivors of war adopt a refugee consciousness, they become refugees not only for themselves but also for others" (1993: 7). Said, one of the most outspoken exponents of the dangers of romanticizing exile (whether one's own or someone else's), warns that

to think of exile as beneficial, as a spur to humanism or to creativity, is to belittle its mutilations. Modern exile is irremediably secular and unbearably historical. It is produced by human beings for other human beings; it has torn millions of people from the nourishment of tradition, family, and geography. (1984: 50)

While the Dalai Lama asserts that when you are a monk, any place that is habitable becomes your country (Gyatso 1980: 149), most lay Tibetans in exile feel deeply out of place and often fearful in India.[5] India is *mi yul*, the earthly realm of samsara and human mortality, in opposition to *lha yul*, the heavenly abode of the gods and, figuratively, a blessed country, paradise, Tibet. As Vyvyan Cayley notes, many Tibetans have indeed been able to embrace the "practice of not apportioning external blame [which] makes them relatively free from resentment and bitterness and . . . has helped avoid the refugee pitfalls of apathy and despair" (1994: 3). Indeed, travelers' tales and my own experiences abound with cheerful, smiling Tibetans whose demeanor reveals no trace of anger or cynicism, despite terrible hardships endured.

Unfortunately for intergroup relations in exile, however, many Tibetans, being human, do project their resentment about displacement and their conceptualizations of exile as a source of pollution and suffering onto India and Indians in literal and personalized ways. Although apparently based on the enlightened Buddhist notion of exile as a process of purification, the source of the polluting substance to be cleansed has shifted for many Tibetan refugees away from themselves (that is, from their own karmic baggage from previous lifetimes, as the Dalai Lama suggests) to exile itself, with the result that Indian (and, to a lesser extent, Western) influences in exile are demonized and contrasted with the purity of the remembered and imagined homeland. "There are those," a recent *New York Times* article about Dharamsala reported, for example, "who fear that the years here will have fatally corrupted the Tibetans, addicting them to materialistic values they say were foreign to the old Tibet" (Burns 1996). The construction of India as physically, culturally, and spiritually polluting or corrupting is further bolstered by the emphasis, at both official and personal levels within the Tibetan refugee community, on preserving tradition and shunning assimilation.

DECONSTRUCTING TIBETAN REFUGEE "ALOOFNESS"

Clutching difference like a weapon to be used with stiffened will,
the exile jealously insists on his right to refuse to belong.

Edward Said

Melvyn Goldstein, a Tibet scholar who took an early interest in the "Indo-Tibetan interface" has since turned his energies toward documenting Tibetan experiences within Chinese-run Tibet, summarized the early strategy of the Dalai Lama's government-in-exile as a three-part program focused on: (1) the development of intense feelings of Tibetan cultural and political nationalism among Tibetans; (2) the maintenance and expansion of the charisma and stature of the Dalai Lama; and (3) the fostering of social, political, and economic boundaries (1978: 410). The Dalai Lama, whose word as a "living god" often carries more weight than would any legally binding restrictions, has consistently encouraged Tibetans in exile to regard their residency in the different host countries in which they have been resettled as temporary. This antiassimilationist position, which deters most Tibetan refugees from seeking Indian citizenship, is fundamentally linked to the persistent hope shared by the Dalai Lama and most Tibetan refugees that one day a nonviolent solution to their dilemma will enable them to return to a "free Tibet," a vision threatened by the possibility that the refugee community could, over time, dissipate into tiny depoliticized and/or sectarian pockets all over the world. The "boundaries" referred to by Goldstein are, then, as much a strategy for "keeping in" as for "keeping out."[6]

Structurally, Tibetans in India construct boundaries in a number of ways—most notably by means of settlement patterns, institutional segregation, and official position statements regarding employment and citizenship—all strategies that are impossible to unlink from psychological investments in ethnically defined divisions. Since descriptions of these aspects of Tibetan refugee life in India have been published elsewhere, I will only summarize them as background information to a discussion of more personal and aesthetic aspects of Tibetan-Indian relations in and around Dharamsala today.[7]

After an initial period in transit camps and road work crews in Nepal and northern India, many of the Tibetan refugees who escaped in or shortly after 1959 were relocated to new agricultural settlements scattered all over India. Land for these isolated settlements was provided by the government of India with the dual hopes of bringing uncultivated jungle acreage into productive use and of enabling Tibetan refugees to provide for themselves within a relatively short period of time, thereby relieving India of the burden of financially supporting them. Forty years later, these settlements are well-established Tibetan communities using modern agricultural equipment and employing local Indian, as well as Tibetan, labor. In most cases, the camps have created a consumer base for new commercial centers, providing new business opportunities for Indians living in their vicinities. The majority of Tibetans in exile now live in these agricultural settlements, with the rest gathered in various industrial and handicraft centers, monastic communities, urban enclaves, hill station communities (such as Dharamsala, Simla, Manali, and Darjeeling), and small "cluster sites" in countries other than Nepal and India.

From the start, the government of India has granted Tibetans a large degree of autonomy in running the internal affairs of their communities, allowing Dharamsala's government-in-exile to regulate welfare programs, an internal voluntary taxation system, schools, employment opportunities, and other aspects of refugee life all over India.[8] Tibetan children attend schools established especially for them, either one of the schools run privately by the Dalai Lama's government and supported in large part by foreign money, or one of the Central Schools for Tibetans still largely funded by the Indian government. As explained in the discussion of traditional music and dance programs in the last chapter, these schools play a crucial role in the development of ethnic pride and identity construction among Tibetan refugee children. Margaret Nowak stresses that the Tibetan school system in India "not only serves to transmit traditional Tibetan knowledge, but by virtue of its modern, diversified curriculum, can potentially aid the young generation in their acculturation" (1984: 53). Sandra Penny-Dimri, however, downplays the assimilative potential of refugee school curricula, emphasizing instead that these institutions simply "support cultural differentiation and the maintenance of separate social groups," a stance she holds to be a significant contributing factor to tensions between Tibetans and Indians (1994: 286).

Wanting to encourage the refugee population to stay together in cluster sites and yet keenly aware of the social and political risks of taking jobs away from Indians, the Tibetan government-in-exile has continually attempted to absorb the refugee workforce emerging out of exile schools and out of various backgrounds in Tibet back into the infrastructure of the Tibetan refugee community, primarily in offices, schools, and handicraft centers. In agricultural settlements, a "farming only" employment policy has artificially controlled economic competition between refugees and local Indians (Goldstein 1978: 417). However, with an ever-increasing number of Tibetan refugees arriving and staying in India, a higher level of education being achieved by refugee youth and the rise in cost-of-living expenses in places like Dharamsala, the government-in-exile is no longer able to provide adequate jobs for its entire community, and many feel overqualified for the limited (and underpaid) opportunities that are locally available.[9] This dynamic has complicated the willingness and ability of many Tibetan refugees to conform to politically informed expectations that they stay in their settlements and shun Indian citizenship. The last five years have witnessed a dramatic increase in the number of young, educated Tibetans finding ways of leaving Dharamsala, whether by moving abroad or by spreading out into Indian universities, cities, and marketplaces.

In locations where Indians are able to benefit financially from the presence of Tibetan refugees—where Indian resentment is "restrained by considerations of economic self-interest" (Penny-Dimri 1994: 289)—relations between Indians and Tibetans are cordial, although generally restricted to the economic sphere (endogamy has, so far, been encouraged and generally practiced by Tibetan refugees).[10] For example, in 1990, Christoph von Fürer-Haimendorf reported that in Karnataka State in southern India

> the Representative of the Dalai Lama did his best to ensure that the presence of Tibetans and their growing prosperity also benefited local Indians. Tractors and trucks bought for the Tibetans were made available for Indian landowners to hire whenever they could be spared. Similarly, poor landless Indians profited from the Tibetans' need for casual agricultural labourers. Shopkeepers and traders in nearby villages and towns derived some benefits from economic development of the region, due in part at least to financial aid provided to Tibetans by the Government of India as well as international charitable agencies channeled to Karnataka by the Dalai Lama's organization. (1990: 77)

However, in other (particularly nonagricultural) settlements, including Dharamsala, relations between refugees and Indians have become notably strained and, in an increasing number of cases, have led to various forms of intergroup conflict. Resentment felt by both groups finds its source almost exclusively in discrepancies deriving from the Tibetans' status as being "outside of the system." Politically, economically, and socially, there are both advantages and disadvantages to being marginally or ambiguously situated in a modern nation-state like India, with its expansive bureaucracy and caste-based social order. These advantages and disadvantages are alternately exploited and resented by both Tibetans and the Indians whose lives and villages are affected by the presence of these refugees.

In his dissertation on the adaptation of Tibetan refugees in Nepal, Ram Chhetri asks: "Can someone inherit refugee status from one's parents?" (1990: 6). For forty years Tibetans have assumed so. The label "refugee" serves an explicit agenda for Tibetans living in the diaspora, because most recognize that, however ironic it may seem, the possibility of stability in the future is precisely dependent on maintaining instability today, owing to the international aid, sponsorships, and attention available to them as refugees. Through this quasi-professionalization of the refugees' status as outsiders in their host societies, the term *refugee* has become integral to the identity of Tibetans all over the world, to the extent, I would argue, that part of "preserving Tibetan culture" in exile now includes inheriting and reproducing the marginal political status of the older generation. In ideal terms, marginality gives Tibetan refugees the "leeway to forge their own community around their leader and religion, with little diversion from the original purpose of flight—to defend the faith and, in the end, to rescue the people left behind in Tibet" (de Voe 1987: 57). What Tibetans might regard as "diversion," however, many Indians regard as fair participation in a society that has generously supported the refugees for decades.

In the early 1980s, for example, Saklani noted that in many places the fact that Tibetans "run almost a parallel economy" has become a "major source of simmering friction between local Indian traders and the Tibetans," since Tibetans tend to buy and sell exclusively within their own group and to undersell Indian merchants (1984: 372). Indeed, during the winter months, nomadic Tibetan sweater sellers spread their wares on blankets on city sidewalks all over India, avoiding the overhead and taxes required of shopkeepers. Kids keep their eyes out for Indian authorities, with the blankets doubling as bundles that can be quickly whisked away if necessary. In addition, Tibetans with established shops can count on the patronage of their compatriots, many of whom believe Indians purposefully overcharge them, taking advantage of their limited Hindi language skills or cultural naïveté and, further, of their lack of knowledge about and access to forms of retributive legal action. When they are obligated to conduct business with Indians who provide goods and services unavailable from within the Tibetan community, particularly those individuals distributing government-regulated items such as permits and propane gas, Tibetans often expect to have to pay bribes to get what they need.[11]

From the other side, Indian resentment of the suspicious, in-group focus of Tibetan refugees is exacerbated by jealousy over the relatively high standard of living enjoyed by these newcomers. In Dharamsala, Tibetans are quite literally fawned over by Westerners, and tangible signs of this affection are visible everywhere in the form of happily bequeathed clothing, hiking boots, bright fleece pullovers, and backpacks. There is, in fact, a running joke among Tibetans about monks who befriend Western tourists, invite them for tea and a dharma chat, and emerge from the café wearing a new pair of Nike sneakers. Less visible gifts to refugees, such as large aid grants to Tibetan organizations, personal invitations to the United States, cash passed in envelopes, sponsorships for school children, English lessons, and business advice are no less obvious to their bypassed and, it would often seem, invisible Indian neighbors.[12] Penny-Dimri notes that Tibetan non- or misrecognition of the source of these privileges—the common attribution by refugees of Tibetan economic well-being to their own hard work and the "kind graces of the Dalai Lama" and of Indian hardship to laziness—adds salt to the wounds of local Indians who know well who holds the purse strings that have allowed Tibetans to flourish economically (1994: 284). Saklani also notes an attitude of superiority and "elitism" among Tibetan refugees (1984: 378), along with the understandable confusion among Indians who believe that refugees are beggars and should not be building new cement houses and driving around in four-wheel-drive jeeps. As it is, Indian beggars now gravitate to Tibetan settlements, particularly on religious holidays like *Saka Dawa*, when merit making is on every Tibetan's mind and piggy banks are broken open for charity.

At the official level, Tibetans and Indians express great respect, even affection, for one another. Local authorities give public speeches on Tibetan Uprising Day praising the Dalai Lama's efforts to keep the peaceful message of Mahatma Gandhi alive, Tibetan school children throughout India parade through towns on "Thank India Day" waving Indian and Tibetan flags, and Indian bureaucrats visiting Tibetan offices on business are served tea in special china teapots reserved for important guests. However, at all age levels, few personal Tibetan-Indian friendships are evident in the streets and cafés of McLeod Ganj. Relations between the groups are generally restricted to the economic sphere (mostly between Indian shopkeepers and Tibetan customers and between Tibetan families and their Indian servant boys),[13] although formal venues for open-minded and empathetic individuals to express their solidarity do exist: For example, in January 2001, a number of Indian activists, including the National President of the Indo-Tibetan Friendship Society, participated side-by-side with Tibetan refugees, and were arrested, in protests in Delhi against the diplomatic visit of Chinese second-in-command, Li Peng, to India. Only a few weeks later, the Tibetan community living in North America presented the Consul General of India with a donation of $23,000 to help the victims of a major earthquake in Gujarat.

The common distrust between Tibetans and Indians in and around Dharamsala is, for the most part, expressed through unrestrained gossip: some slanderous, some derived from a grain of truth. On various occasions, Indian shopkeepers and friends asked if I was aware that Tibetans had the habit of eating their dead when they first came to India ("Ask anyone from Manali! It's not just a local rumor."), that they are all violent and prone to fighting with knives at the slightest provocation,[14] that they are out to convert everyone to Buddhism, that they are all rich and exploit Westerners' sympathy to acquire privileges and wealth, and that they are all dirty and drink too much and are not to be trusted. Tibetans told me that Indians routinely poison newborn girls and bring them to Delek Hospital on the verge

Figure 11.   Gaddi women presenting a traditional dance to the Dalai Lama in celebration of the Tibetan leader's sixtieth birthday.

of death pretending to be upset that they are ill, that they whack off dogs' tails to make sure the animals don't grow too big, that they give and accept bribes ruthlessly to get whatever they want, and that they are all dirty and drink too much and are not to be trusted. With these kinds of sentiments simmering for years in the community, it came as no surprise to many when the resentment and lack of trust between groups finally led to violence.

SINCE APRIL 1994

NEW DELHI, Friday: The Dalai Lama, the spiritual and temporal leader of Tibet, has threatened to move the headquarters of his government-in-exile from Dharamsala, in the Himalayas of northern India, [to Bangalore in southern India], after two local politicians incited Indians to go on a rampage against Tibetan refugees.

The calm of Dharamsala . . . was shattered on April 22 when an Indian youth, who belonged to a caste . . . known as gaddis, was stabbed to death by a Tibetan in a fight over an Indian versus Pakistan cricket match on television.

During the funeral . . . , a politician . . . yanked the shroud off the corpse, reached into the cadaver's open stomach, pulled out a length of intestine and held it high. "This is what the Tibetans have done," he yelled.

> The mourners went berserk . . . the mob stormed the compound of
> the Tibetan government-in-exile, smashed windows, set fires and de-
> stroyed furniture. Then they looted Tibetan shops and beat up refugees.
> . . . Even before the stabbing, the gaddis' resentment against the
> refugees was high. They blamed them for driving up land prices and
> envied the prosperity of some Tibetan shopkeepers. (cited in Penny-
> Dimri 1994: 281)

As a result of the events described above in the *Sydney Morning Her-
ald,* the social atmosphere in Dharamsala intensified overnight, and local
interethnic tensions have remained palpable ever since.[15] The violent outpouring of pent-up resentment by the Gaddis fanned the worst fears of Tibetan refugees and, sadly, confirmed most of their negative stereotypes
about Indians generally. During the rampage, most Tibetan residents of
Dharamsala remained locked inside their homes, and it remains a point of
pride in the community that no Tibetans fought back against the angry Indians—proof, they say, that a commitment to nonviolence and patience is
an inherent Tibetan characteristic and not merely Buddhist rhetoric (in
contrast, it is implied, to Indians, who are overemotional and impulsive).

Penny-Dimri attributes the eruption of interethnic violence in Dharamsala in 1994 to an "accumulation of conflicts" arising from (1) perceived
cultural differences (particularly meat eating, gender relations, and hy-
giene), (2) divergent constructions of group identity, (3) the necessity for
nonjudicial resolutions of conflict due to the inadequacies of the Indian
legal system, and (4) most significant in her opinion, increasingly apparent
socioeconomic inequalities between groups (particularly the current distribution of welfare assistance in the region being based on ethnicity rather
than on need) (1994: 281, 293). This last factor (competition for resources)
was also singled out by Goldstein fifteen years earlier in his discussion of
the dynamics of "ethnogenesis" as being one of the critical factors under-
lying the development of ethnic boundaries operative both within and outside the Tibetan community (1978: 395). In 1978, in rural south India, a
balance seemed to have been achieved, but by 1994 in Dharamsala, the situation had become unacceptable for local Indians.

In the immediate wake of the 1994 violence, the Dalai Lama proposed
moving his government-in-exile to south India to avoid provocation by
the Tibetan community's presence in Dharamsala of any further unrest.
Local (non-Gaddi) Indian businessmen, fearing the overnight transformation of Dharamsala into a ghost town, quickly called a meeting with the
exiled leader and pleaded with him to stay in their district. Some peace-
making gestures were negotiated to limit the encroachment of the Tibetan

community and its groupies on locals, such as a brief moratorium on building, but development has continued to boom ever since.

Although the Tibetan community chose not to pack up and leave in April 1994 and daily life in McLeod Ganj soon resumed an air of normalcy, a clear message had been sent to the refugees, physical reminders of which—broken panes, sturdy new padlocks, and iron window grates—were still evident when I arrived there five months later in September 1994. A sense that any incident could (and most feel someday surely will) trigger a repeat performance of the mob rioting still hangs in the air, seemingly precluding former worries about the great earthquake that is expected to soon level Dharamsala and its environs (within one hundred years after the enormous temblor that destroyed the area in 1905). Many Indians are still resentful, and there is a deep sense of helplessness among Tibetans, who learned from the riots that, without their own law-enforcement agency, there is no one to protect them in such an emergency, since the police are, after all, Indians. In addition, the younger taxi drivers in McLeod Ganj have taken it upon themselves to act as a vigilante gang, meting out justice (usually in the form of beatings) when they see fit. For these reasons, when an Indian shopkeeper who leases his space from a Tibetan family ordered workers to smash down a wall separating his store from his landlord's residence in order to expand, the Tibetan owner stood by, legal documents in hand, knowing that any appeal to the authorities in Lower Dharamsala would be fruitless, since their fellow Indian could bribe them to sign or say anything. "Indians just won't let us live peacefully here," the landlord sighed. Members of the Hindu fundamentalist Bharatiya Janata Party (BJP) have been quietly boycotted by Tibetans since the riots, because of the gruesome antics of BJP politicians described in the newspaper article above. One BJP-affiliated storekeeper, who conducts a booming business developing film and selling souvenir photos of the Dalai Lama to tourists was generally believed to have marched in the rampage, yelling "Death to the Dalai Lama!" although he has publicly denied this accusation. Individuals now strongly represent their community through their actions: a drunk Tibetan tarnishes the reputation of all Tibetans, a dishonest Indian grocer makes his colleagues up and down the street suspect. Accusations have, therefore, deep implications. A major furor ensued, for example, following the rape at knifepoint of a German dharma student in the forest above McLeod Ganj soon after I arrived. A local newspaper described the suspect as a "Tibetan youth," although the victim had only told police that her assailant was from "from Nepal." Tibetans in McLeod Ganj were sure that no Tibetan would do such a thing and that the Indian press was just trying to fan the flames of interethnic tension by making them look bad. As a further projection of their fears, for months I was warned by Tibetans not to walk alone in the forest, in case I were to run into an Indian man.

Despite efforts by Tibetans at both official and personal levels to distance themselves physically and culturally from India and Indians, these refugees do live in India and have, because of a combination of necessity and choice, incorporated many local practices and even values into their lives. In a sample of households in Dharamsala, Clement Town, and Majnu-ka-Tilla, Saklani found great confusion among Tibetan refugees over what having a "distinct identity" actually means. Either respondents were "parrot-like and mechanically re-echoing others" or "being emotionally effusive," leading Saklani to conclude that "clear thinking on this delicate and important point could hardly be seen in any quarters" (1984: 349). Regarding the gap between preaching and practice among Tibetan refugees, she further states:

> To any observer it comes as a shock that the Tibetans are allowing themselves to be easily overwhelmed by the forces of change in spite of their strongly professed attachment to the pristine Tibetan culture. It is rather ironical to see them doing what is diametrically opposite to what they should seem to mean by separate identity. (1984: 350)

The most obvious example of willing (even eager) Tibetan participation in Indian culture is the widespread popularity of Hindi films and their signature pop songs among refugees of all ages living throughout the Tibetan diaspora. Given the amount of energy the Tibetan community puts into advocating "cultural preservation" and the amount of tension commonly simmering between Tibetan refugees and their Indian neighbors, the extent to which Tibetans truly enjoy this particular aspect of Indian culture, and their feelings about the foothold Indian popular culture has taken in their lives, are important (though, I would argue once more with Saklani, hardly "shocking") developments.

FILMI GEET!

For songs of unbridled love and playfulness, Tibetan refugees generally turn to Bombay more often than they do to the homeland or to the West. Indeed, the flirtatious lyrics and catchy tunes of Hindi film songs seem to be as irresistible to Tibetan refugees as they are to the rest of South and Southeast Asia. Tibetans eagerly line up with local Indians to see the latest films at the "Himalaya Talkies," a large cinema housed in an old hall in

Dharamsala's lower bazaar, transcribe song lyrics into ruled notebooks, and crowd around the doors of dark video halls in McLeod Ganj or their own televisions, hoping to catch a glimpse or a tune. Tibetan children throughout India and Nepal know the words and sexy dance movements to all the top film hits and are often called on to perform these routines for the amusement of visitors and relatives.[16]

Hindi films are so popular among Tibetan refugees for many of the same reasons that they are popular among Indians of all castes, classes, and regions: the extent and ease of exposure to films, the crosscultural accessibility of the genre, and the satisfying correspondence between the actual content of Hindi films and the psychological needs of their audiences. There are also, of course, many unique ways in which Tibetans enjoy and use Hindi films that can only be understood from an ethnographically informed perspective concerned with not only *what* this particular genre "means" to Tibetan refugees but also *how* and *why* it means what it does. Therefore, to explore the ways in which the songs are consciously and unconsciously maintained as "theirs" (Indian), even as playful imitation seems to slip into nonironic identification, I focus the remainder of this chapter on the Tibetan consumption and production or performance of Hindi film songs in India, analyzing the songs' migration from commercial screens to local stages. Considered within the wider context of Tibetan concerns with cultural purity and nonassimilation and the rhetorical casting of India as polluting, I argue that live performances of Hindi film songs by Tibetans are acts of transgression that, like many forms of mimicry, simultaneously underscore (1) the differences between the original and the mime—when a mood of mockery or parody prevails, thereby disrupting and alleviating anxieties about the pleasure this Indian music invokes in Tibetans—and (2) the similarities between the original and the mime, when the easy assumption of Indian roles and aesthetics by Tibetan performers and audiences stimulates anxiety over the extent to which hegemonic Indian pop culture has, in fact, become naturalized in this refugee community.

To a certain extent, the appeal of Hindi films to exiled Tibetans can be explained quite simply by the fact that, despite their efforts to live in separate settlements, they do live (and many have *only* ever lived) in India. And to live in India is to live within earshot of the cinema, to the extent that one Indian film music composer can claim: "Whether one likes it or not, most waking hours of an average Indian are, aurally, totally engulfed by this music" (Chandavarkar 1976: 109). Indeed, because of the distribution of preview cassettes, the release of the films themselves, and the music videos and movie reruns aired continually on Asia's primary cable station (Star TV) and in local video halls, it is virtually impossible to live in South Asia, particularly in India, and not be familiar with the current hit film songs. The sounds blare at high volumes from most roadside tea stalls and buses, and colorful layer upon layer of movie posters cover village walls and huge urban billboards throughout the country. Film songs, the artistic and financial pulse of the hundreds of movies produced every year in Bombay (also called "Bollywood"), acoustically wallpaper the Indian subcontinent, and Tibetan refugees, despite their isolationist efforts and refusal to partake officially in India's public life, are nevertheless part of the audience served by their host country's commercial pop culture industry.

Residence in India accounts for the degree of exposure Tibetan refugees have to Hindi films, but it does not account for their popularity. The appeal of these films even to foreigners may be explained in part by their accessibility, the same accessibility—made possible by a strong emphasis on predictable plots, cross-cultural music, evocative dancing, and visual effects—that allows Indians of different language groups and backgrounds to enjoy them. The same features that have made Hindi films the backbone of a national popular culture that plays a crucial role in uniting India across caste, class, religious, linguistic, and regional boundaries, then, also allow monolingual Tibetan grandmothers in Dharamsala and Tibetan children resettled in the United States to enjoy fully the spectacle and, more or less, to follow the story line. With minimal linguistic knowledge, any of these spectators can pick up the simple lyrics of sentimental Hindi film songs. In addition, the film plots themselves are highly conventionalized, since "a comprehensive world-view imposes a highly stylized and formal format" (Saari 1985: 24). Equally conventionalized, in turn, are the expectations of Hindi film audiences who, through an "aesthetics of identity"[17] have become "aesthetically initiated" to know what to expect and to expect it (Lutze 1985: 13–14). Similarly, Mira Binford points out the "enormously powerful system of social feedback" underway when a "seminal audience" is provided with a cinema of its own that can cater to its desires and needs "with an unrivalled efficiency in a wonderfully varied set of choices" (1983: 3).

The majority of story themes in contemporary Hindi films do cater to (and certainly simultaneously help create) their audience's desires by drawing inspiration primarily from common intergenerational tensions, tensions between "traditional" and "modern" lifestyles, and hero-villain conflicts. These general themes are presented through elaborate, often quite outrageous, dramatizations of mundane matters of the heart and home (arranged versus "love" marriages, dowry negotiations, challenges to patrilocality by educated young couples, greedy relatives or business partners, the exposure of a corrupt landlord or boss, and so on).[18] Although Tibetans living in exile generally emphasize their differences from Indians, the two groups in fact share many concerns such as these, mostly resulting from the recent and rapid modernization of both their traditional societies and the resulting confusion and sense of injustice these changes have invoked. These personal concerns account in large part for the popularity of Hindi films among older Tibetan women, particularly matriarchs who spend a lot of time at home watching television while caring for small grandchildren. Unlike the younger generation of refugees, it seems the *amala* who watch these movies are primarily interested in the story line rather than the hoochy-koochy songs, especially since in the movies, unlike in real life, wayward ones return to the fold, and good always triumphs over evil.

Although it can be argued that the themes of Hindi films have a certain degree of social and psychological relevance to their diverse audiences, most critics share Narendra Sharma's fundamental concern that "movies are wishies" (1980: 61). Perhaps even stronger than the desire or need for mindless entertainment and escape through dazzling spectacle—common explanations offered for the popularity of commercial Indian films deemed to be "inane potboilers" (Karanth 1984: 45), "moronic" (Rinki 1984: 15), or "monstrous" (Ghatak 1987: 41)—is the hunger for witnessing fantastic solutions to social and economic problems that are all too real and relevant to most film viewers. These films are particularly suggestive and powerful, then, precisely because their themes are based on familiar facts but are unfettered by familiar restraints.[19] Actors and actresses express the inexpressible, "dramatizing feelings that cannot be stated directly" (Dickey 1993: 59). In this way, Sara Dickey states, "Viewers are active participants in the construction of a spectacular image that both represents them and allows them to escape who they are" (1993: 176). Many critics—few, if any, of whom have faced the hardships that are commonplace to the average filmgoer in India—continually express outrage at the political, social, and psychological effects of melodrama they perceive, including inertia, fatalism, and passivity. In an article titled "What Price Entertainment?" P. K. Nair laments:

> The luck element is a recurring motif in most of our films, so much so, that it makes the average man believe in the futility of hard work and the necessity to pin all his hopes on the "hand of luck," which will de-

scend on him one day to remove all his worries. Unfortunately, most of our films, in the name of providing popular entertainment, are transporting our audience to a dream world where all their social, sexual and economic frustrations find an easy outlet. When they come back to the real world outside, they find the going not so smooth. Therefore, to escape from the hard realities of life they drown themselves in the dream world of films. And so the cycle continues till they are reduced to imbeciles and their whole outlook on life gets distorted. (1976: 65)

It is generally acknowledged, however, that a Hindi film's plot really serves only as filler between songs, that the six new songs typically featured in any new film are what patrons are mostly paying to see and hear, as evidenced by the raucous shuffling one hears after hit songs in the cinema hall made by viewers satisfied that they have seen the best part of the movie and can now leave. In fact, the majority of the highly choreographed song-and-dance routines have nothing at all to do with the unfolding story, and this sharp dichotomy between plot and song has become the key generic feature of Hindi films.

WITHIN THE SONG-SPACES

Within the resulting "song-spaces" (Ranade 1980: 7), anything goes: an actress with a husky speaking voice clumsily lip-synchs Lata Mangeshkar's high clear strains; she wears black Lycra shorts under an erotically shredded costume inspired, perhaps, by hula girls in 1960s Hawaiian beach party movies, as she cavorts in a horse stable with a macho man in leather. The hay stops flying and suddenly—because "it is not uncommon these days to have each line of a lyric sung against a different scenic background" (Ray 1976: 74)—the couple is lunging at each other and pulsing their hips on the stairway of a marble mansion or driving a sports car through a rustic village among a chorus of colorful peasant women drawing water from a well. The same practice of appropriating and juxtaposing traditional and modern visual images with unrestrained abandon characterizes the film music that drives the pulsing spectacle. Most contemporary film songs are uncanny exercises in sampling, giving a new meaning to the term "world beat" by borrowing one beat, it often seems, from every part of the world.[20] Violins well suited to a Hollywood screen adaptation of a Jane Austen novel swell behind a reggae beat pounded out on Indian tabla drums. A woman's a cappella introductory aria incorporates the melismatic slides typical of so much traditional Indian song and leads listeners into a dreamy space before the deep thwacks of an electric bass catch her tune on the upbeat and whisk them all away to a place where a pulsing disco beat and frantic jazz flute flurries prevail.

The "catholicity" (Lutze 1985: 5) of popular film songs (and the films more generally) is a source of pride and enjoyment for fans as well as a target of scorn from many intellectual critics, although a handful, like Satyajit Ray, confess to admiring the genre's "brashness and verve" (1976: 75). The freedom and license with which composers and arrangers borrow from here, there, and everywhere is often justified and linked to patriotic understandings of a modern and secular India, with multicultural music as a "natural allegory to Democracy" (B.C. Deva, quoted in Chandavarkar 1976: 110). By being true to no tradition in particular, the songs celebrate all traditions, with the result that the genre has not been "marooned in little islands of orthodoxy" (Chandavarkar 1976: 111). In this way, advocates suggest, films are able to function as a "cementing act" (Ranade 1980: 7) within Mother India and elsewhere:

> Beyond the borders of India, the film song has even acted as a roving ambassador of goodwill and good cheer for India. In this direction the Indian film song has outstripped even the Maharaja of Air India. (Sharma 1980: 56)

Filmmaker Basu Bhattacharya extends the potential for films to engender intercultural understanding even further:

> Political and economic imbalance has not only divided the world, it has broken the human into unidentifiable pieces. But the art of cinema with its universal appeal can wipe out the geographical and political separating lines from the human mind. (1984: 6)

Indeed, a knowledge and love of Hindi film songs often act, perhaps ironically, as agents of cultural reunification and ethnic solidarity among Tibetan refugees scattered throughout the diaspora. Isolated in Texas, Vermont, or Berkeley, away from the interethnic tensions of many of the refugee camps in South Asia, Tibetans living in double exile often gather to watch rented Hindi films and include Hindi songs centrally in their community celebrations. At Tibetan New Year parties I have attended in both Austin and Berkeley, after nightfall when the prayers and eating and displays of Tibetan traditional dancing were finished, a microphone was passed to individuals known to be keen on film songs. For hours, the audiences sang along, and sometimes danced, to the Hindi favorites being performed by the least shy among them. The songs evoked a demonstrative joy that revealed a frankly inclusive fondness and nostalgia for things Indian that caught me by surprise after a year living deep within the intensely Tibet-oriented nostalgia of Dharamsala. On many occasions since returning to the United States I have had to remind myself that India is, after all, the last home (and in some cases, the only home) Tibetan refugees in this country have actually left behind and that Indian pop songs provide a sensory link to that very real, rather than imagined, past.

The inclusive nature of Hindi pop culture that makes it accessible to such wide audiences is not, however, appreciated by everyone. Critics such as Ashok Ranade maintain that the seeming advantages of "greater abandon, more tonal colour, variety and polish" have come at the price of making popular film music "transient, rootless and artificial" (1980: 11). The effect of becoming less and less culture bound, becomes, from this perspective, a sure and tragic sign that India has simply caved in to a success formula that depends on a globally mass-produced, commercial aesthetic. Similarly, Peter Manuel attributes the accessibility and cultural transposability of Hindi films and their songs to the particular circumstances of their production, namely top-down commercialism. He points out that, in contrast to many forms of "public culture" considered by theorists such as Stuart Hall and Simon Frith to be hotly contested territory, Indian pop style, centered as it is on big-budget Bombay films, has not "evolved in connection with alienated youth or class subcultures" (Manuel 1993: 10). Rather, Indian pop songs are "Trojan horses for the values of the hegemonic class and/or region" (1993: 137), namely the Hindi- and English-speaking urban middle class. Others, including Sara Dickey (1993), who researched Tamil cinema and Ritwik Ghatak (1987), a Bengali filmmaker, similarly complain that Hindi language films are wiping out cultural diversity in India by imposing a highly formulaic and hegemonic genre on the entire continent. Considered in this light, India's commercial film culture undermines, rather than reinforces, a sense of community and alienates all audience members but the tiny handful whose lives are, in fact, represented by the international glamour portrayed.

Again and again, within and between these various arguments, a fundamental question is raised that applies to the Indian film audiences who are the central concern of most critical voices and to the Tibetan refugee audiences on whom this study is focused: What are viewers actually *doing* with the "fantastic dreams of sin and modernity" (Das Gupta 1981: 8) presented on the silver screen? My sense is that most viewers do not return to the daily grind transformed into inert morons or consumed with frustration because they cannot buy their own sons red Ferrari convertibles. Hindi films do draw on the average person's fascination with wealth and modernity, and without doubt have created real desires, in youth particularly, for material signs of such in the form of scooters, sunglasses, and leather jackets. Yet by virtue of their very extravagance and impossible grandeur, these films do simultaneously seem to mock the capitalistic excesses of the wealthy, Western-oriented elite and launch the whole representation far into the realm of make-believe, rather than letting it dangle within reach of the average viewer's serious aspirations. This potential discouragement of identification with the rich and famous is further supported by the highly romanticized celebration in most films of the untouched rural village life and traditional values that prove to be eternally right and good even in new contexts such as skyscrapers, beach resorts, and discotheques.[21] Whether or not mockery is the intent of the moviemakers in Bombay (who themselves are an exceptionally glittery lot), the way these films "reduce objects and fashions from the Euro-American civilization into caricatures adorned with the shape, colours, and awkwardness of the Indian urban landscape" (Saari 1985: 25) do often have a humorous or parodic effect.[22] Indian filmmakers, Anil Saari asserts, "plagiarise Hollywood; but everything they plagiarise, they distort and caricature, thereby trying to prevent a straight imitation of life in the west" (1985: 27).[23] Films, then, at once play on a viewer's fantasies *and*, at least potentially, confirm the evil (waste, vanity, immorality, and so on) of late-twentieth-century capitalism, as compared with the simple, traditional village life of India romantically celebrated in the agrarian scenery and traditional drumbeats that fill so many song-spaces. For only a few rupees, a viewer gets to satisfy his curiosity about modern lifestyles; yet, in the end, "he has not sinned himself . . . he has merely inspected the sins of others before condemning them" (Das Gupta 1981: 6).

INSPECTING THE SINS OF OTHERS

Why do people go to see films? Because they want to see other
people. Through the experience of other people, they have a sense
of experience. They go to see not what happens, but how it
happens. After all, what can happen is limited.

                    Chidananda Das Gupta

The opportunity to "window-shop," to inspect the beauty, foibles, vices, and follies of different classes and cultures, is a fundamental appeal of many forms of entertainment. The concern of many Indian film critics, as with many Tibetans worried about cultural preservation, is the degree to which a film viewer's exposure to a smorgasbord of "ways to be" in fact reaffirms or fractures his or her own way of being. When that person's "way of being" has become highly prized and politicized within, for example, the context of a cultural group deeply concerned about maintaining its unique identity in exile, the slippery slope between entertainment and role modeling is unsettling. Whereas playful (or sometimes unkind) mimicry of an "other" can be a powerful tool for consolidating in-group identity, identification or the nonironic desire actually to become the "other" threatens to foreground similarities over differences between groups, thereby blurring boundaries and weakening group solidarity. The ways in which Tibetans "use" Hindi films as a source of entertainment, as a tool to underscore intergroup differences and tensions, and as a source of ideas about different "ways to be" now need to be explored.

It can be argued that Hindi films and film songs are just entertainment for Tibetans who, like Indian viewers, enjoy being transported from their daily work and worries into fantastic mansions and the uninhibited exhibitions of emotions that occur therein. For refugees (and anthropologists) who are from time to time keen on transcending the daily reality of being in India, these films are foreign enough from the surroundings in which they are shown to provide a sense of escape. One afternoon while shopping for kitchen utensils in Lower Dharamsala, Lhanzom and I spontaneously decided to ditch our afternoon work plans and catch a matinee at the "Himalaya Talkies." Lhanzom had seen the feature film *Hum Aapne Kaun Hain?* (Who am I to you?) only two days before but was happy to sit through the silly family comedy again rather than return to the tensions of her household and business up the hill. Perched tentatively on the exposed springs of the hall's folding burlap seats and seeking maximum exposure to the air currents produced by the roaring ceiling fans, we giggled along with the Indian women seated with us in the Ladies Section at the histrionics of a meddlesome mother, haughty daughter, and worried father and tapped our toes during the songs (during which bright red lights flashed around the perimeter of the screen, adding to the spectacle). Walking up the mountain later in the evening light, Lhanzom told me that this film, which utterly lacks violence or sex, had taken everyone by surprise by becoming a major hit for no apparent reason, except that it was "just for fun," an amusing "time-pass."

Most Hindi films, however, with their stock murders, rape scenes, and networks of corruption are not quite so tame. Even the lighthearted song-and-dance routines often border on the pornographic and provide a glamorous stage for machismo and promiscuity that would be impossible, perhaps even criminal, in real life. These scintillating transgressions account, as I have mentioned, for both the popularity of films among the Indian poor (whether as vehicles of escape and/or opportunities to smirk at decadence) and for the morally outraged, often patronizing, criticism of elite critics concerned about the psychological welfare of innocent viewers. The behavior of most film characters seems equally as outrageous to Tibetan refugees in the audience, and a similar dynamic of attraction and rejection can be noted among them. At one level, as outsiders, Tibetan viewers can be titillated by the extravagance and naughtiness of India's pop culture without much concern, since the society that produced the devilish men and seductive nymphs who populate that fantastic culture is not theirs. They can thus, in Chidananda Das Gupta's terms, inspect the sins of India (and make generalizations about national character instead of viewing them as the particular sins of the urban upper class or of certain kinds of women, as an Indian viewer might specify) and then condemn them, at once confirming their worst fears and suspicions of their host country and distancing themselves from Indians. My implication here is not that every Tibetan refugee watches Hindi films in a "resistant" manner, drawing literal parallels between mad staged plots and the course of his or her own daily interactions with Indians in the shops of McLeod Ganj. However, extensive exposure to stock movie characters does accrue in viewers' minds in the form of stereotypical Indian "types"—the greedy landlord, the overbearing matriarch, the passionate son, the religious fanatic, the corrupt politician—fledgling versions of which can be found in any town. Of course, these characters can be found in any Tibetan community as well, but these individuals are criticized, even ostracized, by Tibetans as *individuals,* not as *Tibetans.* In communities marked as Dharamsala is by interethnic tensions, any excuse to generalize from the maladjusted or wicked individual to the community at large is capitalized on by members of the other community.

At another level, however, there are plenty of signs that films are giving Tibetan refugees—particularly children and young adults—new ideas about "ways to be" that are not being readily dismissed. More than the glimpses of ultramodernity or gaudy materialism offered by Hindi film songs and films, it is their celebration of hybridity that strikes me as the key to understanding the appeal of this genre to young Tibetans in particular. Raised within communities keen on protecting their traditional culture from hybridization, Tibetan youth generally feel most at liberty to experiment with and elaborate on *other* people's traditions, traditions with roots that are not, ultimately, theirs to tend.

Narendra Sharma summarizes the quality of freedom in film music that I am claiming is fundamental to its appeal to refugees, for whom a strong investment in their own origins is essential to their ethnic and political identities and cannot be easily set aside in the context of their own communities:

> In order to get accepted by many, the film song accepts much from many sources of tradition and trade. It gladly and gratefully accepts what the lowest common denominators in music, poetry and human sensibility may offer. Rather than aspiring to be authentic, the film song seeks to be effective. For this reason it readily yields to improvisation. . . . Kipling's East and West present no problems of essential cleavage in philosophies of life and culture and civilisation to a film song of universal acceptance. . . . The film song is completely catholic in its choice of drawing inspiration or borrowing from the common fund of conserved or observed music of the human race. . . . *All love of originality has to be got over*—in order to get on (in favor of universality and generality). (1980: 56, emphasis added)

The dilemmas experienced by young Tibetans who are well aware of the tensions between "originality" (which can displace the importance of roots) and "origins" (which can limit respect for innovation) will be further discussed in chapter 5 in the context of their creation of "modern" Tibetan music. The goal of "universal appeal" is a risky one to pursue in a community invested in articulating ethnic difference. The result in Dharamsala is, to a certain extent, a separation of cultural spheres and even personal identities—one traditional, one modern—whereby "authentic" Tibetan ways may be protected and useful or appealing foreign trends embraced.

Owing to the relative financial advantages enjoyed by many Dharamsala refugees, some of them, unlike poorer local Indians, are able to act on their cinematically hatched desires and refashion themselves accordingly, keeping in synch from their mountainside with middle-class urban Indian youth on the plains. McLeod Ganj, along with the other Tibetan settlements in India and Nepal, is full of cool Tibetan Shah Rukh Khan wannabes: young men wearing nearly opaque dark glasses, black leather jackets or vests, blue jeans, white tank tops, silver jewelry, and head scarves (despite erroneous claims by the same young men that Indian films are primarily enjoyed by women). The look is enhanced or Tibetanized by long hair worn loose or in a ponytail, a little turquoise, and the ubiquitous woven "freedom bracelets" worn by youth throughout the Tibetan diaspora. It is true that conservative sex roles among Tibetan refugees—

defined by Margaret Nowak twenty years ago as "normative expectations regarding gender-appropriate appearance, activities, and self-definitions for male and female members" (1980: 219)—seem to have somewhat slowed the influence of female Indian movie stars on the public self-styling of Tibetan girls and young women in exile, but many now redden their hair with henna and wear *kajol* (black eyeliner or kohl), and the vast majority know the words to dozens and dozens of songs. Although she does not specifically mention the influence of Hindi films in her brief analysis of changing sex roles among young Tibetan adults in India, Nowak states that the most significant changes in female sex roles in exile have, rather, involved notions of "propriety." Among these changes from traditional Tibetan female behavior, she notes

> the studied shyness of coeds when interacting with young men in public places; the manipulating of a Hindi kinship term (*bhai*—brother) to disclaim or prevent the possibility of any supposed, implied, or attempted sexual relationship; the newly learned unease of many young women when they have to walk or travel unescorted. . . . All of these behavior patterns are being shaped by social guidelines and expectations that are characteristically Indian. (1980: 223)

These indications that Indian culture has come to be behaviorally embodied in Tibetan refugee youth underscore concerns about the effects the consumption of Indian popular culture is having on youngsters throughout the diaspora. These concerns regarding the extent to which images can become identities are intensified when Tibetan youth start *producing* this foreign pop music, to some extent making it their own by blurring the genre's boundaries between audience members and performers.

PERFORMING THE SPECTACULAR OTHER

Although film songs have emerged from the background to become "free agents" (Ranade 1980: 10) independent of their original cinematic context, they still remain dependent for their full effect on the images that originally accompanied them and linger in listeners' minds. The "picturization" (Das Gupta 1981: 34) of these songs as they are heard allows fans to relive the film scenes' sexual tensions (fanned by the Victorian prohibitions of Indian censorship laws) and the release from these tensions provided by the flirtatious songs (what Das Gupta calls "musical ejaculation" [1981: 34]), even if they are now being replayed perhaps as one stares out a dirty bus window, cleans house, or shops for lentils in the bazaar. That these songs are, in every sense of the word, spectacular, accounts in good measure for their successful transposition into casual or locally staged performances. Live performances or "covers" of hit film songs, even when offered by musicians as utterly different from the original stars as the Tibetan Yak Band, reintroduce the visual dimension of the genre, reembodying the popular voiced melodies and lyrics in new forms. As familiar memories of the films mix with past knowledge and novel impressions of the new performers and performance contexts, the field of experience for listeners bursts wide open again. As a result, interpretations of these performances vary greatly, especially since these judgments are themselves further dependent on individual interpretations of contemporary Tibetan-Indian relations and of the goals of the Tibetan exilic paradigm of cultural preservation, the complexities of which have already been discussed.

With the popularity of Hindi film songs among Tibetan refugees and the omnipresence of this musical genre in their communities established, the significant shift in this community from on- and off-the-screen (cassette) *consumption* of these foreign film songs to their onstage *production* by in-group members must be considered. For many years Tibetans in exile have included Hindi film songs as *masala* (spice) during wedding celebrations, New Year's parties, and in song and dance competitions between Tibetan government-in-exile staffs or schools, all casual public performances that have been a source of great delight for those involved. At parties, these are very unprofessional, spontaneous offerings by fun-loving solo singers willing to utterly embarrass themselves to get a laugh or two. Without musical accompaniment, these singers generally drift off key by the first chorus and sometimes have to be prompted with the lyrics when stage fright suddenly hits mid-verse. In competitions, it is more typical for performers to lip-synch songs blasted from a portable cassette player on stage. The emphasis in these contexts is on attempting to imitate perfectly a well-known film song performance, from the details of costume, facial expression, and demeanor to the hip-hop-inspired dance steps choreographed in a Bombay studio. These performances are infrequent and create a real sensation in the community, even when the more promiscuous body movements are significantly toned down (as they invariably are). People in Dharamsala still speak enthusiastically, for example, of the young pharmacist from Delek Hospital whose uncanny imitation of an Indian superstar at one such competition a few years ago set a new standard. It seems a little of the star's aura rubbed off on him that night, even though he is back to filling prescriptions.

The emergence of two fully equipped rock-and-roll bands in Dharamsala a few years ago ushered in a new local venue for musical performances—the live concert—into which Hindi film songs were quickly incorporated. Although the primary focus of the Yak Band and TIPA's Ah-Ka-Ma Band was the creation and performance of modern Tibetan songs, as will be further discussed in chapter 5, both groups have regularly included popular Indian songs in their concerts as "salt and pepper" to diversify their set lists. Unlike the amateur performances mentioned above, these bands are, through a combination of technology and skill, able quite faithfully to copy the complete instrumentation and overall effect of famous hit songs, providing their audiences with a unique opportunity to experience these numbers being performed live.

An irony here is that these young Tibetan musicians are breathing life into a genre that, in fact, was never performed live, complicating assumptions about originality or the authenticity of prior forms. In his study of "cassette culture" in northern India, which focuses largely on the off-the-screen afterlives of hit film songs, Manuel points out that these pop songs initially emerge as a "studio-based art without live audiences" (1993: 48). The music is highly dependent on electronic special effects rather than on live musicians (a trend facilitated by the capability of modern keyboard synthesizers to imitate any instrument, or a full orchestra, at the command of a few fingers), actors and actresses lip-synch over carefully recorded soundtracks produced by invisible singers, and all this is captured on film to be shown in two dimensions to viewers dispersed around the world. The layers of mediation involved in this genre are further enhanced by the fact that there are often spectators watching the song-and-dance routines in the film scenes in which new songs are debuted—spectators staged as guests at a party, villagers gathered around gamboling visitors, patrons in a nightclub, and so forth—so that even the "original" version of a song is already literally framed as a performance or spectacle-within-a-spectacle. All this layering means that when a Tamil-speaking musician performs a regional version of a pop Hindi song, embedding new words in a famous tune, or when Tibetan refugees stage sincere "covers" of that same song, the distinction between straight imitation and playful parody is greatly complicated. As Manuel notes:

> While Walter Benjamin speculated on the fate of the "aura" of a live performance when it becomes mass-mediated, here we are concerned with the reverse process, namely, the degree to which an entity borrowed from the mass media retains its "commercial" aura in live performance. (1993: 137)

"Imitation" might be a sign of a desire among some Tibetans to become the other, indicating that the alienated and alienating aesthetic generally assumed to be embodied in hegemonic pop culture has caught on with individuals living in the peripheries of India's political sphere, to the extent that their musical efforts to copy pop genres are ultimately serving to reinforce conventional power relations. "Parody," on the other hand, implies a deliberate distancing from the original, suggesting the possibility of resisting and interrupting the dominant discourse (or melody) by altering its "aura" altogether.

A whole body of literature exists that addresses the ways in which parody and mimicry are used in empowering ways by individuals and groups who are subjugated economically, socially, and/or politically.[24] Mockery and parody are common ways of taking on the "other," deliberately playing with stereotypes and taking familiar (and often despised or resented) practices to burlesque extremes to deride those who actually wield authority outside the realm of play and to resist and disrupt normal power relations. Particularly within postcolonial theoretical explorations, there is also, however, interest in the ways that mimicry can serve to *support* dominant systems of representation and confirm colonialism's "authorized versions of otherness."[25] Diana Fuss (1994) treads between these interpretive discourses and resists psychoanalytic theories of identification that insist that "every imitation . . . is also an incorporation," drawing attention instead to the easy two-way slippage that often takes place between a "mimicry of subversion" and a "mimicry of subjugation":

> Given the various and continually changing cultural coordinates that locate identity at the site of both fantasy and power, one would have to acknowledge, at the very least, that the same mimetic act can be disruptive and reversionary at once. Folded into one another, these two notions of mimicry together suggest that context is decisive in registering the full range of political meanings one might attribute to even a single identification. The deceptively simple details of who is imitating whom and under what conditions stand as the most insistent, intricate, and indispensable questions for a politics of mimesis. (1994: 25)

Although Manuel does not assume that parodies always have pejorative or satirical connotations, he regards the existence of regional language versions of hit Hindi songs as evidence of a local "creative resignification process" with "potential for subtle social critique, affirmation of identity and humor," rather than as evidence of "capitulation to commercial, dominant-class aesthetics and values" (1993: 140–42). What about Tibetan performances of the same songs? A close look at contextual detail opens up the possibility that these staged presentations of the "other" could have a parodic tinge, even though the music and lyrics generally remain unaltered.

Although the musicians and audience members at a Yak Band concert enjoy Hindi film songs, there remains among many Tibetan refugees (particularly in Dharamsala) a sense that they should *not* be enjoying the songs as much as they do. The result is a tense flickering between straightforward participation and aloof distancing that makes it particularly complicated to address standard categories of performance analysis such as "intention" and "reception." Some youth exude joy during the performances by singing along and dancing, other audience members watch the band with stunned looks on their faces, others prefer to watch the youth exuding, and others, of course, opt not to attend these events at all as statements of their disapproval of cultural assimilation. After participating in and observing dozens of film song performances in various Tibetan communities, I have come to the conclusion that the usefully ambiguous nature of these events—the quality about them that allows Tibetans, essentially, to have their cake and criticize it too—is made possible by a combination of the issues of boundary maintenance I have claimed most Tibetans feel a responsibility to keep in mind and the inherent characteristics of the film song genre itself.

Perhaps ironically, to perform a perfect imitation of Hindi film stars "singing" hit songs, as a talented and charismatic showman like the Yak Band's leader Thubten can and does, is at once gratifying to those who loved the original version *and* hilarious to those who didn't or to those who did but feel at some level that they shouldn't have. Because of the melodramatic, exaggerated affect of the "original" performances, any faithful imitation automatically reveals the excesses of the whole film song genre and, by extension (for those inclined to take an oppositional position to signs of assimilation), the excesses of the culture that produced the genre and can easily slip into parody. Further, to behold a Tibetan refugee assuming the playful affect of an Indian performer—winks, smiles, supple body movements, a general jocularity—and hear the silly, overtly amorous lyrics of a film song coming from a Tibetan mouth ideally presumed to be accustomed to the more serious activities of shouting political slogans or praying may not so much constitute a mockery of Hindu pop culture as a striking (and entertaining) physical enactment of the radical differences between stereotypical Tibetan and Indian styles of self-expression. Embodying this flashy genre, which is so deeply "other," has the potential, therefore, of subverting it, even without ironic intention on the part of the performer. A faithful imitation of kitsch may retain or even exaggerate its kitschiness. Thubten does not need to assume the standard strategies of parodic performance—exaggeration and "making it one's own"—to open up a space for playful interpretation. This point is perhaps better made by noting what happens when a Tibetan performer *does* attempt to alter the original genre to fit within Tibetan expectations of expression and performance style. To perform Hindi songs seriously, as the school teacher Tenzin Dolma does, removing the playful affect of the original and concentrating instead on the beauty of the melody as a vehicle for displaying the beauty of the female voice, can make the performer, rather than the genre, look ridiculous. One is struck foremost by the fact that one is watching a Tibetan failing to sing a Hindi film song "right." Tenzin Dolma's decision to eliminate references to the original spectacle of film songs, to disembody them so thoroughly, seems to disappoint segments of Tibetan audiences perhaps by emphasizing (by their absence) the aspects of Indian pop films Tibetan refugees love most. Or it may be that Tenzin Dolma's performances are so lovely musically that they make the audience nervous, deprived of any reason at all to distance themselves from the enjoyment her very Tibetan interpretation of the genre evokes and validates. Once the effects of these divergent performance styles are understood, audience reactions to duets sung by Thubten and Tenzin Dolma make more sense. It is far less troubling, and therefore more appealing, to go along with Thubten's style that allows for cathartic fantasy, pleasure, and, if one is so inclined, self-conscious humor.[26]

The role of film songs in Tibetan parties, staged competitions, and concerts may be regarded in the same way that these songs are understood in the context of movies, namely as non-sequitur "vitamin injections" (Segal cited in Dickey 1993: 59), interludes from the serious stuff of political struggles or convoluted screenplays. However, as has been the case with the movies, the *masala* or "salt and pepper" has, in the words of a concerned member of the Yak Band, become the "bread and butter." Just as film viewers come and go from the cinema to catch their favorite songs or fast-forward their VCRs between song-spaces, Tibetan musicians are aware that a large segment of their concert audiences is just waiting for the next "injection" while the band plays the original Tibetan songs it has created specifically for the community's sake. As will be further discussed in the closer analysis of Yak Band concerts in chapter 7, although Thubten himself loves Hindi film songs, he is very concerned about those segments of the Tibetan refugee population—particularly adolescent males and small children—whose hunger for these songs seems insatiable and stubbornly sincere or nonironic. Although his performances open up a space for playful interpretation, as I have said, this does not guarantee that the space will be explored by those to whom it is offered. For critics within the Tibetan community, this is the risk of ambiguous acts of cultural transgression. Because Hindi films and film songs are easily categorized as mere entertainment, a myth of separation between these cultural products and real life is maintainable, along with the illusion that, in Gail Chung-Liang Low's words, the "promise of 'transgressive' pleasure" can be fulfilled "without the penalties of actual change" (quoted in Fuss 1994: 25).

THE VAMPIRE'S KISS

The fear of playful transgressions that do, in fact, lead to change brings us full circle to dominant rhetorical Tibetan refugee understandings of the fragile purity of their heritage and of the polluting influence of India. This notion of cultural pollution or infection is akin to what film scholar Charles Ramirez-Berg claims is captured in the cinematic metaphor of the "vampire's kiss" (1996). The vampire's kiss sucks the life out of others to fill up the "undead," spiritually empty corpses that hang on without a life force of their own and need the blood of others to sustain themselves. The vampire thereby inverts his victim's relationship to otherness by causing her desires to be like his. Such an inversion is an extreme description of what Tibetans with strong commitments to cultural preservation feel could happen to refugee youth if they became dissatisfied with their own heritage and are seduced by what the foreign cultures around them have to offer. It is feared that once a taste for otherness is established, commercial pop culture, itself transient and rootless, will suck the life force out of vulnerable ethnic bodies. A more appropriate metaphor for this particular perspective might be the wet sari, a standard feature of erotic scenes in Hindi films. Like the wet sari, Indian films are clinging to Tibetan refugee bodies and suggestively revealing things that many would rather not behold.

In her discussion of a 1986 Tibetan opera performance in Dharamsala into which a politically savvy actor incorporated a snippet of a Hindi film song to ridicule indirectly a government official, Calkowski noted that "while certain Tibetans in exile might effect a cultural superiority by harshly criticizing any sign of Westernization in Tibetan youth, none took the least notice of the effect Hindu culture had on their lives" (1991: 650). Since this performance more than a decade ago, there has clearly been a shift in attention in Dharamsala's concern with the containment of foreign influences. The community's relationship with India and Indians inevitably remains, however, confused. A child monk I knew was severely whipped by his superior until he collapsed vomiting after being caught in a video hall in McLeod Ganj watching Hindi movies with his lay peers. Yet a few minutes' walk away from this scene, monk-students at the Institute for Buddhist Dialectics watch Hindi movies together every Sunday afternoon. At issue, one monk explained to me, is not, as one might expect, the movies themselves so much as a concern among the older sangha that lay members of the community find it offensive for monks to entertain themselves in public. Discouraged from playing sports or frequenting cinema halls for this reason, the Institute's monks are limited to renting an occasional video and gathering around the television donated to them by the Dalai Lama years ago to encourage the students to keep up with world news.

The distinction between private and public consumption of Indian pop culture may well be the key to making sense of the wide range of opinions and habits concerning Hindi films in Dharamsala. After returning from a two-month tour to south India during which the Yak Band performed an unusually high proportion of Hindi film songs in their concerts because of strong audience demand, the Yaks faced stern criticism from official sources, family members, and friends back at home for having catered to the desires of Tibetans smitten with the Hindi film "craze." Many of these same critics spend significant amounts of time watching Hindi movies at home in the evenings but found it improper that the musicians were publicly endorsing, even promoting, Indian pop culture at explicitly Tibetan public gatherings. The difference seems to hinge on the degree to which willful participation in mainstream Indian culture can be understood as a private or individual choice versus a community preference that is displayed for all to see. The latter situation, exemplified by public concerts attended by Westerners and a handful of Indians as well, threatens the image of distinctiveness or immunity (or, from another perspective, "aloofness") that the refugee community's dominant public voices have deemed crucial to the preservation of Tibetan culture in exile and to the cause of independence.

■ ■ ■

One morning, Tsering Lhanzom and I walked up to the Tibetan Children's Village to meet with Ugyen Choedon, a tiny older woman who is an accomplished traditional musician and has taught Tibetan music and dance in exile schools for many years. After she played a few original songs for us on the *dranyen* that had only been sung once or twice at specific school functions, I asked in the near-whisper her diminutive manner seems to require of those around her how she thought refugee songwriters could make new songs that would really catch the fancy of Tibetans in exile, especially young audiences who seem to prefer foreign entertainment. Without a pause, she suggested that someone should start making videos of Tibetan historical plays, with old and new songs interspersed between the scenes. These educational and entertaining productions could then be aired on the local cable station. I laughed and said, "Tibetan *filmi geet?*" "*Los, los, los,*" she affirmed, smiling at the obvious irony inherent in the idea of modeling a tool for Tibetan cultural preservation on Hindi film songs, the very genre that most directly appears to be supplanting Tibetan music's place in the community. It was ironic, but perhaps very wise, I told Lhanzom, as we walked back down the rocky path from the music teacher's home to the school basketball court where the TCV's Spring Fete was going on. While Lhanzom fished for a Coke bottle and I urged on a baby chick I had picked to win a race through a cardboard maze, I tried to picture what the effect of meshing the lyrics to a Tibetan folk song or the Yaks' "Rangzen" with the spectacular effects that fill Hindi film song-spaces would be. I thought, too, about the many times Tibetans had told me, perhaps a little defensively, that the only reason they watch Hindi films so much is because they have no choice, since there are no Tibetan alternatives, no popular or "modern" Tibetan culture other than that being pumped out of Chinese studios in Tibet.

Ugyen Choedon's idea captures one of the greatest challenges of living in exile: how to create new strategies for staying the same (meaning distinct from others, rather than unchanged) in a new context in the "here and now." A fundamental irony in the investment Tibetan refugees have in their outsider status is that by adamantly retaining and even nurturing their identities as refugees, Tibetans in exile must constantly resynthesize a distinct identity for themselves. In order to remain "distinct," it seems they must constantly change, rearticulating themselves in conversation with the changes taking place among and around them. Taking a close look at the constant shimmerings that characterize most Tibetan refugees' relationships with India and Indians—shimmerings between gratitude and resentment, cooperation and fear, identification and parodic distancing—brings to light the daily dilemmas and decisions that embody such catchphrases as "cultural preservation" and "maintenance of identity" and, rather than making a mockery of those processes, promotes understanding of the challenges they pose.

Thubten, Tenzin Dolma, the Delek Hospital pharmacist, the little kids wiggling at government staff picnics, Dharamsala teenagers, and even monks with VCRs and Ugyen Choedon are all figuring out how to make sense of their relationships to the Indian cultural context in which their "here and now" is embedded. They are all, to different degrees, grappling with the difficulties and opportunities presented by dwelling in India, even as they are also negotiating relationships with other influences, including those from the West.

4 The West as Surrogate Shangri-La

Rock and Roll and Rangzen
as Style and Ideology

> The issue here is not just musical meaning, but also the slipper-
> iness, the power, the idea of *"America"* itself.
>
> Simon Frith

> And then the most scary poster was Alice Cooper, life size, you
> know. Huge one. His eyes were dyed. A huge snake, python on
> his hand. And his torn leather pant. His hair was all . . . And
> what happened one day was there was a family friend, who was
> like a sister to my mother. And she was from Ta-Yup, in Kham,
> Ta-Yup. And she knew my mother right from when she came
> over to Darjeeling. She was very . . . We were like one family . . .
> She became a nun, but was living along with her son. She's ex-
> pired a long time back . . . she died. So she used to sometimes
> come home . . . and she used to shout, really, "What are these
> posters? Especially this one!" She used to scold us in Tibetan.
> Like *"Dong day!" "Day!"*
>   —What's that?
>   —"*Day*" is you know like evil, scary, evil spirits and all this.
> So if you put such posters this will sort of draw all kinds of un-
> wanted spirits. That was her kind of—
>   —But you liked it.
>   —I liked her a lot.
>   —But you liked the posters too.
>   —Poster too I liked a lot.
>
> T. Paljor Phupatsang,
> describing his childhood bedroom to me

One afternoon I took a cab up to Naddi where the Yak Band lived and found they had their equipment set up on the front porch for a change. As usual, they had put an incredible amount of work and money into that evening's party—the furniture had been rearranged to make a banquet room, lots of food and drink had been prepared, and boys from the nearby TCV school had been hired to help. That night we jammed like we had never jammed before, largely thanks to the presence of "Jackpot," a French friend of the band's, who is a great guitar player. He plays so confidently that the band clicks into whatever he's doing—he's the best kind of teacher for them. We played a few of our favorites from our concert set list and serenaded an incredible Himalayan sunset with the snow mountains glowing pink. It was really cold, so the guests (random Tibetan guys, some other French people, the TCV kids, a couple of dogs) squatted around a little charcoal fire in the dirt yard while we played. We got into a great riff that included the blues, boogie-woogie, and, for some reason, Paljor imitating Joe Cocker singing Eagles songs.

> Welcome to the Hotel California,
> Such a lovely place (such a lovely place).
> Plenty of room at the Hotel California.
> Any time of year, you can find it here.

The Eagles welcomed me in living rooms in Darjeeling, restaurants in Dharamsala, teahouses in Rajpur, hotels in Manali, cabs in Delhi, cabs in Kathmandu, cafés in Lhasa. "Hotel California" followed me everywhere I went and, through a process moving from sentimentality to irritation to intrigue about why this song had become so popular so far away from any Spanish mission bells, became something of a theme song for my year in South Asia. Being from California, I was repeatedly called on to clarify the strange lyrics to this song, to explain its obscure meaning, to transpose its basic riffs.

For Tibetans born in exile, particularly those who grew up in Kathmandu, Darjeeling, or Dharamsala, the Eagles' lyrics, Paul McCartney's voice, and Eric Clapton's guitar playing have been part of their lives since childhood. Surveying the selection of Western music cassettes available in even the tiniest music shop in north India or Nepal, one realizes that Western music has been "out of place" for so long that it has become a common part of the Himalayan soundscape. I even heard about Grateful Dead guitarist Jerry Garcia's sudden death in 1995 from a vendor in Darjeeling's marketplace before a fax from home reached me with that news at the post office.

Figure 12.   Monk and youths at an "international music" shop in Bodha, Nepal.

∎ ∎ ∎

One afternoon I was draped over a cold Limca soda in a dusty Tibetan settlement, having just explained to those around me my interest in music.
An old Tibetan man said to me, between gales of sympathetic laughter and
verses of a Pink Floyd song blaring in his son's village café, "It seems,
friend, you have come all the way here just to hear American songs!" Actually, I had, at least in part. How "out-of-place" rock and roll was being
enjoyed, played, and discussed by "out-of-place" people had proven to be
an extremely fruitful area of inquiry that was allowing me to explore some
of the most difficult issues that lie at the heart of Tibetan refugee life as
well as many of the complex issues that face ethnomusicologists interested
in studying local song genres today. If I had not, however, expected to hear
Pink Floyd on a back-roads, premonsoon afternoon in Uttar Pradesh, the
moment would have been quite devastating. At times like these, it is very
tempting to admit that predictions of a homogeneous world crafted by
Rambo and the invisible hands behind Pico Iyer's "Coca-Colonizing
forces" (1988: 5) have, indeed, been realized. But extended time in the field
denies one the ability fully to embrace such cultural quips in good con-
science, however compelling they might be.

Thus far, Dharamsala has been established as the hub of Tibetan refugee life, and the echoes from contemporary Tibet and India that continually complicate and vitalize the processes of cultural preservation and identity construction in exile have been discussed. This chapter attends to echoes from the "West," the last segment of this book's geographical mandala to be considered before taking a close look at the modern music being *created*—not just listened to and loved—by young Tibetan refugees living in and inspired by the nexus of this tangle of sounds.

For Tibetans of all ages living inside and outside the homeland, the "West"—generally understood to include North America, Europe, Australia, and New Zealand—is a friend and a source of hope, support, and inspiration. It is also powerful living proof that there exist viable social alternatives to the models of feudalism, theocracy, and/or Communism most Tibetans have experienced firsthand, which adds credibility and prestige to the Dalai Lama's own democratic experiment in exile. For Tibetans, the West is categorically, and reductively, opposed to China. Further, the West offers the best of India—democracy and freedom of speech, in particular—without, it is believed, the hassles of corruption, caste, filth, and overcrowding. The West has become for many Tibetans something of a substitute Shangri-La, a dream one can actually see and know, unlike the Tibetan homeland whose current inaccessibility and elusiveness are more in keeping with the traditional myth of a hidden heaven on earth. It is as if some of the love and trust felt for Tibet has been projected onto the West, a place that is, in fact, likely to provide some immediate gratification for those refugees lucky enough to obtain tourist visas or green cards. Luckily, perhaps, for Tibetans, the feelings are mutual. The West has a well-documented, centuries-old romance of its own with Tibet, a love affair whose flames have been fanned to a new level of intensity over the past decade.

I am particularly interested in understanding the power the West holds for all Tibetans as an icon of freedom. Because of the musical emphasis of this book, I specifically argue that for Tibetan refugee youth rock-and-roll music is a phenomenally powerful, accessible, and visceral example of that coveted freedom, a piece of the West that can be brought into the most private spaces of one's humble life to be examined, experienced, and enjoyed. However, rock music is more than an ambassador of the West; it is the engine for a virtual reality machine that can transport its listeners into a substitute Shangri-La. In keeping, then, with the theme of considering songs as icons of places, this chapter explores the appeal of rock and roll—as a style and as an ideology—for Tibetan refugee youth seeking to experience Western-style freedom while the homeland remains occupied.

My understanding of rock music as a cultural medium builds on British sociologist Bernice Martin's thesis that it

> has the classic function which Durkheim (1975) attributed to "the sacred," that of celebrating and reinforcing group integration, and paradoxically doing so through a *common* pursuit of the symbolism of disorder and ambiguity. (1979: 89)

Martin sees rock music as a late component in a mid-twentieth-century process that she, following Talcott Parsons (1975), calls an "Expressive Revolution" (1979: 88). The values of this revolution—spanning impressionism, expressionism, Dada, and surrealism—involved the "promotion of personal expressiveness and experiential richness such as had perhaps been the privilege only of an elite minority in the past" (Martin 1979: 89). Rock music's importance, Martin argues, is that it works those values into a mass medium that also serves to bond individuals to one another. Because of this paradox, rock music is

> stretched over the frame of a double contradiction which at times works as a symbiosis and at times threatens to tear the fabric apart. (1979: 102)

Many contemporary Westerners and Tibetans are rethinking and negotiating their culturally prescribed commitments to self and to community. Further, at this particular historical moment, both groups seem to exemplify the paradoxical challenge Martin identifies as central to living in an advanced industrial society. On the one hand, she states, people face the danger of anomie or feelings of rootlessness and confusion about norms; on the other, they enjoy the possibility of enhanced and intensified individuation and self-realization (1979: 88). Given their unique histories, Westerners and Tibetans are at different, perhaps complementary, points in this process. To generalize, there is strong behavioral and discursive evidence that many in the West are seeking community and connections, while Tibetans are increasingly experimenting with "Western-style" individualism, a trend that is intensifying as contact with Western culture and values increases. The relationship between the dual desires for self-expression and belonging is generally assumed to be tense or counteractive. However, many Tibetans are seeking to increase their personal freedom—economically, artistically, socially—without abandoning their commitment to their community's struggle for freedom of a different kind. Many youths, in fact, see the development of their own individuality as instrumental in achieving group solidarity rather than as threatening to that end.

In the West, rock music has historically played a role in both the "sacralization of the symbolism of disorder" (Martin 1979: 89) *and* the solidification of group identities, and it seems to have acquired a similar role in the development of Tibetan youth culture as well. At a certain level, Tibetan youth are only "playing with liminality" (1979: 109), as Martin asserts is the case with most American teenagers, but they feel, too, that rock music is truly empowering in the real political struggle for *rangzen* that their generation faces. The question of what Tibetan youth in South Asia are doing with Western rock and roll—the extent to which they are being sucked in by global capitalistic forces or actively making the music into a useful cultural medium of their own—raises the debate exemplified, according to David Sanjek, by the positions articulated by theorists Theodor Adorno and Walter Benjamin:

> In the case of [Adorno], virtually all culture (certainly any statistically popular form of expression) constitutes the hegemonic control of the powers that be over the consumer, while [Benjamin] observes in the erasure of the "aura" of ineffable artifacts the opportunity for individuals to make sense of and even transform their lives. The one condemns popular culture as nothing more than a mass-manufactured commodity, while the other contends that the demise of the "original" and the proliferation of the copy democratizes the very process of consumption. (1996: 347)

In many ways, rock and roll as a sound and as an experience is prenarrated as oppositional in both Western and non-Western discourses on modernity and youth culture. These sounds bring along with them, therefore, as much cultural baggage as the traditional Tibetan music, Chinese-influenced songs, and Hindi film music already discussed in other chapters. The oppositional aura of rock and roll is certainly part of the music's appeal to Tibetan youth, as it is for young adults all over the world eager to test the boundaries of the authorities who have raised them. And plenty of taboo-breaking is certainly involved in locally creating and partaking in the culture of rock within an Asian refugee community: it is loud, technological, often angry, openly amorous, and deeply foreign.

There is also, however, a general tendency in cultural studies to interpret the expressions of youth *only* within the framework of "resistance" or "deviance." This means, as Stanley Cohen warns, that "instances are sometimes missed when the style is conservative or supportive" (1980: xii). Cohen is referring to instances when a style is taken over "intact from dominant commercial culture," when "changes in youth culture are manufactured changes, dictated by consumer society" (1980: xii). In these cases, kids are "manufactured dummies" being duped by corporate machinations rather than "creative agents" reworking, negotiating, and transcending dominant values.

Certainly for many Tibetan youth, rock music is simply a sonic component of the broader stylistic category of "pop culture." Its sounds are an accessory to a cool, desired "look." Some young Tibetans, however, take a strong ideological interest in rock music as a vehicle for social change. Significantly, they are not so much seeking change within their own immediate communities as they are within China. For this reason, I have determined that many youth are actually using rock music in a conservative way that is, perhaps, surprising. They hope that its amplified sounds will contribute to the achievement of group solidarity, freedom, and cultural survival while also satisfying their own contemporary aesthetic desires. Obviously, not all Tibetans have such noble aspirations, and a number of rock fans in the exile community simply become preoccupied with their own lives and neglect the "Cause," but these claims are generally true for the youth with whom I worked most closely.

Resistant and *duped* are, of course, the extremes on a continuum. Both terms are certainly relevant descriptions of some aspects of youth culture in the Tibetan diaspora, but they would be misrepresentative labels for most of what constitutes these young people's daily lives. Appadurai, Korom, and Mills offer a statement that captures well a middle path in contemporary cultural theory that negotiates between the extremes of radical innovation and global "whitewash":

> The deep, creative force that now drives the reproduction of cultural forms in South Asia, and elsewhere, is the friction between singularization and commodification, as the culture industries seek to commodify and domesticate local voices, and local voices seek to incorporate the very commodified forms they are forced to consume. This global cannibalization of sameness and difference constitutes a complex dynamic. (1991: 23)

Graham Murdock further contributes to a perspective that tempers the same extremes:

> The dynamics of globalization are of course more complex than the cruder characterizations of "cultural imperialism" allow for. To argue that they impose alien cultures on indigenous peoples simply revives the "dominant ideology" thesis. It is more productive to see them as changing the terms of existing struggles by introducing new discursive

formations and new points of identity and pleasure and by facilitating new kinds of cultural practice. (1993: 86)

The mutual fascination and romanticization (some would prefer the term *cannibalization*) between Tibetans and Westerners that in part fuels the "dynamics of globalization" and affects cultural practice is, of course, based on reality and fantasy and represents a complex phenomenon that has merited its own studies.[1] For the purposes of this study, the *causes* fueling the current Tibet mania in the West are important to consider next, since they are part of the larger Western-Tibetan dialogue so crucial to the self-perception and self-presentation of many Tibetans in exile, as this chapter will convey. There then follows a discussion of the counterpoint to this Tibetophilia, namely the appeal of the West (and rock and roll) to even the most politically committed young Tibetan adults. Their lives embody this dual affection that both integrates them into their community and threatens to alienate them from it.

TIBETOPHILIA

I will begin with a summary of the channels of communication and fantasy between Westerners and Tibetans. As mentioned in the introduction, the West's interest in Tibet has dramatically increased in recent years and seems to be more than a passing cause célèbre. In terms of publishing, this growth has, until very recently, been focused on very particular topics and audiences (primarily spiritual guidance tailored to the New Age movement),[2] but a more general look at the situation reveals the current intrigue with Tibet to have a more broadly based public grounding.

Briefly, practical and philosophical texts about Tibetan Buddhism have proliferated in the West since the 1970s, primarily owing to the "Beat Generation's" interest in Buddhist teachings (dharma) and the resettlement of a substantial number of Tibetan monks (lama) in Europe and the United States, many of whom have established Buddhist centers. In the last decade, public interest in Tibet has been further boosted and extended beyond religious matters by a convergence of specific historical events and the particular interests and needs of a segment of the populations of Western countries (hunger for spiritual advice, feelings of alienation in Western technological societies, and concern about human rights and environmental issues). In addition to sporadic news coverage of developments in Tibet under Chinese rule, recent events that have put Tibet in the public spotlight in the West include the granting of the Nobel Peace Prize to the Dalai Lama in 1989, the Year of Tibet activities in 1991, actor Richard Gere's plug for the Tibetan Cause in his acceptance speech at the 1993 Academy Awards, Tibetan hunger strikes on the steps of the United Nations (a body in which Tibet has no autonomous voice), the clumsy and abusive treatment of the Tibetan delegation to the Beijing Women's Conference in 1995, the continuing confrontation between Tibetan and Chinese authorities about the identification of the reincarnation of the young Panchen Lama, former President Clinton's firm stand to unlink China's human rights record from its economic privileges, four annual Tibetan Freedom Concerts in major U.S. cities, the self-immolation of an elderly Tibetan in protest of Indian police interference in a lengthy hunger strike in Delhi in March 1998, the escape of the eminent young Karmapa to India in January 2000, and extensive international protests against China's bid to host the 2008 Olympics because of its humans rights record.

Further, many people in the United States now personally know Tibetans because of the U.S. Resettlement Project that has made possible the incorporation of one thousand Tibetan immigrant families into the schools, neighborhoods, and workplaces of a handful of American cities. Tibet's popularity has also been tapped into by the popular media, thereby sending information, along with cultural stereotypes, out to a vast audience that was probably unfamiliar with Tibet's existence before the 1993 release of Bernardo Bertolucci's film *Little Buddha*. Tibetan monks have appeared in television ads for Nike shoes and Apple computers and have been recorded as backup singers for the Beastie Boys rock group. Two more Hollywood films—one an enactment of Heinrich Harrer's 1953 book *Seven Years in Tibet* directed by Jean-Jacques Annaud, the other (*Kundun*) the story of the Dalai Lama's life directed by Martin Scorcese—were released in 1997. The latter film, in particular, introduced a remarkably authentic and sensitive representation of Tibetan history, culture, and aesthetics into the American mainstream.[3] The widespread effect of these big-budget films was supplemented by the release in 1999 of two more modest and ethnographically sensitive films, Paul Wagner's *Windhorse* and Khyentse Norbu's *The Cup*.

Although a good number of the public representations of Tibetan culture that have resulted from this fascination with Tibet are exclusively interested in either "spirituality" (what can Tibet do to save me?) or "politics" (what can I do to save Tibet?), Calla Jacobson (1994) points out that most, such as the rhetoric used by the international network of "Free Tibet" campaigns and the Dalai Lama himself, support political agendas calling for Tibetan independence and human rights with an argument about Tibet's spiritual legacy to the world. Jacobson has argued, and I agree with her basic point, that the "crystallized, popularized essence of contemporary imaginings about Tibet" at once naturalizes and departicu-larizes Tibetans to such an extent that the current and widespread glorification of the "Tibetan spirit" that emerges is "dehumanizing, per-haps no less so than more obviously racist essentializations" (1994: 2–3). Jacobson summarizes the essential image of Tibet today, an image gleaned from a wide variety of publications and media, as one that replaces Tibet's turbulent worldly history (including its various consensual relationships with China) with a stable, deeply spiritual and environmentally conscien-tious society maintained in an ancient timelessness. The dominant image, she adds, also glosses over social and cultural differences between people now uniformly considered "Tibetan," a denial of internal diversity due, in part, to a strong political investment in presenting Tibet as a bounded and distinct national and cultural unit counter to Chinese claims and due, in part, to a spiritual investment in Tibetans as nonviolent, compassionate beings. The extension of Western fantasies about Tibet onto Tibetans themselves—expectations of enlightened behavior and nonmaterialist lifestyles, for example—are largely responsible for the outpouring of sup-port for these refugees. This transference has also frequently resulted in severely disappointed *Injis*, many of whom feel betrayed when the Ti-betans they have helped turn out to be rather ordinary and fallible human beings.

Although it is certain that Tibetans have materially benefited from and played a significant role in creating and perpetuating this rhetoric of glorification,[4] there is growing skepticism and concern among Tibetolo-gists and Tibetans themselves about the effects of popular interest in and representations of Tibet, along with the burden and frustration of trying to meet the expectations of Western sponsors and supporters. Propelled by the conviction that it is their moral responsibility as refugees to share their culture and religion with all who are interested, in order to educate the world about the plight of Tibet and to ensure the preservation of their tra-ditional culture, some Tibetans have been dismayed at and confused by the results of their efforts. Debated events have included the decontextualiza-tion and public display of sacred sand mandalas in museums and sky-scraper lobbies and the transformation of monastic dances and chants into choreographed performances by touring groups of monks. The concerned voices are, however, largely academic. As long as Western audiences want access to Tibetan Buddhist culture and Tibetans want access to Western ears and hearts, these events are a perfect match, even if the access gate is a ticket window at Madison Square Garden.

While a shared interest in Buddhism has opened many fruitful dialogues between Tibetans and Westerners, the exchange has not always been a responsible one. In his *Dreams of Power: Tibetan Buddhism and the Western Imagination*, Peter Bishop describes his sense of disquiet about the way Tibetan Buddhism has been established in the West:

> There seemed to be a complete lack of critical reflection on the immensely complex cross-cultural problems associated with the transfer of a system of wisdom/knowledge from one culture to another. At one extreme this resulted in an unquestioning and naïve adulation, whilst at the other end was an arrogant picking and choosing of the bits that could prove useful. Both attitudes, I believe, sprang from the same source—a kind of cultural imperialism, with all its associations of power and guilt. (1993: 9)

An infatuation with, or even seduction by, Tibet and all things Tibetan was also pointed out, and mocked by, the one character in James Hilton's classic 1933 novel *Lost Horizon* who remained skeptical and "rational" during his group's unintended sojourn in "Shangri-La" (a valley somewhere in Tibet). Here he is trying to knock sense into a fellow Brit who has, he fears, fallen under the place's spell:

> "After all, man, you're a critical sort of person—you'd hesitate to believe all you were told even in an English monastery—I really can't see why you should jump at everything just because you're in Tibet!" (1933: 169)

Bishop's *The Myth of Shangri-La: Tibet, Travel Writing and the Western Creation of Sacred Landscape* (1989), which is methodologically based on archetypal psychology, offers an analysis of *why* Westerners jump at everything Tibetan by examining the "inner meanings that Tibet came to hold directly for a considerable number of Westerners and also indirectly for their cultures as a whole" (1989: vii). In this book, Tibet emerges as a "site of contending fantasies" (1989: viii) rather than as the coherent whole typically imagined by contemporary Westerners and exiled Tibetans. Bishop posits a diachronic transformation of Tibet (as imagined by Westerners) over the centuries from a geographic rumor into a sacred place and, finally, following the invasion and exposure of Tibet by the Chinese, into "Shangri-La" or a placeless utopia. The territory's usefulness as an image of unknownness, he argues, was shattered by its realization (literally, by its having been made real via roads, planes, and video footage). This process of familiarization happened gradually, with the site of the West's fascination with Tibet's mysteries shrinking from the whole landscape of the "roof of the world," to the "forbidden city" of Lhasa, to the Potala Palace, to be finally entirely concentrated within the person of the Dalai Lama himself. Bishop regards Hilton's 1933 image of "Shangri-La" as a fitting conclusion to this dual process of symbolic concentration and geographical abstraction. "Shangri-La" is just an idea now. The fantasy of Tibet, the actual place, as a utopian society, a "possible exemplary model for a West desperate and in decline," Bishop concludes, is "rarer than sightings of the yeti" (1989: 245).

Bishop's metacommentary is based on foreign accounts of Tibet from 1773 to 1959, the year the present Dalai Lama fled to India.[5] He suggests that in that year, more than forty years ago, a whole new process of "Shangri-La-ization" began in exile.[6] That new process has been distinctly dialogic, engaging Tibetans for whom the West has become their own site of contending fantasies. This mirror effect and the personalization of contact have greatly intensified the relationship between real and imagined domains.

INJI FEVER

In many Tibetan refugee homes one finds displayed a framed copy of a photo of former president George Bush shaking hands with the Dalai Lama. This image has achieved the status of a cultural icon, a reassuring souvenir of a moment when the Tibetan Cause seemed spotlighted, attended to, and taken seriously by people who could make a difference. Bush met with the Dalai Lama after the Buddhist leader was awarded the 1989 Nobel Peace Prize, another moment of great hope for Tibetans everywhere that is commemorated annually with pride. Many refugees' hopes were again boosted when former president Clinton made strong public statements about Tibet during his 1998 visit to China urging President Jiang Zemin to "assume a dialogue in return for the recognition that Tibet is part of China" (Burns 1998: A9). The Dalai Lama firmly supported the Clinton administration's strategy of changing China through engagement, rather than punishment, a policy that resulted in the unlinking of economic and human rights issues and the consistent renewal of China's Most Favored Nation trading status with the United States. Clinton, in turn, supported Tibetan "autonomy" within China, which the Dalai Lama now deems more realistic than full independence. Optimism among Tibetans was renewed when Secretary of State-elect Colin Powell asserted at his confirmation hearing that George W. Bush's administration would show a genuine interest in expressing solidarity with the Dalai Lama and the people of

Tibet and in reenergizing discussions with the Chinese that will promote reconciliation in the region. Indeed, space may have to be made on the walls of Tibetan refugee homes for a photo of the meeting between the younger Bush and the Dalai Lama that took place on May 23, 2001, despite Beijing's strong objections.

In these and many other lower-profile ways, the Western world has sent strong messages that it cares about Tibet and disapproves of China's behavior there, if not its claims to power. And, in general, Tibetans living in exile and in the homeland have a deep faith that the West will one day save them from their current troubles, despite the lack of critical diplomatic action by Western governments terrified of angering China. Since 1959 Tibetans have, in fact, received extensive material and philosophical support from Western individuals and, to varying degrees at various times, from Western governments. European countries in particular responded immediately to the refugees' plight, setting up emergency camps and providing medical help. Many Tibetan children were assigned Western sponsors who supported them through school, and a significant number were sent abroad to Norway and Switzerland, where they have stayed and raised their own families. Small populations of Tibetans have been allowed to emigrate to Canada and Australia over the years as well. Tibetans remain deeply grateful for all these past kindnesses and extend a gracious attitude of indebtedness to most Westerners they meet.

Until fairly recently, the number of Tibetans living in the United States was not significant, generally limited to religious leaders and their aides and families, along with a few individuals who had obtained residency for other scholarly and professional reasons. In the past ten years, however, the attention of Tibetans seeking alternatives to their lives in South Asia has shifted from Europe to the United States and, most recently, to Canada. This shift was triggered by a single event: the 1990 approval of a special act by the U.S. Congress that allowed one thousand Tibetan heads of household and their families to resettle in the United States as immigrants with green cards rather than as refugees. The Tibetan government-in-exile immediately put out a call for applications to exiled Tibetans everywhere and selected the lucky one thousand by lottery.[7] The chosen group was, as intended, diverse, including aristocrats, new arrivals, long-time Dharamsala residents, uneducated street vendors, bachelors, elderly government officials, and young mothers, among others. Efforts were made to group the emigrants so that each "cluster site" had people skilled in various aspects of Tibetan culture to facilitate the replication of traditional communities. Now that the drawn-out process of family reunification is completed, approximately eight thousand

Tibetans call America home.[8] As a result of this project, many Tibetans living in exile now have some connection with friends or relatives who are, in fact, living the American Dream working in hotels, pizzerias, and donut shops in cities such as Berkeley, Chicago, and Salt Lake City.

When the U.S. immigrants return to Dharamsala to celebrate the Tibetan New Year, one can walk through the streets and visibly distinguish those Tibetans who have connections abroad from those who do not. Those who do walk stiffly in new Levi's, towing children in bright ski jackets and new boots. Women can be seen trying to navigate their way in high-heeled shoes or steer completely impractical new baby strollers down rocky, potholed streets. These accessories may seem superficial, but they have, in fact, fomented deep jealousies and rifts in the exile communities. What one might even call new class distinctions in Dharamsala and elsewhere seem to be displacing the social order that has developed there over the decades. Children of lottery losers desire the toys they are seeing, and their parents envy the comfortable futures their absent friends and neighbors are bound to enjoy. The gleam others see is further polished by the fact that those resettled in America never reveal the hardships and humiliation many of them have suffered in the West—cleaning toilets, enduring intense loneliness, barely saving anything after paying the rent, buying gifts, paying long-distance phone bills and international airline fares. Tellers of such honest tales would be harshly accused of being ungrateful or of squandering a precious opportunity bestowed on them.

Those left behind in India and Nepal, personally unconnected to the West, often console themselves by pointing out that they are the ones who have remained loyal to the Tibetan Cause, sacrificing short-term material gains to continue working for the Dalai Lama's government, for example. The resettlement project caused a devastating and continuing "brain drain" that hollowed out school faculties, administrative staffs, and offices and is still deeply resented by those who thought their colleagues were committed to their work. Those left behind also do not hesitate to point out the moral decay they perceive in those who have moved to the West. They cite in particular the high percentage of divorces and extramarital affairs that took place during the years of separation before family reunification and the poor Tibetan language skills of children being educated in America's public schools.

Despite these and other proud critiques, some of which are well founded, the fact is that the resettlement project has set into motion a frenzy of tourist visa applications at the U.S. Embassy in Delhi, as Tibetans left behind in Dharamsala and other settlements scramble to ride the coattails of their compatriots' successes in *Ari* (America). Most are successful, needing only a sponsorship letter and bank statement from an American acquaintance and proof of personal or professional obligations in India that will necessitate one's return. In the United States, most visitors move in with friends and quickly find illegal work to bring in the *jang khu* (dollars, literally the "green") that is so valuable in India. Some return, but many stay on, illegally or by seeking political asylum, and others are continually coming over. As a result, the Tibetan refugee "community"-in-exile is experiencing a major reconfiguration, with new liminal centers emerging in unexpected places like Minneapolis and Albuquerque and tilting the focus of exilic Tibetan attention to the West.

Readers of the Dalai Lama's autobiography and viewers of recent films about the Tibetan leader are charmed by descriptions of this high lama's childhood fascination with the West, particularly as a source of wristwatches, movies, and cars. The Dalai Lama retains a deep respect for and intellectual interest in Western culture and philosophy and often articulates how much his people and Westerners can learn from one another. However, he does not condone the emulation of Western ways:

> I always tell these young Tibetans: "You are Tibetan, whether you live
> in America or anywhere else. No matter how hard you try, you cannot
> turn Western 100 percent. If you forget about your own culture completely, the final result is that you will be neither Tibetan nor Western.
> It is far better, simply in your own interest, to maintain Tibetan ways."
> (Gyatso 1980: 149–50)[9]

Yet, for many reasons, the West clearly holds a strong appeal for many Tibetans, including the Dalai Lama himself, building on long-term historical connections and exchanges between the two regions and the powerful mutual attraction between the desires and needs suggested above. Insecurities about their refugee status in an increasingly conservative and Hindu-centric India and wavering confidence in the possibility of self-rule in the homeland are also "push factors" that are contributing to Tibetan pursuance of real and imagined opportunities in the West. For young Tibetans in particular, there is a direct correspondence between the real contemporary challenges they face as refugees and their unprecedented efforts to tap into the West as a cultural, economic, and political resource for personal and political change.

DHASA TEENS

Adolescence and young adulthood in Dharamsala and elsewhere in the South Asian diaspora are stressful, even grim, in many ways, and Tibetans in exile are growing increasingly concerned about the future of the waves of young people being well educated through high school and beyond who find they have few opportunities open to them once they finish their formal schooling. The Tibetan government-in-exile was once able to absorb all the brightest, trilingual graduates of Tibetan schools into its own offices and community projects. This was an ideal arrangement, for a time. Now the supply of qualified Tibetan workers far exceeds the government's needs, resulting in an increase in out-migration from Dharamsala and other settlements and a rise in local unemployment. Further, many of the most qualified young Tibetans the government would like to retain are unwilling to work for the meager stipends offered by their refugee community's organizations and are applying instead for scholarships and other opportunities abroad. Those who do accept government positions often consider these jobs as stopgap measures or as stepping stones to other opportunities. Many well-meaning youth are very confused about what to do, having been raised to put group needs before individual desires but now finding themselves unable to imagine how to be of use to the community *and* make a living. Others have become disillusioned with the "community" and are pursuing their own dreams instead.

After four decades in exile, the majority of young Tibetans living in India were born there. However, the flow of children out of the homeland still continues, ebbing and flowing as Chinese policies and border patrols change. According to the Tibet Information Network (TIN) in London, about nine hundred Tibetan children under the age of eighteen arrived in Nepal in 1996 on their way to seek asylum in India. Nearly 80 percent of these children, TIN reports, were sent across the Himalayas unaccompanied by their parents, who had entrusted them to guides or other refugees in the hope that they would be taken to one of the schools run by the Tibetan government-in-exile in India (Tibetan Information Network 1997). In fact, most of those who arrive safely and are not repatriated by Nepali police or handed over to the Chinese do eventually end up being scrubbed and shorn by a dorm mother and fitted with a British-inspired school uniform, complete with neckties for boys and girls. A foreign sponsor is immediately sought for each student to help defray the costs of educating these needy children. In the interest of anonymity and propriety, school staff monitors correspondence and gifts exchanged between the children and their sponsors so much so that children are not even given the name and address of their "godparent" when they graduate. These relationships instill in many Tibetan youth a deep sense of gratitude and indebtedness to *Injis*. They also instill in some an expectation of continued support from

Westerners and a comfort with dependence and favor seeking, in one form or another.

Many of these newly arrived children do not intend to stay in exile and only wish to fulfill their parents' desires for them to receive a modern education and to have the opportunity to receive the Dalai Lama's blessing. A great number of young adults from Amdo and Kham in Eastern Tibet have been arriving in India during the past ten years with similar motivations, seeking short-term benefits from an excursion into exile. Many pass their time at the Suja School in Bir, in the valley below Dharamsala, a special facility set up to educate new arrivals in their teens and twenties who need remedial education. Others take short-term English conversation classes, which are casually taught by volunteer Western tourists, at the Tibetan Library in Dharamsala. The classes gather in small circles on the library's scrubby lawn to discuss the weather or their escape stories or to ask their young teachers long-burning questions about the West. After class, the students linger around the teashop run by monks from the Nechung monastery, hoping to join other Westerners for lunch and to interest them in private English tutoring. These new arrivals are hungry to learn and are extremely entrepreneurial in the way that the most recent wave of refugees often is. Some do return to Tibet, although doing so has become increasingly risky. The Chinese have become suspicious of Tibetans who have been influenced by the "separatist ideology of the Dalai clique," and most returnees expect to spend at least a month in jail before being allowed to return to their homes. Others remain in exile, eventually marrying or moving on to opportunities in other countries, an option often easier for them to exercise as Chinese passport holders than for Tibetan refugees born in exile.

Most Tibetans now in their teens or twenties who were born in exile or carried out of Tibet as small children have been well educated, in the Tibetan Children's Village schools run by the Dalai Lama's government, at the Tibetan Homes Foundation in Mussoorie, in one of the Central Schools for Tibetans run by the Indian Government, or in one of the many private missionary schools run for needy children in India. Only those students planning to attend college continue past Class 10. Most leave school at this point, at about age sixteen, and have to make a life for themselves.

There is very little in the way of job counseling for Tibetan refugee youths, and their options are limited. A handful of teenagers will be accepted into teacher-training programs at TIPA or the TCV. Only the brightest students from good families will land the poor-paying but honorable jobs in the exile government's offices. Some boys will join the In-

Figure 13. Uniformed school children at the Tibetan Homes Foundation in Mussoorie, India, preparing letters to send to their Western sponsors.

dian army for a while, although this option is not as popular as it was twenty years ago. Many young graduates will return to their families' settlements in India or Nepal and help with their petty businesses (shop keeping or selling sweaters on the streets in Indian cities). Girls in particular often return to the rural settlements to care for their parents or to get married and care for their husbands' parents. Those students who are orphans or semiorphans or who have left their families behind in Tibet usually have some connection with kin in exile on whom they can rely at least for housing and food.

In Dharamsala and most Tibetan settlements, not surprisingly, a good number of young men hang about the streets and cafes with nothing much to do. Most are just getting by on the generosity of friends and the odd job until their luck runs dry; some get *Inji* girlfriends and find themselves living in France or Australia until their passion and/or tourist visas expire. Other young men have consciously marginalized themselves from the Tibetan community and have developed a community of their own based on a shared critique of the status quo. Their haunts attract young Western backpackers with extra cash, cassettes, and cigarettes to share and are fertile ground for rock-and-roll fantasies.

The Zoha Café and the Freedom Café are located physically and socially on the periphery of McLeod Ganj, beyond the last shops on the rough road out to the waterfall at Bhagsu Nag. I got to know these makeshift hangouts a bit through Hannah, a pink-cheeked eighteen-year-old student from England spending a year abroad before starting college. She had been placed by her volunteer organization as an English teacher for students at the Tibetan Institute of Performing Arts. She was fulfilling her duties responsibly, but had quickly grown weary with the institute's conservatism and rigid structure. Most evenings found her up and out of her dorm window absorbed in the late-night culture of the self-named "Yeti," alternately known as "Roamers" by most Tibetans in town. The Yeti are a group of young guys who hang out, get high, listen to the Rolling Stones and the Doors, play the spoons, write poetry, and talk about *rangzen*. Their activities spell a rejection of their limited alternatives and of the Tibetan establishment in exile, and Western music and friends are their vehicles for escape. The Yeti are strongly critical of materialism and just get along by "making friends with people." They had recently sold someone's guitar for three thousand rupees to finance a trip to Goa, but they had spent two thousand of them on food and drink at the local Hotel Tibet celebrating the transaction and couldn't go. Many of them have young *Inji* girlfriends who hang out with them until their visas expire, laugh at their jokes, enjoy the tunes, and live out their own dreams of independence far from the pubs of Manchester.

After hours, the Yeti shut the doors of the cafes and convert the benches into beds. Two of the Yeti—the new leaders of the group since its founder fell off a building to his death—actually live in a small house provided for them by the Tibetan Welfare Office. One used to work for the Tibetan government-in-exile but quit because he felt everyone but the Dalai Lama was looking in the wrong direction and making themselves too comfortable in India. He loves Jack Kerouac and Jim Morrison and writes poetry in English, including a few verses about Westerners in Dharamsala. One poem's basic message to *Injis* seemed to be stop pretending to be into the dharma and just hang out and smoke pot with us. At the end of his notebook is his will: "When I die, don't mourn." During the autumn I was in Dharamsala, he was busy collecting signatures for a protest march from "Dhasa to Lhasa"[10] and, as an unattached bachelor with no job and no possessions, was fully prepared to be arrested by the Chinese for attempting to enter Tibet on foot. "I have no religion, I have no country, and I don't believe in the dharma," one Yeti told an American friend.

The Yeti have chosen, or created, a life that is extreme in its rejection of traditional family, work, and community networks. While young guys who fit into this subcultural niche are not the norm, neither are they as unique as is implied by their self-proclaimed, elusive mascot. While most young Tibetan refugees somehow find a way of participating in traditional social networks, many who do so are still concerned about and constrained in various ways by the same issues that have so fully absorbed the minds of their more radical peers: regaining the dignity of having a country, being well liked by friends, having access to modern tunes and styles, making *Inji* friends, and learning English well. Above all, virtually every young Tibetan is deeply invested in achieving freedom, or *rangzen*, but their understanding of this concept and their means for realizing it vary widely. Generally, this freedom is understood to mean political independence for the homeland, but it is increasingly inclusive of more typical adolescent dreams of self-assertion and self-expression as well, interpretations that are not always compatible with one another.

RANGZEN

Young people's search for relevant themes and heroes brings their "Tibetanness" face to face with nontraditional pop culture.

Margaret Nowak

Understanding the concept of *rangzen*—a Tibetan neologism variously translated as self-determination, independence, or freedom—is essential to understanding the framework of young Tibetan refugees' lives and the choices they make in the process of creating a distinct Tibetan youth identity. It is the slogan shouted in front of Chinese consulates all over the world by Tibetans protesting their country's occupation, the anchoring lyric for innumerable songs and poems written in exile, the name of the Tibetan Youth Congress' publication, a two-syllable mantra for Tibetans everywhere, a cementing agent that binds generations, and a ticket to prison in Tibet.

In her important doctoral study of Tibetan refugee youth, Nowak explores *rangzen* as *the* "root metaphor"[11] for Tibetan refugees, since the term embraces the concept of independence "as a *meta*political image, that is, as a metaphor suggestive of a range of meanings going beyond the notion of political autonomy" (1984: 33). She elaborates:

> Whether taken in the literal sense of the Tibetan morphemes *rang* ("self") and *bstan* ("power") or interpreted metaphorically as a metapolitical image of independence, this concept directly impinges on two of the most critical problems Tibetan refugees must confront today: that of *self*-definition (either as individuals vis-à-vis others, especially Tibetans,

or as Tibetans vis-à-vis the rest of the world) and that of de facto and de jure relationships of *power* (again, in reference to both intra-Tibetan and Tibetan–non-Tibetan relationships). (1984: 136–37)

This multivalent concept, whose ambiguity Nowak deconstructs at length, is the result, she explains, of "twentieth-century events, ideology, and experience" (1984: 31) and is useful to Tibetans (and to anthropologists) interested in exploring how issues of modernity, democracy, and hybridity are being incorporated into their lives both publicly and more privately, regarding both Tibet's political struggle and individual self-definition.

In some ways, Nowak maintains, the concept of *rangzen* fits well with and even enriches certain traditional Tibetan feelings and ideas nurtured in school: compassion (*nying jay*), respectful behavior (*ya rab chö zang*), patriotism (*gyal zhen*), and avoiding shame (*ngo tsa*) (1984: 137–38). However, it is evident that these qualities can easily conflict with one another. Striving to uphold all of them has led to a certain amount of frustration and "psychological anguish" for many young Tibetans trying to integrate old traditions and ideology with new ways of thought derived from their own lived experiences.

The difficulty of exemplifying traditionally valued personal qualities in a setting so ripe with alternate ways to be is compounded for young people in the diaspora by a growing frustration throughout the community with the marked lack of progress in negotiations with the Chinese government. The Dalai Lama himself has acknowledged that, although he still believes in the path of nonviolence and cannot condone any other method of diplomacy, his approach has not been successful. His rhetorical shift during the past decade to working toward "genuine autonomy within China" rather than "independence" sent shock waves through Tibetan communities everywhere, compromising as it seems to, much that Tibetans living in and out of Tibet have been fighting for over the past forty years. This "accommodationist" stance has inspired among the more radical factions in exile an unprecedented level of skepticism about the Dalai Lama's tactics, with the most extreme among those disappointed—often members of the Tibetan Youth Congress—actively ignoring his advice.[12] Yet even the most radical Tibetans, the cool Yeti included, still hold deep respect for the leader and acknowledge the importance of striving for a unified Tibetan resistance effort. To the credit of everyone involved, an open dialogue has been maintained with the Dalai Lama regarding what is best for the future of all Tibetans everywhere. His critics generally acknowledge that if constructive negotiations ever do take place between Tibetans and the Chinese govern-

Figure 14.   Youth calling for *rangzen* with "Independence Only" banner made for Dharamsala's annual Tibetan Uprising Day procession.

ment, they will likely occur through his office. The Dalai Lama's continuing confidence in his people's faith in him was revealed in a statement made in response to former president Clinton and President Jiang Zemin's surprisingly frank conversations about the Tibet Question, a comment in which the exiled leader emphasized that the Chinese should take advantage of the opportunity to negotiate with him personally:

> In 20 years' time, I'll be 83, just an old man with a stick, moving like a sloth bear. While I'm alive, I am fully committed to autonomy, and I am the person who can persuade the Tibetan people to accept it. In 10, 20 years' time, the Dalai Lama will die, and then who can persuade these radicals? Then, who will be in a position to cool them down? If the Dalai Lama is not there, the Tibetan issue can go completely out of control. (Burns 1998: A9)

At issue here is not only a strategic political debate over Tibet's autonomy or independence from China but also an internal debate over the degree of autonomy or independence attainable or desirable by Tibetan "radicals" in relation to the Dalai Lama and mainstream Tibetan exile society. Layered over this is the broader issue of how much autonomy or independence

Tibetan culture can or should expect to pursue vis-à-vis the rest of the world at a time when cultural preservation is a pressing concern and yet deep regrets over Tibet's past isolation are being felt and acknowledged. Relevant to all these personal and public struggles to define and attain *rangzen* is the Dalai Lama's call for cooperation, a broad outlook, and the willing assumption of what he calls "universal responsibility" (looking beyond one's own immediate concerns):

> In ancient times each village was more or less independent; there was no need for others' cooperation, because they did everything themselves and they survived. But now the situation has completely changed. National political boundaries seem important, while actually they are not. Something that happens in one area has an impact or implications beyond the boundaries of that area or country. So we need a broader outlook these days, and the need for a sense of Universal Responsibility is connected with this. (Gyatso 1995: 7–8)

For many "radical" Tibetans—generally young and male—a consoling confirmation of the permeability of political borders has been the diverse music that has provided a soundtrack for their lives. In particular, rock music has become for them, as it has for youth all over the world, a powerful "resource for the articulation of their arguments as well as a vehicle for their effective involvements" (Brace 1991: 44). For some youth who are frustrated with the limited opportunities available to them yet are politically and socially committed to crafting their lives in accordance with local possibilities, participation in rock and roll does seem to be a passport to a wider community without borders. Rock music is marked, in Martin's words, by its "devotion to the cause of boundary violation," sending out its tentacles and drawing in material from wherever it can (1979: 117).

Tapping into electronic sounds from faraway continents greatly expands the size of a Tibetan teenager's world, whether or not he or she actually leaves the community. Although rock music feels satisfyingly naughty and oppositional to young Tibetans (and, indeed, can lead to radical styles and behavior), certain genres of rock are also appealing precisely because they are politically acceptable, given the ways the songs ideologically align with many of the Tibetan refugee community's concerns, such as justice, freedom of expression, and world peace. The Dalai Lama is aware of this conservative core in Tibetan youth culture and is therefore quite tolerant, sometimes actively supportive, of the ways young people are scrambling for new tactics and voices and strategies precisely, in most cases, to regain their country and strengthen their own cultural mooring post.

THE HOPE OF ROCK AND ROLL

In 1968 a tape recorder was hardly ever seen in India and certainly
not in the Tibetan settlements, and when music was heard coming
out of the tape recorder at my place people were very surprised.
Whenever there was a marriage ceremony or some other
celebration they would invite me—maybe it was not so much me
as my tape recorder they were interested in! . . . In fun [the
guests] said to me: "Okay, we have done our dancing and singing.
Now you foreigner, you do your song." I had some really moving
rock 'n' roll songs on tape, including some by Elvis who was our
favourite, so I played the songs loudly and did some modern
Western dancing to go with them. Every woman there covered her
face—although some were peeping through their fingers—and
they were screaming and yelling in surprise. . . . Many of the
community members came to look at my dancing, and later they
gave it a nickname which translated from the Tibetan means
something like "madness" or "nervous twitching."

Ugyan Norbu

Gradually, rock-and-roll music has moved out of the West and into a global
diaspora of its own, creating a vast jam session or karaoke party with a part
for anyone seeking solidarity. Like any immigrant, rock music has managed to make elbowroom for itself via both honorable and scrappy tactics
in all its new surroundings, and it has become part of everyday life for people everywhere. Further, it is part of many people's understanding of their
own contemporary culture, wherever in the world they may be.[13] Therefore, efforts to stylistically, socially, or politically position oneself at the
margin of one's community by embracing the alternatives offered by
Western pop culture is, then, as much a move to "join with" as it is a move
to "distance from." That is, those who pursue liminality and "embrac[e]
anomia for the sake of creative possibilities" (Martin 1979: 99) are also
often pursuing community and aggregation. Similarly, British sociologist
Simon Frith has noted that young consumers "have a sense of being part
of a common audience, whether a generation or a cult" (1981: 9). Among
Tibetan refugees, this international camaraderie seems to be pleasurable at
the level of style for both sexes in this case and particularly validating for
politicized young men at the level of ideology.

Traditional Tibetan clothes are still commonly worn on holidays and are
worn daily by all older Tibetan women and young women employed by
the government-in-exile. But in Dharamsala and other refugee communities, there is plenty of evidence that young Tibetans, like youth all over the
world, desire to emulate Western pop culture, including fashion. Many

young Tibetan men and women are hybrid, hip, hennaed, and bell-bottomed, cruising town in Doc Martin boots and platform sneakers. One evening years ago, I spied a Tibetan boy with his Chicago Bulls baseball cap on sideways and knew it was only a matter of time before it, and all the other caps in town, would move around backward in true hip-hop fashion. This is *rangzen* at the level of style: freedom to shock elders and conform to peers, to buy teen magazines and relatively expensive manufactured clothes in Chandigarh and Delhi.

In her study of young Tibetans in exile, Girija Saklani rather harshly dismisses the self-fashioning of her refugee subjects as the result of the difficulties of resolving the conflict they face between the traditional and the modern:

> The youth that come out of such a system mostly have an inner hollowness and modern exterior; they betray emotive repercussions rather than intellectual conviction. The Tibetan youths' emotional rejection of their traditional social identity may be ascribed to the above factor. Their orientation to the symbols of western progress is so passionate and compulsive that they not only look down upon their own social milieu but also of their host country. What is more disturbing is that their attitudes are based more upon the quirks of emotion than on any critical or constructive dialectic. (1984: 325)

She further berates young Tibetans for not possessing an intellectual understanding of the historical development of the styles they are inspired by, rendering their efforts into

> more or less a fashion and spirit of bravado, a stint at aping rather than an appreciation of and absorption in the ideological background of the western youth movements. (1984: 327)

While Saklani is both overestimating the ideological impetus behind Western pop culture and underestimating young Tibetans' motivations, there is, no doubt, a certain amount of fantasy at play in the efforts of young Tibetans to experiment with popular Western images. However, the fantasy is not limited to the material products that physically alter one's appearance. Another factor involved for many youth (generally male) is precisely the fantasy, informed by rock music's history, that by listening to and playing the sounds of rock and roll one can tap into the genre's original social energy and be a revolutionary too. This fantasy can, in turn, have "real" effects. Peter Wicke describes how rock music acquires a true "*media* character," taking the concept of "medium" in its "original, scientific, meaning: an agent, a material substance in which a physical or chemical process takes place" (1987: 181).

Politically, listening to and producing rock and roll is a way for young Tibetans to express solidarity with a wider struggle for both mobility and stability through sounds that have a historical relationship with social change—hence their fixation on music from the mid-1960s and early 1970s. Sitting in bedrooms adorned with posters of Western musicians torn from youth magazines, young Tibetans discuss their love of songs by the "Bobs" (Dylan and Marley), Pink Floyd, and others specifically in terms of the relevance these artists' lyrics have to their own struggle for political independence and for dignity despite their status as refugees. With only a few exceptions, most of the favorite *Inji* songs in Dharamsala contain key words and phrases that resonate with these young refugees' learned and self-consciously nurtured identities as nonviolent ("Mama, put my guns in the ground"), yearning to return to their parents' homeland ("Get back, get back to where you once belonged"), yet rebellious and cool ("We don't need no education"). A space in the local aural scene has been created for these songs owing to their political relevance and their potential to test, reinforce, and remind the community of its commitment to liberation. The word *rock*, Frith tells us,

> draw[s] attention not just to a sound and a beat but also to an intention and an effect. Rock, in contrast to pop, carries intimations of sincerity, authenticity, art—noncommercial concerns. (1981: 11)

In his discussion of Chinese rock star Cui Jian, Brace similarly notes that that musician's appropriation of rock-and-roll ideology

> lifts it out of its Western context and expands its meaning by making it a transnational ideology: not restricted to a particular culture (the West), but tied to a particular musical genre (rock-and-roll). Cui Jian's insistence on the ideological dictates of rock-and-roll becomes embodied within the music itself: style is ideology objectified. (1991: 56)

This belief that a musical genre can be "lifted" out of one culture and can "dictate" the nature of its reproduction—not only formally or technically but also in its entirety as an ideological force—simply by plugging it into another country's electrical circuits is, indeed, a fantasy. Interestingly, even ironically, it is a fantasy shared by musicians like Cui Jian all over the world who embrace rock music as locally liberating *and* by critics who insistently refer to the geographical origins of rock music (or any "Western"

cultural product) to dismiss it as evidence of cultural imperialism. Both ignore the historical specificities of creation and performance that give musical sounds meaning in order to preserve their respective models of transna-
tionalism and global flow that effectively wash out difference. That is, they
disregard the local and current "when and why and how" of cultural practice. Imitative fantasy, yes, but also potential for real cultural and social
transformations:

> Rock music is a mass medium through which cultural values and
> meanings circulate, through which social experiences are passed, and
> which reach far beyond the material nature of the music. The "content"
> of rock songs cannot be reduced to what is directly played or even what
> appears to be expressed in the lyrics. For listeners these aspects only
> form the medium of which they themselves make *active* use. They in-
> tegrate them into their lives and use them as symbols to make public
> their own experiences, just as, seen from another angle, these aspects
> give the experience of social reality a cultural form conveyed by the
> senses and thereby influence that reality. (Wicke 1987: ix)

During one especially long and cold blackout at the Yak Band's house,
we all sat around on pillows on the floor having a late candlelight dinner.
The Yaks somehow got to talking about their dream of playing their original rock songs about freedom and independence in front of the Potala
Palace in Lhasa with a huge Tibetan flag flying overhead. They all thought
about this grand scene for a while, each lost in his own visualization, occasionally shaking a head or offering a detail out loud. Then, almost in anticipation of my warning that they shouldn't hold their breath or get their
hopes up, their comments came one right after another, each one more and
more absurd and fantastic than the last: "And we've got the latest Marshall
equipment and we've flown Keila in from America to play fifteen layers of
keyboards—some with her feet—and Phuntsok's got a bass with two
necks . . . " They were all grinning madly by now and rolling about laughing. "And," Phuntsok added, reluctant to dismiss the whole scene as illu-
sionary, "I've got a gray beard down to here and a cane, and Paljor's twelve
sons will all be there." It *is* all possible, he was saying, but probably not for
a long, long time.

Why Tibetan youth love rock and roll (and why local bands have started
playing it) surely involves a degree of fantasy like Cui Jian's, but this dis-
covery does not negate the possibility that rock music can, in fact, enhance
and consolidate subcultural group identities in non-Western contexts like
Dharamsala. To dismiss the Yak Band and other non-Western rock musicians as dupes and ignore the ways in which rock music is actually experi-

enced by Tibetan youth (the locally grounded resonances and personally experienced histories that inform their enjoyment of plugged-in sounds) is its own kind of theoretical imperialism. Communications scholar Donald F. Roberts argues that

> [w]hatever the effects of music media on adolescent attitudes, values, and behavior, there remains popular music's most important "consequence"—its capacity to involve youth. Adolescent listeners invest prodigious amounts of time, money, and ego in the pop music habit. Music matters to adolescents, and they cannot be understood without a serious consideration of how it fits into their lives. (1997: 43)

A powerful confirmation for young Tibetans that rock and roll remains a medium for positive social change and community building has been the responsiveness of a number of famous rock and pop musicians to the Tibetan Cause. It has been deeply moving and affirming to many young Tibetans to learn that the seemingly unreal icons of pop culture can also be audience members who listen to and are affected by the Tibetan community's stories. The loop is powerfully complete when the very musicians young Tibetans listen to as a source of inspiration begin to write and sing specifically about *them*, taking on their dreams and broadcasting them far and wide. In their song "The Update," the Beastie Boys rap:

> The past is gone, the future yet unborn
> But right here and right now is where it all goes on
> I know we can fix it and we're not too late
> I give respect to King and his non-violent ways
> I dream and I hope and I won't forget
> Someday I'm gonna visit on a free Tibet

For four consecutive summers (1996 to 1999), the Milarepa Fund, co-founded by Beastie Boy Adam Yauch, produced Tibetan Freedom Concerts in major cities around the world. Yauch is committed to promoting awareness about the situation in Tibet among American youth in particular and has chosen to reach them through famous rockers like Smashing Pumpkins, the Red Hot Chili Peppers, Rage Against the Machine, Yoko Ono, and Sean Lennon. In between the big-name acts, monks chant, Tibetan individuals speak about their experiences in prison, and Tibetan performers now based in the West present their dances and songs. By jumbling "punks and monks" (Whiting 1996), mandalas and mosh pits, Yauch has attempted to make young Westerners think twice about violence and allow themselves to admire and emulate examples of nonviolent conflict resolution. Also linking music and consciousness-raising, a benefit for the nonprofit Tibet

House in New York is held annually at Carnegie Hall. Aimed at a mellower, older, wealthier crowd, the event's headliners have included Emmylou Harris, Natalie Merchant, Philip Glass, David Bowie, and Laurie Anderson. Contemporary musical events like these reinforce and perpetuate the cycles of desire and affection that have characterized Tibetan-Western relations for so long.

ROCK MUSIC'S PLACE IN THE LOCAL SOUNDSCAPE

Rock and roll's place in Dharamsala's local soundscape remains controversial. Its presence, although it would be impossible to silence now, is so far primarily justified by (and thus far limited in the public sphere to) its contribution to local political awareness and activism, although pleasure-centric youth dance parties are common. It is considered by its listeners to be powerful, sincere, and thought provoking, and it is never distanced or parodied the way Hindi film songs are. Tibetan youth do, of course, listen to plenty of vapid Western love songs as well, but these have not yet found a justifiable niche in the *public* sphere. For example, although Tibetan bands like the Yaks frequently play covers of Marley and Dylan tunes during their concerts, they never perform Western rock or "country" love songs, even though they know dozens of them. Toward the end of the year during which I played keyboards with the Yak Band, we did, in fact, try playing a love song by the Eagles during one of our concerts in Dharamsala, and it was a complete fiasco (described in the next chapter). Interestingly, Frith has suggested that perhaps it is a healthy idea to downplay Western love songs and avoid the "sentimental ideology of capitalist society" (1988: 109) that suggests love is the solution to everything.

To be accurate, plenty of Tibetans of all ages feel that Western pop and rock music have no place in a community engaged in an intense battle for cultural survival. For example, I met a relatively small number of fiercely patriotic young Tibetans who were "100 percent against the Yak Band" because of its Western pretensions. Interestingly, most of these young adults had recently arrived from Tibet and had far less exposure to rock and roll and far more exposure to anti-Western propaganda than have their peers in exile, perhaps making it seem more threatening or foreign to them. They praised other young artists who are putting their efforts into "reversing the tide" of cultural change by researching and learning traditional forms.

Other more intellectual members of the community are less concerned with the presence of rock-and-roll sounds and lyrics in the air than with what they perceive to be a general lack of creativity and integrity in the

Figure 15.   Paljor, Keila, and Phuntsok enjoying a rock-and-roll moment before a concert.

way it is listened to and made by young Tibetans. Reflecting on the popular Tibetan music being made in exile, Jamyang Norbu, for example, has confessed that "the results of these efforts somehow seem to me insipid, possessing neither the energy of good Western pop music nor the charm of the old Tibetan traditions" (1992). Others sense in the young generation in general a great deal of revolutionary posturing rather than the constructive political work they remember taking place when they were young in the 1970s. For example, Tibetan historian Tsering Shakya expressed his despair in an article titled "Exile Creativity Wasted by Tibetan Youth":

> But what can we say about those of us who have grown up in exile? We
> have been in exile for over thirty years, since then two generations
> have grown up and made homes in exile. The word "exile" has a certain
> romantic resonance. It conjures up images of exiled writers, painters,
> poets and revolutionaries dreaming of new worlds, but where are the
> Tibetan writers, poets, scientists and revolutionaries? All the years we
> have been in exile and the generation that has been bred in the refugee
> camps have failed to produce our writers and visionaries. Have our
> youthful years also been wasted like the torrent of rains of a monsoon
> gushing to no purposeful end? (1996)

These differences of opinion raise issues that are central to understanding the experiences of refugee youth. What, for example, has the young generation born in exile actually lost? What is the nature of their suffering as compared to that of their parents? What, for that matter, is the nature of their pleasure? What are appropriate ways of expressing pleasure without appearing to be insensitive to the community's history or simply decadent? There is a great deal of disagreement and confusion among young refugees about how to be good Tibetans. For some, it seems easiest and safest to satisfy their adolescent urges for experimentation and self-expression—for personal *rangzen*—by trying on aspects of other people's cultures rather than by risking offense by meddling with traditional Tibetan styles. These youth, in turn, bond with their Tibetan peers in their common pursuit of ambiguity, and, in many cases, it is rock music that gives their quest a rhythm and a style.

The question that had nestled in the forefront of my mind after about six months in the field was: What would music sound like that really felt "Tibetan" to people but tapped into the power of rock and roll? On the one hand, there are very strong, politically informed reactions against any Tibetan music that sounds too Chinese, too Hindi, or too Western. On the other, many Tibetan youth respect traditional Tibetan music but find it boring. How could a young composer rise to the challenge and bridge this divide? Listening to terribly reproduced Indian dubs of classic Western rock cassettes at Dharamsala's frequent youth dance parties, trying to pick out the chords of solos on a guitar in a café or in their homes, or (only recently possible) attending live rock concerts, Tibetan youth raised with the Beatles *and* with a real personal responsibility to "talk about a revolution" are becoming aware of the tensions between imitative fantasy and creative political work, even if the distinction between them is not always clear. It is a tension that truly preoccupies them as heirs to a political struggle as idealistic as it is crucial to keep alive, a tension that resonates in the rock sounds that some Tibetan musicians have chosen, and their audiences have generally accepted, as appropriate to accompany the political poetry they sing.

5   The Nail That Sticks Up Gets Hammered Down

Making Modern Tibetan Music

The task for the exile, especially the exiled artist, is to transform
the figure of rupture back into a figure of connection.

Michael Seidel

As Raymond Williams always insisted, culture is ordinary. It is
the extraordinary in the ordinary, which is extraordinary, which
makes both into culture, common culture. We are thinking of the
extraordinary symbolic creativity of the multitude of ways in
which young people use, humanize, decorate and invest with
meanings their common and immediate life spaces and social
practices—personal styles and choice of clothes; selective and
active use of music, TV, magazines; decoration of bedrooms; the
rituals of romance and subcultural styles; the style, banter and
drama of friendship groups; music-making and dance. Nor are
these pursuits and activities trivial or inconsequential. In
conditions of late modernization and widespread crisis of cultural
values they can be crucial to the creation and sustenance of
individual and group identities, even to the cultural survival of
identity itself. There is work, even desperate work, in their play.

Paul Willis

From the moment I arrived in Dharamsala, I kept a binder of original Tibetan song lyrics and music that eventually included quite a remarkable collection of compositions, some recorded, some popular, most the result of private moments of creativity never shared before. I hoped to publish a
songbook in tandem with my dissertation (a project that unfortunately remains on my "to do" list). Despite the fact that by the end of my stay in
Dharamsala the binder's rings had broken and its contents—everything
from tidy computer printouts to photocopies of squiggly handwriting to
notes on napkins—were spilling out on all sides, I decided to leave no stone
unturned and formally solicit original Tibetan songs from the community,

just in case I had missed anyone. Eager to see who would come forward, I plastered the town with Tibetan and English versions of the following flyer:

> Have *you* written
> a song or poem lately?
> We are making a songbook of new,
> original Tibetan songs. We would
> like to include *your* songs in it!
> All styles are welcome:
> traditional, rock, pop, country.
> Any subject matter:
> political songs, love songs, songs about Dharamsala,
> Tibet, the environment, anything!
> Tell your friends!
> This book is a chance for *everyone* to share his
> or her songs with Tibetans everywhere.
> Please sign up at Friend's Corner Restaurant
> before Friday, June 16th.

June 16, the deadline for submissions, found me leaning on the counter of Friend's Corner Restaurant, a cool yogurt *lassi* in hand, feeling depressed that everything I had either determined on my own or had been directly told about Tibetan social pressures appeared to be true. I had hoped that the young people in town, many of whom were by now familiar with me and my project, would come through. However, the only submission I received was from a monk friend who, in the process of helping me translate the poster into Tibetan, had been inspired to return immediately to his monastery and compose a short praise song (really just a poem, since he wasn't a musician) for the young reincarnation of the Panchen Lama being held under house arrest in China. The owner of Friend's Corner further dashed my stubborn hopes and offended my lingering faith in the situation by insisting that the problem was that I had not offered to pay people money for their songs. Later in the afternoon, I consoled myself, as I had many times before, with the thought that things that don't happen, people who don't show up for appointments, news that's not spread, sounds that aren't made, are all "data" too. *The revolutionary consciousness as manifested in nonaction,* I wrote that evening in my field notes.

■ ■ ■

The story behind "modern Tibetan music" is largely a story about the social and artistic challenges young Tibetan refugee musicians face in their efforts to convince their community-in-exile that there is room for a new musical genre alongside, or even within, the politically charged paradigm of cultural preservation presiding in Dharamsala and elsewhere in the Tibetan diaspora. It is, put more generally, the story of determining what it means to be "modern" in Dharamsala and, further, what the role of contemporary music might be in answering this question.

As has been discussed, the dominant exilic understanding of the "rich cultural heritage of Tibet" is heavily oriented toward the "there and then" (pre-1959 Tibet) and toward the distant future (dreams of a "free" Tibet). Most young Tibetans are very invested in these temporal and spatial mooring posts as well, but some are expressing their relationships to their community's past and future in nontraditional ways. The relationship many youth raised in exile have managed to maintain with *both* the conservative political and cultural paradigm of their community and with foreign and modern ways sends a confusing message to older and less acculturated refugees in exile who are particularly sensitive to signs that youth in exile are dissatisfied with or becoming alienated from their heritage. In this context, some Tibetan refugees are unsure how to react, for example, to Dharamsala's Yak Band, a rock group whose music is deeply patriotic and yet is also adamantly grounded in the "here and now" (exile) with its tangle of cultural influences, opportunities, and anxieties. Many refugees, on the other hand, are avid Yak fans and hear in the new music a hopeful message of continuity and commitment from the generation raised in exile.

This chapter considers how modern Tibetan music, a rock-influenced sound that has developed during the last ten years, fits into the mix of sounds in Dharamsala that has been discussed thus far. Traditional Tibetan music, Chinese-influenced songs, Hindi film songs, and Western rock music have been presented as sonic icons of places that flow through Dharamsala and inform the character of the Tibetan capital-in-exile and the tastes and identities of the town's residents in a variety of ways. Modern Tibetan music has grown out of this mix and is understood here to be a soundmark of the exile experience itself, an icon of displacement considered *as a place*. This claim is based on the assertion that Tibetan "displacement" is, after all, happening in geographical places that locate or localize refugee experiences and provide a tangible setting for the complex flow of people, sounds, and ideas that stream in from around the world and interact. For several decades Dharamsala has been the hub of this activity—hence its placement at the center of the mandala presented in the introduction—but, as recently as in the last five years, even this center of displacement is being fractured as Tibetan refugees fan out into the world in significant numbers. The fact that most of the musical innovation taking place today in the Tibetan exile community is *not* actually happening in Dharamsala anymore is only one indicator of the extent and nature of this rediasporization.

Because the development of modern Tibetan music has not been documented elsewhere, I will begin by narrating the brief but important history of this musical genre. I will then consider this story in the immediate cultural context of the Tibetan refugee community in Dharamsala by taking a close look at the experiences of the Yak Band. I focus on this group because of their centrality to the trends discussed and because of my close involvement with this band during my year in India. From a local perspective, the narrative of modern Tibetan music's development reveals many of the constraints and opportunities that aspiring musicians face in this refugee community, including challenges posed by Tibetan cultural expectations regarding status and modesty. It also, however, reveals the positive influence musicians like the Yaks can have as role models for Tibetan children. A wider perspective on the development of modern Tibetan music reveals the important role Tibetan musicians are beginning to play in the emergence of a diaspora-wide Tibetan youth culture that is unique and yet shares important common ground with other youth cultures around the world, links that many young Tibetans—the "hope of Tibet"—find personally and politically empowering. This double orientation toward the unique and the shared informs my notion of "folk music made possible by global flow" that will be introduced and discussed below.

THE HISTORY OF MODERN TIBETAN MUSIC

The general consensus in Dharamsala is that the very first "modern" (Western pop or rock-inspired) Tibetan song heard by the local public was performed by a group of Tibetan refugee students visiting from their host country, Norway, in around 1970 (or was it students returning from an auto mechanics training course in Japan?—it's the subject of some debate). Attired in dark suits and ties and snapping their fingers to a casual beat, these youngsters made a dazzling and long-lasting impression on the local refugee community. In response to the audience's enthusiasm, the group repeated its new love song three times at this history-making performance, and it was quickly learned by Tibetan schoolchildren everywhere. This first modern song— "Khey Ni Tseden Lhamo" (You are my dearest Lhamo)—is so ingrained in the refugee community's aural history that, twenty-five years after its original performance, an elderly poet delighted everyone at my farewell party in Dharamsala's Dreamland Restaurant by spontaneously rising to his feet to sing it, complete with vaguely remembered dance movements.

The first modern Tibetan songs composed locally in India were, perhaps ironically, written by young artists at the Tibetan Institute of Performing Arts around the same time as the youth group from Norway appeared. These songs, usually accompanied by simple chord progressions on a Western guitar or paralleled by a melody line plucked on the *dranyen*, circulated quickly throughout the Tibetan diaspora and have remained favorites. "Pha Yul dee Ngatsö Tsangma Ray" (This land belongs to all of us) is one of the earliest modern Tibetan songs that is still learned by school children in exile and is well loved. With lyrics written in the 1970s by Jamyang Norbu, a writer and intellectual who would later become a controversial director of TIPA, this popular song is set to the tune of Woody Guthrie's American classic "This Land Is Your Land."[1] In the early 1970s, a 45 rpm record featuring four Tibetan songs was produced by TIPA (then called the Tibetan Drama and Dance Society). The popularity of the only original or "modern" song on the record, "Dzaypa'i Rinzin Wangmo" (Beautiful Rinzin Wangmo), is demonstrated by the fact that this love song is as well known today in Tibet as it is in exile and has even been featured on recent commercial recordings produced in Lhasa. These versions, however, are invariably sung in the smooth, orchestrated karaoke lounge style that the Chinese have so successfully introduced to the Tibetan capital.

BEAUTIFUL RINZIN WANGMO

When I glanced over there,
My Rinzin Wangmo,
Also glanced back
From beneath her eyelids.
Karma caused our connection to happen.

Having a good heart,
Listen, my Rinzin Wangmo.
I feel like going with you.
Even if I don't have soles on my shoes,
Beautiful Rinzin Wangmo,
I can still go slowly, slowly, slowly.

In the middle of big crowds,
Listen, my Rinzin Wangmo.
Don't show that we are in love.
If your father knew about us,
Beautiful Rinzin Wangmo,
He would surely scold me.

What is in your heart,
Beautiful Rinzin Wangmo?

Say it clearly to me.
Truly, my Rinzin Wangmo,
I am thinking about you.[2]

In the early 1980s, Dharamsala was occasionally exposed to live rock music by groups of Western Buddhists who jammed under names like "Subterranean Vajra Hammer" (earlier known as "Rock Bottom") and the "Dharma Bums." Vajra Hammer, most of whose members were dharma students and/or translators living in Dharamsala, made its first public appearance in 1980 at the government-in-exile's office complex. According to a news item in the *Tibetan Review* written at the time, they "kept a crowd of nearly 200 Tibetans, Westerners and Indians dancing till 2 A.M." Most of Vajra Hammer's performances were benefits for local projects, including the youth literary magazine *Lotus Fields*, the TCV, and TIPA. At a 1982 concert given to celebrate the end of a Buddhist course for Westerners, the group bestowed on Dharamsala a dose of homespun wisdom about the relationship between rock and roll and dharma when Western Buddhist monks and nuns in the audience changed from their robes into T-shirts and jeans and, to the disbelief of Tibetan onlookers, "got on the dance floor with wild abandon." Band bass player and spokesman Glen Mullin, now a widely published Tibetan scholar, defended the event in these words:

> Personally, I feel that in Tibet the Gelugpa order laid such stress on the *vinaya* (monastic discipline) largely as a reaction to the apathetic indulgence and non-adherence to the proper vinaya of the other traditions. However, Western Buddhists tend to pay more attention to the original thoughts of the Buddha and to leave as much of the Tibetan culture as possible to the Tibetans themselves. The Buddha never said that dancing was bad as long as it was done in proper situations and without motivation of lust. . . . The monks [among the students of the course] would have been terribly shocked and disappointed were they to be banned from such an event, held in their honour and performed by their friends, for no other reason than Tibetan mediaeval attitude. . . . In the West certain types of music are considered spiritual and "rock n roll" belongs to this category because it tries to permit the full intensity of the moment. (Wangyal 1982: 11)

Despite these inspiring and legitimizing words, it was not until 1988 that the first cassette of original Tibetan songs influenced by the Western folk-rock sound was recorded and produced in exile by Tibetans themselves. This cassette, titled *Modern Tibetan Folk Songs*, was released by three young refugees living in Dharamsala who called themselves

"Rangzen Shönu" ("freedom youth"). Their songs, which covered topics from political independence to the eating habits of Tibetan nomads, were set to acoustic guitar supporting simple vocal harmonies. The group's accomplished guitarist and songwriter, Tsering Paljor Phupatsang (referred to as "Paljor" in previous chapters), had grown up listening to Western hits like "Rhinestone Cowboy" and "Tie a Yellow Ribbon 'Round the Old Oak Tree" in the context of Christian missionary schools in Darjeeling. Inspired by a young monk who sang John Denver and James Taylor songs for the students, Paljor picked up the guitar in the eighth grade and with practice was soon able to work out any song by ear. His newfound love proved to be too distracting, however, and caused him to fail school that year. He was immediately transferred to the local Central School for Tibetans, although his Tibetan language skills were still very poor. In high school, he hung out with older Nepali musicians who had started rock bands and attended their occasional concerts at Darjeeling's historic Gymkhana Club. With 250 rupees, Paljor bought his first guitar and began singing Neil Young songs at school talent shows. At St. Joseph's College, he started up his own band called "Ultra Vires"—"It's Latin, something to do with political science," he later told me—and began competing in the regional "beat contests" where West Bengali bands vied to impress judges and win prizes with their covers of Elvis, Deep Purple, and the Rolling Stones. One year, Paljor's group paid local street kids who had learned how to break dance by watching Michael Jackson videos to join them on stage as flashy sidekicks to their act. Despite these efforts, "Ultra Vires" never won a beat contest, but the members gained notoriety and were, briefly, "treated like stars" in the Darjeeling area.

During this same period, Paljor and his Tibetan college friends were composing songs to accompany the original Tibetan lyrics being written by their Tibetan professor at St. Joseph's, a former abbot who wanted live music to accompany a Tibetan historical drama his students were performing for refugee communities in the hilly Darjeeling-Kalimpong-Gangtok area.[3] These student-teacher collaborations resulted in the first Tibetan rock/pop songs ever written. When I finally met Professor Jinpa in Darjeeling during the last weeks of my year in India, he laughed out loud to learn that I was interested in researching "modern Tibetan songs." "Modern Tibetan songs!" he exclaimed. "Paljor and I *invented* this thing called 'modern Tibetan songs'!" Years after these songs were first composed, after Paljor had moved to Dharamsala to work in the Dalai Lama's Security Office, he met up with the college friends with whom he had performed

Figure 16.   Paljor, Yak Band guitarist, singer, and composer.

these songs, and they decided to make a recording. The resulting cassette was the landmark *Modern Tibetan Folk Songs* mentioned above.

Paljor went on to produce a solo cassette called *Rangzen Sön Tsa* (Seed and root of freedom) in 1990. When all the songs for this project were ready—some were repeats from the first cassette; others his own original efforts—he borrowed a guitar from an *Inji* friend and took the overnight bus to Delhi. He rented a studio space for two nights, recording all the songs in six hours the first night and then filling in the additional tracks of guitar solos and harmonies in six more hours the second night. He sold two thousand copies of the cassette to pilgrims at the Kalachakra ceremony in Varanasi and easily distributed the remaining one thousand cassettes to Tibetan shops in India. Paljor's musical career then went on hold for a few years until he was invited to join Dharamsala's Yak Band in 1994.

In 1990, the same year Paljor's solo cassette was released, TIPA's newly formed modern music group recorded a cassette in celebration of the Dalai Lama's 1989 Nobel Peace Prize. This experimental tape, simply titled *Tibetan Songs*, features an uneasy mix of traditional and new songs set to the soulless beat of a synthesized drum machine. Although technically far less competent than Paljor in Western genres, particularly with regard to his impressive ability to improvise, the TIPA group's most important contribution to the development of modern Tibetan music has been, and still is, its dedication to incorporating traditional instruments, vocal techniques, and folk tunes into pop-rock compositions.

At the beginning of 1995, two new cassettes were released in Dharamsala that in some ways broke through the formulas that had been quickly established for modern Tibetan songs: one was *Rangzen* by the Yak Band, and the other was *Modern Tibetan Songs* by the Ah-Ka-Ma Band.[4] Unlike earlier recordings, these two cassettes, with their electric lead and rhythm guitars, bass guitars, and drum sets, fit squarely into the category of "rock and roll." The Yaks included a keyboard and male vocalists, while Ah-Ka-Ma, drawing from its members' traditional training in Tibetan performing arts, incorporated both the *dranyen* and the *gyu mang* (hammered dulcimer) and added female vocalists to its sound. The Yak Band and the Ah-Ka-Ma Band—commonly referred to by their Dharamsala fans as the "only two shows in town except watching tourists"—have very different histories that have informed the development of their musical sounds and the trajectories of their respective careers in exile.

Briefly, Ah-Ka-Ma is a small subset of the official "modern music group" at TIPA that takes elements from Western music, usually instruments and rhythms, and incorporates them into songs whose melodies are inspired by traditional folk tunes.[5] The status of this band as part of a government organization has both boosted and constrained its achievements, just as the Yak Band's independence from the Tibetan government-in-exile has been alternately perceived as a benefit and a disadvantage by its members. For example, some of the profits from TIPA's successful international performance tours have underwritten the exorbitant cost of electronic equipment in India, outfitting Ah-Ka-Ma with an impressive array of instruments, speakers, amplifiers, and special-effects machines. The band also often enjoys exposure at "official" events—"to contrast," according to the government-in-exile's official website (www.tibet.net), "with the tradition and provide a reminder of culture as dynamic and ever changing." These opportunities include high-profile evening rock concerts during TIPA's annual traditional opera festivals, and the broadcasting of the band's cassettes on other special community occasions. When Ah-Ka-Ma went on tour to Nepal in the early 1990s, however, the band had to book performance venues under the false name "Ex-TCV Band" owing to the tight influence the Chinese have on any cooperation between Nepali organizations and the Tibetan government-in-exile. Artistically, Ah-Ka-Ma's governmental affiliation has in some ways compromised the aesthetic potential of its creations, for example by often pairing the group's musically interesting songs with dry lyrics commissioned for formal institutional purposes, such as praising TIPA's teachers and honoring the institute's anniversaries. However, the band's latest release, *Akama 2000*, produced in honor of the sixtieth anniversary of the Dalai Lama's enthronement, demonstrates a remarkable improvement in the group's overall musicality and confidence. The music is relaxed but lively, featuring strong male vocals; smooth integration of the traditional flute, dulcimer, and lute; and only a few moments of uncomfortable experimentation with smarmy electronic effects and Andrew Sisters–style harmonies.

During the past decade, approximately a dozen other individuals and groups from throughout the Tibetan diaspora (besides those already mentioned) have released cassettes featuring original Tibetan songs. In the early 1990s, many of these productions were imitative of either Rangzen Shönu's mellow "folk-rock" acoustic guitar sound or of smooth Asian pop music "of the most whiny and tinkly sort" (J. Norbu 1992) featuring keyboard synthesizers and solo vocalists heavily dependent on echo effects. More recent releases, such as the six popular cassettes produced since 1997 by Tsering Gyurmey in Nepal, reflect the increasing influence of Hindi film music and Nepali pop songs on modern Tibetan music, while others reflect the growing popularity of American rap music among Tibetan youth. Gyurmey, a graduate of TIPA's one-year teacher-training course, is a solo artist who hires professional bands in Kathmandu to back him up or occasionally collaborates with other young Tibetan musicians in Nepal when he records an album. These musicians are, in turn, largely dependent on programmable keyboards able to imitate any sound or style at the push of a button. At a recent concert appearance in Dharamsala, Gyurmey compensated for his unfamiliar isolation on stage by popping a cassette of the musical track to his latest album in a stereo and singing along with it, karaoke style. Reflecting another trend in recent releases, a former music teacher from Nepal aspiring to become a professional recording artist recently wowed a Tibetan New Year's party in Berkeley, California, with a live performance of a Tibetan rap song featured on his cassette. Indeed, when I asked a Tibetan musician friend what he thought of the idea of circulating a questionnaire among Tibetan kids resettled in the San Francisco Bay Area to find out what kind of music they listened to in their free time, he responded, "Let me save you the time—it's a one-word answer: rap."

Of note during this decade of musical experimentation and recording by Tibetan refugees were the 1991 cassette titled *Rainbow Tibetan hJah*, the 1999 CD *Renewal*, and the 2001 CD *PhaYul*, which feature contemporary Tibetan music played on traditional instruments composed and recorded by a group of ex-TIPA artists living in North America. Two of these artists—Tashi Dhondup ("Techung") and Sonam Tashi—are founding members of Chaksam-pa, a successful Tibetan dance and opera company based in San Francisco. In addition to his dedication to preserving traditional genres ranging from opera to beer-drinking songs, Techung has recorded his own CDs of original songs: *Yarlung: Tibetan Songs of Love and Freedom* and *Sky Treasure*, a collaborative effort with pianist Kit Walker. Because of his diverse talents, entrepreneurial spirit, success in the West, and continuing commitment to presenting and teaching the traditional Tibetan performing arts, Techung is at the forefront of the Tibetan music scene today and is deeply admired by the international Tibetan community. Chaksam-pa was invited to participate in Tibet House's annual fundraising concert at Carnegie Hall and was featured at the Smithsonian Folklife Festival in Washington, D.C., in the summer of 2000.

Other contemporary artists living in "double exile" in the West have found market niches for themselves in the international music scene, reaching out to audiences beyond the Tibetan community. Flutist Nawang Khechog, for example, has created a place for himself in the New Age market, tapping into the spiritual expectations Western audiences in particular have of Tibetan culture and earning himself a Grammy nomination in 2001 for his album *In a Distant Place*. Khechog, who incorporates instruments from all over the world in his recordings (Japanese Taiko drums, South American rain sticks, Indian drums), has recently invented what he calls the Universal Horn, a combination of the Tibetan ritual long horn and the Australian didgeridoo. Yungchen Lhamo has recorded haunting a cappella songs meant to inspire her listeners to awaken their spiritual awareness, and a Tibetan nun named Chöying Drolma has teamed up with American guitarist Steve Tibbetts to provide Western audiences with appealing adaptations of sacred Tibetan chants.

In Lhasa itself, a small handful of Tibetan musicians are also creating modern music. It is extremely difficult, however, for these artists to pursue musical careers independently of official, Chinese-run institutions. One determined young pop star, the late Jampa Tsering, managed to release several successful cassettes with private financial backing before his premature death, but he was not allowed to stage public concerts. He had been selected at a young age to study piano in Shanghai and was later assigned to perform with the official government performing arts troupe in Lhasa. The troupe's leadership was unhappy with Jampa's persistent interest in popular music and insisted that he either cease playing *mang shay* (popular songs) or quit the troupe. He resigned, a risky testimony to his dedication to his original music, in large part because he knew that music can cross borders people cannot, and he wanted youth in exile to know that creative energy still exists in Lhasa. A few other musicians trained in Chinese-ruled Tibet have found some popularity among Tibetans living in the diaspora, although for political and aesthetic reasons their fans are generally limited to those refugees who have recently escaped from the homeland. These performers include Dadon, a singer who escaped from Tibet in 1992 and whose life story is told in the 1999 film *Windhorse*, and Yadhong, a very popular Tibetan musician living in China (outside the Tibetan Autonomous Region) who is walking a fine line by recording and performing both Chinese and Tibetan songs. In part because of Dadon's successful escape to the West and subsequent activist work for Tibetan freedom, the Chinese government has denied Yadhong permission to go on tour.

Despite the seeming diversity and energy behind this story of modern Tibetan music's development, the number of musicians involved in the movement is very small, and the amount of new music being produced has been limited mainly because of a number of social, cultural, and financial constraints that aspiring musicians face both in Tibet and in the Tibetan refugee community and that will be discussed later in this chapter. At the moment, the Tibetan musical world is, according to Jamyang Norbu, "splintered, confused, and lacking in confidence and energy" (1992). The same dozen cassettes are heard everywhere in the Tibetan diaspora, and no single Tibetan performer or band has yet caught the hearts of the young generation by overcoming the existing challenges and finding the perfect balance between old and new, unique and shared, sounds. Here is the story of one group that tried.

THE YAK BAND

The Yak Band locates its roots in the early 1980s in a Tibetan regiment of the Indian Army stationed in Ladakh. Several young Tibetan soldiers purchased equipment with a loan, became the Snow Lions, and started playing at army parties in exchange for rum (which the band would sell to buy more equipment). The group first played in Dharamsala in 1989 when it was invited to participate in the local celebration of the Dalai Lama's Nobel Peace Prize and, interestingly, it donated all profits from that concert to the Tibetan Institute of Performing Arts. After being discharged from the army in 1992, three of the Snow Lions resettled in Dharamsala and set up a cable television business there, bringing Hong Kong–based Star TV to the community. Soon after, the group attended an audience with the Dalai Lama, who encouraged the band to make new Tibetan music as a way of holding on to their roots while also "modernizing" and moving into the world community. Between 1992 and 1996, the group, which changed its name to the Yak Band, staged several concerts a year in Dharamsala and other Tibetan settlements, some as commercial ventures and others as fundraisers for local organizations. When I met Paljor in October 1994 and agreed to play keyboards in the Yak Band, the group included four young men—Thubten, Paljor, Phuntsok, and Ngodup (and this hierarchy was clear)—whose life experiences, I came to realize, were representative of very different, though all quite typical, youth realities in exile. The Yaks were having personnel problems when I left India in the summer of 1995, and by that winter the group had permanently disbanded.

In the absence of Sangay.la, the founder of the original Snow Lion Band (who had won the lottery and resettled in Chicago before I arrived), the band's leader was a loveable trickster in his late thirties named Thubten. Thubten was born in Shigatse, Tibet, in 1957 and escaped with his family to Kalimpong as a small child. His Khampa father died shortly after the family arrived in India, leaving a destitute family with many children behind, so Thubten was sent "to eat and sleep" at a children's hostel run by Christian missionaries. He attended a Nepali-medium school as a day student until, at the age of sixteen, he and a friend left home, went to Dehra Dun, and enlisted in the Indian Army "to fight the Chinese." For seventeen years, Thubten served in the Tibetan regiment of the army, primarily in a unit patrolling the disputed border on the Siachen glacier between Pakistan and India. "In the army," Thubten told me, "our hearts were only thinking for freedom," and music was a way for him and his friends to continue that commitment after being discharged from the military in their early thirties. Musically, he has little knowledge of what he is up to on the guitar, but he has enough natural talent to get away with it, and he can sing well in several languages. Until the end of the winter of 1994 to 1995, when he decided to leave the band and move away from Dharamsala, Thubten stoically kept his complicated personal life a secret from me. It was not until several months after I joined the band that I even learned that Thubten was married to his sister-in-law, who had been jilted by his brother. It was not a love marriage, and his wife, who strongly disapproved of Thubten's involvement with the Yak Band, lived far away in the tough refugee camp in Delhi with her young daughter. The arrangement was the fulfillment of a duty, the honorable righting of a wrong committed by his relative, a modern twist on traditional Tibetan polyandry. Thubten's life was constrained in many ways like this by the consequences of acts initiated by his natural kindness and generosity. Thubten is charming, loyal, funny, talented, hard working, frustrated, and sad. He has lived a hard life and sees things for what they are.

Paljor was a semiorphan whose father, an important Tibetan chieftain in the region of Kham, had been killed by the Chinese during a botched CIA maneuver. Paljor was raised by his mother in Darjeeling and primarily educated in local Christian boarding schools. Married with three sons, he worked for more than ten years in the Dalai Lama's Security Office and at the government's Reception Center in Dharamsala. Musically, he was the anchor of the band, playing lead guitar and singing most of the group's Tibetan songs (many of which he composed). He had learned to play everything he knew by ear and could transpose any song, imitate any voice. He has musical ambitions that we all knew would outlive the Yak Band and is the only member of the band with the skills to pursue a solo career. A little beer or whisky in his system took away the last layer of self-consciousness to astonishing musical effect; a lot of beer or whisky made him difficult. In his ideal life, he would have practiced his music all day long; in his real life, he pushed the limits and practiced more than his extended family could tolerate. Rehearsals ran late and were held far from his family's crowded apartment in the government complex halfway down the mountain. Even without the band, he had a lot of responsibility, including a sick mother to care for and a strong-willed uncle who had wrested away any paternal authority Paljor might have otherwise enjoyed. The three small boys consumed the time and energy of his wife, who had a full-time position of responsibility in the government's Planning Council. Though the family never attended any of our concerts, I came to know them well over time and was often included in family evenings drowned out by the Hindi movies Paljor's elderly mother loved so well. Paljor has a deep respect for tradition and he finds daily religious practice indispensable, despite the insurmountable contradictions between his Western-trained rationality and his Buddhist faith. Whenever walking, Paljor fingers his rosary; when playing guitar, it sways around his neck or rests coiled around his wrist.

Phuntsok was the local boy, to the extent that a refugee community has such a thing. He was born in Dharamsala and schooled entirely at the Tibetan Children's Village just down the road from where he would eventually end up living and rehearsing with the Yak Band. He was a young bachelor, with a network of relatives in town with whom he didn't seem to spend a lot of time. He chain-smoked, played the bass confidently with intense but understated pleasure, and had an innate understanding of all things electrical and mechanical. Because of the band's motley array of new and used equipment and its dependence on undependable Indian electricity, "technical problems" were a moment-by-moment concern for the Yaks. At the slightest electronic squeal or puff of black smoke, Phuntsok would be squatting on the floor, his Buddha belly balanced on his thighs, ripping apart some cords and splicing together others until he gave a sign to one of us to "try it out," knowing full well he had it all solved. Because he had been a cook in the army and had learned how to feed the masses, Phuntsok also fed the band, creating huge vats of *thukpa* (noodle soup) for our late-night dinners eaten as we huddled around on pillows in cold rooms. Once in a while, his competence would falter and he'd sulk, stomp off to be insecure alone, disappear on his motorcycle into the night, not show up when expected, and then return without ever talking things out, screwdriver and soldering iron in hand, all revved up and ready to jam. He has a great, wide smile between enormous cheeks and is eager to learn, always slightly lovesick, and deeply patriotic.

Ngodup was the baby of the band, everyone's favorite little brother who got lost in his drumming and managed to stay out of all the squabbles, take no sides, and create no problems, though he understood everything that was going on. An orphan schooled in Darjeeling with siblings scattered about Nepal, Ngodup was the one most dependent on the band to keep him, pay him a monthly stipend, house him, and feed him. He had left friends and a band in Darjeeling specifically to join the Yak Band at their invitation. He had no possessions, no motorbike, and no family, and he spent a lot of time sitting, skinny legs folded under him, on the stoops of shops in McLeod Ganj, smoking and chatting with friends. He'll be taken care of always. A child of rock and roll, cool without trying to be, he is from a different generation than the rest. I loved to turn away from the audience and watch Ngodup play the drums during one of his favorite funky Hindi film songs—eyes closed, blissing out, in perfect synch with everything. He fancies himself a singer, too, and would occasionally venture to the microphone and offer one of the two songs he had practiced in his high falsetto voice again and again and again.

These were the Yaks, though there were other peripheral characters who supported the band in various ways. Sangay.la visited from Chicago, bearing new equipment and some cash, creating confusion about who was in charge of the band. His brother, "Uncle," kept an eye on the group in Sangay's absence and, since he was the Dalai Lama's audio-visual technician, he helped out when the band was recording or setting up a local concert. Tenzin Lodo, the debonair teenaged nephew of the Dalai Lama, loved being with the band and often worked as our sound man. I often thought it must have been a wonderful outlet for him, a rare context in which he could just be one of the guys, joke and banter, stay out late. His influential parents were supportive of the band, for which the Yaks were extremely grateful, but the musicians managed to treat their son as a peer (though they generally did call him "Kush" which vaguely translates as "prince"). Kusang kept the band's cable TV business running out of its second-floor office in McLeod Ganj. When he wasn't fiddling with antennae on precarious roofs, this man of few words would hang out at our rehearsals, help with the cooking, haul equipment from here to there. And there was Tenzin Dolma, a high school English teacher and the only other woman involved with the band, who showed up to rehearse a few days before each concert, with her well-worn notebook full of Hindi songs.

CHALLENGES FACING ASPIRING MUSICIANS

Any Tibetan refugee, like those introduced above, who hopes to act on the conviction that young Tibetans should be able to enjoy and make modern music sung in their own native language faces certain challenges that are all fundamentally related to the overarching challenge of working within a community that is so concerned about cultural preservation. As has been emphasized throughout this book, in the "collective search for identity,"

> nostalgia looks backward rather than forward, for the familiar rather than the novel, for certainty rather than discovery. (Davis 1979: 107–8)

The emphasis, at once nostalgic and practical, on preservation in musical performance and training in Dharamsala has been so dominant that composition classes, for example, are not offered at TIPA or in Tibetan schools. The result is that neither troupe artistes, teacher trainees, nor high school graduates with a keen interest in music have the theoretical or technical knowledge to create original songs, whether in traditional or innovative modern styles. When a new arrival from Tibet who had been thoroughly trained in Western music theory and notation in China offered to teach TIPA students how to read and write music, believing that this skill would be a crucial aid in documenting traditional music familiar to only a few surviving individuals, her suggestion was flatly turned down. Currently, therefore, only a few Tibetan refugees who have been abroad on Fulbright scholarships or who have shown individual initiative to educate themselves can read or write music and articulate how the songs they have memorized are constructed. There are, of course, potential risks here in making judgments informed by Western assumptions that value "originality" and favor written over aural acts of transmission and documentation. The observations made here are included because they arose repeatedly in conversations with Tibetan musicians and audience members who expressed frustration with the fact that, partly as a result of limited technical knowledge and skills, most original Tibetan compositions are in fact highly predictable and imitative of prior material, and institutional learning remains focused on rote repetition.

Yet the constraints informing the predictable and imitative quality of much modern Tibetan music cannot be accounted for entirely in technical terms. A young drummer in the Ah-Ka-Ma Band who also had a lead role in TIPA's 1995 opera made the profound observation that there is a fundamental link between creative freedom and political independence. His thoughts on this relationship were inspired by his experiences living in India, a country where he feels music has radically diversified specifically since the nation won its independence from Britain in 1947. He explained that with independence Indian musicians have gained the confidence and freedom to borrow new ideas from here and there, to experiment and thereby expand the range of sounds encompassed by the adjective "Indian," without their artistic eclecticism being perceived as a threat to Indian culture. Indians are managing, in his opinion, to develop a variety of modern sounds *and* to maintain traditional music simultaneously. In contrast, he noted, Tibetans have neither a strong desire for nor tolerance of artistic creativity because, out of necessity and taste, their energy and resources are earmarked for preserving Tibetan culture. If musicians in the exile community do not perpetuate traditional genres, it is argued, who will? This young musician's thoughts were very provocative to me, and remain so, particularly since they directly challenge so many popular assumptions about creativity burgeoning out of the pain of exile. Without the backup guarantee of a *place* where Tibetan culture (how this is defined is the crucial thing) is alive and well, any change appears frightening. This drummer and I agreed that an unintended consequence of this dynamic is that, without vibrant Tibetan options, Tibetan kids are attracted instead to the Western and Hindi alternatives within earshot.

In addition to the generally conservative wariness of innovation implied by this community's investment in traditional ways, certain *social* constraints also affect all contemporary Tibetan performers in Dharamsala (and, to varying degrees, throughout the diaspora). The primary social issues that present challenges to Tibetan musicians are rooted in commonly shared notions of status (with its attendant focus on financial earnings) and modesty, concerns that largely determine the degree to which any Tibetan can devote him- or herself to making music of any kind.

Regarding the issue of status, the perception of music making and any form of entertainment work as an inferior position of service has deep historical roots and affects traditional musicians training at TIPA as well as rock musicians like the Yaks.[6] In the dozen or so refugee communities I visited in India and Nepal, lack of support from family members concerned that music making is neither a lucrative nor a respectable way to spend one's time was a standard constraint alluded to by aspiring musicians through stories of guitars purchased with saved-up snack money and stashed in friends' cafés, songs written in private, and lyrics never shared. One young woman I know who is a gifted singer was strongly advised by her parents, both music teachers in Tibetan schools, to pursue a teaching career in a core subject like English, which is respected. Another acquaintance who dabbles in songwriting anticipated early on that I would have trouble tracking down informants. "If I tell someone what I'm up to," he said, "their response is always, 'Why are you doing *that*?'"

Because of these attitudes, many of the arts teachers, TIPA administrators, and young artists I have interviewed are concerned about the mixed message Tibetan children living outside Tibet are receiving. Specifically, the children learn that they are entirely responsible for preserving Tibetan culture, but those who commit themselves to the arts in an amateur or professional capacity are stigmatized. Family pressure generally wins, despite repeated statements from the Dalai Lama himself about the important role of artists in the world:

> Generally, I believe artists, like the musician, have big responsibility to serve, or to help to serve humanity. . . . Unless, you see, the good spiritual things develop within oneself, then in spite of material development or all other facilities, our human society may not have inner peace or inner deep satisfaction. So therefore I think it is the responsibility of all entire humanity, particularly you, as a musician or artist, through your own profession, to give people hope and give people the ideas. Sometimes people here, a little bit too much frustration, discouraged, and always complaining and lose self-confidence and the desire to

change that unhappy situation. So, give them hope. Usually, we have good potential if we open up our mind, make effort, we have the ability to overcome all these problems, all this suffering. So I think if you visualize your role as a professional and from that way give the people the new idea, new hope, a sense of responsibility.[7]

At a less philosophical level, the fact is that very few young musicians are able to pursue their artistic interests once they marry, have children, and/or start full-time jobs, because they are hard-pressed to justify to their families and employers the time needed for rehearsals and the money needed for equipment or financing a cassette. It is, in fact, a no-win situation. If a musician does experience success—for example, selling out a concert or a cassette—disapproving gossip whirls through town on the next breeze. If these songs are being written "for the Tibetan Cause," people feel, the musicians should not be "getting rich" off them. Prices for concert tickets and cassettes must be kept at nominal levels so that Tibetans can feel assured that no significant profit is being made. As a result, only a few Tibetan musicians living in exile have ever broken even in any of their ventures.

Additionally, while most Tibetan musicians feel that time spent writing Tibetan songs is time spent contributing to the fight for cultural preservation and political independence rather than mere recreation, the real and imagined associations of Western-influenced music (rock and roll, in particular) with alcohol, drugs, and bad behavior deeply inform the perceptions of a musician's older relatives. These perceptions can, further, easily be confirmed through the personal observation of shaggy Western backpackers during tourist season in McLeod Ganj and of the peripheral cafés in town where "roamers" (young Tibetan men without jobs or local families) smoke and sleep and revel in the moods of Led Zeppelin and Guns 'n' Roses. The cultural baggage of rock music is difficult to counter, even by part-time musicians who hold government jobs or teach, when coupled with the community's generally derogatory feelings toward musicians of any kind and the disappointment, even shame, caused by relatives who pursue this vocation.

In August 1995, the *Tibetan Review* featured a photo and a short paragraph titled "A Star Is Born" about a five-year-old Tibetan boy in south India described as the "singing sensation of the Tibetan community in exile." The child was pictured singing joyfully into a microphone the length of his torso, the cord held professionally and casually in his chubby left hand. I enclosed the article in a letter to Paljor filled with questions about the child because I had never heard of him during my fieldwork. Paljor's responding letter was filled with news of other things and contained only a poignant, sad, and slightly jealous comment about how lucky that boy in the newspaper is, since his career (unlike Paljor's) is obviously being supported by his relatives.

In addition to family concerns about status and money, musicians are also subject to scrutiny by fellow Tibetans who, on the whole, are socialized to downplay, even disapprove of, solo achievements or behavior that appears to be self-praising. This dynamic translates into shared social expectations of extreme modesty, along with the deferential treatment of others and sometimes into a paralysis of individual initiative. Tibetan audiences freely jeer at and boo performers, even if they are actually enjoying the show (their behavior can become abusive if they aren't), taking advantage of the unusual opportunity to act out publicly in the safety of an auditorium's darkness, show off for friends, and test the performer's ability to cope with the attention he or she has voluntarily accepted by getting onstage.[8]

Dharamsala does, in fact, harbor quite a few songwriters and musicians, but few will share their music publicly, in however casual a setting, because: "What would people say?" Even experienced performers like the Yaks only play their songs in formal concert settings or in the privacy of a friend's home. While I was living in Dharamsala, some Westerners suggested that a restaurant owner in McLeod Ganj should have an "open-mike night" once a week to give locals a chance to try out their music in a casual setting and to provide some much-needed evening entertainment for the town. The woman liked the idea but predicted that no Tibetans would agree to perform for fear that people would think they were "hard up" and singing for money. A number of inquiries made to likely participants confirmed her predictions. Even Paljor, who I assumed would volunteer, refused on the grounds that he had the good name of his family and his standing as a government employee to consider.[9]

Fundamental to this resistance to public exposure is the stigma in Tibetan society of being set apart from the group, whether voluntarily or involuntarily. "The nail that sticks up gets hammered down," one folk saying plainly reminds all youngsters. In Tibetan schools, naughty children in class or assembly are simply asked to stand up while the lesson or announcements continue. That moment of isolation amid a sea of seated peers is mortifying, and the child bends over with shame or *ngo tsa* (literally, a "hot face"). Despite the obvious differences, the experience of standing on stage in front of an audience is similar enough to the shame sanctions of childhood to evoke the same reactions in the performer and the crowd. My first exposure to this tortuous dynamic was at a TCV Inter-School Song and Dance Competition. The solo singers were terrified, so their voices started wavering off key and cracking. The audience began howling with laughter, even booing the children. The worse they found the performance, the louder they clapped at the end in a wildly sarcastic display. I really wondered why any teacher would subject his or her students to this kind of humiliation. The power went out during one student's song, and he kept singing in the dark, his voice growing bolder and more beautiful without the spotlights on him. There was only a little spattering of applause for this act—he hadn't messed it up, so it hadn't been particularly entertaining, I supposed.

Months later, I had the misfortune of finding myself at the receiving end of this dynamic when Paljor and I made the mistake of playing a Western love song during a Yak Band concert. I had coaxed Paljor into including the Eagles' "Peaceful, Easy Feeling" in the night's set list, since it was so well loved by the community and had sounded great when we fooled around with it at a recent jam session. We'd play a quiet duet, provide a break from the heavy rock and roll. Paljor strummed his guitar and began to sing, in his quiet husky voice: *I like the way your sparklin' earrings lay against your skin so brown. And I want to sleep with you in the desert tonight, with a billion stars all around . . .*

We performed it alone, or so I thought. One verse into the song I realized that Tenzin Lodo (normally the sound man) had jumped onstage behind us and was playing the basic chords on someone's guitar. Perhaps he was playing "air chords," since he doesn't actually know how to play the guitar. In retrospect, I believe he may have been trying to save the day. About the time I started to think, belatedly, about the fact that the lyrics were, in fact, very embarrassing for Paljor to be singing apparently *to me* onstage, the audience started the slow clapping and sarcastic cheering that is the Tibetan warm-up to booing wildly. At a certain level, I wasn't too surprised and I felt pretty unfazed by their reaction, but I was worried about Paljor. And we had a long way to go yet. *I found out a long time ago what a woman can do to your soul . . .*

It had been my idea to perform this popular song, and Paljor probably didn't have the heart to say, "Absolutely not," as he clearly should have. As we plodded through the remaining verses at the excruciatingly slow tempo we had chosen, committed to ushering the song through to the bitter end, I scolded myself for having imagined that we could ever recapture the spontaneous joy and funkiness of our first whisky-sodden, winter-night experiment with this out-of-date pop love song weeks later on a public Dharamsala stage. *I get this feeling I may know you as a lover and a friend . . .*

Too embarrassed to look up at the whistling audience and too afraid of what would happen if I caught Paljor's eye, I put my fingers on autopilot for the final chorus and set to thinking. Why are they booing, anyway? They must *really* be uncomfortable with this if they are openly ridiculing Paljor, a respected community member from a good family, an *Inji* and, for heaven's sake, the Dalai Lama's own nephew. This is bad. It's too slow. They are amped up and want rock and roll or Hindi titillation. It's a love song. It makes them squirmy. It's too quiet. It's boring. They know we're reading off the sheet music, which means we don't know what we're doing . . .

To Paljor's credit, considering that he was the one who had to keep living in this community, he sang the song all the way through. The crowd cheered wildly, as thrilled as we were to be released from this tortuous experience, and Paljor smirked at me as Phuntsok rushed onstage to recapture our alienated audience's hearts with a particularly raunchy, metallic version of "Smoke on the Water." As we were packing up our equipment later that night, Paljor informed me matter-of-factly, "For that, you owe me a music scholarship to America." Grateful that that apparently seemed to be all Paljor, with typically diplomatic Tibetan reserve, planned to say about what had happened, I cocked my head, Indian style, with a smile and said, "No problem."

Related to the issue of modesty and downplaying individual achievement or ambition is the fact that little attention is paid in this community to authorship. Rarely is there agreement about who wrote any particular song, a situation that posed real challenges in my attempts to document the development of the modern song genre. Copyright consciousness has not arrived in Dharamsala either. This fact, combined with the frugality of Tibetans and their determination to ensure that musicians do not get rich off them, means that every cassette that is actually sold to a Tibetan for thirty or forty rupees (approximately one dollar) is the mother of a dozen dubs, effectively undermining any musical business venture immediately. This situation prompted Techung, the ex-TIPA artist now living in California and performing internationally, to include the following plea on the liner notes of his cassette titled *Yarlung: Tibetan Songs of Love and Freedom*:

> Music Tibet needs and requests support in educating others not to duplicate and pirate our music. The livelihoods of Tibetan creative artists must not be threatened if the Tibetan musical tradition is to flourish in the face of Western and Indian popular music and thus contribute to the perpetuation and development of Tibetan culture. We shall be grateful for the support of everyone interested in the future of Tibetan music.

To sum up, I am convinced that the heckling and scrutinizing of musicians on stage are not actually mean-spirited, though the daily economic sabotage and gossip can get prickly, unmoored as they are from the performance context and the physical presence of the artist. The source of much of the audience's reactions at live performances seems genuinely to be a sense of awe at the performer's willingness to go ahead and put on a show, despite all the constraints at play. Most Tibetans love to listen to music but just don't want the performer to be related to them or interested in marrying their children. Within the community there is, certainly, admiration for musicians, but it is often expressed in all sorts of inverse ways that never ceased to amaze me. This lack of overt support truly discouraged the Yaks and other musicians I knew. In this tight-knit refugee society, it takes someone of enormous resilience and conviction to pursue his or her interest in music, let alone step into the spotlight to share it.

Despite all the constraints and hurdles described, however, a taste for, even love of, modern Tibetan songs (both those influenced by rock and others inspired directly by traditional genres) has clearly developed. Modern music cassettes are played in shops and restaurants in settlements all over India and Nepal, and unlabeled and smuggled dubs are enjoyed quietly and at great risk in homes in Lhasa. Dharamsala's rock-and-rollers and other recorded musicians throughout the diaspora are becoming well known and admired by Tibetan youth in particular—school children carry around dog-eared lyrics to the Yak songs in their uniform pockets, and student bands are forming in high schools—confirming the belief shared by these musicians that locally made modern music addresses a void not fulfilled by other local heard sounds. However, because the whole idea of "modern Tibetan music" (particularly Tibetan rock music) is still relatively new for many refugees, musicians like the Yaks and Ah-Ka-Ma bear the responsibility for, and take the social and financial risks involved in, educating their audiences by exposing them to rock and roll as a sound and as a social experience and by crafting songs and concerts that local communities can, they hope, gradually embrace as their own.

MUSICIANS AS ROLE MODELS

As might be expected, Tibetan children do not share many of the social and financial concerns felt by their older relatives about music making. On the contrary, Tibetan musicians find their most supportive fans among their peers and schoolchildren. To balance out the rather discouraging environment described above, I have included a few stories here that reveal the

Figure 17.   Yak Band drummer Ngodup with young fans in Dharamsala.

positive influence Tibetan musicians like the Yaks can have as role models for youngsters in the diaspora and, if they are within earshot, in Tibet. Unlike American rock or other sounds that could be described as "mass music," modern Tibetan music still enjoys a close relationship with its consumers. Anyone living in Dharamsala, for example, knows all the Yaks at least by sight and probably by name. For youngsters, this accessibility creates an important bridge between the sounds they consume and the realities behind creating those sounds. The normalcy of the musicians in day-to-day life makes the dreams some of them have of being in a band, daring to try something risky and new, seem less fantastic.

When I was staying at the Tibetan Homes Foundation school in Mussoorie in the spring of 1995, a number of young students recognized me with great excitement as the keyboard player in the Yak Band. They had been on pilgrimage to the Kalachakra ceremony in South India with their families during the winter holiday and had seen us perform. After a rehearsal of traditional Tibetan dancing, one young boy approached me shyly and asked if I would please teach him the chords for "Yetok ki Tromo.la" (roughly, Girlfriend who stole my heart), the Yak Band's one and only love song. "Sure," I said. He quickly produced a tiny battery-operated keyboard from inside his green school blazer. "And 'Pha Yul' (Fatherland)? And 'Mi Yul' (Foreign land)?" A small group of students had crowded around me by this time, and the center of attention in the auditorium had shifted away from the dance rehearsal being led by a young teacher who had earlier expressed to me his disgust with modern music that just slaps Tibetan words into any kind of song. The kids seemed unconcerned about making the teacher mad, so I followed their lead. They finally insisted that I come downstairs to listen to the school band practice. The "Freedom Band" had an electric guitar and a drum set and the battery-operated keyboard, and they were eager for advice. So I tuned the guitar and taught everyone how to play the Yak Band's most popular song, "Rangzen." When I found out that this group was supposed to perform a song or two at the school's graduation ceremony in a few days, I promised to help them get their act together the following day.

The Saturday rehearsal was held in the bachelor pad of the school librarian, a young teacher who played guitar in the band. Posters of Michael Jackson, Bob Marley, Bon Jovi, and Charlie Chaplin wallpapered the small cement room, now packed with equipment, bodies, and noise. The singer, who was graduating the next day, put a warped copy of the Yak Band's new cassette into a boom box, and we listened for a while to the song they hoped to perform. As the keyboard player noodled, trying to echo my keyboard strains, and the singer followed Thubten's voice by reading the cassette's badly printed liner notes, I realized that there was a whole other layer to what the Yaks were accomplishing with their band beyond entertainment and politics, an important consequence of which even the musicians themselves were quite unaware. They were, simply, saying to young Tibetans, "See? There is such a thing as Tibetan rock and roll! Try it!" If the youngsters in the Freedom Band were not learning to play rock music, I realized, most of them probably would not be making music at all. These thoughts filtered the dreadful sounds that were emanating from every corner of the room and inspired me to help them hone their act. We sorted out which key they should play in, and I transposed the song, wrote out the chords, tuned the instruments, and bossed them around. "Stand here! Listen to him! What are you *doing*? Try again." The song gradually came together, and they were thrilled. I called it quits and headed back down the steep steps to the guest house, leaving them to practice.

The next day, the whole school gathered in the auditorium for graduation. The headmistress gave a short speech in English, the main point of which was: "No matter how much you achieve in your works, your morals and virtues will make you respected and well loved, wherever you may sit, whether it's in a high place or a low place, or under a tree." The principal, general secretary, and class representative gave speeches, too, while the monk disciplinarian paced up and down, mallet in hand, staring down the little ones in front who were starting to squirm. Blessing scarves were presented to the embarrassed graduates, and then the Freedom Band took the stage. The Yak Band song went fine, but an Ah-Ka-Ma Band song they had spontaneously decided to include was a disaster. The speakers were squealing and the librarian was in his own key, but the musicians were engaged and happy, and the cross-legged audience even bopped up and down a bit. We cheered them off the stage and were released for the graduation tea party.

During my year with Tibetan refugees, I experienced many sweet moments of this kind, when the Yak Band's influence as a sound or an idea surfaced and reinforced my feelings that, despite all the troubles and complications, what my friends were doing was worthwhile and was having lasting effects that they might never fully know about. Waking to the boy on the balcony below mine working out the melody to a Yak song on his Casio keyboard, passing a classroom window and hearing a Yak song being sung by newly arrived students in preparation for the Dalai Lama's sixtieth birthday celebration, being shyly approached here and there by young Tibetans wondering if they recognized me from the band all testified to the band's influence. The Yak Band's cassette, which will be discussed next as an illustration of the challenges and rewards of being a Tibetan musician, has, like all commodities, taken on a life of its own.

MAKING AND MARKETING A CASSETTE

In anticipation of a major religious gathering of Tibetans from all over the world to be held in southern India in January 1995, the Yak Band had been planning for months to produce a cassette of their original songs that they could sell to the thousands of pilgrims who would attend the teaching. Shortly after I met the Yaks, the band borrowed money from the Tibetan government-in-exile's small business opportunity fund to finance the production of the cassette. For two weeks, we gathered up at the "Yak Shack" every night to record eight songs, with the expert help of "Uncle" and the government-in-exile's multitrack mixer.

The challenges of recording live rock music in a small cement house at the mercy of the erratic power supply of an Indian village at seven thousand feet made for slow progress, although the frustrations of waiting in the cold for the lights to come on were often dissolved by candlelit hours filled with acoustic improvisation sessions and Thubten's masterful quadralingual storytelling. Because of the difficulties, however, there was not time to rerecord

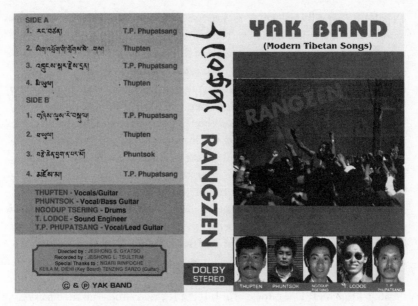

Figure 18.   Original cover of the Yak Band's 1995 cassette *Rangzen*.

each song until it was perfect; just to capture a whole song on tape uninter-
rupted was an accomplishment in itself. When we were done, the master
tape was sent to some disreputable place in Delhi to be quickly and cheaply
reproduced and packaged—so quickly and cheaply that many of the tapes
were badly distorted and could not, ultimately, be sold.

The original cover of the cassette, designed by the band members, featured a well-known photo of a severely burned monk with his fist raised,
held high on the shoulders of Tibetans demonstrating in front of a flaming
police station in Lhasa. The photo was taken by a tourist during the 1987
political unrest that resulted in severe crackdowns in Tibet. Below this
image, which has become a familiar symbol of the continuing struggle for
Tibetan independence, the cassette cover features grim head shots of the
four members of the Yak Band, along with a photo of the Dalai Lama's
nephew meant to lend credibility to the project. I was acknowledged in the
liner notes for my contributions at the keyboard.

As soon as the boxes of cassettes arrived, the Yak Band loaded its equipment on a train bound for Mundgod, a Tibetan agricultural settlement in
Karnataka State two thousand miles away. For fifteen straight nights, we
performed the new songs featured on *Rangzen*, along with Hindi film hits
and rock and roll favorites, to huge audiences of Tibetans from India,

Nepal, Bhutan, Sikkim, Tibet, and overseas. During the day, everyone attended the Kalachakra initiation being given by the Dalai Lama (see chapter 7 for full ethnographic description of these concerts).[10] At night, the pilgrims had the choice of resting in their tents or attending live shows: either traditional opera performances or the Yak Band concerts. During this time, band members took turns hawking their cassettes from a roadside stand, blaring our songs from dusty boom boxes. The cassettes sold steadily, but so slowly and cheaply that, despite the profits from concert ticket sales, the Yak Band still lost money on the venture (though they managed to repay the government's loan). After this tour, the remaining cassettes were distributed to Tibetan shopkeepers from various refugee settlements in Nepal and India to be sold. Within weeks, of course, homemade dubs of the cassette with pale Xeroxed covers were on sale in Tibetan settlements, and a few months later in a Kathmandu market stall I was shocked to find a pirated version of *Rangzen* made in faraway Singapore with all the names and photos of the Yaks removed.

Soon after I left Dharamsala (in July 1995), two American men actively involved in the Free Tibet movement in the United States arrived in Dharamsala. They had heard *Rangzen* playing in a Dharamsala restaurant and, being musicians, asked the owner if what they were hearing was really Tibetan rock and roll. They sought out Paljor and Phuntsok and soon found themselves jamming with the Yaks in Naddi, as I had done. The two men, one of whom was superstar rapper Adam Yauch of the "Beastie Boys,"[11] resolved to support the Yak Band and, simultaneously, to use Dharamsala's locally produced rock songs to raise awareness about Tibet among American youth.

I first learned of this fortuitous encounter when I was contacted in November 1995 to help put together a new version of *Rangzen* for the U.S. market. After corresponding with Paljor, I wrote the liner notes and provided the photos and one live recording that are part of the new *Rangzen*. Including my photograph on the new cassette was the decision of the band's former leader who now lives in Chicago and was consulted about every aspect of production. The original, blurry recordings made in the Himalayas were digitalized and cleaned up by professional sound engineers, and the cassette was rereleased on March 10, 1996, the thirty-seventh anniversary of the 1959 uprising in Lhasa that triggered the Dalai Lama's flight from Tibet.[12] This version of the cassette was advertised in the Snow Lion Press catalog, which most Americans interested in Tibet and Buddhism receive, but sales were slow. Rock and roll is not what *Injis* are seeking when they shop for Tibetan cultural merchandise.

The Yaks were thrilled with the "new and improved" cassette, despite their quick realization that it would never be a money-making prospect. They all share a dream of visiting the United States, and having their music set loose in America seemed a close approximation of actually being there in person. As refugees severely restricted from traveling by their lack of diplomatic papers and raised never to forget that they are living on the wrong side of the highest mountains in the world, the Yaks are well aware of the power of boundaries. They are also aware that musical sounds, like the elaborate cast of ghosts that populate Tibetan lives, are immaterial and can travel more freely than people can. A few years ago, during a routine office interview with a young man who had just escaped from Tibet on foot, Paljor learned that the youth had fled for fear of being arrested after singing a Tibetan independence song at an illegal demonstration in Lhasa. Paljor later told me that while listening to the stranger hum the song, his heart soared, because the tune was one of his own.

The story of the making and marketing of the Yak Band's *Rangzen* cassette provides a profound illustration of the interplay of local and, perhaps surprisingly, global forces at play in even a modest, small-scale project in a community that is the focus of keen political and cultural attention from a variety of sources. Impossible to label definitively as a "success" or "failure," the cassette was the catalyst for unprecedented musical enjoyment and appreciation as well as the cause of intense disappointment, depression, and discord among those directly and indirectly involved in its production and promotion.

FOLK MUSIC MADE POSSIBLE BY GLOBAL FLOW

For ideological and stylistic reasons explored in the last chapter, rock music is the structural backbone of most amplified modern music in Dharamsala, such as that made by the Yak Band and the Ah-Ka-Ma Band, but the development of modern Tibetan music—the range of what Tibetan rock does (and, also important, what it *doesn't do*)—has been significantly informed by the presence of other musics as well. Now that I have discussed the social and political contexts that inform how Tibetan refugees listen to and produce traditional Tibetan music, Chinese-influenced Tibetan songs, Indian film songs, and Western rock and roll, the locally understood borderlines between these genres and the notions of appropriateness that have developed in exile regarding the acceptable motivations for participating in these different kinds of music making should be coming into focus for the reader. These characteristics of the local musical environment in turn directly influence the subject matter, lyrics, instrumentation, and performance contexts of the modern Tibetan songs being made by refugee musicians today.

Increasingly, both indigenous cultural policy making and contemporary cultural research in non-Western contexts require paying critical attention to commercial Western expressive genres that have become locally meaningful, albeit still somewhat "foreign," elements of daily life. The patriotic rock songs of the Tibetan refugee Yak Band in northern India are representative of a new example of what I call "folk music made possible by global flow" that raises dilemmas for the highly politicized Tibetan paradigm of cultural preservation in exile and for current theoretical celebrations of blurred boundaries and hybridity.[13] The dilemma hinges on the ways this music complicates received understandings of the "local" and the "foreign," challenging the usefulness of deferring to a sound's origins to determine its native-ness, refusing to land squarely on familiar or alien ground.[14] This paradoxical notion underscores how close ethnographic work is the only way to understand how musics are actually experienced and thought about by those for whom the "field" is "home."

Fifteen years ago, Roger Wallis and Krister Malm proposed the term *transculturation* to describe the kind of interaction between music cultures and subcultures that has resulted, as of 1970, from the worldwide penetration attained by music mass media. Through the transculturation process, they argued, "music from the international music industry can interact with virtually all other music cultures and sub-cultures in the world" (1984: 297). Wallis and Malm went on to suggest that this process—carefully distinguished from cultural "exchange," "dominance," or "imperialism"—was the basis of an explanation for the "almost simultaneous emergence of what could be termed 'national pop and rock music'" in all the countries they studied. Almost universally, the researchers found that this music was not initially accepted by the establishment in those countries, with politicians being particularly slow to realize the value and importance of this development, particularly for young people. After ten years or so, local forms of pop and rock had been incorporated into the countries' mainstream cultural consciousness, making the slow migration from informal youth audiences to national mass media.

The coming-of-age of the first generation of Tibetan teenagers raised outside the homeland coincided, interestingly, with this moment when local language pop musics were burgeoning around the world, a time described by Wallis and Malm, and remembered by many musicians, as "a very creative period in small country cultural history" (1984: 303). And it appears that modern Tibetan music is gradually developing into an accepted local genre, although there are signs that the place that has been made for it in the public domain and the vision of the music's makers are, in fact, both quite carefully circumscribed. The social and financial challenges of being a musician are surmountable with determination and resources, but the community's overarching worry that anything new necessarily undermines the old is difficult to overcome. It seems, however, that the acknowledgment, even encouragement, of artistic creativity and innovation need not be at odds with the goal of maintaining and replicating Tibetan genres of artistic expression in exile. In fact, restrictions on the elaboration of Tibetan artistic genres—in this case, modern Tibetan songs—may actually be increasing the appeal of the various foreign genres within earshot.

Tibetan refugee youth are creating what Gil Bottomley describes as "counter-memories" or "narratives about the multiplicities of identity" (1992: 134), shifts in lifestyle and attitude that often cast an air of radicalism on the younger generation. But these changes are generally based on these youth's own experiences as refugees, the naturalization of local or culturally hybrid practices over the course of forty years in exile, and the incongruities between their institutional socialization and their experiences after they graduate from Tibetan schools (cf. Nowak 1984), rather than on intentionally confrontational choices. In a fluid refugee community like Dharamsala, cultural change cannot be accounted for in simple generational terms (youth versus their parents), since in exile Tibetans of all ages are being (re)socialized to live in new ways, a process that varies greatly depending on the location and conditions of resettlement.

To invent, borrow, play, and experiment with cultural forms become highly marked undertakings in a displaced community intensely invested in a faraway homeland and concerned about disappearing into melting pots. In this situation, the cultivation and enjoyment, or even public acknowledgment, of cultural ambiguity—for example, setting the poetry of ancient Tibetan god-kings to American rock music or singing Hindi film songs at local weddings—can seem self-defeating, perhaps a luxury of other cultures whose foundations cannot be shaken by such mingling.[15] And yet some non-Tibetan popular music and some new Tibetan cultural forms that have emerged specifically out of the experience of displacement, such as Tibetan rock and roll, are extremely popular among refugees of all ages and cannot be ignored for the sake of maintaining a desired cultural profile. It is this dilemma, a contradictory and as-of-yet unresolvable tension between a desire for both distinction (Tibetan culture) and participation (Tibetan culture as culture-in-the-world),[16] that informs the choices Tibetan refugee musicians developing a "modern" Tibetan sound, and others, make in their personal lives and in their artistic work. Tibetan intellectuals at the Amnye Machen Institute in Dharamsala articulate this dilemma, and the hesitancy to innovate, as a direct result of the community's remarkable success in preserving its ancient culture and religion in exile:

> [Their] very success in this task, coupled with their traditional conservatism, has resulted in an unfortunate closing-in of the national mind from further investigation, discussion or movement towards the cultural and intellectual changes necessary to making Tibetan institutions and ideas viable in a rapidly changing world.[17]

The next chapter turns from how modern Tibetan songs sound and are made to what they *say*, emphasizing the processes of negotiation behind the creation of contemporary lyrics that are meaningful and acceptable to Tibetan refugees.

6 "Little *Jolmo* Bird in the Willow Grove"
Crafting Tibetan Song Lyrics

And so the question remains: why and how do song words
(banal words, unreal words, routine words) work?

Simon Frith

Jampa Gyaltsen Dakton.la, who was at the time of my fieldwork a fifty-eight-year-old official astrologer for the Tibetan government-in-exile, seemed quite happy to have company on a Saturday morning when Tsering Lhanzom and I finally stopped by to interview him after we had had many interesting conversations on the roadside. The professor (playfully nicknamed "Asterix" by his friends) was apparently unmarried, so he lived alone in rooms provided by the Medical and Astrological Institute, where he taught. Notably, his living space was one of only a few I visited during my stay in Dharamsala that housed bookshelves full of books. By the end of this meeting, a good number of these books and even more cassettes were scattered all over the table and bed, as Dakton.la pointed out a reference from here or played a song fragment from there.

Dakton.la grew up in a village near the Bhutan border and was studying astrology when he escaped to Bhutan on foot in 1960. After working for the Dalai Lama's office there until 1967, he moved to Dharamsala, where he finished his studies at the Tibetan Medical Institute.[1] With his interest and skill in Tibetan poetry, writing song lyrics in exile on commission for musicians or government organizations or simply for himself had become a hobby. It's what he does, he told us, when he sits alone.[2] Many of the lyrics are based on historical stories, such as the famous seventh-century scene in which the Tibetan foreign minister tries to convince an extremely reluctant Chinese princess being sent to marry King Songten Gompo of all the good things about Tibet. But the range of topics covered in his handwritten portfolio is diverse. His love songs in particular caught my attention and led us into a very informative and amusing discussion of the differences between how Tibetans and Westerners express their romantic feelings.

Dakton.la started by explaining the process of writing a love song for TIPA's Ah-Ka-Ma Band, whose songs are musically inspired by traditional Tibetan tunes. Formally, each line must have a fixed number of syllables to fit the music (although he doesn't know the tune the band will use in advance, he knows the genre).[3] Rhetorically, the lyrics must be "Tibetan style." At least in the domain of formal poetry, Tibetan lovers don't directly shout, "Hey, I love you!" like Americans, he joked. They always try to give poetic examples from the natural world to convey their feelings. Only at the end of the song or poem might the lover finally tell you what he or she is trying to say. You must, he emphasized, think of the "opposite side" of the words to find their true meaning. The Ah-Ka-Ma Band included one of Dakton.la's Tibetan-style love songs on its cassette titled *Modern Tibetan Songs*:

FRIENDSHIP SONG

Little *jolmo*[4] bird in the willow grove
With a sweet-sounding voice,
Please think deeply.
I wonder if it is really as it seems.

Little fish belonging to the Turquoise Lake
With golden eyes,
You are flexing to please me.
Is it really true?

Little bird in the willow grove
If you really want to stay here,
I will certainly allow you, bird of the willow garden,
To be its owner.

Fish with golden eyes and quick movements
If you really want to go to the lake,
Of course, I will take care of you.

"So sweet!" Tsering Lhanzom exclaimed with delight when Dakton.la finished reading these lyrics. He kindly turned his notebook around so she could copy out the words. "So nice!" she repeated as she worked. Sharing her pleasure, I realized what a gift such well-written Tibetan songs are to younger generations.

For the purposes of comparison, having shared with us a "Tibetan-style" love song, the professor then spoke of his collaborative work with the Yak Band. Dakton.la wrote the words for most of the new songs Paljor included on his second cassette (including the "Tashi Delek Blues"), as well as a number of songs on the Yak Band's 1995 release *Rangzen,* so these young musicians had a well-established working relationship with the astrologer. Dakton.la explained that the Yaks had asked him to write the lyrics for a new love song about a girl who is very "fancy" and doesn't seem to love the boy in return. Familiar with the 4/4 beat of the Yaks' Western rock music and with the directness of *Inji* rhetoric, the professor produced the following song, translated here from the original Tibetan:

> Hey, Beautiful! Listen to me carefully—
> Don't pretend to be what you're not, Beautiful!
> By applying many colors and spreading a lot of scent,
> You, who fill the place with a smell by walking around.
>
> If you please, don't pretend you don't want it,
> even when you do.
> Come over here to me, and listen well
> to what I have to say.
>
> Mother's daughter, Tseden Lhamo.la,
> If the boy of your desires is not me,
> Who else could you possibly meet?
> It seems like I'm the one!

Because she was giggling so hard, Tsering Lhanzom could hardly translate for me as Asterix read the words from his notebook. The old man was grinning too, aware of how outrageous the presumptuous attitude of the young man he had invented sounded in Tibetan. As if to provide solid documentation of the cultural appropriateness of these naughty lyrics for a Western-style band, Dakton.la leaned across the room and dropped an unlabeled cassette into the boom box sitting on the table by his bed. One of the most surprising moments of my fieldwork unfolded as the heavy I-IV-V chord progression of the twelve-bar blues filled the old man's room. "Johnny Lee Hooker," the old man stated matter-of-factly, mirroring my incredulous smile. "Ah, you know this song?" Tsering Lhanzom asked me, noting my excitement. "No." "It's your favorite singer, then?" "No." "Then, why are you so happy?" she wanted to know, having exhausted the two reasons for going nuts over a popular song. "It's just a style I know well." I was just happy to hear the blues, as always, but I was also happy to learn that Asterix apparently loved the blues too.

I was confused that I had never heard of "Hey, Beautiful," despite my close involvement with the Yak Band, until I learned that it was precisely because Dakton.la carried out his assignment so well that this song had never seen the light of day (or the spotlight of the concert stage). It was written specifically for the Yaks in a direct Western style, but when the hip elderly poet showed it to Paljor and Thubten they apparently balked and said that they couldn't perform it, that they were too afraid the girl (it seems they had someone specific in mind) would get too embarrassed and be mad at them. The poet just shrugged his shoulders and commented that although they play Western music well, the Yaks are obviously still Tibetan boys inside. I couldn't help agreeing, thinking to myself that the Yaks were the ones who would be embarrassed by performing the song. The audience, on the other hand, would have loved its sassy attitude.

As an afterthought, Dakton.la reached across the room and produced a basket of stale *kabsay* (deep-fried biscuits) left over from New Year's and offered them to us while explaining, by way of closing our afternoon together, that just as a Tibetan boy playing rock and roll is still a Tibetan boy, an *Inji* song with Tibetan words is still an *Inji* song.

■　■　■

In an essay titled "Why Do Songs Have Words?" Simon Frith (1988: 105–28) surveys the ways in which song lyrics have been analyzed in the twentieth century. He moves from the near-exclusive preoccupation of scholars with song words in the 1950s and 1960s—a perspective based on a theory of "reflection" that assumed a direct connection between popular lyrics and the social forces that produced them—to the general acceptance of Robinson and Hirsch's 1972 conclusion that audiences don't, in fact, actually listen to the words of pop music and that a song's meaning lies principally in its sound (beat and melody). Frith is not convinced by arguments dismissing the importance of lyrics, pointing out that they must be doing *something,* since purely instrumental hits are rare. However, he stresses the need to attend to a song's words not simply as bearers of semantic meaning but also as the "sign of a voice" (1988: 120) conveying emotion and character, constructing both singer and listeners, through performance conventions. Having been preoccupied for so long with lyrics and their referentiality, sociologists of pop music, Frith argues, have neglected to analyze the "ways in which songs are about themselves, about language" (1988: 121). Although ethnomusicologists Steven Feld and Aaron Fox hold that Frith himself remains overinvested in song texts, they agree with him that "ethnographic treatments of song texts have tended to treat songs as verbal art, and to background the question of why and how certain texts are sung" (1994: 31). While Frith maintains that "lyrics give songs their social use" (1988: 123), Feld and Fox praise recent scholarship that critiques an overly textual conception of voice and an overly discursive conception of the social construction of meaning by exploring "polysemous, associative, iconic, presentational, ostensive, reflexive, ludic, emotive and embodied dimensions of sociability" (1994: 43).

I share Feld and Fox's preference for a wider focus on forms of musical expression as "total social facts, saturated with messages about time, place, feeling, style, belonging, and identity" (1994: 38) and therefore have chosen to devote the greater part of my research and writing to discussions of how musical sounds resonating in Dharamsala contribute to the making of Tibetan refugee identity, community, and culture. However, such an analysis would be incomplete without a separate discussion of the lyrics of modern Tibetan songs, extracted from their musical settings.[5] While I would not claim that lyrics are a source of meaning that should be favored over other aspects of a song (musical, social, and so on), texts are given special attention here because of the marked attention to, even prioritization of, the linguistic features of songs shown by Tibetan refugees themselves. The nature of Tibetan refugee attention to song lyrics highlights the importance of broadening the analysis of words to include the ways they can carry and evoke a whole range of meanings including, but also going beyond, the literally referential domain typically emphasized in scholarly work.

With respect to the diverse ways in which Tibetan song words speak to Tibetan listeners, I have, for the purposes of this discussion, differentiated between the attention Tibetan refugees pay to lyrics first as powerfully evocative sounds and, second, as carriers of semantic content. While these qualities of a given song's lyrics may not in fact be experientially separable, song words do often work simultaneously as sonic embodiments of this community *and* as a vehicle for expressing specific issues of local concern. The most evocative or successful songs are those that incorporate and extend both aspects of the Tibetan language's communicative potential—the sonic and the semantic—to their fullest. Tibetan audiences never complain if an instrument is out of tune or if an amplifier squeals painfully and distorts the music, but they leave a concert or turn off a cassette disappointed if they have not been able to understand the words of a song. I initially assumed this reaction indicated a keen interest in the subject matter of the songs, given the close links between modern song lyrics and the community's political struggle. In some cases, listeners were indeed frustrated by their inability to comprehend the literal meaning of the words; but in other cases they were, I came to learn, primarily disappointed not to have clearly *heard* the words. The value often attributed by Tibetan refugees to the aesthetic or somatic experience of Tibetan lyrics as sounds, sometimes separate from the task of intellectual comprehension, will be explored here.

Affectionate and critical local attention to native linguistic expression is hardly unique to Tibetan refugees. Particularly in communities dealing with the rapid loss of traditional knowledge, language acquisition and use are particularly sensitive and marked issues. For Tibetans living in the diaspora, particularly in Dharamsala, where centralized decisions regarding education and cultural preservation are made, a keen sense of urgency surrounds language issues as Chinese, English, Nepali, and Hindi squeeze their way into local conversations (as the sources of loan words to Tibetan and as alternate languages). The urgency and complexity of the Tibetan refugee language situation are particularly notable and unique for reasons stemming back to pre-1950 Tibet—particularly due to the historical status of the Tibetan language as sacred (*tsawa chenpo*)—and for reasons that have developed as a result of this group's insecure social and political situation in exile.

TIBETAN FLUENCY AND LITERACY IN EXILE

To understand the average Tibetan's relationship to the Tibetan language, it is necessary to distinguish between the individual's exposure to and associations with what are generally referred to as "literary Tibetan" (written, printed, or chanted texts in *oo chen* ["big head"] script) and "colloquial Tibetan" (spoken and, less frequently, written in *oo meh* ["headless"] or *kyug* ["running"] script). Although this is not the place to explore thoroughly the visual, grammatical, social, and historical differences that inform this formal linguistic division, it is important for the present discussion of Tibetan song lyrics to convey a sense of the complex layers of ways of "knowing" Tibetan that exist among any given group of Tibetans. In brief, literary and colloquial Tibetan are different enough that they are generally taught as separate subjects. Speaking Tibetan and being able to read and write Tibetan are distinct skills. In fact, verbal fluency may prove to be a hindrance to gaining literary proficiency: because of the language's complex orthography, words do not look like they sound, and many grammatical structures are only found in printed texts. From this situation arise the jokes about Western Buddhist scholars who arrive in India proudly *speaking* the literary Tibetan they know so well, only to confuse Tibetan listeners with their unintelligible sputterings: "I am hungry!" for example, is spelled *Nga grod khog ltogs kyi 'dug!* but is actually pronounced something like *Nga drokok toki doo!*

Because the difficulty of literary Tibetan requires the student to devote exceptional amounts of time to memorization and practice, and because monks and aristocrats have historically been the custodians of this knowledge, most Tibetan refugees over the age of forty-five are illiterate (although most can sound out and recite the syllables of printed religious texts, a special relationship to the language that will be discussed below). Despite the efforts of Dharamsala's Amnye Machen Institute to encourage literacy and reading among Tibetans by publishing a (now-discontinued) secular monthly newspaper, *Mangtso* (Democracy), and translating Western classics into Tibetan,[6] the written Tibetan word is still confined to government offices, schoolbooks, and monasteries in this refugee community. In Dharamsala, most children fortunate enough to attend one of the Tibetan Children's Village schools run by the Dalai Lama's government and largely funded by overseas sponsors do learn to read and write *oo meh* (the informal cursive script used for everyday purposes such as letter writing) and can at least slowly read *oo chen* (the formal printed script used in religious texts and official documents) as well. The ability to write *oo chen* is less common among youth, although students who show artistic talent are encouraged to practice calligraphy.[7] Interestingly, in early 2001, the government-in-exile launched an email service (www.tibetmail.net) to enable and encourage Tibetan refugees to write to one another in Tibetan script, with the goal of preserving the Tibetan language in exile and reducing the general dependence of the refugee community on English for written correspondence.

"Colloquial Tibetan" encompasses the wide range of sometimes mutually unintelligible spoken regional dialects, many of which have been brought together for the first time in communities in exile. Many older Tibetans and "new arrivals" from the regions of Amdo, Tingri, Ngari, Kham, and elsewhere in Tibet still speak in their village tongues,[8] while the government-in-exile has made an effort to use a standardized form of Lhasan Tibetan in schools and offices. This effort has not, however, been unopposed by regional groups wary of the perpetuation in exile of the historical hegemony of elite, urban Tibetans over other segments of the population. Owing to centralized educational programs, conscious efforts by parents to speak Tibetan in the home, and the constant influx of refugees from Tibet, the Tibetan language is still this refugee community's internal medium of verbal communication after four decades in exile. Indeed, it is safe to say that all Tibetan children living in Nepal and India are verbally fluent in their parents' native language, although all, except for the most recent to arrive, have also learned Hindi and/or Nepali simultaneously. All Tibetan children in Dharamsala speak Tibetan, although one commonly hears disparaging remarks about a new "TCV dialect" developing among school children, a variety of Tibetan characterized by its rapid pace, sloppy use (or total absence) of honorific vocabulary, and liberal peppering with Hindi words. This dialect has developed so much that children arriving at the TCV from Tibet and kids raised in Dharamsala often cannot understand one another.

For foreigners like me who have devoted significant time and energy to learning Tibetan and have despaired over its infamous difficulty, it is something of a relief to realize that most Tibetans find it very difficult as well. But this initial consolation is soon mitigated as one becomes aware of the centrality of linguistic issues to what have become quite bitter community debates. The crux of these debates involves "traditional" and "modern" perspectives on the religious versus secular nature of the Tibetan language. For example, there is a severe rift in Dharamsala over whether the language should be simplified and modernized to increase the likelihood that the younger generation will actually learn to read and write or whether to dilute the language in this way is to fail to preserve it properly.[9] Although it is beyond the scope of this book, I will suggest that at stake is the hegemony of a definition of Tibetan culture developed from a highly literate, monastic perspective, an issue that points directly at the larger difficulties of reconciling the historical religiopolitical structure of the Tibetan government with the democratic ideals embraced in exile by the Dalai Lama himself. Generally, the authority of the traditional perspective is not questioned, but some school administrators, teachers, government staff, and intellectuals are outspoken with their concerns. In a statement recorded by Vyvyan Cayley, the late K. Dhondup, an important intellectual figure in exile, included a critique of the incorporation of religious authorities into the secular education system:

> The Administration in Dharamsala decided to replace the Tibetan lay teachers with Tibetan monk teachers. That is I think one of the biggest mistakes our Government made . . . What appeared right to them was not necessarily right for the students. Tibetan monks went into Buddhist philosophy in great detail but they did not study lay literature which could have been useful for Tibetan children. I think our generation was lucky because we had lay teachers, but the education of those that came after us was a little imbalanced. Perhaps that is one reason why with so many schools in our community and with all their facili-

ties, we are not producing Tibetans who will serve the Tibetan society in a multi-dimensional, more democratic way . . . Previously the emphasis had been on dance, Scouts, Guides . . . and that had made us very lively. We had had some monks and nuns but they were a subdued section of the school. Under Samdhong Rinpoche [name of a high-ranking monk], the school developed a strong community of monks and nuns and he issued a decree that all students above 12 or 13 years of age had to memorise the Lam-Rim text, which is a long religious text. It scared me, because the decree declared that those who failed to recite it by memory would undergo certain punishments, which sounded draconian. (quoted in Cayley 1994: 90–91)

Similar issues were raised by the experience of a Tibetan friend who is fluent in English and has taught himself to write Tibetan well. Not long ago, he took an exam administered by the Tibetan government-in-exile to staff members hoping to be promoted to managerial status in their offices. As a college-educated layperson who had worked for the government for a decade, he was dismayed by the number of questions on the exam concerned with dharma and requiring knowledge of esoteric religious terminology. He wrote to me that he was "ashamed" to report he had failed the exam, adding that only one monk schooled at the Institute for Buddhist Dialectics had passed.[10]

Tibetan refugees of different ages, social classes, educational histories, and regional backgrounds have, then, complex and uneven relationships with the Tibetan language as a literary tradition, as the local dialect of one's family and village of origin, as sacred, and as mundane. These linguistic ideas and experiences all inform how a Tibetan hears lyrics sung in his or her native tongue. I turn now to a discussion of Tibetan lyrics as sacred and secular *sounds,* focusing on the ways the Tibetan language itself can move displaced listeners by evoking a deep sense of familiarity (in the sense of something both known and shared).

TIBETAN WORDS AS SACRED SOUNDS

The Tibetan writing system used today was developed in the seventh century by a Tibetan minister who had been sent to India by King Songten Gompo specifically for the purpose of learning Sanskrit and facilitating the translation of Buddhist texts into Tibetan. For several centuries, the development of written Tibetan was fully focused on the work of textual translation, particularly on the difficulties of reconciling the existing spoken Tibetan language with the refined, scientific grammatical structure of Sanskrit. Literacy during this period was limited to males engaged in monastic training, and, with the exception of private schools for artisto-cratic boys in Lhasa, this remained the situation until 1959. This intense relationship between dharma and language caused H. Jäschke, compiler of a Tibetan dictionary published in German in the 1870s and in English in 1881, to note that the "sanctity of the religious message conferred a corre-sponding reputation and tradition of excellence upon the form in which it was conveyed" (1992: iv). This holy correspondence is still assumed by most native Tibetan speakers today. While the Tibetan language is not the original language of revelation, it *is* the language that enabled the Bud-dha's teachings to spread to Tibet.

In religious Tibetan contexts, the specific referential words of prayers are often blurred—intentionally, in the case of secret esoteric teachings, or unintentionally, by virtue of their chanted medium—into sounds (mantras and melodies) as they are intoned, leaving the literal meaning of the verses behind for all but the most scholarly present. According to Rakra Tethong, rather than distracting from a prayer's power, this smooth transition be-tween the spoken and the sung, the literal word and the metaphysical syl-lable, reinforces the holiness of the Tibetan language for ritual participants.

> We always have to begin our singing from one word, a mantra: often *Hüm* and sometimes from *Om, Ah,* or another mantra. The melody is based on these. For example, the Tantric Colleges have some of the most famous *dbyangs* [11] in Tibet; each person sings two or three notes at once. Now, if you listen carefully when they sing, not paying attention to the words, you don't hear the words at all, but just the sound of "Om Ah Hüm." Of course, their texts are secret and they can't make the words clear, but still, you understand, it is very significant that they should be able to change their words into these mantras. (Tethong 1979: 18)

Although the words of monastic texts may not be intellectually under-stood by everyone participating or listening, the valuable message of the verses is not, according to Lobsang Lhalungpa and others, lost:

> Musical sounds, canonically ordered, affect a man's psychic condition in such a way as to render him more receptive to the truth. The same ap-plies in the visual arts: a painted ikon, in which every detail corresponds to some aspect of enlightenment, is a powerful instrument in promoting the contemplative spirit and so is a *sonorous ikon*—the nature of all truly sacred music is such; it pertains to method, its aim being to awaken a corresponding wisdom in the soul. (Lhalungpa 1969: 6)

Lhalungpa's conceptualization of sounds as *useful* is particularly interest-ing. Syllable by syllable, otherwise illiterate laypeople sound out and recite sacred texts at temples, children chant prayers learned by rote in schools, and there is merit to be gained in the practice, in the method and mindfulness, of such efforts. Similarly, devotees attend high Buddhist teachings to gain merit by being in the presence of the Dalai Lama and to recite in an echo of his voice the fundamental mantras of the ceremony. In response to my questions about the efficacy and purpose of an esoteric Buddhist teaching like the Kalachakra for uneducated Tibetan laypeople or foreign practitioners without any knowledge of Tibetan, a Buddhist nun explained to me that those who do not fully participate in the teaching—which includes all but a few advanced scholars—are still receiving an "imprint" of the ceremony's difficult concepts, a subliminal preparation of the soul that will facilitate enlightenment the next time around . . . or the next.

An example from the secular musical domain will serve to underscore the degree to which song and prayer are intertwined for Tibetan refugees, a cultural pattern that informs the public's unproblematic acceptance of hearing, even singing, words in one's native tongue that are, in fact, unintelligible to the average person.

In an article in the Delhi-based *Tibetan Review*, Tibetan translator Dhawa Dhondup reflects on the fact that the meaning of the Tibetan national anthem ("Pö Gyal Khab kyi Gyal Lu"), like other popular nationalist songs and the symbolism of the Tibetan flag, is far too profound for common folk to understand, although every Tibetan knows the words by heart and sings them frequently. The "highly spiritual" lyrics of the national anthem are believed to have been penned by the late Kyabje Trijang Rinpoche, the junior tutor of the Dalai Lama who accompanied the leader into exile (and whose preadolescent reincarnation was living in a British-style bungalow in Dharamsala during my fieldwork). Dhondup explains the difficulty:

> To understand versified Tibetan—marked by a heavy blend of metaphysical outlook—it requires a certain degree of literacy and an acute familiarity with the sophisticated discipline of Buddhism. *"Si-Zhi"* (existence/mundane/tranquil/transcended), the opening two words of the Tibetan national anthem, for example, are very complex epistemological concepts (that's speaking non-religiously). (1993: 14)

All Tibetan school children memorize such difficult song texts by means of rhythmic rote exercises, echoing patient music teachers charged with staging patriotic pageants on Tibetan holidays. Rather than moving on to critique forms of patriotic expression that are clearly not "of the people," as a Western reader with a secular conceptual understanding of nationhood might expect, Dhondup concludes that "such richness of the contents must be recognized as a distinction, indicative of a highly evolved culture" (1993: 14). His point is that, unlike most national anthems that celebrate bloody acts of vengeance and the glorification of tyrants, the Tibetan anthem maintains its relevance at a time when global concerns are competing with the "neighbourly enmity" of reclusive nations. Even if Tibetans cannot understand or explain the literal meanings of the words, they all know that their anthem is a statement of humanitarianism, of faith, and, ultimately, of the inevitable victory of Buddhist dharma over the "destructive camp" (alternatively translated as "dark negative forces"). Pushing the sober rationality of semantic content aside, Dhondup admits that the "kick" of singing such songs may be "more in the symbolism that the very act of singing a common anthem (or a struggle song) injects: a euphoria of nationhood, a common belonging" (1993: 14). This community-affirming aspect of Tibetan songs derives, I argue, from both the sound and the sense the lyrics carry for listeners and performers.

TIBETAN WORDS AS SOUNDS OF CULTURAL SURVIVAL AND IDENTITY

Considered from a more secular standpoint and from an exilic perspective, the *sound* of Tibetan has become a powerful symbol of identity for refugees—as a unique aspect of their culture (Tibetan is an extremely unusual language, only related distantly to Burmese) and as tangible evidence of cultural survival in exile. Given the ease with which Tibetan refugee children have picked up the languages of their host countries and their enthusiasm for non-Tibetan popular culture, language loss in exile is a key concern for Tibetans. The preservation of linguistic knowledge among children born in exile is deemed especially urgent by many because of the rapid rate of language loss documented among Tibetans living in Chinese-ruled Tibet, few of whom are now educated in their native tongue.[12] Attachment to the preservation of a "pure" Tibetan language in exile is also fueled by changes in the Tibetan language in Tibet, particularly during the Cultural Revolution (1966–1976) when, according to John Avedon, "Tibetan writing and even the language itself were targeted for destruction, replaced by a bizarre, mainly Chinese patois called 'the Tibetan-Chinese Friendship language,' the grammar and vocabulary of which were incomprehensible to most Tibetans" (1986: 289).[13] Cultural survival in exile is often more widely conceived by Tibetan refugees as the urgent effort to preserve Tibetan culture anywhere at all. Hearing original Tibetan verses sung by refugee youth sends a strong, reassuring message to many audience members that the struggle, and the most appropriate language in which to articulate the struggle, are both alive and well. For many Tibetan concertgoers, particularly older refugees or recent escapees for whom rock music itself, as a sound, has no special meaning in the way that it does for youth raised in exile, the Tibetan lyrics of modern songs are where their value, their personal and cultural relevance, lies.[14]

In addition to the pleasure of hearing Tibetan verses performed and the relative novelty of hearing Tibetan words sung in a concert setting, the lyrics (still being considered as sounds) are a vehicle for other information as well. The voice that delivers a song's words tells the audience a great deal about the performer as an individual. Because the Tibetan language is so closely associated with the issue of cultural preservation (which includes the preservation of Tibetan Buddhism), and since all Tibetan refugees in South Asia have the opportunity at least to learn to speak Tibetan, one's linguistic competence in the native tongue can be interpreted as a tangible sign not only of what kind of Tibetan a person is (class, region of origin, and so on) but also of that person's commitment to the "Cause." Particularly in the identity-conscious context of Dharamsala, it follows, then, that lack of linguistic competence can compromise one's perceived "Tibetanness" and qualify one's participation in the community. A singer's accent, manner of delivery, and (moving from the domain of sound into that of sense) chosen subject matter are all of great interest to a public curious to see and hear what an individual confident enough to get on stage has to say for him- or herself and *how* he or she goes about saying it. Dharamsala is a community intensely (many would say *too* intensely) conscious of regional, sectarian, and class differences within the refugee population, differences generally rooted in an individual's family background in Tibet. Although the personal backgrounds of most regular performers in Dharamsala are common knowledge among residents, when newcomers attend concerts or when bands go on tour "out of station," accents and verbal style matter greatly.

In the case of the Yak Band, listeners generally expressed to me a preference for Thubten's singing voice over Paljor's. While I suspect that this preference is informed in no small part by the fact that Thubten sings all the Hindi songs (which nearly everyone knows by heart anyway) and the Yak Band's only Tibetan love song, fans commented that Thubten's voice is richer and deeper and that they could clearly make out the lyrics when he sang. They often asked me to confirm their impressions that he had a Nepali accent, which he does, having been raised by poor parents in the border town of Kalimpong and schooled in a Nepali-medium day school. On the other hand, listeners often expressed frustration trying to follow the lyrics when Paljor sang, variously claiming that he mumbles, sings like a girl, and speaks Tibetan a little oddly. In fact, the only Tibetan Paljor heard and spoke until he entered a Tibetan high school in Class IX was the extreme Khampa dialect of his mother and other relatives in Darjeeling. In addition, he is naturally soft-spoken and he suffered a serious injury to his upper palate as a child, which he blames, with a typically ironic twist, for his trouble enunciating song words clearly enough:

PALJOR: And I was pretty naughty, you know, in school.

KEILA: You?

PALJOR: I was going around—

KEILA: Really? I can see you being a very good boy.

PALJOR: No, I was naughty.

KEILA: Like Pema.la.

PALJOR: I think I was worse than my kids. Really. From one story [of a house] I have fallen down three times. Got this all smashed. My nose smashed up. Finally the last naughty thing I did was I got a huge big long bamboo right through my—

KEILA: Oh, God, you told me this. Through your throat, in your mouth. Oh, God, I can't stand it. That's horrible!

PALJOR: You can imagine, I had my second life. I would have died. It was a miracle I survived. So after that incident, I have this . . . When I speak you can still . . . I have this nasal kind of —

KEILA: Maybe that's why people say when you sing they have trouble understanding the words.

PALJOR: I have this nasal—

KEILA: The words aren't very clear . . . because you shoved a bamboo up your nose!

PALJOR: I was trying to, you know, imitate Bob Dylan . . . It didn't work out.

KEILA: No, you weren't!

Physical constraints aside, the majority of young Tibetan adults in exile, even those educated in Tibetan schools, are notably insecure about their Tibetan language skills. Because they are so aware of their responsibility to preserve Tibetan culture, most are ashamed by their lack of proficiency in reading and writing their "native" tongue, even though most have had no opportunity to develop these difficult skills properly. Most youth avoid the issue by using either English or Hindi when they are absolutely obligated to write something down. One friend, for example, writes Tibetan song lyrics phonetically in his notebook, using the Devanagari script of Nepali and Hindi with which he is most familiar.[15] Since there is next to no lay literature available for lay Tibetans to read in Tibetan, weakness in this skill does not pose regular problems, until a curious Westerner comes along, needing help translating songs. Indeed, much of my understanding of the issues of linguistic competence discussed in this chapter arose out of my efforts to get musicians to translate their own songs. I was amazed to learn that Paljor, for example, had not sung on his first trio cassette at all, because at that point in his life (in 1988), he did not fully understand the lyrics and felt insecure about his accent. Similarly, I noticed Thubten would summarize a song's story for me instead of going through the lyrics line by line. Young friends who felt obligated to help me usually took the song texts home for long periods of time, waiting for an opportunity to pass them on to a visiting older relative or monk.

The linguistic insecurity of young adults has significantly affected the form and content of modern Tibetan songs. Because the sound and sense of modern Tibetan song lyrics are attended to so closely by Tibetan audiences, musicians must put great effort into the selection of song topics, the appropriateness of the language used to express them, and the clear articulation of the words in performance. As will be shown, the importance and inherent solemnity of the topics that have become accepted as appropriate for this modern genre demand an elegant and artistic use of the Tibetan language that is far beyond the skills of most Tibetans, including young quadralingual Tibetans like the members of the Yak Band or the Ah-Ka-Ma Band. My emphasis thus far on the evocative power of the *sound* of Tibetan words for Tibetan listeners has been intended to expand the reader's understanding of how lyrics "work" in modern Tibetan songs. By now it should be clear that the religious, patriotic, and personal resonances of these sounds significantly contribute to, inform, and often intensify the overall meaning that a song's words carry more literally. I turn now to consider Tibetan song lyrics as carriers of semantic meaning, in terms of their referentiality.

WHAT MODERN TIBETAN SONGS ARE ABOUT

With few exceptions, the niche for modern Tibetan songs in exile has been limited to their use as a musical medium for expressing the specific experience of displacement out of which the genre was born. Therefore, contemporary song lyrics are generally patriotic calls for Tibetans to put aside their differences, unite, and fight for independence. Other common related topics include historical stories, expressions of sadness over the loss of a beautiful homeland and loved ones who have passed away or been left behind, and devotional poems for the Dalai Lama and other religious figures. Whereas folk songs in pre-1950 Tibet addressed a wide variety of topics and served many purposes (setting the rhythm for manual labor, negotiating marriage arrangements, expressing political satire, and so on), Dhawa Dhondup has noted, and my own fieldwork confirms, that a "three-part combination" of themes—the freedom struggle, rigorous Red China–bashing, and nostalgic recalling of the solemn past (the golden era of the three ancestral spiritual kings)—has somehow "stuck" as the only source material for most expressive culture in exile (1993: 14). Continuing his critique with the confidence that rhetorically marks Tibetan intellectuals who have removed themselves from the conservative fishbowl atmosphere of Dharamsala, Dhondup (who lives in Australia) further speculates:

> Perhaps the very concentrated habitation in exile, with our conscience focussed on and emitting from Dharamsala, has shaped the exile culture into a regimentally uniform one, not unlike suburban monoculture. Consequently, when it comes to public vocalization of our patriotism and nationalism we all have remained abreast, by and large, with those three pieces. (1993: 14)

The idea of thematic "pieces" that have become fundamental to the umbrella genre of modern Tibetan songs brings to mind Frith's claims that pop songs work as "recruiting symbols" (1981: 36), with songwriters drawing on a communal language to create a sense of community.[16] Modern Tibetan songs derive their inspiration from the patriotic sentiments of Tibetans and, in turn, often confirm and augment those same sentiments in performance, thereby strengthening the community's shared memories and goals. This is the fundamental give-and-take dynamic by which genres are formed, transformed, and abandoned, a process described in literary studies as a meeting between the "horizon of expectation" of the reader and a "model of writing" for the author (Todorov 1990: 18) or as a "social contract" between a writer and a public created to specify proper use of a particular cultural artifact (Jameson 1981: 106). A genre can at least partly be understood, then, as a choice that a given society has made conventional (Todorov 1990: 10).

In a relatively short period of time, contemporary Tibetan song lyrics have become conventionalized as the exiled community's most effective secular public voice for expressing its pain (*na tsa*), sadness (*lo pham*), pride (*pö pa*), and right to political self-determination (*rangzen*). The composition, live performance, and consumption[17] of these modern lyrics comprise a "ritual re-enactment" (Connerton 1989: 61) of exile that specifically preserves and reanimates (and certainly alters and sometimes even creates) the shared memories of displacement, violence, loss, and vulnerability that are central to feelings of solidarity in the Tibetan diaspora. One of the most interesting features of the Tibetan refugee situation is precisely the way in which it challenges the common assumption that social order decreases as tension and instability within a group increase. Tibetans living in exile have, in fact, developed many practices that recharge the group's sense of liminality and vulnerability precisely *in order* to maintain social order in their diaspora. The form and content of many exilic musical compositions, such as this typical contemporary song, confirm this observation:

> Our misery is bigger than a mountain.
> Our tears flow more than the ocean.
> Our relatives have been killed by the Chinese.
> Brothers and sisters, please try to exert yourselves!

> Our beloved lives must be highly valued.
> Our leader and protector is His Holiness the Dalai Lama.
> We are being tortured by the Chinese.
> Brothers and sisters, unite!
> Tibet is like a rocky mountain.
> Brothers and sisters, try to exert yourselves![18]

Paul Connerton describes rituals of reenactment as "actions which are explicitly represented as re-enactments of prior, prototypical actions" and are, therefore, "of cardinal importance in the shaping of communal memory" (1989: 61). Indeed, this song (and numerous other songs similar to it) was composed specifically to be performed by Tibetan students during a patriotic staged school event.[19] Performances like these are, following Connerton's argument, "celebrated" or "exemplary" recurrences that create the "experience of recapitulative imitation" through a rhetoric of reenactment (1989: 64). It is through such evocative representations that new songs based on personal and social knowledge and experience express and confront the group's identity as "refugees" as much as their identity as "Tibetans." Further, by reanimating or indexing the group's experiences of injustice, modern Tibetan songs examine and generally confirm the refugees' commitment to the Buddhist ideals of nonviolence (*tse may shi wa*) and compassion (*nying je*) embodied for them in the person of their leader, the Dalai Lama. Written in 1990, just after the Dalai Lama received the Nobel Peace Prize, this song, for example, remains one of the Yak Band's most popular offerings:

COMPASSIONATE HOLDER OF THE LOTUS

The great loving *phyagna padmo*[20]
May his wishes be fulfilled.
The happy sunshine of the land of Tibet
Is shining once again.

Nowadays, the wise men of the world
Have conferred the Nobel Peace Prize
[on the Dalai Lama].
While everyone is congratulating him,
The enemy is complaining.

Great Tenzin Gyatso,[21]
For receiving the Nobel Peace Prize
All we Tibetan people
Offer prayers of good fortune.

All the money from the prize
Relieved those tormented by hunger and thirst,
Laying the foundations for peace.
All sufferings were removed.[22]

The announcement of the Dalai Lama's Nobel Peace Prize in the fall of 1989 marked the greatest moment of joy and optimism in this community's time in exile, a flash of hope after decades of frustration and despair. The leader's principled commitment to nonviolent conflict resolution, which had proved fruitless in improving relations with Chinese officialdom, had at least finally been honored by the international community. The prize put Tibet on the map (and the Dalai Lama's face and voice all over the media) just when Tibetans were wondering why the world was ignoring their situation. Although little has changed on the diplomatic front regarding the Tibetan situation, the memory of December 10, 1990—now an annual holiday marked with celebrations of song and dance—serves to remind most Tibetans that their leader's Buddhist philosophy and tactics are right and good. The Yak Band's song regenerates this pride and reminds each Tibetan of his or her responsibility to try to live up to the ideal established by the Dalai Lama for the good of the world, despite Chinese derision and the diplomatic passivity of supposedly sympathetic nations.

As might be expected, given the close relationship between politics and modern Tibetan songs, this new genre has been enthusiastically embraced by many tendrils of Dharamsala's bureaucracy as a way of acknowledging, commemorating, honoring, celebrating, dedicating, and thanking specific individuals and events important to the community. As a result, local music teachers are regularly requested to produce new songs with appropriate and inspirational lyrics for various anniversaries and holidays. Produced and performed within the framework of Tibetan officialdom, a political sphere of activity marked by its highly conservative and deferential social and rhetorical customs, this subgenre of modern songs does not stray from the canon of predictable themes and attitudes that has developed over the years. Most of these official songs are never recorded, and many are only performed at the specific occasion for which they were commissioned, but some do make their way into the public acoustic sphere. For example, in the process of translating the songs on the Ah-Ka-Ma Band's cassette of "modern Tibetan songs," I was surprised to find that the lyrics to a very pleasant tune I had always enjoyed, and which could be heard all over town because of the cassette's popularity, were actually an awkwardly prosaic example of institutional promotion:

ON THIS DAY

On this day,
The thirty-sixth anniversary of TIPA's founding,
On this big occasion,
The musical committee wishes you greetings of "*Tashi delek!*"
The musical committee wishes you "*Tashi delek!*"
His Holiness the Dalai Lama
With broad thinking established TIPA in 1959.
And TIPA has so far preserved the culture,
Performed well, and spread it very widely in today's world.
By performing it well,
Tibetan culture has been spread very widely.
The musical committee wishes all the audience "*Tashi delek!*"

It is quite certain that a song so blatantly "official" would only be included on a cassette produced, as this one was, by a government organization (the Tibetan Institute of Performing Arts). According to many listeners, the song's appeal is in its sound, the rock-and-roll influence incorporated into a traditional tune, which accounts for the cassette's popularity as a whole, not in its specific lyrics, which can be ignored once they have become familiar. However, it is important to note that the linguistic and topical conservatism that marks the lyrics of "official" songs such as "On This Day" is also common in the majority of modern songs composed and enjoyed by lay youth, a conservatism or hesitancy to innovate that is a theme running through this study of the expressive culture of Tibetan refugees. The boredom expressed by Tibetan youth helping me translate song after song off their favorite cassettes—songs made silent by our focus on the words alone—drew my attention to the possibility that precisely *because* of this community's deep awareness of the historical and contemporary significance embodied in the Tibetan language, it is often used very timidly and in reassuringly familiar ways. It is, it seems, being preserved by many, but is only being creatively used and kept alive by a few who have the confidence and skills to do so. Jamyang Norbu's "Pha Yul dee Ngatsö Tsangma Ray" (This land belongs to all of us) was repeatedly presented to me as an example of poetic, yet accessible, lyrics that are evocative rather than boring:

THIS LAND BELONGS TO ALL OF US

At the top of a high pass,
We did a fire *puja*.
Having raised prayer flags,
We tossed *tsampa* in the air.
The protector deities told me:
This land belongs to all of us.

Tibet is yours.
Tibet is mine.
From Tartse Do in the east
To Tö Ngari "Kor Sum"
From the blue lake of the north
To the forests of Kongpo in the south,
This land belongs to all of us.

When I rode a winged windhorse
in the Chang Tang,
With those cool breezes,
There was a smell of sage.
From the blue skies,
The birds told me:
This land belongs to all of us.

Tibet is yours . . .

After many years,
When I go home,
There is a golden carpet of wheat fields.
When the farmers harvest,
They sang pleasing songs.

When they made conversation,
They said:
This land belongs to all of us.

Tibet is yours . . .

After traveling around many countries,
I reached Lhasa.
After going to a bar,
I met a friend.
We drank delicious *chang*.
Then he sang this song:
This land belongs to all of us.

Tibet is yours . . .

Despite popular appreciation of this song's lyrics, the songs with "boring" words still make up the core of modern Tibetan music and reveal a great deal about the ideals of young musicians, the circumstances within which they compose, and the ways a genre is restricted in certain phases of its development over time. The near-total dependence of contemporary song-writers on tried-and-true topics has significantly contained modern Tibetan songs, limiting their potential to express musically the full range of issues and feelings that are meaningful to their listeners and thereby certainly contributing to the appeal of other kinds of music.

BRINGING SOUND AND SENSE TOGETHER

Having separately discussed Tibetan song words as evocative sacred and secular sounds and as carriers of meaningful semantic content, it is time to explore how various songwriters bring these different aspects of song lyrics together. As I mentioned, the most successful songs are generally the handful that incorporate and extend both the acoustic and the referential aspects of the Tibetan language to their fullest, songs that display both a learned and poetically sensitive mastery of the language *and* a deep commitment to the fundamental themes that resonate with the contemporary refugee community's concerns.

Because of both the political and patriotic motivations of most modern Tibetan musicians and their need to justify their novel and often electrified sounds to culturally conservative segments of their community, the younger generation has for the most part stuck closely to the three early thematic trends identified by Dhondup. At least, that is, the songs that today's young musicians choose to perform publicly and to record adhere to and thereby perpetuate these generic expectations. In fact, many Tibetan musicians write love songs as well, but most are reluctant to perform them on stage. Even these songs, however, generally incorporate one of the above themes (for example, lovers separated by the flight of one partner into exile or by bad karma). As I have discussed elsewhere, partly because of the risks inherent in steering a genre that has become deeply associated with political and religious discourse in the direction of mere entertainment, love is, for the most part, taken care of in the public sphere by Hindi film songs, rather than by Tibetan songs.[23]

The commitment to singing about the inherently solemn topics that have become accepted as appropriate for modern songs—independence, the homeland, praiseworthy religious figures, famous martyrs, and so on—poses a dilemma for most of Dharamsala's young musicians. By nature of their cultural and political importance, these topics demand a formal and correct use of Tibetan that is, generally speaking, far beyond the literary skills of the younger generation in exile. A handful of young musicians do write their own Tibetan lyrics, but, with few exceptions, these songs are highly predictable, rhythmically heavy, and devoid of the references to specific locations in the Tibetan landscape and the use of tools of indirect speech, such as metaphor, that characterize traditional Tibetan poetry and are particularly gratifying to Tibetan listeners.

One of the few young Tibetan musicians I met who writes all his own lyrics was Jippy, the math teacher at the Lower Tibetan Children's Village (TCV) in Dharamsala, whose original school play was discussed in chapter 2. Born in India in 1964 and educated at the Upper TCV, Jippy is an extremely emotional patriot whose own sentimental songs rarely fail to bring tears to his eyes. While teaching in Ladakh (where he had been sent to recover from a near-fatal case of spinal tuberculosis), Jippy started playing around on his roommate's guitar, "partly just to annoy him." Pretending to be reading, Jippy often watched and memorized his friend's chord positions and technique, practicing when the instrument's owner was on leave. He wrote his first song—titled "Bö kyi Den Lu" (Tibetan memory song)—on the occasion of an ex-TCV party in Leh and thought to himself: "Maybe I have a little talent and should work to unearth it." Most of the thirty-seven songs he had written by the time I met him in 1995 were about freedom and unity, some were written specifically for schoolchildren, and a few were love songs.

Musically, Jippy's songs are based on the standard chord progressions of Western popular music, occasionally including a well-rehearsed solo melody line between verses. He doesn't actually listen to much music, preferring to spend any free time he has making his own. He expressed a definite dislike of rock music, but he thought "country" groups like the Eagles made nice songs that "make you feel like you're going up a hill, reaching a peak and then coming down at a good speed," thereby emphasizing the emotional crescendos of the lyrics and the song's eventual release (whether happy or, more common in his songs, devastatingly sad). The following song, written by Jippy in response to a song composed by a nun imprisoned in Tibet, is representative of the highly sentimental and literal rhetoric typical of his generation's Tibetan-language poetry:

NOWADAYS

The way this wind is blowing, it seems it came from Tibet.
My brothers and sisters, how is their health?

In former times it was a religious and peaceful country.
Nowadays it has changed into a Chinese prison.
The blood of my brothers and sisters,
Came out and flowed like a river.
And for the freedom struggle,
Many gave their lives.

But still, our willpower and courage
Are growing like a burning fire.
And we have to bring the peace
of the sun and the moon to our nation.

My grandparents were from Tibet.
Whether or not we are beautiful, we have this heritage.
If I don't work for precious freedom, who will?
And if we don't get this jewel, then who will?
Happy country is the country of Tibet.
It is a sacred country.

Even if we have to stay in the hands of butchers,
It is not possible that we will lose our courage and willpower. And the
    young generations should work for and get *rangzen*.
We have to bring back peace to the country.
Even though there are so many water outlets,
They are all collected in one ocean.
The Chinese torture us in many ways,
But Tibet will prevail!

Since few local musicians have Jippy's Tibetan language skills, the solution most of them have embraced involves a separation of tasks—the partnership of a musician and a poet—in the process of making a new song. Occasionally, musicians turn to the better-educated members of their peer group, including young monks, for Tibetan lyrics. However, these sources are limited. While a good number of youth in Dharamsala enjoy writing poetry and have notebooks full of verses, more often than not these young secular poets write in English. In addition to having received more formal education in English than in Tibetan, primarily due to the status of English as an official language in India, youth expressed to me a greater sense of freedom when not writing in their native language.[24] To err grammatically in English is locally unimportant, whereas to err in Tibetan can be, as I have explained, a risky advertisement of one's failure to preserve the culture. A disadvantage of these English poems, however, is that they rarely go public, getting passed around instead among friends in cafés. Perhaps not surprisingly, there seems to be a consensus among musicians that English is not an appropriate medium for the public expression of patriotic and religious sentiments to local audiences. I never heard a Tibetan musician publicly perform an original song in English, although with considerable embarrassment Jippy agreed to sing this composition to me in his room. It is meant to be sung by a group of school children to their peers:

THAT'S MY COUNTRY

As we walked up the street,
Many people passed by us
With smiles on their faces
And flowers in their hair.

At a corner we saw a boy
With tears in his eyes.
Asked him why he was sad
Told us he'd got nowhere to go.

To which country you belong?
Told us it's in Asia.
On the roof of the world.
Called it *"Bö Jong."*

T-I-B-E-T, Tibet!
That's my country.
We are the children of Tibet.
I'm the son of Tibet.
We are the future of *Bö Jong.*
We are the future of *Bö Jong.*

We are missing you, Mother.
We need peace and your love.
Sad being away from home.
From Shangri-La.

Hand in hand we'll walk on
To the country we belong.
Though the roads may be rough,
Yet the heart is full of love.

T-I-B-E-T, Tibet!
That's my country.
We are the children of Tibet.
We are the sons of Tibet.
We are the daughters of Tibet.
We are the future of *Bö Jong*.
We are the future of *Bö Jong*.
We are the future of *Bö Jong*.

As should be evident by now, there is a strong connection for Tibetan refugees between the subject matter of a song and the language in which it is sung. To sing of *rangzen* in Hindi, for example, would be absurd. Interestingly, I never even encountered a song that incorporated the code-switching among languages that typically characterizes everyday speech among the "children of Tibet" in Dharamsala. The same young men who write careful and clichéd Tibetan songs about the "sun of happiness rising in Tibet" will spend long evening hours bantering in four languages, sharing their enjoyment of wordplay and multilingual punning, revealing a reluctance to mix up or corrupt the Tibetan language in a public context or permanent form (a written/sung song that is traceable to its author/performer).

IN PARTNERSHIP WITH ELDERS

Because of the combined topical and linguistic constraints on the creation of new songs, it has been most common since the production of the first modern cassette in exile for those young musicians with hopes of performing and recording to invite erudite older aristocrats or religious scholars in the community to compose lyrics for them, often providing these elders with a topic idea and rhythmic structure for the song. This practice not only compensates for (or even hides) the younger generation's linguistic insecurity, but it also lends prestige and credibility to the music by involving the older generation in its creation. In many cases, however, the poems are so well written that few people, including some of the people who sing them, can fully understand the lyrics of these "popular" songs, since the formal poetry of the lyricists is quite beyond the linguistic abilities of the average Tibetan speaker. The inability of fans to sing along with their favorite songs—the impact of linguistic competence or lack thereof on performative participation—has caused some concern among musicians;[25] however, as follows from the above discussion of the importance of the Tibetan language as a sound, rather than discouraging listeners, the formal beauty of literary Tibetan often seems to add to the song's value, its "Tibetan-ness," for listeners. Two Tibetan elders in particular have cooperated extensively with young musicians in exile by creating lyrics for the new genre of "modern" music. The late Professor Jampa Gyaltsen Dakton, introduced in the story at the start of this chapter, was closely involved with the development of modern Tibetan songs in exile up until his death shortly after I left Dharamsala. The name of a second elder, Professor Ngawang Jinpa, came up many times in conversations with Paljor about his music making, usually in the context of Paljor reminiscing about his early experiences playing rock and roll in his teens. After barely squeaking through high school at Darjeeling's Central School for Tibetans because of his weak Tibetan language skills and strong preference for playing guitar rather than studying, Paljor returned to an English-medium environment for postsecondary studies in 1981. While enrolled at St. Joseph's College, a Jesuit institution in Darjeeling, he participated in college-sponsored events oriented specifically toward Tibetan refugee audiences in the Gangtok-Kalimpong-Darjeeling area of Northeast India. Paljor's rock band provided musical interludes for original Tibetan dramas written and directed by St. Joseph's prestigious Tibetan language teacher, Ngawang Jinpa.

Professor Jinpa earned his *geshe* degree at Drepung monastery in Lhasa in 1959 and was abbot of Tharpa Choeling Monastery in Kalimpong (West Bengal, India) until 1963. He then resigned from his position, left the monkhood, and became a lecturer at St. Joseph's College. He currently serves as well on the faculties of the Manjushri Institute of Tibetan Culture and the Chakpoori Institute of Tibetan Medicine in Darjeeling, where he teaches Tibetan language, poetry, Buddhist philosophy, and history. Recognized widely as an important elder in exile, the professor was recently honored with a role in *Kundun*, the Hollywood film about the Dalai Lama's life. When I finally met Professor Jinpa in Darjeeling, during the last weeks of my year in India, he laughed out loud to learn that I was interested in researching "modern Tibetan songs." My flagging late-fieldwork interest in my research topic was boosted by his enthusiasm for the project: "This is really different, really special, not the normal dharma and grammar things people usually come to me for help with!" After conveying news about Paljor's family—"Ah! He who has three sons will rule the district!"—we made our way back to the topic of music, via stories of his former student's recent adventures with the Yak Band. The professor was clearly pleased that Paljor was pursuing his love of music, recalling that one of his primary motives for writing those first songs was to get his students interested in making Tibetan music, without depending on the traditional repertoire that the youth seemed to find boring. Four of the songs written by Jinpa.la during Paljor's college years were included on Paljor's first cassette (to the professor's great surprise).[26] This teacher's enthusiasm continues to bear fruit, since his son Namgyal is an amateur singer/songwriter who led Darjeeling's talented Choksum Band for a while before emigrating to Canada. Musicians in Dharamsala—particularly Ngodup, the Yak Band's drummer, who formerly played in the Choksum Band—acknowledge that this Darjeeling band had a distinct advantage over other Tibetan musical groups in that all their song lyrics were composed by Namgyal's accomplished father. While "boring" lyrics are remarkably tolerated by Tibetan listeners, beautifully poetic lyrics are truly appreciated.

This chapter has been concerned with what the lyrics (*shay tsig*) of modern Tibetan songs communicate to Tibetan audiences and, further, with *how* they communicate. As sacred sounds that index the holiness of the Tibetan language, as secular sounds associated with the political and cultural struggles of the community, as carriers of meaningful semantic information, and even as theoretically old-fashioned "reflections" of the social forces that in part produced them, the lyrics of modern songs contribute significantly and diversely to the ways in which Tibetan audiences listen to and appreciate this new musical genre. Further, the historical and formal attributes of the Tibetan language and the varying relationships Tibetans of different ages and backgrounds have with their "native" tongue have all influenced the form and niche of the modern song genre in exile. Attending to song texts within a larger analysis concerned with the dialectic nature of artistic expression gets us closer to, rather than farther away from, an understanding of how music creates sociability and of the "why" and "how" of the creation, performance, and consumption of sung sounds.

7 A Peek Through Ragged Tent Flaps and Heaven's Door
Concerts That Rupture and Bond

Having toured the different sounds that contribute to the musical environment of Dharamsala, and the Tibetan refugee community more widely, this final chapter focuses on the public concerts that uniquely bring many of these sounds together in a single place and time. These events—generally referred to as "rock concerts" because of their amplified technology and inclusion of Western music, although they always include modern Tibetan, Indian, and Nepali music as well—are considered here as profoundly revealing cultural performances in which many of the social dynamics and community-wide challenges raised throughout this book are enacted. Loud evening concerts offer a new way for this refugee community to come together, adding to the list of familiar public gatherings that includes religious teachings, political demonstrations, folk operas, school performances, New Year rituals, and annual holidays such as the Dalai Lama's birthday. Each of these kinds of gatherings foregrounds different aspects of the community's life, and rock concerts have added a new form of self-representation, and self-critique, to the mix.

As mentioned earlier, Bernice Martin has likened rock concerts to Victor Turner's liminal ritual stage, in the sense that they are "crucibles for social experimentation" (1979: 98). Like rock music itself, she argues, concerts both create *communitas* and expose or stimulate antagonism among participants. Indeed, as social events, Tibetan rock concerts provide an unprecedented forum for these refugees to enact their relationships to one another as kin or tightly bonded compatriots, resulting in deeply felt moments of solidarity. The concerts also, however, invite participants to reveal through their pleasure the inevitable (but carefully managed) fact that many practices and ideas borrowed from the foreign cultures that inform their daily lives as refugees have become deeply, even fondly, incorporated into their lives. Their pleasure risks revealing that the oppositional stance to otherness institutionalized by the dominant paradigm of cultural preservation and residential isolation in exile now raises for Tibetans the awkward question of when and how it is appropriate or necessary to oppose one another.

By juxtaposing the many ways of being Tibetan in exile, concerts provide a new and controversial venue where refugees can express their appreciation for Tibetan *and* non-Tibetan musics, revealing a level of comfort with cultural ambiguity and a passion for foreign culture that is worrisome to some in the community, including, ironically, many of the musicians themselves. As messengers or mirrors of fearful aspects of contemporary refugee culture, it is the musicians themselves who are often blamed for the trends displayed at their concerts. Because they create a venue for expressing controversial behaviors, many assume that they are the cause or catalyst of those behaviors, and they are thereby made into scapegoats for the community's "failings."

While my observations regarding the cultural and social dynamics of Tibetan rock concerts are informed by all the concerts I attended and participated in during my year in India, this chapter primarily presents ethnographic material from a fifteen-night series of concerts staged by the Yak Band in January 1995. Although this event took place two thousand miles away from Dharamsala, in a large tent erected at the Mundgod refugee settlement in South India, it played an important and lasting role in the community's cumulative impression of what rock and roll, rock concerts, and rock musicians are and the place they should or should not have in Tibetan cultural life.

Albeit intensified over the course of several weeks, the dynamics at the Kalachakra concerts were very similar to those seen at concerts in Dharamsala—in fact, a significant number of Dharamsala Tibetans attended—so it is useful to include this event in an analysis of Dharamsala's musical life and the investments Tibetan refugees have in cultural boundary making.[1]

This concert series also provided a unique opportunity for me, as anthropologist and keyboard player, to study a musical event again and again in the same context and from an onstage perspective. Further, the extended time frame enabled me to note and experience the truly dialogic nature of performance, since the content and performer-audience relations of each concert reflected the previous nights' experiences and anticipated the remaining concerts yet to come. Each day the band members had time to react to the last concert, reflect on the successes and failures of the tour as it unfolded, and rethink their plans for the next performance. The audiences, too, developed expectations via rumors and repeat attendance and brought these with them through the tent flaps. As a result, every concert was remarkably different, while each contributed to the narratives of the tour the band members ultimately carried away with them and still tell today, a social process by which this important event has been personally and publicly remembered. This chapter is one of these narratives, tracing the band's pilgrimage into the diaspora, its unforeseeable, bizarre, and troublesome experiences on tour, and the rough welcome received upon returning to Dharamsala. The Mundgod experience made the spring of 1995 a grim time for the band, a period during which the members painfully processed the insights into their community provided by the concert tour. Although my own narrative about and involvement with the Yaks goes on and remains unfinished, this chapter closes at a July 1995 concert held at Dharamsala's main temple in honor of the Dalai Lama's sixtieth birthday, an event that, in retrospect, marked the beginning of the end of the Yak Band, as well as the end of my time in Dharamsala.

A PILGRIMAGE INTO THE DIASPORA

In December 1994, the members of the Yak Band and their assistants loaded the group's bulky equipment onto a train in Delhi and traveled for three days to Mundgod, an agricultural Tibetan settlement in Karnataka State in south India. The Yaks had just recorded their first cassette (*Rangzen*) and were planning to release it for sale at the sacred Kalachakra teachings and initiation ceremony being offered by the Dalai Lama at Mundgod the following month, an event that fifty thousand Tibetan pilgrims from all over Nepal, Sikkim, Bhutan, India, Tibet, and overseas were expected to attend (including a significant percentage of Dharamsala's population).[2] The band had reserved in advance a barren cornfield at the hub of the rural settlement to stage a two-week series of rock concerts to promote their new Tibetan songs, raise money from ticket sales to cover travel and production expenses, and entertain the pilgrims. The journey was Herculean, highlighted with unreal images of lines of porters carrying electronic equipment across crowded train platforms and, at one point, five hundred new cassettes spilling out into puddles of winter rain. Once in Mundgod, the cornfield had to be leveled, an electrical generator and massive tent were hired and set up, and signs advertising the concerts and cassette were posted before the pilgrims even began to arrive.

Perhaps greater than the logistical difficulties of getting to Mundgod and setting up the concert stage were the personal and financial hurdles the Yaks had to overcome before even leaving Dharamsala, many of which are

Figure 19.   The Yak Band's concert tent in a winter cornfield at the Mundgod refugee settlement in southern India.

good illustrations of the specific constraints on musicians that have already been discussed. For those band members with families and employers skeptical of the trip's importance, the required two-month leave had to be negotiated through insecure promises of financial gains from the tour, on the one hand, and acceptance of leave without pay, on the other. The band's application to the Tibetan government-in-exile's small business opportunity fund for an advance loan for the recording and production of the cassette was only approved in time after the intervention of the Dalai Lama's brother (whose son is a friend of and occasional participant in the Yak Band) in the bureaucratic process. Bolstered by positive *mo* divinations by an eminent local rinpoche,[3] the band members pursued the project out of a belief that the community gathering at the Kalachakra was an appropriate venue for sharing their songs of praise for the Dalai Lama, longing for a homeland they have never seen, and compassion for their compatriots left behind in Tibet. They also hoped it would be a ripe opportunity to make the band financially viable, after years of dependence on personal loans and volunteerism.

For the Yaks, this tour represented a nearly two-month pilgrimage, venturing away from the center of the Tibetan exilic world far into India and

the diaspora. Unlike Dharamsala, Mundgod is rural, flat, humid, hot, isolated, and untouristed, and its Tibetan residents are primarily engaged in
agricultural work rather than commerce. In a sense, the Kalachakra event
recreated the diaspora in miniature in one place, since Tibetans from all
over the world gathered there. For this reason, the Yaks regarded this religious teaching as a prime opportunity for them to share their music and
their message with "brothers and sisters" they might never otherwise
meet. On setting out from Dharamsala, the band had multiple financial,
political, cultural, and personal goals. These hopes were all factored into the
overarching dream that if the tour were a success, it would legitimate the
Yak Band's musical mission in the eyes of the musicians' families, employers, and the wider community. Last, but not least, the Yaks, like all pilgrims
to the event, looked forward to receiving the long-life blessing offered by
the Dalai Lama at the end of the Kalachakra teachings.

I arrived in Mundgod as the first waves of pilgrims streamed in. This
normally quiet settlement was already buzzing with activity and excitement, since the Dalai Lama had arrived the previous evening, accompanied
by an unseasonal, and therefore extremely auspicious, light rain. The pilgrims, laden with huge bundles of provisions to last at least a fortnight,
made their way in family groups to the homes of friends and relatives scattered throughout the settlement's vast camps or to the temporary tent village that had been set up for visitors near the center of activity in Camp
Three. Across a free-flowing irrigation ditch from the tent village, I found
the Yak Band's enormous concert tent made of bamboo and brightly patterned expanses of red canvas. Inside, the Yaks were having tea on the elevated stage, surrounded by their familiar equipment, working on the set
list for that night's concert. We greeted each other happily and exchanged
news of the few weeks we had been apart. After they had filled me in on
their plans for the upcoming concert, I set off to find a room to rent in time
to return to perform.

The Yaks had already started selling their cassettes from a roadside table
equipped with speakers blaring out their new songs. Several other Tibetan
music groups from southern India had had the same idea, rendering the
dusty main thoroughfare of Camp Three into a festive and cacophonous
zone of sonic marketing. These stands were but a few in the sprawling
makeshift bazaar that had sprung up to serve the event and would soon
evolve into a capitalistic carnival. Indian *subjiwalla* had traveled from
nearby towns with vegetables to sell, monasteries throughout the diaspora
had sent representatives to campaign for contributions, entrepreneurs sold
Tibetan goods carried from Lhasa or Nepal, charities ran lotteries and

games, and dozens of families had set up makeshift restaurants with massive pots of noodles boiling on open fires. For two weeks, this market both grew and deteriorated as more merchants, beggars, and street performers joined in and as the presence of fifty thousand campers took its toll on the camp's weak infrastructure and on the landscape. In the midst of this dusty chaos, the Yaks quickly settled into something of a routine taking turns selling cassettes, sporadically attending the teachings, performing every night, eating late dinners in a friend's restaurant tent, sleeping on the stage (I slept in a monastery in the next camp), and occasionally making the ten-mile trip to town for supplies, cool *lassi* drinks, or a good protein-rich meal.

Across the road from the Yak Tent, beyond the bazaar, the Tibetan Institute of Performing Arts troupe had also set up a large canopy and stage for their own nightly performances of traditional Tibetan songs and dances. Although the group members never said anything antagonistic to one another, the competition between TIPA and the Yaks over audience turnout and cassette sales became evident and was made palpable through a subtle increase in volume each night (which actually said more about the size and condition of each group's rented generators than about its popularity). In reality, most pilgrims attended both performances, perhaps several times over, since there was nothing else to do for entertainment after the teachings ended each afternoon. Indeed, after the Yak Band's first concert, which was rained out, both tents were filled to capacity nearly every night for two weeks.

Despite their loudness and lateness, the Yak Band's rock concerts were not youth events as might be expected; rather, they were inclusive community performances. Pilgrims of all ages paid twenty rupees each to hear, most for the first time, live modern Tibetan music, and the band members interpreted the diversity and size of their audiences as an encouraging sign of widespread interest and support. Old refugees fingering prayer beads and clad in thick wool sat cross-legged in the front row, eager to find out what these young Tibetans were up to, unaware of the enormous speakers looming only a few feet away until the band plugged in for a sound check. Groups of young women sat together giggling and chatting midway back in the audience, while their male counterparts, wearing jeans and bandannas, squatted around the edges eager to leap up and dance. Families attended, with several generations gathered together on picnic blankets. Kids gathered around the front of the stage, occasionally fiddling with equipment and the coils of wires or tugging on the singers' pants to ask a question or pull a funny face. And, for the first few nights, young monks from the local monasteries attended the concerts in droves, turning the audience into a sea of maroon robes, until their abbots found out and imposed a strict curfew on them.

THE POLITICS OF THE SET LIST

The Yak Band concerts always opened with an uplifting, extended version of the popular title song of the band's cassette, during which the audience was encouraged to sing along with the song's repeated calls for *rangzen:*

> The main responsibility of we, the Tibetan people,
> Is to regain our national independence.
> All of us Tibetan people must do
> What we are required to do.

Starting sweet and plain, "Rangzen" gently draws in the audience, creating an intimate feeling in any situation. Intense and immediate *communitas* was always evoked by this gentle song, whose lyrics, written by the elderly astrologist Asterix, go straight to the heart of the Tibetan Cause and remind each Tibetan of his or her role in the struggle. It was a powerful and artful beginning to the performance.

> Regaining independence,
> That is the one and only thing.
> Not only must it be achieved,
> It is worth doing, and it can be done.
> Independence! Independence! Independence!

We loved this song, too, and played it well, though never the same way twice. The strong chords of the chorus contrast perfectly with the melodic verses and invite the audience to sing along with Paljor's calls for independence.

> One wonders, after seeing endless blood flowing like a waterfall
> And the whole countryside filled with human corpses.
> Generally, that is the way.
> But we, according to His Holiness's wishes,
> By the peaceful, nonviolent way of truth and honesty,
> We must endeavor to the ultimate end.
> Independence! Independence! Independence!
> Independence! Independence! Independence!
> Independence! Independence! Independence!

By the end of the song, Paljor's solo breaks were loud and wailing into the night. Fans raised their fists, some even shed quiet tears, and many sang along. Paljor was always reluctant to let the song go, repeating the chorus until the moment's magic finally started to fade. *Rangzen! Rangzen! Rangzen!*

From there, the evening's entertainment unfolded over the course of two hours with a set list carefully crafted by Thubten, the band's leader, to include their original modern Tibetan songs (50 percent), "English" rock songs (25 percent), and Hindi and Nepali songs (25 percent). The first set generally featured all modern Tibetan songs, almost exclusively drawn from the band's new cassette. During this part of the concert, the audience showed its appreciation for songs titled "Fatherland," "An Appeal to Those Left Behind," "Holder of the Lotus," "Foreign Land," and "Girlfriend Who Stole My Heart" by listening quietly and attentively and clapping very briefly at the end of each tune. Almost as if the event were a continuation of the afternoon's religious teachings, the audience sat still during these sets with passive expressions on their faces, thinking, apparently, about the losses and sorrowful challenges the song lyrics urged them to remember. I had become accustomed to this listening style in Dharamsala, but I had to keep wrestling with the impression that our audiences were simply bored, or stunned by the noise. Even Paljor yearned for more overt signs of appreciation from his fellow Tibetans while he performed his original songs. "They just sit there like a bunch of *torma!*" he complained to me one night. *Torma* are phallic-shaped ritual sculptures made out of butter that jiggle ever so slightly when jarred. This image so aptly described our audiences during these first sets that for nights after Paljor made this comment I could hardly look out at the crowd and keep a straight face. One of the only times any discernable reaction was elicited from the audience during the first set (other than during "Rangzen") was when a large cobra was detected in the fourth row and our volunteer ticket collectors dramatically wrestled it into a burlap sack while we played on.

After the intermission, this whole dynamic changed. During the second set, Thubten creatively mixed rock, reggae, blues, Hindi film songs, Nepali tunes, and other modern Tibetan songs, creating a palpable air of anticipation in the tent with this randomness. Set lists from these sessions read like a postmodern celebration of global flow: Bob Dylan's "Knockin' on Heaven's Door" drifted into a blues number sung in Tibetan, followed by a macho Hindi film tune, Bob Marley's "Buffalo Soldier," and a blessing song for the Dalai Lama's long life. The audience was mesmerized, confused, and thrilled all at once by this rapid-fire juxtaposition of genres that index such different emotions and such a variety of cultural commitments and connections for them. While a good portion of the audience managed to maintain its reserve, many in the audience cheered and hooted, young men and

boys danced, and the crowds grew larger every night. The band was satis-
factorily fulfilling its various roles as activist-entertainers, the audiences
were enjoying themselves, and the tour seemed to be off to a successful
start.

After the first week, however, the Yak Band's well-planned balance between Tibetan and other kinds of music gradually began to shift. Increasingly during the thoughtful first set, even before the last chords of a Tibetan song had faded away, bold voices from the crowd started calling out
and pleading for Hindi film songs by name. The Yaks ignored this feedback
for a while, profoundly hurt that, even in the context of a sacred cultural
and religious gathering, their fellow Tibetans openly preferred silly Indian
love songs to the band's original Tibetan offerings. However, as cassette
sales during the day slowed down after an initial burst and concerns about
breaking even on the tour grew, the "salt and pepper" for the concerts
gradually became, in one band member's words, their "bread and butter."
By increasing the number of Hindi songs in the set list (at the equal expense of Tibetan, Western, and Nepali numbers), the band brought people
back night after night, curious to hear which new film songs the Yaks
might play and eager to have their favorites repeated. Indians who had set
up stalls in the bazaar, taxi drivers, and even locals from the town ten miles
away from the refugee settlement started attending the concerts in small
numbers too, as word (and the sounds themselves) spread out from the Yak
Band's tent. The Yaks did not go along with their fans' desires without resistance. They had intended the film songs to play a similar role in these
concerts as they do in Indian films, where there is distinct dichotomy between plot and song. Seated cross-legged on the outdoor stage counting
ticket stubs after each evening's performance, the Yaks expressed disappointment in their Tibetan audiences and frustration at being compelled to
compromise the group's politically and socially informed goals of creating
and promoting *Tibetan* music.

The musicians' confusion about their audience's contradictory expectations—enthusiasm for the unique experience of seeing and hearing young
Tibetans performing modern music coupled with demands that the very
Tibetan-ness of the event be overwhelmed by foreign sounds—was evident in their own contradictory responses to the Mundgod crowd. By increasing the number of Hindi songs they played—actually, by playing
Hindi, Western, or Nepali songs at all—the band had clearly established its
willingness to expand its repertoire beyond "modern Tibetan music." The
Yaks had also thereby established their willingness to open up their concerts to the tensions that inevitably accompany culturally jumbled prac-

Figure 20.   Yaks working on the next concert's set list over a pot of Tibetan soup *(thukpa).*

tices in this refugee community. In fact, perhaps because of the extended holiday feeling of the whole Kalachakra event, its suspension from routine in a place that was home to few, these tensions were being thoroughly enjoyed by the audience. Unexpectedly, it was finally the band itself that donned the conservative mantle and stepped in to scold the public for its tastes and behavior, first through parody and eventually by deferring to traditional authority.

By the beginning of the second week of the concert series, the careful cultural balance Thubten had aspired to maintain had been completely upset. The crowds were enormous, topping out at 1,100 people one night, at which point the canvas walls literally bulged and ripped, allowing even more curious pilgrims to squeeze in. The Yaks spontaneously played so many new Hindi and Nepali songs each night without rehearsing beforehand that I found myself sitting off stage more and more, watching the crowd or wandering around, until someone shouted for me to jump back up behind the keyboard to play my part in one of our old standards. Every night young boys crowded in front of the stage wearing sunglasses and bandannas tied around their heads, gyrating their hips in imitation of the macho man who sings the film hit "Mast, Mast" (Sexy, sexy), small packs of Indian men moved through these same dance steps here and there in the audience, and one night a Tibetan businessman with a disastrous voice somehow convinced Thubten to let him stand at the microphone and passionately sing his favorite song with the band jamming dutifully behind him.[4] We even received a pink letter through the mail from a Tibetan pilgrim from Kashmir—"To The Director, Yak Band, Camp No. 3"—requesting, very formally, specific songs on the specific nights the writer expected to attend:

> Sub: Request for playing the song of a film
>
> Dear Sir,
> We heartily request that kindly [sic] take some trouble to play the song of film we are mentioning below. We will be highly grateful to you.
>
> Film: 1. *Phul our Angeor*
>
> 2. *Dalal* and
>
> 3. *Khudhar*
>
> 4. Ladakhi song
>
> Any one song from the above mentioned song. Please play it on 11th or 12th of Jan. 95. We will come to your band on these both days. Thanking you in anticipation.
>
> Faithfully yours,
> Tsewang Ngochuk and Party

The word was out, and things were getting tense on stage. The situation had taken on a life of its own, and we were all feeling increasingly distanced from what was happening each night, so far was the scene from anything we had imagined back in Dharamsala. The local beer (called "Knock Out") was playing an increasingly fundamental part in keeping up the confidence of certain band members, to extraordinary musical effect but much to the detriment of in-group relations. Thubten, who didn't drink and objected to having the band's scarce rupees being spent on alcohol, kept his group of homesick, dispirited, tired, and grubby musicians together. He proved himself to be a master at reading the audience—keeping them coming and keeping them under control—and, as band leader, made big decisions informed largely by the boxes of unsold cassettes stored backstage[5] and the outstanding government loan he had worked so hard to obtain. He was also deeply depressed by the scene, however, and, despite his natural charm on stage, barely veiled his resentment as he cranked out hit song after hit song, thrilling the crowds. As he later told me, "If we'd only played Tibetan songs one night, the next night the tent would have been empty."

During one concert that had been punctuated throughout with desperate calls for various film hits, Thubten, who sang all the Hindi numbers, finally gifted the audience with an extremely popular film song called "Holé! Holé!" While singing the chorus, the trickster in him took over and he began coyly flicking his cheek with his index finger in rhythm with the music. Although the words have no referential meaning in Hindi (they could be glossed as "Wow! Wow!" or "Oh! Oh!"), in the Tibetan language they roughly mean "Shame on you!" when accompanied by this cheek-flicking gesture. It is most commonly used by mothers dealing with mischievous children; often the gesture alone, along with a stern look, is enough to rein in restless kids in a quiet setting like a temple. With a huge grin on his face and singing in the flirtatious manner of Indian film stars, apparently participating in the audience's ecstasy at having coaxed the band to play this Hindi favorite, Thubten simultaneously and openly scolded the crowd for enjoying themselves so much. But Thubten's satisfaction from this parodic turn was only momentary and seemed to actually increase the naughty thrill of the moment for the young Tibetan men and boys who invariably jumped to their feet and wiggled their hips upon hearing the first trumpeting notes of this song emerge from the keyboard synthesizer.

Frustrated, the Yak Band finally decided that some integrity could be restored to the whole project if the band's founder, who had come from Chicago to participate in the Kalachakra concerts, took the opportunity during intermission to recount to the crowd his personal story of presenting the Dalai Lama with the idea for a modern Tibetan band years earlier and receiving his blessing. Every night for the remainder of the series, therefore, the band's stout elder eloquently presented the group's origin myth in the somber rhetorical style of formal Tibetan speeches. These brief orations aimed to legitimize the band's commitment to creating and playing modern Tibetan music by deferring to the authority of someone adored by everyone present—the teacher and leader they had come all the way to Mundgod to revere and learn from—and attempted to reaffirm the Tibetan refugee community's shared responsibility to support its threatened culture. The comments were heartfelt, coming from a young man with a U.S. green card who, as he explained, now had an outsider's perspective on the Tibetan community-in-exile and could see very clearly the vulnerability of his people's ancient culture. The speeches did, momentarily, succeed in defusing the tension that built up between the performers and the audience each evening (particularly during the first set, which Thubten still made an effort to keep completely Tibetan). However, rather than encouraging the audience to hoot and cheer and dance to the Tibetan numbers, these sober reminders of each Tibetan's responsibility to respect his or her heritage only increased the solemnity and concentration with which they listened to the Tibetan songs, probably making the emotional release of the Hindi film songs in the second set all the more welcome. Privately, the band's founder likened the Yak Band to Elvis Presley, explaining to me that, like the "King," the Yaks weren't the best musicians in the world but they were trying to do something new that the audience was still unsure of. Once they broke through the barriers, like those posed by the Mundgod crowds, he told me, the band could work on refining what it is doing.

The complexity of these moments—a Tibetan refugee rock band calling for cultural commitment from a film-crazed yet patriotic audience while fragments of TIPA's high-pitched traditional opera arias drifted out of another tent across the fields under a balmy night sky in India—was not lost on the band members. The dilemma fueled many conversations during the days and months following the tour, revealing a growing awareness among the Yaks and others that their modern rock songs and live concerts were addressing borderlines other than the geographical one defining their status as political refugees.

Most Tibetan refugees are only gradually allowing themselves to confront the ambiguities that exist in their community and in their lives. By juxtaposing a variety of musics and providing a place for Tibetans to express their different relationships to these sounds (and to the respective cultures they represent), rock concerts are bringing the boundaries that have both arisen and dissolved between these musics (and between Tibetans and other ethnic groups) to a conscious level, thereby opening up a space for defensive, constructive, angry, and reflexive discussions about the usefulness of these distinctions and revealing fissures between the ideal and lived relationships most refugees have with those boundaries. Rather than the songs themselves, the radical aspect of the modern Tibetan music movement in Dharamsala has proven to be the way live multicultural music performances put the community itself on stage, an unintended consequence that has taken the musicians by surprise as much as anyone else.

KNOCKIN' ON HEAVEN'S DOOR

While the Yaks and their lay audiences were engaged in the intense nightly negotiations just described, another drama was unfolding in and around the Yak tent that would further complicate the band's attempts to gain acceptance as a cultural and political voice for the Tibetan community-in-exile. The band's highly visible (and highly audible) contributions to the party atmosphere in Camp Three made it a focus of attention for those disturbed by the increasingly obvious tensions at the Kalachakra between the sacred and secular aspects of the event. Indeed, no one present could fail to note the ironic contradictions between the context and content of the Dalai Lama's holy afternoon teachings held under white canvas canopies in a field and the dusty scene in Camp Three a kilometer away, where many of the pilgrims lived, shopped, ate, gossiped, defecated, entertained themselves, and slept the other twenty hours of the day. The contrast between the profound explication of a high tantric initiation ceremony by the Dalai Lama draped in saffron and gold seated high above a quiet expanse of high lamas, monks, and lay devotees and the crush of jeeps and bodies, dust and screeching loudspeakers nearby was physically and emotionally shocking. The event was clearly serving many purposes at once, including, as it turned out, providing a welcome interruption of routine for the thousands of young monks who live permanently in the large Tibetan monasteries located in the Mundgod settlement.

From my perspective onstage, it seemed that the entire audience at the first Yak concert in Mundgod was, somewhat surprisingly, made up of monks. *A sea of robes,* I wrote in my field notes late that night. The monks were young. Some were surely serious about their studies, but, as I came to learn, many here in the south were newly arrived adolescents from Tibet with little Buddhist training who had found the monasteries to be an appropriate source of free food and lodging until they decided what to do with themselves in exile. Those present in the Yak tent that night clearly enjoyed themselves, although in a very understated way, pulling their robes up over their heads to cover entranced smiles. Still tired from my train journey the night before, and happy to be performing again, I found the unexpected scene wonderfully amusing. Dylan's "Knockin' on Heaven's Door" took on new dimensions for me that night, as we bopped through its trancelike refrain for these aspirants to nirvana.[6] The monks seemed especially fond of Ngodup, the young drummer who occasionally stepped forward to sing a song in his high falsetto voice, and they called for him to do an encore. *"Oooh Baby, I love your way, everyday"* he shyly crooned, swaying, to the few dozen monks who lingered around after the show had ended. I returned to my room after the concert in a jeep crammed with happy religious novices humming the tune to "Rangzen."

On the second night, the first ticket holders to line themselves up on the front row of mats were again young monks. No sooner had they settled in, however, than they leapt up in a panic, dashed backstage, and fled out of a gap in the tent in a maroon blur. They literally dove through our equipment and out of the curtains into the dry cornfields beyond, having somehow sensed that one of their teachers was approaching. Word had evidently gotten out among the authorities that a significant number of monks had had a lot of fun in the Yak Tent the night before, so now our audiences were being patrolled by *geshe* (teachers) bearing large sticks and official badges. After making sure the tent was monk free, the *geshe* guarded the entrances. Halfway through the concert, these disciplinarians created a stir in the audience when, during Eric Clapton's "Living on Tulsa Time" or some equally incongruous song, a line of six of them entered the tent and processed methodically through the audience, stepping over our fans, and across the front of the stage, peering into the audience to catch a glimpse of maroon. I was truly afraid they would find a monk-fan and beat him up on the spot, but luckily their charges had been forewarned. Soon after the teachers left, the power went completely dead and the lights and sound fizzled away, even though the rented generator (named "Shiva," after the creative and destructive energy of the universe) was still running out on the cornfield. Phuntsok quickly set to work fixing the connection, which we all suspected had been disrupted when one of the young monks squatting in the darkness behind the tent, peering through holes in the canvas, had accidentally tripped over it.

We were very surprised, after this drama, to find the tent once again packed with monks a few nights later. I asked the band's founder if we should warn them about the disciplinarians, and he said he had heard that today was a holiday for the monks. His understanding, however, was that they had only been given permission to attend the traditional TIPA performance across the way, which he thought was ridiculous. If the concern is about "entertainment," he argued, then they should be consistent and ban everything. Despite this rumor, the evening went smoothly, without any trouble for the monks. A week later, out of the blue, they were back again. It was another holiday, we assumed. The *geshe* only made one more appearance during the concert series, when they paraded through the tent without warning one night, ruining "Rangzen" by creating a spectacle when they dramatically dragged a monk disguised in plain clothes out of the entrance by his ear. The song fizzled, and we stopped mid-chorus shaking our heads until the crowd settled down.

Financially, the absence of monks night after night was a real blow to the band, although many did buy cassettes. Without them, the audiences settled at about four or five hundred people, compared with more than one thousand when they were there. The band was confused by the seemingly erratic

Figure 21.   Refueling "Shiva," the Yak Band's generator.

manner in which the monastery authorities were controlling their students' concert attendance. Already feeling rejected by the their lay audiences, the band could only take the bans as an overt sign of official disapproval and lack of understanding of the band's mission. During a break in the teachings one afternoon I asked a monk friend his opinion on the matter. He felt that TIPA's *lhamo* was acceptable for monks to see, because the operas tell stories that are about real life, educating people about historical events and teaching them how to deal with real emotions and the existential trials of samsara. On the other hand, he continued, rock music just "disturbs the heart by creating desire." I refrained from sharing with him my existential experience playing "Knockin' on Heaven's Door" a few nights earlier and instead asked what he thought about rock music with Tibetan lyrics about

His Holiness and Tibetan freedom. That stumped him a bit, as it does most people, but he maintained that listening to music is generally disruptive to attempts to maintain an "ethical monastic life."

I later learned from the director of TIPA, Ngodup Tsering, that the monks were, in fact, forbidden to attend *any* concerts after the first night. The director had challenged this decision immediately by complaining to the Minister of Religion and Culture, Kelsang Yeshi, a former monk himself. Ngodup Tsering argued that TIPA's traditional material is "for all Tibetans" and not just laypeople. The minister then met with the abbots of the Drepung and Gomang monasteries and convinced them to grant one free night to their monks to allow them to attend special TIPA performances for monks only. I surmised that those were the nights when the Yak tent had been packed with monks who had been set free but had opted for an alternate show. The Yaks had, evidently, received some residual benefit from TIPA's plea of cultural integrity. Back in Dharamsala, Kelsang Yeshi elaborated to me that the abbots' concern was not specifically about the content of the TIPA performance (the Yak concert was never considered permissible); rather, they were worried about the impressions it would give the laypeople at the Kalachakra if they saw monks intermingling with women at a public nighttime performance. Once out and about, of course, the temptation to then linger at the shops and cafés in Camp Three would also be great. The abbots were evidently confident that they could control their own monks, but they were worried about the behavior of unknown monks visiting from other places, over whom they had less authority. The minister felt that so many monks had sneaked over to the Yak tent because of the novelty of the event, the lure of the unknown, since most know what to expect from TIPA. He was not surprised by their choice and seemed aware of the risks of cultural preservation, including the possibility that highly choreographed "traditional" performances eventually lack vitality and cause audiences and artists alike to become bored. The crux of the Kalachakra dilemma concerning monks and entertainment, he concluded, was concern for the reputation of the sangha in the public eye, which accounts somewhat for the showy comportment of the disciplinarians. Unfortunately, he observed, as in Dharamsala, the only monks people see are the ones roaming around town wearing high-top sneakers and watching videos. The ones studying in their rooms are invisible.

The abbots had, without doubt, genuine grounds for concern about the Yak Band's Kalachakra concerts, with their mix of rock and pop and general craziness. The band's modern Tibetan songs, however, extracted from the controversial setting of live performances like those described here, remain

Figure 22.   Monks buying Yak Band cassettes at the Kalachakra gathering in Mundgod.

very popular among Tibetan monks everywhere. These unlikely fans, the band feels, are the ones who may have the most genuine understanding of the motivations and sentiments behind their patriotic songs.

THE RETURN TO LIMINALITY

By the final days of the concert series, the physical and emotional infrastructure of the Yak Band had all but collapsed. Camp Three itself was a disaster area, with food supplies running short, litter carpeting the fields, and water for bathing and laundry all but dried up. The irrigation ditch that had been flowing freely through the fields when I arrived a fortnight earlier was clogged with plastic bags and sat stagnant. Even the Indian street performers lining the road had gotten weirder, the latest arrivals having necks, cheeks, and chests punctured with various pieces of metal and spending their afternoons in the bazaar whipping themselves to the beat of a drum. Although this scene was enough to make anyone pray fervently for a quick release from consciousness, all the tens of thousands of pilgrims (including the Yaks who had hardly attended any teachings thus far) dressed up in traditional *chuba* and walked across to the ceremonial tents to make offerings of biscuits, bananas, sweets, and bread and partake in the long-life *puja* that marked the end of the Dalai Lama's holy presence at the Mundgod settlement.

The following day everyone lined up for miles to see the sacred sand mandala that had been created by the Namgyal Monastery's monks while the Dalai Lama had been guiding his followers through its visualization. Later that afternoon the intricate and colorful creation would be casually swept up into a gray pile and poured away, an enactment by the monks of the fundamentally important quality of nonattachment to which Buddhists aspire. I waited under umbrellas in the heat and dust with Phuntsok, the band's bass player, who was quite dismayed to hear the Ah-Ka-Ma Band's cassette of modern Tibetan songs blaring from the same temple speakers that had, for the past ten days, been broadcasting the Dalai Lama's teachings. While it seemed clear to me that Ah-Ka-Ma, as part of TIPA, was deemed safe and official (unlike the Yaks), Phuntsok was sure that if the authorities had a copy of the Yak Band's cassette they would be playing it as well. His hunger for the band's acceptance was admirably persistent, and I reflected while waiting in line on the mixed messages the group had received recently from its community.

Our fifteenth and final concert was a delirious carnival, made all the more festive when thousands of lottery tickets were dumped on the stage during an intermission drawing. During the beloved "Holé! Holé!" people scooped up armfuls of tickets and threw them in the air in celebration. I shouted something to a volunteer backstage about what a mess we would have to clean up, and he shouted back for me not to worry: "When they plow the fields again, it will all get turned under!" Such was the ambiance of the night. In the morning, men came in a rickety truck, rolled up the massive, battered tent, and gathered the bamboo poles. Beyond, exhausted families were piling into jeeps, cabs, buses, and bullock carts to begin their long journeys home, and the bazaar was flattened into heaps of bundles. By nightfall, we were left camping amid our boxed equipment on a stage now isolated in a snowdrift of discarded lottery tickets in the middle of a trampled field. In the predawn light, we packed up the back of a gaudily painted Goods Carrier truck Thubten had somehow managed to procure in town and rumbled off to the city of Miraj, where we hoped to catch any train north.

Back home in Dharamsala after the long journey, I settled for a while into a quiet routine in the extreme cold and calm of the off-season. The Yak Band's return to the capital-in-exile was, however, less serene. For a start, their families were not greeted with envelopes stuffed with profits. Despite resentful local rumors that the band had gotten rich in the south, the band in fact came up fifty thousand rupees (approximately $1,500) short after Thubten had paid their expenses and distributed five thousand rupees "pocket money" to each musician. The Yak from Chicago had to forward the money to pay off the debt and keep the band afloat until the remaining cassettes could be sold or distributed at below-wholesale prices to Tibetan shops throughout northern India and Nepal. In addition to these troubles, some residents of Dharamsala—perhaps those same individuals Marcia Calkowski observed assuming the role of "cultural censors" who take it upon themselves to "judge the appropriateness of particular cultural items or events" (1991: 648)—had strong criticisms of the band's rumored sell-out in Mundgod to Indian pop culture. When the Yaks pointed out the audience's role in the situation, many Dharamsala Tibetans distanced themselves from the Kalachakra fans' behavior, insisting that Tibetans in the south have become embarrassingly "Indianized," whereas Tibetan ways have been better preserved in the capital-in-exile. Obviously, I consoled the band, these people have never attended one of your concerts in Dharamsala and witnessed the same glee over *filmi geet* that derailed the Mundgod tour. As one old Tibetan saying reminds us, "When you point your finger to blame someone else, three fingers are pointing back at you."

To make matters worse for the band, the Dalai Lama himself included some critical comments about "getting the habits of other people" in his annual speech to the Tibetan parliament in February 1995, which some of the band's critics and relatives latched onto to bolster their complaints. The band was so paranoid at this point that they wondered who had planted a bug in the Dalai Lama's ear after the Kalachakra debacle:

> In Dharamsala and other places like it that are a little "fast," . . . per-sonalities are changing in this society. There is nowhere to lay the blame. We are staying in someone else's land and getting the habits of other people . . . For example, it seems that in our society we like the music, dance, and customs of other countries. I think this doesn't affect one's character that much. However, if things do gradually affect one's character, then what? I see this as a very great danger.

The Dalai Lama's comments, along with the criticism from outspoken community members and relatives, had several band members convinced that the Yaks would never be able to perform again in Dharamsala once the speech was published. When I suggested that they were overreacting, one Yak said I was obviously a terrible anthropologist and had not learned anything about how his community works, about "how people in Dharamsala like to bring other people down."

In addition to the unfounded gossip, better thought-out and constructive critiques of the Yak Band were forthcoming from individuals in the
community with an informed perspective on the situation. TIPA's director
expressed to me his disappointment that the Yaks had played so much
Hindi music at the Kalachakra, since the Dalai Lama had supported the
Yaks as a *Tibetan* band and they therefore had a responsibility to stick to
their stated mission. They had, he said, a responsibility to lead or educate
the audience, teach them to appreciate Tibetan songs, and not simply cater
to the current "Hindi craze." While he had ready explanations for the appeal of Hindi film songs to Tibetans—among them, the media cult created
around movie stars, the eclectic diversity of the music, and the accessibility
of the genre's themes and lyrics—he found the situation in the south "de-
pressing" and returned to Dharamsala resolved to send more TIPA artistes
on tour around the rural settlements to increase the familiarity of Tibetans
in the south with their own traditional culture. Another friendly critic of
the band, a young scholar with radical aspirations, told me he felt the Yaks
were "too tame" and "too constrained by what other people think of
them." We talked at length about the connection between rock and roll and
revolution, and my own culturally informed and long-suppressed disappointment in the Yak Band for always playing it so safe, despite my understanding of the challenges they face, made its way into the conversation.
We half-joked that it seemed, despite all the political rhetoric circulating in
the community, that the average Tibetan's notion of revolutionary activity
often seems simply to involve praying very hard that the Dalai Lama will
come up with a solution to everything soon.

When Thubten announced in early February that he was leaving the
band and moving to faraway Kalimpong, we all knew that it was, to use one
of his favorite expressions, "chapter closed" for the Yak Band. Before starting my fieldwork, I had read that villagers in "old Tibet" sometimes used
their precious yaks ritually as scapegoats for their community's misfortune and confusion by means of a "ransom-substitute ceremony"
(Palmieri 1970: 76). According to Richard Palmieri, a chosen animal was
symbolically saddled with the guilt and evil spirits of the community by
means of magical formulae and literally driven away with sticks to be
killed by whomever came across it or to become the prey of wild animals.
In this way, the animal assumed the guilt for sins believed to have caused
whatever misfortune had occurred. This bit of folklore haunted me as I
reflected on Thubten's decision and the combination of forces that had led
him to make such a bold move.

Leading the Yak Band had been Thubten's full-time job in Dharamsala, and the burden of dealing with the logistics of the disappointing cassette and tour projects had largely been his. The band's situation was only one of a number of urgent personal and professional motivations behind moving on, and he had chosen simply to tell everyone that he needed to "fulfill his duty as a son and take care of his old mother in Kalimpong." Two days before he left, Thubten came by my house to chat openly about his life and his decision to leave in a way he had never done before. Motorcycle helmet under his arm, cheeks stuffed with tobacco, he settled in my chair for three hours, refusing tea and twisting his mustache, and told his story.

He talked about his family and about the members of the band, but, ultimately, Thubten was in fact most dejected by the lack of official and community support for the Yak Band. He observed, by way of comparison, that

> in America, if a kid is good at sports, then his school supports him, and the government gives him scholarships so he can develop his skills. They do this because when he becomes world famous or wins a medal, everyone says, "American!" I want the band to succeed so people will say, "Tibetan!" not "Thubten!"

He also felt disgusted with himself for giving in to the Kalachakra audiences, remembering that when he was serving in the Indian army, his heart "was only thinking for freedom." Making political Tibetan music had been a way of continuing that struggle after being discharged from the military, but

> now we make a cassette of Tibetan songs called "Rangzen" about *rangzen* and out of fifty thousand Tibetan refugees attending the Kalachakra, one thousand buy a cassette. What's going on? People have forgotten everything!

He paused, looking so forlorn I expected him to howl out loud in despair, but his eyes landed on the red knotted blessing cord I had worn around my neck since attending the Kalachakra teachings. We all had them and planned to wear them until they fell off on their own. His eyes lit up. "Mrs. Anthropologist, you know why it has nine knots?" he prodded, brow furrowed in mock condescension. "No, please tell me, sir." And the old Thubten was back, going on about hungry witches and kids trapped in boxes and eight close calls with death and the evil forces giving up just then, "which is why you need *nine* knots to protect you." He rose to go, the mischievous grin back in place, and ordered me to be up at the Yak Shack the next evening at 7:00 "English time," meaning five minutes early.

The band members met at the taxi stand and rode up to Thubten's farewell dinner together on motorcycles. The evening light was clear and made the snow peaks shimmer white and then pink against the blue of the Himalayan winter sky. The house was warm and the mood quite somber as we drank tea, listened to our cassette, told stories, and nibbled on the snacks that emerged one by one from the kitchen where Phuntsok was choreographing a banquet. Fearing thieves and animals, he had actually padlocked the tiny kitchen during the day because he had bought so much meat. We settled ourselves on the mattresses that had been arranged in a rectangle in the altar room, and soon Sangay.la, the band's founder from Chicago, stood up and made a very formal speech, using the same intonations as he had during the intermissions in Mundgod. Everyone listened with downcast eyes as he expounded on the old Tibetan saying, "All things that come together must be separated." Thubten stood when asked and bent over deferentially as Sangay.la draped around his neck a silk *khata* that reached the floor and was decorated with the eight auspicious symbols. Thubten accepted a *thangka* painting rolled up in newspaper and mumbled a few comments in response. He sat down and wiped away his tears with the end of the *khata*. There was a moment of silence. Eventually, someone said something funny, and Paljor pulled out his beat-up guitar and played a musical *"Tashi delek"* for Thubten, filling the space during which no one could think what to say. Then the food came—mutton curry, pork ribs, roasted chicken, noodle salad, rice, red hot chili sauce, and the wok-baked chocolate chip cookies I had made earlier in the day. After dinner, Tenzin Lodoe ("Kush") drove "Uncle," Paljor, and me home down the mountain in style in his mother's government-issued Gypsy jeep. Good-byes to Thubten were deferred until the next day when we would put him on the overnight bus to Delhi buried in more *khata* and good wishes. As the bus pulled away in a cloud of diesel smoke, I consoled myself by remembering that other prize yaks in "old Tibet" were occasionally purchased from the butcher and liberated as a way for individuals and communities to earn extra merit.

FOR HIS HOLINESS THE DALAI LAMA

The town became preoccupied with *Losar* celebrations, and the band members spun out in their own directions, preoccupied with jobs and families or simply hanging out more on the steps of friends' shops in McLeod Ganj. We got together to jam a few times and socialized over meals, but I turned my attention to other aspects of my research that had been shelved for months by this time. At the end of March, Thubten, who had only gotten as far as the refugee camp in Delhi by that time, came back to Dharamsala for a visit, so we spontaneously put on a concert in the TIPA auditorium. The tickets sold out immediately and the applause was loud, which gave the band a boost in morale—they *were* popular, just not exactly for the reasons they had hoped.

I traveled a lot in April and May, visiting other Tibetan settlements in the Himalayan foothills, and settled back down in Dharamsala in June. Catching up on the news with Paljor on my sunny cement roof one day, I learned that a member of the original Snow Lion Band had recently moved back to Dharamsala after abandoning a romance in France. He had none of Thubten's musical ability or charm but was a "senior member" and expected to be accommodated by the band. There followed some agonizing rehearsals in which Paljor patiently tried to teach Tenzin the basic chords to the Yak Band's well-known songs and other rock-and-roll standards. Paljor allowed himself to pass me a desperate look as we plodded through the Rolling Stones' "Can't Get No Satisfaction" one afternoon, and I nodded back in sympathy. I was on the verge of offering to play rhythm guitar myself to save us the embarrassment of ever performing publicly in such a weakened state, but I knew it was not my place to contradict the path the Yaks felt obligated to follow out of respect for someone with whom they did not actually want to play. We all missed Thubten greatly during this time.

The Yaks were forcing themselves to get their act together, despite the circumstances, because of the upcoming celebrations for the Dalai Lama's sixtieth birthday (*Trungkar*). In honor of the event, the town's Welfare Office was organizing a morning of performances by community groups eager to make song and dance offerings to the Dalai Lama, who would be in attendance. The Yaks had submitted a request to be added to the program and, as a well-established and popular fixture in the town, fully expected to be included. I was eating a plateful of tofu and vegetables at Friends Corner when Paljor turned up in a bad mood, sat down at my table, and ordered a Coke. The uncharacteristic Coke meant he was having stomach troubles, which meant he was upset. The Welfare Officer had just called Paljor at his office to say that he was sorry but he had "completely forgotten" to put the Yak Band on the official program for tomorrow's activities at the temple. I could see the ghosts of the Kalachakra experience awakening in Paljor; he clearly suspected that the omission had not been accidental, and the effect this doubt had on him was devastating. He had, in fact, hung up on the Welfare Officer, an unthinkable act that had rattled him even more. For weeks the band had been anticipating *Trungkar*, convinced of the importance of having the Dalai Lama see and hear for himself what the band was doing, since the leader had not heard them perform live since 1989.

After an afternoon of bureaucratic negotiations, the Welfare Officer proposed that the Yak Band could take over the stage at the temple after the official program was over. While this meant that His Holiness would no longer be in the audience, which was a great disappointment, it did mean that we could play as long as we liked, rather than fitting into the tight schedule of the official program. We rehearsed late into the night, borrowed jeeps from friends at the Namgyal Monastery, and transported our equipment down the mountain to the central temple under a full moon.

I dressed in my best *chuba* and met Tsering Lhanzom at Friends Corner for an early breakfast. It was a bittersweet holiday for us, since this was also my last day in Dharamsala, and we asked her father-in-law to take photos of us in his rooftop garden. Everyone in town was flowing down the steep main road to the temple, enameled thermoses in hand and silk blouses of every color flashing as the crowd moved. Although the Dalai Lama's birthday had actually taken place a week earlier, he had been away from Dharamsala at that time, so the celebrations were being repeated to welcome him home. According to the astrologers, the past year had been a particularly vulnerable one for His Holiness, and the relief that he had made it through a potentially difficult time without illness or misfortune was palpable. We bought *sha palay* (meat pies) from the students at the Dialectics Institute near the gate of the temple and squeezed our way up onto a roof, where we had a good view of the courtyard and the cheerful crowd. Throughout the morning, group after group presented traditional songs and dances to the Dalai Lama, who sat smiling on the temple's balcony: school children, village associations, new arrivals, TIPA artistes, Gaddi villagers, and others honored the leader with their musical offerings, and official speech making was, uncharacteristically, kept to a minimum. At the end of the program, the Dalai Lama returned to his residence across the courtyard, and I scrambled down from the roof to help the Yaks quickly set up their equipment on the temple steps before the crowd had a chance to disappear.

Paljor greeted the crowd, whose members seemed very happy to have an excuse to extend the festivities, with a hearty *"Tashi delek!"* He dedicated the performance to the Dalai Lama and moved right into "Trungkar," a long-life prayer for His Holiness. We played it joyfully, loud and clear, with the hope that the Dalai Lama might hear it from his nearby palace:

From the land of Tsongkapa in the east.
Among the mountains of Amdo,

Figure 23. The Yak Band performing at Dharamsala's main temple in celebration of the Dalai Lama's sixtieth birthday.

> From Takster, the land of God,
> The reincarnation of His Holiness, Gyalwa Rinpoche, was born.
> In the Iron Dragon year,
> He was placed on the Golden Throne.
> The sun of happiness in the land of snows
> From that time shone once again!

There had been drizzles all morning, but moments after we began playing, it started to rain and then to pour. In retrospect, I realize that it never occurred to us to stop playing, and no one in the audience ran away. Those of us not singing were laughing out loud at the scene. The long-awaited monsoon had suddenly begun, instantly relieving the dense humidity that had enveloped the area for weeks. Umbrellas of all colors popped open everywhere, and soon the courtyard and surrounding roofs were entirely canopied. Some older *amala*, small children, and boy monks scurried up the temple steps and joined us under the upstairs balcony, finding shelter against our amplifiers and behind the drums. Paljor, who hardly seemed to notice the toddlers crawling between his legs and entangling themselves in the microphone cords, sang on:

Figure 24.   Dharamsala concert audience accommodating the start of the 1995 monsoon.

His Holiness the Dalai Lama (the all-protecting, wish-fulfilling gem),
Whatever his life's achievements,
They are for the benefit of Tibetan people and all sentient beings.
Thinking about this, we should all be grateful.
Always remembering this gratitude,
We should strive to fulfill his wishes
In happiness and joy.
Please commemorate the day properly.
May his Holiness live long!
May his achievements flourish!
Next year we will all peacefully
Celebrate his birthday in Tibet!
The birthday that we celebrate today,
May be celebrated hundreds of times!
The happiness that we have today,
May it not set! May it last forever!

We played song after song, resolved to perform every modern Tibetan tune we knew until the crowd either had had enough or had been simply swept away by the deluge. Without discussing it, we all knew that the context and occasion were perfect for the Yak Band's original music, and each song was literally being dusted off and reenergized as it was performed.

The audience, though drenched, was happy, and no calls for Hindi songs shattered the cultural space that had been created over the hours by the celebrants. The ghosts of the Kalachakra were, for the time being, in retreat. I could see the relief on Paljor's face as he played and sang and was sorry that Thubten wasn't with us to see and feel what was happening today in the Tibetan capital-in-exile. Perhaps we ran out of songs, or perhaps Paljor was a little giddy and thought it would be humorously appropriate in the temple setting, but he eventually led the band, without warning, out of our all-Tibetan set list and into "Knockin' on Heaven's Door."

> Mama, take this badge off of me
> I can't use it anymore.
> It's gettin' dark, too dark for me to see
> I feel like I'm knockin' on heaven's door.
> Knock, knock, knockin' on heaven's door.
>
> Knock, knock, knockin' on heaven's door
> Knock, knock, knockin' on heaven's door
> Knock, knock, knockin' on heaven's door

I was already feeling overwhelmed by the happiness of the birthday celebration, the band's renewed spirit, my imminent departure from Dharamsala, and the cool relief of the rains. Adding Dylan's classic to the mix nearly undid me. Even without all the associations that had become attached to it during my year in India, it is a powerfully simple song, as music critic Paul Williams has described:

> This is a trance record. It puts you under instantly, I mean instantly, and holds you there lovingly for hours if you just let it play over and over on the phonograph. And if you only hear it once, you'll walk around all day in a half-trance, wondering why the air seems richer and the afternoon light has such an unusual quality. The background voices and the "knock, knock, knockin'" refrain have something to do with this, I'm sure, and the perfect compact imagery of the title and the six short lines (count them) that make up the text of the verses. "Take this badge off of me . . . It's getting dark, too dark to see . . . " Yeah. But mostly what's happening here is that a crack in the universe has opened up. Dylan spotted it lying on a coffee table in the recording studio that day, and picked it up and passed it along to us . . . I am staring with my ears into this gap between worlds now. Time is stopped, as Mr. Dylan promised it would be. And as if I myself were about to die, I feel a kind of comradeship with every one else who has been in this place. It's an astonishing feeling. (1993: 157)

Many things were indeed about to die, but the moment was sweet. The Yak Band would perform a few more times in Dharamsala, but the musicians' persistent artistic and financial insecurity, fear of being misunderstood, and family pressures would finally contribute to the band's final breakup early in 1996. Asterix, the elderly poet-astrologer who penned the lyrics of most of the modern Tibetan songs performed by the Yak Band would soon pass away. And a revered senior lama and two young monks would soon be found murdered in their rooms only footsteps away from where we were performing, opening up a painful investigation of sectarian violence within the Tibetan refugee community.

> Mama, put my guns in the ground.
> I can't shoot them anymore.
> That long black cloud is comin' down.
> I feel like I'm knockin' on heaven's door.
>
> Knock, knock, knockin' on heaven's door
> Knock, knock, knockin' on heaven's door . . .

Thubten once told me it is good to make changes when everyone is *sem karpo* or "white hearted," feeling settled and clean and good. As I played music for the last time with these friends, I felt sure that this was, indeed, the perfect time for me to leave Dharamsala and enter a gap between worlds. The participant in me had finally out-muscled the observer, most rough patches had been muddled through, and the streets were now too muddy to navigate in search of new sounds anyway.

> Knock, knock, knockin' on heaven's door . . .
> Knock, knock—

We jerked to a stop. Shaken from my reveries, I looked at Paljor. Paljor looked at his guitar and shrugged, and Ngodup's drumming stuttered to a halt. *Lo min dook*, a young monk behind me stated matter-of-factly. *No electricity*. The sweet moment fizzled, the celebration had run its course, the soggy crowd dispersed in search of tea and shelter, and we started to pack up.

Conclusion
Echoes, Cycles, and Their Implications

All of us speak of *awda*, "return," but do we mean that literally, or do we mean "we must restore ourselves to ourselves?" . . . But is there any place that fits us, together with our accumulated memories and experiences?

Edward Said

One Sunday in March, during the slow weeks after *Losar* when a reluctance to let go of the holiday season and resume the busy pace demanded by offices, shops, and schools hangs heavy in the air, Tsomo and her husband invited me to an all-day mah-jongg party at their government-owned apartment down the mountain. They had told me to come at 11:00 A.M., so I got there around 1:00. After six months in Dharamsala, I had learned that being two hours late was usually about right for this sort of event. A few women were gathered on the beds in one room with their kids, absent-mindedly flipping through Tsomo's family photographs (including new snaps of "Tsomo as grocery bagger" wearing a black bow tie in front of mountains of citrus fruit at the Fiesta Mart in Austin). Tsomo, home on holiday from the Tibetan resettlement site in Texas, commented now and then but mostly attended to keeping everyone's teacups full.

The men gradually arrived and arranged themselves around the low table in the other room. And I, feeling awkward because of my incomplete understanding of the women's gossip and unsure about getting too involved with the men's gambling, was seated by Tsomo's gracious husband, Phuntsok Namgyal, in a chair near the door frame between the rooms. As a sure indication of both his confusion about what to do with me and his unsurpassable hospitality, he placed both a cup of tea and a glass of strong *chang* on the table at my side. Perched awkwardly in the literal limen, neither bird nor beast, I wondered what I could possibly do with myself all day at this event. So I drank the butter tea, moved on to the homemade beer, and stayed put, having decided that if these people were not embarrassed to have me lurking around the peripheries of their pleasant Sunday, then I wouldn't be embarrassed either. As I sat and watched, I was amused by the thought of a generation of anthropologists avidly working so hard to reject the old stereotypical image of fieldworkers as flies on the wall. On a sleepy afternoon, with a pint of fermented barley water in my belly, the wall was, in fact, a rather comfortable place to be. But soon I began to feel guilty about not making more of an effort to participate in some way in the party, if only by moving in closer to the other guests.

I sat for a brief time with the women, hoping in vain as usual that some-one would introduce me to someone else or ask who I was, while my friend the hostess busied herself in the kitchen out of sight. Perhaps they already knew everything they needed to know about me. Under the pretense of getting more tea, I ended up, as I always eventually did in these situations, settling in cross-legged with the men. They had thrown a plaid wool blan-ket over the table and were well into their second round of *sho* (a Tibetan gambling game), a pinch of snuff balanced by the forces of second nature on yellowed left thumbnails all around. I watched a long game in its en-tirety, happy for the opportunity finally to figure out the rules of when and how to move the small tropical shells and dark, greasy coins from the British Raj worn smooth, even thin, from decades of Tibetan men passing Sunday afternoons in this way. At last, this was something constructive for me to do.

Perhaps it was the *chang* (the foreign guest's conundrum: if my glass is always full, can I have drunk much at all?) or the intensity of my attention to the game for lack of anything else to do, but I soon became completely transfixed by the movements going on in this dim inner room. In turn, each player swirled the die in an oily fruitwood cup in his right hand, let-ting out the high-pitched rhyming puns and pleas that sprinkle from win-dows all over Dharamsala on days like this, followed by a "Slam!" as the cup hit the leather pad upside down, sometimes shifting it enough to reveal corners of one hundred–rupee notes stashed underneath. The gambler's fingers linger for a moment on the bowl's underside as if for extra luck, until he lifts the tip of his index finger and his lefthand neighbor removes the cup, revealing the die. The shells and coins move so rapidly. There's no need to count; it's all visual for them by now. Then hands, coins, voices, slams. Everything was moving in circles. Auspicious circles of shells and coins and snuff in Kodak film canisters traveling around the table, flashes of hands rippling round clockwise. The gradual inching around the tartan table of the always-unclosed circle of game pieces. A circle with no break, no beginning, no end. Like the women's circle dances, which rarely close or exclude, and appear to never enclose. I just melted into the cloud design of

Figure 25.   Arms linked in a traditional circle dance.

the plush carpet I was sitting on, enjoying my *chang*-induced spherical hallucinations again and again until someone finally won the game. I was brought back into the moment by the swoop of a hand pouring the game pieces into an old leather bag and folding up the blanket. Time for lunch.

But during the meal, the circles persisted. The women joined us and ten left hands turned small bowls around and around as right hands kneaded *tsampa* (roasted barley flour) and tea into an edible dough. Pa.la kept pouring tea and *chang,* starting up with the first person again, as soon as the last had been served, politely skipping his own cup, keeping a gap. A cleaver for the fatty thigh on the platter in the middle of the table was passed along. Soon sated on the *churra* (dried cheese) and *sha khampa* (dried yak meat) Tsomo had carried out of Tibet only the week before in hand-sewn canvas sacks, the guests allowed the dishes to be swirled away with tilts of their heads, eyes modestly closed, and the snuff resumed its orbit. I was on the verge of dismissing my experience as absurd, so well trained to be suspicious of the order of such patterns and one's own desire for them, when four guests snorted powder into their noses in a perfect clockwise order, and I burst out laughing.

■   ■   ■

The fundamental belief of Tibetans in the cyclic nature of existence and in its premise, impermanence, significantly shapes and orders their experiences as refugees in many literal and philosophical ways, ranging from firm confidence in the inevitability of eventual return to the homeland to belief in the reincarnation of all sentient beings. For this reason, I have foregrounded this local understanding in this book and used it as a framework on which to hang my observations and analyses. In particular, I chose the theme of echoes to link the idea of cyclicity to this study's focus on music. Various genres of music echo off of one another in the daily lives of Tibetan refugees, as do ideas, habits, and languages. These reverberations are not faithful to their sources, however, with each projection shaping and being shaped by its echo. In this manner, the ways different musics resonate with and against one another for Tibetan refugees reveal both subtle and remarkable changes that have generated tensions and ambiguities in this community-in-exile, despite the profound desire for clear boundaries felt by many Tibetans.

This study of Tibetan identity, community, and culture in exile is intended to contribute to the relatively sparse literature on Tibetan refugees an accessible and well-grounded ethnographic account of the daily experience of extended displacement in a particular place at a particular moment. By writing about the daily lives of Tibetan laypeople living in exile in the mid-to-late 1990s, I have attempted to bring attention to and begin to fill in areas that have not been well represented either in Tibetan Studies, a discipline that—despite recent signs of constructive, self-reflexive critique from within the field—remains largely focused on traditional Buddhist texts and rituals or in the limited literature written thus far by Tibetans themselves. Specifically, using sound as its point of entry into Tibetan refugee life, this book has explored musical tastes and experiences in order to complicate narrow and reified notions of "Tibetan culture" as well as understandings of culture as something that is either preserved (keeping alive a while longer the dream of "Shangri-La") or simply lost. These notions have developed both independently and through a process of mutual reinforcement in Tibetan refugee communities and in academic and popular documentation produced for the most part by Westerners.

Certainly, it is my hope that this book will also be useful for the Tibetans it is about, as a compassionate but critical documentation and analysis of their refugee community's current social and cultural profile, the Tibetan government-in-exile's hegemonic public representation of the group's identity and aspirations, and the less heard and increasingly disparate voices emerging from within the private sphere. Fundamental to achieving this aim has been the investigation of the potential risks of a hyperliteral understanding of the concept of "cultural preservation" that this book opens up. A particular concern of mine has been to grapple with the creation of a canonical understanding of the "rich cultural heritage of Tibet" and the ensuing devaluation or dismissal by many Tibetans of the potential for culturally syncretic or nontraditional forms of expression by young Tibetans in India and Nepal, "new arrivals" from Tibet, and refugees resettled outside South Asia to further those interests that are, in fact, widely shared by many Tibetans (political self-determination, the Buddhist tenets of compassion and nonviolence, and so forth). While the preservation and transmission of traditional Tibetan culture is crucial psychologically, politically, and historically, it is worthwhile seeing what happens to these processes when "tradition" and "culture" are rethought and understood to be the consequences, *as well as* the origins, of contemporary lifestyles, aesthetic forms, values, and ideas. With these thoughts in mind, I hope that this book has underscored the importance of the performing arts, and music especially, as a crucial site where official and personal, old and new, representations of Tibetan culture meet and where different notions of "Tibetan-ness" are being confronted and imagined. Any increase in social and financial support for those interested in dedicating time and energy to the arts will only enhance the heritage of future generations of Tibetans that is being simultaneously preserved *and* created in exile and in the homeland as this is being written.

Moving beyond the specific case of Tibetan refugees, the reader has been provided with stories that get at the heart of current discussions in anthropological and popular forums concerning the relationship between place and culture, as well as debates about the relative influences of local and global constraints and opportunities on identity construction. For example, the popular modern music being made by Tibetans living outside their homeland provides an interesting case study of what happens to culture "on the road," of musical creativity unhooked from a particular geographical place. In fact, the boundaries of cultural practices rarely coincide (and have rarely *ever* coincided) with the lines drawn on geopolitical maps. Refugee culture can, in this sense, be regarded as an extreme example of the very common twenty-first-century experience of living multilocal or mulitcultural, hybrid lives. Considered in the context of this case study, the local/global binary reveals itself to be reductive and, finally, quite unproductive, except as a starting point to deconstruct. What is "local" for teenaged Tibetan refugees raised in North India? Tibetan, Hindi, Nepali, Chinese, and Western sounds have floated around on the Himalayan breezes for stretches of time that encompass the lifetimes of Tibetan teenagers and even their parents or grandparents.

Even just contemplating the wide variety of "Tibetan" sounds being made today and the passionate debates concerning their authenticity and appropriateness goes a long way in challenging any faith in categorically consigning cultural practices to here or there, self or other. Think back on the village drinking songs offered so heartily at weddings by the *chang ma*, the highly choreographed interpretations of traditional songs and dances offered on international stages by the artists at the Tibetan Institute of Performing Arts, the heartfelt independence songs belted out by pilgrims from Lhasa possessing Chinese passports and an ear for Hong Kong pop music, the well-disciplined drummer boys celebrating their school's anniversary, the polished songs performed by Dadon at Carnegie Hall, Nawang Khechog's New Age recordings on the transverse flute, the original compositions of Sonam Tashi and Tashi Dhondup of Chaksam-pa, and the Yak Band's amplified praise songs for the Dalai Lama. Heard in juxtaposition with one another, and in juxtaposition with all the other sounds that contribute to Dharamsala's soundscape, the purity implied in discussions of cultural hybridity, the artistic freedom frequently associated with the exile experience, and the radicalism assumed by discussions of youth culture and campaigns for self-determination go largely unrewarded when sought out in practice, in the field. And yet, for many reasons, some of which have been explored here, a gap, a space, exists between the modern and experimental lives many Tibetan refugees are privately living, and even enjoying, day-to-day and the marginality, aloofness, tradition, and ethnic enclavement embraced by many in the public spheres of their lives. As has been discussed, there are powerful local narratives informing Tibetan refugee understandings of change and innovation as failure, as the unfortunate consequences of refugee life, as polluting consequences of living in the wrong place. This compartmentalization of people and their practices, as represented by the geographical and musical mandalas offered in the introduction, is powerfully reassuring and understandable, to be sure. It is also, however a cognitive strategy, however unconscious, that belies the ambiguity and porosity of boundaries and, ultimately, mutes the echoes that energize individual and community identities. For Western academics or Tibetan refugees themselves to expect things to be otherwise—to privilege and value lives that are (or appear to be) seamlessly noncontradictory—is to ignore the fact that the ways the conditions of marginality and multiculturalism will be experienced in today's world can not be scripted, just as the effect a song—whether frozen in a recording or performed live on stage—will have on a

Figure 26.   Tibetan refugee youth at Chaksam-pa's music camp in Pacifica, California.

listener can never be anticipated or necessarily repeated. That's what music, and this book, are all about. Sounds and places and pleasure and loss. Movement and being moved.

■ ■ ■

Even while larger cycles remain unresolved, smaller cycles do close as surely as new cycles open. The blues-loving Paljor who has never seen his homeland did come to the United States in 1997 and was able to hear the real thing with me at Eli's Mile-High Club in Oakland. For a year, he worked eighty-hour weeks as a busboy in a Chinese restaurant in Virginia, forwarded most of his earnings to his family, but treated himself to his first electric guitar before returning to his job in the Dalai Lama's Security Office in Dharamsala. He returned to the United States in 1999 and, along with his wife, was recently granted political asylum in Canada, where he hopes to start up a new Tibetan band and produce more modern recordings. He expects to bring his three sons over from India soon, finally reuniting their family after several years.

Phuntsok, the bass player, now works as the audio-visual technician at TIPA, touring abroad with the institute's troupe and playing in the Ah-Ka-Ma Band. Thubten bought a periwinkle-blue taxi jeep with his brother and is driving the perilous road between Kalimpong and Gangtok (Sikkim) every day. He worries about the limited future he and his family have to look forward to in this rough, remote area of northeast India and frequently visits local temples to make offerings to Buddha and other deities seeking their blessings in return. Ngodup, the drummer, came to Berkeley on a tourist visa and was recently granted political asylum by the United States. At age thirty, his boyishness is gone—his waist-length hair and a scraggly goatee make him look older, wiser, somehow—but he still likes to be taken care of, often returning home from his job painting houses just in time for dinner so he doesn't have to cook. Tenzin Dolma, the shy school teacher and singer of Hindi songs, was awarded a Fulbright scholarship to get an M.A. in the United States that will help her set up a youth guidance center in Dharamsala.

And hundreds of Tibetan children now live in the United States, as they have gradually joined their parents who resettled here in the early 1990s. They are struggling to find their way linguistically, academically, and socially, often in huge, urban public schools. Their cassette collections of Hindi, Tibetan, and "English" songs offer a profound source of continuity—a familiar soundscape—between their new life here and their early childhoods in refugee camps in South Asia or in Tibet as well as a source of joy to share with their new friends and with one another.

Notes

PREFACE

1. In Tibetan, the honorific syllable *la* is added after names, except when another title is already included in the form of address and in informal situations.

2. The term *Inji*, derived from the word *English*, is used in colloquial Tibetan as a noun to refer to a "Westerner" and as an adjective to describe anything originating in the "West."

INTRODUCTION

1. Composer and scholar R. Murray Schafer coined the term *soundscape* in *The Tuning of the World* (1977) to refer to a given sonic environment. The concept is closely linked to Schafer's interest in "acoustic ecology," or the study of the effects of acoustic environments on the physical responses or behavioral characteristics of creatures living within them, the study of sounds in relationship to life and society. While Schafer's particular aim is to draw attention to imbalances in a given soundscape that may have "unhealthy or inimical effects" (1977: 271) and, in turn, to design healthy sonic environments, I use the term more generally to evoke the ethnographic richness of the aural/sonic dimension of a given field site. I focus here on consciously crafted musical sounds.

2. Each of these musics will be discussed in the following chapters, with the exception of Nepali folk and pop songs. These are, in fact, very popular genres among many Tibetan refugees, but my field research in this area was not extensive enough to warrant a detailed analysis of the appeal and influence of Nepali materials on exilic Tibetan musical culture.

3. Tibetans in Dharamsala generally use the English word *modern* to describe any song written in exile after 1959, regardless of its style. "Modern" songs are being made by Tibetans of all ages and backgrounds living all over the world, both in exile and in Tibet, and will be discussed further in chapters

5 and 6. This book specifically addresses the new Tibetan pop-rock music being made in Dharamsala, but it is informed by my work with Tibetan musicians in the United States, Nepal, and Tibet as well. This is by no means, then, a complete review of the range of contemporary sounds being created by Tibetans, although many of the constraints and opportunities that inform the experiences and compositions of Dharamsala's musicians are relevant throughout the diaspora and in Tibet.

4. Lavie et al. offer the following succinct explanation of Victor Turner's concept of *communitas*: "The term 'communitas' refers to the potential fullness of human encounters, both within and beyond the social group. Human action in its plenitude embraces cruelty and tenderness, rage and compassion. It involves forms of knowing that are at once cognitive, affective, and ethical. Both cerebral and heartfelt, communitas allows thought to shape feeling and feeling to inform thought. In its full plenitude, communitas encompasses the turbulence of human life as well as the warmth of friendly fellow feeling" (1993: 2).

5. See Gilad 1990, Long 1993, Malkki 1995, and Nowak 1984.

6. Along these lines, Arif Dirlik offers an important examination of postcolonial theory and its assumed "universal applicability globally" (1997: 8). We are now, Dirlik suggests, dealing with two separate worlds that are at odds with each other—"the world of cultural criticism and the world of newly reconfigured geopoliticized essentialisms" (1997: 10)—which are, it seems, generated by the same processes.

7. The Tibetan case provides an interesting challenge to this claim, in that, through a process of reification of cultural authority, many Tibetan refugees regard themselves as the true or authentic representatives of Tibet (as opposed to their compatriots still living in the homeland and, presumably, polluted by the influence of the Chinese).

8. Many Tibetan refugees, especially schoolchildren, monks, and nuns receive financial support from individual Western sponsors through either privately or institutionally managed arrangements (see de Voe 1983 and Klieger 1989, 1992).

9. Meg McLagen (1996b, forthcoming) examines the kinds of "willful misunderstandings" that exist between Tibetans and their Western supporters in the activist context. She argues that both groups operate with sets of assumptions, perceptions, constructions of the other that are often incorrect but that serve to advance their mutually shared goal of promoting the Tibetan Cause. In other words, McLagen contends, problematic issues of cultural translation exist among Tibet activists, since there is often an advantage to *not* translating certain cultural categories, practices, and concepts that do not fit or work well with their exile situation. A similar dynamic of "mutual seduction" is described by Vincanne Adams (1996b) in her study of how Sherpas and Westerners mirror each other's desires.

10. See volume 30 (2000) of the journal *Public Culture* for critiques of the "global" as it is constructed in academic discourse.

11. This assumption is, of course, the essential idea behind the anthropologist's time in the field, during which he or she lives as a participant-observer, and the workings of an alien culture (and his or her own culture) are, to some degree, revealed.

12. Lavie et al. admit, though, that Turner risks favoring the liminal as *the* site of cultural innovation (1993: 5). For Turner, "novel configurations of ideas and relations" or "anti-structures" may arise in the liminal realm but are generally left behind when the novice reenters the newly reinstantiated structural realm (Turner 1967: 97). Although I value the dialectical and processual qualities of Turner's model, I find its unidirectional trajectory problematic because of its overly holistic conceptualization of the integrated stage and its lack of attention to the appearance of totally new or even radically changed cultural practices in mundane situations.

13. See Feld 1990, Keil 1975, Roseman 1991, Seeger 1987, among others.

14. See Brenneis 1987, Diehl 1992, Feld 1995, Hebdige 1987, Waterman 1990.

15. Of course, the Chinese have also aggressively harnessed the energy and appeal of Tibetan-style folk performances for their own political ends (see Calkowski 1997 and Samdup 1992).

16. The major exception to this observation is the amount of attention devoted to the music of the African diaspora in the Caribbean, perhaps because this region was the focus of many efforts to transpose understandings of syncretism gained from the study of pidgin and Creole linguistics to other realms of culture, including music.

17. Drawing from the work of Jacques Lacan, Hamid Naficy broadens the childlike experience of exile even further:

> The psychic process involved in the transplantation of an emigre can be analogized to the entry of the child from the Imaginary (homeland) into the Symbolic (exile), which reduces the function of the mother. . . . Thus, through identification with the fixated images of the past, the splitting of the subject in exile (Where do I belong? Where do I stand?) is thwarted as he/she returns to the narcissism of the Imaginary, united with the "mother"land. In this way, during the liminal stage, the exile remains psychologically whole, and home remains partially repressed as a fetish. Through controlling "there" and "then," exile can control "here" and "now." (1991: 102)

This, he claims, is "the impulse to return—of reunion with the object of fetish, the (m)otherland, of regression into the prelapsarian narcissism of childhood" (1991: 107). Renato Rosaldo also writes of the general assumption that learning a second culture replicates learning the first one, a belief that results in the "reinfantalization" of displaced people (1988: 83).

18. There are, of course, exceptions, primarily in the area of education, literacy/language acquisition, and governmental policy/children's rights (cf. Foley 1990, Heath 1983, Schieffelin and Ochs 1986, Stephens 1995).

19. By encouraging a reevaluation of the local value of new or foreign genres, this book is not intended to undermine the importance of continuing the transmission of traditional cultural knowledge from one generation to the next, nor

is this an effort to judge the degree to which traditionally trained performers and schoolteachers have succeeded in their difficult mission to preserve traditional native Tibetan songs and dances and foster a knowledge and love of these genres in young refugees.

20. A landmark indicator of the increasing self-reflexivity of Tibetologists regarding their own role in perpetuating myths about Tibet was the collection of papers (originally published in German as *Mythos Tibet*) that came out of the Seventh Seminar of the International Association for Tibetan Studies held in Gratz in 1995. The collection has recently been translated into English (Dodin and Räther 2001).

21. Contrary to most accounts, Snellgrove and Richardson interestingly attribute Tibet's resistance to Western visitors to nineteenth-century *Chinese* xenophobia, thereby giving it a relatively recent origin (1968: 227).

22. For example, there is a growing literature on Tibetan and Western women's roles in Buddhism (Allione 1984; Aziz 1976, 1989; Havnevik 1989; J. Willis 1987), as well as ethnographic scholarship on religious practices in Tibetan refugee settlements in India (Calkowski 1988, Cantwell 1989, Cech 1987, Schrempf 1997, Ström 1997).

23. These include studies by Canzio (1978), Crossley-Holland (1968), Dorje and Ellingson (1979), Ellingson (1974, 1979abc), Helffer (1979, 1983, 1985, 1994), Kaufmann (1975), Pertl (1992), Scheidegger (1988), and Vandor (1976a, 1976b), among others.

24. What has been published is well summarized by Crossley-Holland in his "State of Research" article (1986). Notable contemporary work on lay music includes Crossley-Holland's own early work on folk song (1967), brief articles on Lhasa street songs by Goldstein (1982) and Samuel (1976), and a handful of publications about Tibetan folk opera (*lhamo*) by Dorjee (1984), Foley and Carter (1988), Snyder (1979) and Yao (1985). Studies of the Sixth Dalai Lama's famous songs (Phuntsok 1990, Sorenson 1988, 1990) and the songs of the saint Milarepa (Heruka 1983) treat earthy materials that interestingly blur the distinctions between the sacred and secular. In addition to the *Asian Music* issue already mentioned, two other collections of articles have been published that include, to date, the most interesting and scholarly work on Tibetan lay music. These are *Soundings in Tibetan Civilization* (1985) edited by Aziz and Kapstein and *Zlos-Gar* (1986) edited by former TIPA director Jamyang Norbu.

25. See Calkowski (1991, 1997), Harris (1999), Klieger (1992, 1997), McGranahan (1996), McLagan (1996b 1997), D. Norbu (1997), Nowak (1984), and Ott-Marti (1971, 1976), among others, for scholarship on Tibetans that moves beyond description to critically address complex anthropological issues.

26. Exceptions include the recent and important work by Vincanne Adams on Tibetan medical theory and women's health issues (1998, 2000, Adams and Dovchin 2000), Melvyn Goldstein on Chinese birth control policy, Tibetan history, nomadic life, and Buddhist practice (1991, 1997, Goldstein and Beall 1990,

Goldstein and Kapstein 1998), Toni Huber on pilgrimage (1999), and P. Christiaan Klieger on tourism (1988).

27. Included in this category would be the classic works by Bell (1928, 1931), Stein (1972), and Waddell (1895), among others.

28. As discussed by McLagen (1996a), computer technologies such as email, websites, conferences, and newsletters have played a crucial role in keeping information from sources other than the Chinese government flowing in and out of Tibet.

1. DHARAMSALA

1. The number of Tibetans living in and around Dharamsala is difficult to estimate because of the fluctuating nature of the refugee population. The figure ten thousand has been circulating for years but is difficult to substantiate. Because the local Indian population has been estimated to be 15,000, the lower Tibetan estimate may be politically informed to downplay the real impact of refugees on the region. The Tibetan government-in-exile's official website estimates that there are 21,000 Tibetans living in the entire state of Himachal Pradesh.

2. The following statement summarizes Grunfeld's take on the Dalai Lama's motives:

> The refugee leadership views itself as a small, embattled entity, fighting the world's lack of interest in helping refugees return to their divinely (as they perceive it) appointed places of rule in Lhasa. Given this attitude, it is not surprising that the leadership expended its major efforts in an attempt to regain power—even risking temporary material deprivation of the people. But it is more complex than that. If the leadership had devoted its efforts to securing a better life for the Tibetans, that probably would have contributed to the erosion of the myth that gives their political existence legitimacy—that they constitute a "government-in-exile," preparing the way for a resumption of power in Tibet one day. In spite of the sacrifice of the well-being of the Tibetan community, the Dalai Lama remains remarkably popular. (1987: 205)

3. Toni Huber (1997) offers an interesting discussion of the strategic development by the Tibetan government-in-exile, Dharamsala intellectuals, and Western supporters of a "Green Tibetan" identity for the past fifteen years in exile, an identity that claims timeless, natural links between Tibetan-ness and ecological consciousness.

4. In a later work, Turner claims further that it is this same "normative communitas" that "constitutes the characteristic social bond among pilgrims and between pilgrims and those who offer them help and hospitality on their holy journey" (1974: 169–70), offering another way of considering the bond between Westerners and Tibetans in Dharamsala.

5. These issues will be explored further in the discussion of social pressures on musicians and local performance dynamics in chapter 5.

2. CONSTRUCTING THE HERITAGE OF TIBET

1. A version of this short piece about Dharamsala's wedding hostesses first appeared in *Chö Yang,* the Tibetan government-in-exile's annual cultural magazine (Diehl 1996).

2. The image of the white crane immediately evokes for Tibetans one of the beloved Sixth Dalai Lama's most famous poems, which he wrote in 1706 when he was being taken away to China by hostile Mongolian forces: "White crane! Lend me your wings. I will not fly far. From Lithang, I shall return." When the Dalai Lama died shortly thereafter, the poem was interpreted as an indication of where his reincarnation could be found.

3. An eminent Tibetan astrologer, the late Jampa Gyaltsen, identified divisiveness as the greatest threat to the Tibetan Cause, stating: "In the calculations, it would seem that the problem is disunity. Given this situation, there is no chance" (quoted in Johnson 1996: 121).

4. de Voe (1983) and Klieger (1989, 1992) thoroughly discuss the historical roots and mutually beneficial dynamics of contemporary Western financial support of Tibetan refugees.

5. See Adams (1996a) for a discussion of karaoke and modernity.

6. While I focus primarily on the ways the paradigm of cultural preservation in exile shapes the ways in which Tibetan-ness is expressed musically (and how this influence is debated within the Tibetan community itself), other published literature seeks to address this issue in other contexts, such as transnational Tibet activism (McLagen 1996b, 1997), Tibetan Buddhism and the West (Lopez 1998, Schell 2000), and discussions of imagining Tibetan nation-ness (Venturino 1997), to name just a few.

7. By "lived experience," I refer to a level of incorporation or embodiment that recalls folklorist Dell Hymes's distinction between "knowledge what" and "knowledge how" (1981: 132).

8. In his preface, the editor of *Resistance and Reform in Tibet* articulates a parallel and related trend in scholarship on Tibet itself: "It became clearer that this new Tibet was a society with its own distinctive character and evolution, matching neither the descriptions of new China provided by Sinologists nor the studies of earlier Tibetologists. There was little I could find in Western academic literature which sought to describe that society as it was then developing" (Barnett 1994: ix).

9. Jeanette Snyder explains that, according to Tibetan scientific theory, the *dögar rignay* comprise one of the five specific sciences (*rignay chungba nga*) included within a larger grouping of five inclusive sciences (*rignay chewa nga*) (1979: 35–37).

10. I emphasize that these strands of expression (public/private, formal/informal, official/personal, self-conscious/spontaneous) are, in fact, only separable as an intellectual exercise for methodological clarity, a porous set of dichotomies to be kept in mind as such. It is the dialectic between these pairs and among these spheres that interests me, particularly the potential for opposi-

tional and private narratives to be heard, articulated, or even imagined in a situation where the hegemonic, public voice is literally divine. (The Dalai Lama is believed to be the reincarnation of *Chenrezig* [in Sanskrit, *Avalokiteshvara*], the god of compassion. He is, then, a bodhisattva, or one who has attained enlightenment but has voluntarily postponed his own entrance into nirvana to help others release themselves from the cycle of rebirth and suffering [samsara] here on earth.) Despite the Dalai Lama's efforts to encourage critical self-consciousness among Tibetan refugees and to decenter himself politically, there is a clear reluctance in the community to articulate, perhaps even to imagine, alternatives to public discourses, since these are automatically associated with His Holiness. Who, one may ask, is dominating whom, when the "people" refuse to stop consenting to an authoritative figure who is attempting to extract himself from politics? The few outspoken oppositional voices in Dharamsala are, in fact, often a vanguard of the Dalai Lama's own aspirations for a politically open society, and their frustration is directed more specifically at the government-in-exile's bureaucrats, who, many claim, tend to play it safe rather than push for reforms.

11. For Gramsci, *common sense* is a collective noun that includes a kind of knowledge halfway between folklore and the philosophic or scientific thinking of experts (1971: 326).

12. See Hobsbawm and Ranger 1983, Wagner 1981, R. Williams 1977, among others.

13. Although I won't discuss it in detail here, the recent establishment of the Academy of Tibetan Culture at Norbulinka Institute near Dharamsala in October 1997 should be mentioned. The academy offers a six-year course in traditional Tibetan studies (philosophy, poetry, literature, and so on) aimed at giving Tibetan students the opportunity to "develop a sound knowledge of their cultural heritage and the ability to place it in global context" (www.tibet.net/eng/norling/academy).

14. In preparation for this event, research teams of residents from each dormitory at TIPA are sent out to other Tibetan settlements in search of old songs and dances no one has heard before. Once the material is recorded, the students return to Dharamsala and rehearse in total secrecy, often in the forest. When I was there, two research teams had planned independently to visit Dekyi Ling, a settlement with many old refugees near Dehra Dun, but they ended up traveling there on the same bus, creating awkward competition for fresh sources of traditional materials.

15. In 1991, Marcia Calkowski described TIPA's troupe as the world's "only professional troupe presenting traditional Tibetan opera" (1991: 646), implying that although *lhamo* is still being produced in Tibet, it has been so heavily influenced by Chinese aesthetics and vocal styles since the 1950s that only the opera being produced in exile can be described as "traditional." In the past decade, Chaksam-pa, a Tibetan dance and opera company based in San Francisco, has produced excerpts from traditional Tibetan operas as well as one full-length opera in Flagstaff, Arizona, in 1995.

16. In the traditional libretto (see Josayma's 1991 translation), there are no ministers from Nepal. TIPA apparently chose to replace the ministers of the King of Tagzig (now Iran) and the King of Bhata (now Mongolia) with ministers from the more-familiar Nepal and Bhutan, omitting entirely the ministers of the warrior King Gesar, who has no contemporary equal.

17. See Calkowski (1997) for details regarding last-minute revocations of visas in deference to Chinese pressure, heckling by Chinese sympathizers and diplomatic personnel, and "tag-team competition" (1997: 54) between refugee Tibetan and Chinese Tibetan musical troupes.

18. Indeed, an older music teacher who had come to India in the early 1990s told me he was not very impressed with TIPA's traditional performances, his literal words being that TIPA "looked like shit compared to village dances at home." He explained his recently acquired fondness for Hindi films by the fact that they were something really new, really different, for him.

19. Implied in this teacher's perceptions is an interesting understanding of Ladakhis as more authentic and traditional than other ethnic Tibetans (having knowledge of traditions that are unfamiliar and therefore more interesting to judges), just as Ladakh itself is often described as "Little Tibet," the only place on earth to get a sense of what Tibet was like before the Chinese came.

20. The decision in 2000 by the members of Chaksam-pa Tibetan Opera and Dance Company in San Francisco to offer a summer music camp for Tibetan children living in the San Francisco Bay Area provides further testimony to the perceived importance of transmitting traditional cultural knowledge to refugee youth (in this case, receiving basic instruction in music, dance, and *thangka* painting) and to the assumed power of that knowledge to inspire affection for and commitment to the Tibetan cause.

21. There is a growing body of literature, described by Feld as focusing on "how spaces are transformed and 'placed' through human action, and, more crucially, how places embody cultural memories, and hence are substantial sites for understanding the construction of social identities" (1996: 73).

22. Contrary to my findings, Calkowski perceived that "Sinicized" music is "well-received in the exile community as not only 'something new,' but also, 'something from Tibet'" (1997: 56). Aside from releases by the already-mentioned Dadon and the late Tibetan pop star Jampa Tsering, I never heard cassettes by contemporary musicians from Tibet played in public or private settings in Dharamsala, except occasionally by "new arrivals."

3. TAKING REFUGE IN (AND FROM) INDIA

1. Lata Mangeshkar (1929–) has enjoyed a six-decade career as a "playback singer," lending her voice to the heroines of more than two thousand Indian films. Until the 1980s, Mangeshkar was recording two songs a day; she is more selective now and has recently begun to protest the loss in modern times of the poetry and decency that characterized the semiclassical genre she popularized.

2. *Tamasha* means "spectacle" in Hindi.

3. The Three Jewels—which can be roughly glossed as the Buddha himself, his teachings, and the monastic community—are resources for worldly prosperity as well as for the achievement of nirvana or release from the cycle of suffering.

4. There is, in fact, a tendency, particularly in contemporary literary studies, to romanticize both the condition of exile and the relationship between emotional suffering due to personal or political traumas and artistic genius. If a writer does not actually live in voluntary or forced exile, his or her experiences are often likened to those of the exile; indeed, these qualities—separation as desire, perspective as witness, alienation as new being (Seidel 1986: x)—often seem essential in the life of an artist.

5. I make this claim with confidence, despite the results of one of Saklani's survey questions, to which 75 percent of the Tibetan refugees who responded chose "India Only" as their choice of country of domicile (1984: 356). Significantly, *Tibet* was not offered as a choice on the questionnaire, and the conditions under which they might be forced to make such a decision were left unspecified.

6. See Barth (1969) for one of the original studies of the cultural significance of boundaries between ethnic groups.

7. See Avedon 1986, Cayley 1994, Goldstein 1978, Michael 1985, Saklani 1984, Penny-Dimri 1994, von Fürer-Haimendorf 1990, among others.

8. Despite these concessions, the Indian government does not (and has never) recognized the Tibetan government-in-exile as the legitimate ruling body of Tibet itself.

9. To give a sense of the pay scale, in 1995, Paljor, the college-educated guitarist of the Yak Band employee who had been working for the Tibetan government-in-exile for ten years, was earning approximately $50 a month. His wife, who has an M.B.A. and had a more senior position in the government, was being paid slightly less. The rent the couple owed back to the government-in-exile for their family's tiny two-bedroom apartment in *Gangkyi* reclaimed half of their joint income.

10. This is generally true, particularly regarding Tibetan-Indian relations, a fact Goldstein ties in with the Tibetans' concern for racial preservation (1978: 414). There were no married Tibetan-Indian couples in Dharamsala when I lived there, and one Tibetan woman whose romantic involvement with an Indian restaurant owner was public knowledge was clearly stigmatized socially. In contrast, sexual relations, and even marriage, between Tibetans and Westerners are not uncommon in Tibetan communities with a high level of contact between refugees and Western tourists and researchers.

11. In a statement belying her own national allegiance, despite earnest attempts to be objective in her study of Tibetan-Indian relations, sociologist Saklani dismisses the Tibetan perception of dishonesty and corruption in India (internationally renowned phenomena) as an "indirect offshoot of the language barrier and also the mental dazedness of the Tibetan refugees after their first landing into a national-society which was completely different from theirs"

(1984: 360). She further surmises that Indians only *seem* lethargic and lazy compared to the machinelike precision and thoroughness of Chairman Mao's China (1984: 361).

12. Why Westerners are so eager to support Tibetans, and, also important, why Tibetans are so comfortable with receiving this support, is a dynamic that has been elegantly analyzed by Klieger (1989, 1992). Briefly, Klieger builds on de Voe's earlier (1983) doctoral work on the historical patron-client dyad in Tibet to articulate the mutually gratifying financial and spiritual relationship between Tibetan refugees and Western institutional and individual aid givers. He argues that, rather than watering down or ruining Tibetan culture and identity, exposure to Western influences in fact supports the Tibetans' stated goals of continuation of traditional cultural patterns in exile, since foreign capital is precisely what allows the Tibetans to maintain their refugee status and resist assimilation.

13. Many Tibetan refugee families in Dharamsala have live-in help from young (ages seven to fifteen) Indian boys who work as baby-sitters, housekeepers, and cooks. The majority of these boys are not local, having been illegally hired by Tibetan families on pilgrimage or sweater-selling trips on the plains (mostly in Bihar). A family I knew well paid their "boy" five rupees a day (approximately sixteen cents a day, or the cost of a cup of tea in McLeod Ganj). Actually, the boys were not paid directly; rather, they were given several months' wages at once to be handed over to their parents on their occasional visits home.

14. The Indian travel agent who told me about Tibetans fighting was not shocked that Tibetans fought so much but that they did it so publicly. This led to a cultural discussion of varying criminal styles, with the following conclusion: Every kind of people does bad things, but Indians always get caught because everyone in the village knows them, unlike the situation for refugees who can move around. In the United States, he added, criminals can just get on a plane and be far away from trouble quickly.

15. These events have also rendered Saklani's romantic conclusions obsolete, at least in the northern areas of India where Tibetans and Indians are living in close proximity:

> The Indian attitude to the Tibetans appears to be changing over the years and interestingly it could be concluded that on the whole a sympathetic and, in a way, pragmatic attitude has been gradually emerging. The earlier inhibition of "purity-pollution" distinction seems to have weakened over the years and this has given place to a growing realization that the Tibetans should not be treated as aliens or poor relations or unwelcome guests but be trusted with heartfelt sense of fraternity and friendship. (1984: 381)

16. Within moments of meeting one music and dance teacher at the Upper TCV, the Tibetan woman urged her six-year-old daughter to dance for me. I was treated to a Hindi film song, complete with chest thrusting and hip wiggling, which the child's proud mother assured me was a folk song her daughter had picked up from the local Gaddi women.

17. Lothar Lutze borrows the concept of the "aesthetics of identity" from J. M. Lotman (1972), who opposes it to the "aesthetics of opposition" (typical of detective stories that depend upon the reader's ignorance).

18. Steve Derné has analyzed how filmgoing "plays out [Indian] men's concerns about masculinity and modernity" (2000: 3), concluding that films' plots and themes at once allow Indian men to imagine and then reject rebellious and individualistic fantasies about love, family control, economic mobility, and so forth, thereby affirming their Indianness and their privileged place in an oppressive gender hierarchy.

19. Some fundamental restraints are, apparently, still generally respected in Indian films: no incest, a son may never kill his mother, and so on.

20. Peter Manuel emphasizes that the concept of music ownership per se is a relatively "insignificant and recent development in India" (1993: 148), a situation he attributes partly to the lax Indian Copyright Act and partly to the historical emphasis in Indian music on improvisation rather than on original composition, the focus of Western bourgeois musical aesthetics.

21. This aspect of the films is often visually confirmed by the peacemaking role of the group shot typically included at the end of these films. Family prevails.

22. Das Gupta has a different interpretation, however. He asserts that although the opportunities films provide poor Indians to smirk at the wealthy appear empowering, these movies are actually further oppressing the poor precisely by reinforcing their attachments to traditional or antimodern ways and deepening the "schizophrenia" between the advanced Indian middle class and the rest of the population. The Indian cinema has, he says, become an immense "obstacle against the development of a positive attitude towards technical progress, towards a synthesis of tradition with modernity for a future pattern of living" (1981: 7), thereby effectively serving to prevent former Prime Minister Jawaharlal Nehru's dream of an East-West synthesis.

23. Saari's larger argument, which leads us into terrain beyond the scope of this chapter, is that, by allowing viewers to regard "the beautiful as gross and ugly and the simple and the ascetic as dignified," films actually can provide the poor Indian with a "useful crutch in evolving an ideology for survival" (1985: 28).

24. For example, Bakhtin 1984, Irigaray 1985, and Taussig 1993, among others.

25. See Fuss 1994 for a discussion of Bhabha's theory of colonial mimicry.

26. I should mention that the Ah-Ka-Ma Band's attempts to cover Hindi film songs have thus far proved quite disastrous. Less talented rock musicians than the Yaks, they are not able to imitate the original songs well enough to be satisfying, none of the band's singers has Thubten's stage presence, and their "failure" lacks the compensating integrity and musical quality of Tenzin Dolma's interpretations. Audiences therefore freely boo and jeer at Ah-Ka-Ma's attempts, thereby providing a form of catharsis nevertheless.

4. THE WEST AS SURROGATE SHANGRI-LA

1. See, in particular, Bishop (1989, 1993), Dodin and Räther (2001), Lopez (1998), Schell (2000).

2. This is true to the extent that Tibetan scholar Jamyang Norbu has declared that "the New Age treacle is well and truly smothering everything of value in Tibetan culture at present, from the highest tantric initiations to the lowest bass register of Gyudto chants" (1992).

3. Orville Schell (2000) has provided a thorough and entertaining discussion of these films, and Hollywood's fascination with Tibet more generally, in his book *Virtual Tibet*.

4. Klieger (1989) and McLagen (1997) have, for example, well articulated the material interest Tibetans have in confirming the spiritual image projected onto them by Westerners.

5. See Sperling (1992) for a critique of Bishop's theoretical framework and his exclusion of non-Western travel accounts.

6. Recently, another process of Shangri-La-ization has become evident, this time (perhaps surprisingly) in China. An article in the *Asia Times* (Forney 2001) reports that Chinese trendmakers are profiting from a current fad called "Tibet chic" by imitating and marketing Tibetan music, clothing, and symbols, none of which would be tolerated if undertaken by Tibetans themselves. These activities, which Forney describes as being "as tacky as white men in redface doing a rain dance," are fueling Chinese tourism in the Tibet Autonomous Region, despite the government's propagandistic representations of the TAR and its native inhabitants as barbaric and unpatriotic.

7. This lottery did not take place without controversy, and many still feel it was not conducted impartially.

8. This figure is taken from the Tibetan government-in-exile's official website (www.tibet.net).

9. The Dalai Lama consistently offers the same advice to Westerners regarding religious conversion, encouraging people to seek strength and wisdom from their own traditions before becoming Buddhists.

10. At the Dalai Lama's request, because he feared that political activism in the homeland would simply result in a crackdown on innocent Tibetans living in Tibet, this project was reimagined, and the group walked instead from Dharamsala to Delhi. The Dalai Lama assuaged the ambitious group's disappointment by joining them for the first mile of the walk down the mountain from his residence to the offices of the Tibetan government-in-exile, where he blessed each walker and sent them on their way to the Indian capital.

11. Nowak explains that, according to Ortner's classification, root metaphors (originally Victor Turner's term) are key symbols that "operate to sort out experience, to place it in cultural categories, and to help us think about how it all hangs together" (Ortner 1973: 1341).

12. A recent act of overt defiance involved the Tibetan Youth Congress's staging of an extended hunger strike in New Delhi in March 1998, despite the Dalai Lama's stated opposition to this tactic.

13. Tim Brace discusses this phenomenon in his study of youth music in China (1991: 44).

5. MAKING MODERN TIBETAN MUSIC

1. The translated Tibetan lyrics to this song are provided in chapter 6.

2. This song, reputedly inspired by a poem by the Sixth Dalai Lama, was written by Thubten Samdup of TIPA, who wanted to write music that ordinary Tibetans (in particular) could relate to.

3. The important song-writing relationship between the young Tsering Paljor Phupatsang and Professor Ngawang Jinpa is discussed again in the next chapter.

4. The Ah-Ka-Ma Band is named after the three Tibetan letters that appeared on the surface of Lhamo Latso Lake in a vision by the Tibetan regent, a sign that led the official party searching for the reincarnation of Tibet's leader in 1935 to the home village of the current Dalai Lama.

5. In a 1993 interview, the then-director of TIPA's modern music group explained that the "modern" instruments used in the band were relegated to the background of songs not because of conservative views and a desire to push the traditional forward, but because the skill level and knowledge of the modern instruments was much lower than it is on the traditional instruments (Yamada 1993: 53).

6. Calkowski has written that this discrimination causes particular distress for young male opera singers who have devoted their lives to preserving Tibetan culture, apparently the most honorable thing a refugee could do, and yet cannot find marriage partners (1991: 649).

7. Unfortunately, I do not know the context in which this statement was originally made by the Dalai Lama. I came across it on an anonymously made, noncommercial cassette of New Age music and Tibetan chanting, interspersed with inspirational excerpts from speeches by the Dalai Lama, that was circulating among Westerners in Dharamsala.

8. Not surprisingly, perhaps, the abuse is stronger for female singers who draw attention to themselves in public. The reality and potential of women's participation in making modern music—including invisible lines between singing and playing instruments—is a larger issue that deserves further research.

9. Five years later, the open-mike-night idea has been revived by a Western couple living in Dharamsala, providing a setting for what the husband recently described to me as "some of the best jamming I've ever witnessed or been a part of in Asia." The musicians who participate include local Tibetans and visiting *Injis* (especially Israelis), who riff on Hendrix and other favorites. This development does not necessarily indicate a change of attitude in the local community: without the initiative and participation of Westerners, these events would not be taking place.

10. The Kalachakra ("wheel of time") initiation is an elaborate Buddhist empowerment ritual, based on extended contemplation of a mandala whose designs symbolize the teachings of the Buddha.

11. Yauch has established the Milarepa Fund to raise funds and awareness to aid Tibet. He has also produced a number of major rock concerts for the same purpose. The polyphonic chanting of Tibetan monks was incorporated into a hit rap song on their 1994 album *Ill Communication*.

12. After the producers have recovered their expenses, should this ever happen, all profits from the sale of this cassette are to be held in an account in the Yak Band's name, to be used at the discretion of the musicians. (A copy of the cassette can be obtained by sending $7.00 to the International Tibet Independence Movement, PO Box 592, Fishers, Indiana, 46038–0592.)

13. Interesting intellectual challenges are presented for the Western researcher as well when dealing with a new genre of folk music that has been made possible by the global flow of pop and rock musics, challenges that require rethinking elements of her "own" culture and treating them as an integral part of the local or "foreign" culture being studied.

14. Interestingly, the artistic director of TIPA, Lobsang Samden, told me that, in his opinion, a song need only have a Tibetan *yang* (melody) and be sung in Tibetan in order to be a "Tibetan song." The instrumentation, rhythm, speed, and subject matter do not matter, he emphasized. "What makes a melody 'Tibetan'?" I asked. "Your ear knows," he answered frankly.

15. In his study of Jews living in Paris, Boyarin found a similar intensification of fear surrounding changes in the young generation: "Loss of homeland and family is a recurrent theme in Jewish popular memory; but the 'loss' of one's children to a different cultural world, common as it may be, remains in large measure an unalleviated source of pain" (1991: 11).

16. Brace articulated this distinction in his discussion of Chinese nationalism (1991: 51).

17. Quoted from www.amnyemachen.org/about/ami.html.

6. CRAFTING TIBETAN SONG LYRICS

1. These biographical details are supplemented by a profile of Dakton.la in Sandy Johnson's *The Book of Tibetan Elders* (1996: 117–18).

2. He wrote spontaneous verses at other times as well. Leaving my farewell party, Dakton.la shook my hand warmly and handed me a scrap of napkin covered with the following verse in swirling script: "Young peacock who came from the Western land, / Today I met you in the garden of juniper trees. / Please show again your beautiful dance and appearance. / I will meet you very soon and wish you auspicious 'Tashi delek.'"

3. See Sorenson (1990: 13–14) for a detailed historical description of meter in Tibetan poetry.

4. The *jolmo* is a songbird with a very sweet voice that is common around Lhasa.

5. Local intellectual and emotional interpretations of modern Tibetan song lyrics in turn deeply inform local understandings of Hindi and English song lyrics, as has been discussed in chapters 3 and 4, respectively.

6. See Venturino (1995) for a discussion of the Amnye Machen Institute's World Literature Translation Project, which serves to "extend the range of Tibetan contact with foreign cultures and their respective ideals, sociopolitical systems, and scientific achievements" (1995: 159). Unfortunately, Venturino does not address the issue of audience and readership, that is, how many Tibetan refugees have actually read (or even would be able to read) the Tibetan versions of Thomas Paine's *Common Sense* or George Orwell's *Animal Farm* now available. See Amnye Machen's website (www.amnyemachen.org) for detailed information about the group's projects.

7. Because of the religious orientation of most Tibetan Studies programs in the United States, language students in this country are generally taught *oo chen*, the assumption being that one studies Tibetan in order to read Buddhist texts, not to talk with or write to Tibetans.

8. Efforts to transcribe our recordings of elderly *amala* and *pala* singing traditional songs nearly drove Lhanzom and me mad. We finally gave up and sought assistance from one of the Dalai Lama's personal translators, a young *geshe* (Ph.D. equivalent in Buddhist Studies) with an interest in folk culture. Even Lhaktor.la made little headway with the rustic lyrics and accents, handing my notebook back with stern advice: "Keila, there are so many songs out there. If some are just too hard to understand, just toss them out!"

9. This debate has been focused recently on the "Tibetanization" program at the TCV, a systematic preservation effort to use Tibetan as the medium of primary education instead of English. For a number of years, the Education Development Resource Center at the Upper TCV in Dharamsala has been creating and publishing new textbooks in Tibetan. The first obstacle to incorporating these new materials was that young TCV teachers, themselves the product of the former Hindi or English medium curriculum, had to be taught how to write Tibetan. After Class VI, Tibetan students in India must take standardized Indian exams, so Hindi and English skills are crucial after that stage. This required trilingualism is the main reason advanced training in written Tibetan is not possible in the lay schools.

10. The common appearance of "high" Tibetan in unexpected places was exemplified for me after I obtained a Tibetan program for my computer at the Library of Tibetan Works and Archives in Dharamsala. The monk teaching me how to convert the keyboard to Tibetan script handed me a typing exercise, something akin to "The quick brown fox jumped over the lazy dog" in that it used every letter on the keyboard. For some reason, a rough English translation of the exercise was provided below the Tibetan version, and it read as follows: "Otherwise, the uncontaminated would arise from the contaminated, the transcendental from the mundane, a buddha from a living being, a holy person from an alienated individual, and so forth. It would never happen like that."

11. Ellingson (1979a) describes *dbyangs* (Sanskrit: *svata*) as a kind of monastic vocal melody based on subtle vowel modifications, changing contours of sounds, rather than scales of discretely separated pitches.

12. According to the Tibetan government-in-exile's official website (www.tibet.net), 25 percent of Tibetans living in Tibet today are literate in Tibetan.

13. Avedon's observation recalls the comments of Jamyang Norbu, one of the founders of the Amnye Machen Institute, quoted earlier in my discussion of Chinese "sound values" in chapter 2.

14. Discussing the explosion of national forms of popular and rock music in small countries all over the world in the late 1960s and early 1970s, Wallis and Malm note: "Singing in one's own language or dialect was a significant change here, since it introduced a new communicative element between performer and listener" (1984: 303).

15. Given the uneven and complex status of the written language in this refugee community, it has been interesting to observe the development of a multilingual language for letter writing between the one thousand Tibetan families who immigrated to the United States in 1990 and their relatives in South Asia.

16. While Frith discusses the use of "recruiting symbols" as both a folk norm (in the sense that "popular" music expresses shared experiences) and as a commercial ploy (based on assumptions of the pleasure of shared consumption), at this stage in the development of Tibetan music, the latter is not a significant motivating factor in the creation of songs. Another description of a similar process of "recruiting" audiences is described in an article on Hindi films as a "correspondence-aesthetique"—matching sounds/music to filmic fact, often using classical raga-rasa theory—by means of which filmmakers exploit association clusters to trigger "stock responses" from viewers (Ranade 1980: 9).

17. I use the verb *to consume* in this context as Feld does; that is, to "socially [interpret] as meaningfully structured, produced, performed, and displayed by varieties of prepared, invested, or otherwise historically situated actors" (1984: 1).

18. This song was performed for me by Ugyen Choedon, a senior music teacher at the Upper TCV. She wrote the music, and Mr. Kusang Paljor wrote the lyrics when he was employed by the government-in-exile's Security Department.

19. See chapter 2 for further discussion of the political and cultural dimensions of such school events.

20. *Phyagna padmo,* or "the one with a lotus in his hand," is another name for *Chenrezig,* the god of compassion of whom the Dalai Lama is considered to be a reincarnation.

21. Tenzin Gyatso is the Fourteenth Dalai Lama's personal name.

22. The lyrics for "Compassionate Holder of the Lotus" were written by Tseden Dorje and S. G. Gyatso.

23. Interestingly, however, the most recent cassette of modern Tibetan songs produced by Tashi Dhondup, a former TIPA artist now living and performing in California, is titled *Tibetan Songs of Love and Freedom* and in-

cludes a number of original Tibetan love songs. That this opening up of the modern song genre to less obviously political material (and to a variety of musical innovations) should happen in "double exile," rather than in Dharamsala, is a significant reminder that the conservative Tibetan capital-in-exile does not always represent the wider diaspora.

24. A journal of poetry written in English by Tibetan youth, titled *Lotus Fields, Fresh Winds,* enjoyed a brief (three-volume) life in Dharamsala between 1978 and 1980.

25. At a time when the Yak Band was struggling to keep its act together because of personal and financial difficulties, "Uncle" (the brother of the Yak Band's manager, who had been left in charge of the band's affairs during this time) complained to me that the band had failed in its mission to create "popular Tibetan music." "Our songs aren't popular," he told me. "You just never hear someone singing the words to themselves as they wander down the street."

26. In my conversations with Professor Jinpa, it was revealed that Paljor.la had never informed his mentor that he intended to record his original songs. Jinpa.la heard about the cassette from a friend long after it had been released. "The truth will prevail!" he declared, after I inquired whether he was bothered by his involuntary anonymity.

7. CONCERTS THAT RUPTURE AND BOND

1. My experiences and observations at Mundgod also suggest that the intra- and intergroup tensions I discuss throughout this book are not phenomena unique to Dharamsala, although they are surely magnified in the capital-in-exile.

2. For detailed historical background, practical advice, and philosophical commentary concerning the Kalachakra ceremony, see Berzin 1997 and Hopkins 1999.

3. It is a very common practice among Tibetans to have a *mo* divination ceremony performed by a religious authority before making or committing to important decisions.

4. Inseparable from images of the stars who sing them and the theatrical dances these idols perform, Hindi film songs are, in every sense of the word, spectacular. This fact certainly accounts in large part for their successful transposition into local staged performances, in contrast with modern Tibetan songs, which are delivered entirely without theatrics.

5. The boxes became a symbol of the tour's failure as well as a physical albatross. Having to lug eight huge boxes of unsold tapes all the way back to Dharamsala added insult to injury after all the difficulties the band had endured. More than once, band members expressed disappointment that the eminent lama who had performed the *mo* divination had advised them so wrongly to produce five thousand rather than two thousand copies of the cassette.

6. I was very amused to learn, two years after my fieldwork, that Bob Dylan himself performed "Knockin' on Heaven's Door" for Pope John Paul II during a live concert in Bologna, Italy. "It's the stuff of which legends are made," the *New York Times* reported. "The rebel who's been knock, knock, knocking on heaven's door meeting the man with the keys to the kingdom" (Associated Press 1997: A3).

Glossary

amala.	Mother.
bak.	Mah-jongg.
chang.	Barley beer.
chang ma.	Wedding hostesses (literally, "beer women").
chuba.	Traditional Tibetan dress.
dranyen.	Six-stringed Tibetan lute.
filmi geet.	Hindi film songs.
gyu mang.	Tibetan hammered dulcimer.
Inji.	Western or Westerner.
khata.	White ceremonial blessing scarf.
kuli.	Laborer or porter.
lhamo (or *achay lhamo*).	Traditional Tibetan opera.
Losar.	Tibetan New Year.
mo.	Divination ceremony.
pala.	Father.
puja.	Religious ceremony.
rangzen.	Independence or self-rule.
sho.	Tibetan dice game.
Tashi delek.	Tibetan greeting.

Bibliography

Abrahams, Roger
　1976　　　Genre Theory and Folkloristics. *Studia Fennica* 20: 13–19.
Adams, Vincanne
　1996a　　Karaoke as Modern Lhasa, Tibet: Western Encounters with Cultural Politics. *Cultural Anthropology* 11 (4): 510–46.
　1996b　　*Tigers of the Snow and Other Virtual Sherpas: An Ethnography of Himalayan Encounters.* Princeton: Princeton University Press.
　1998　　　Suffering the Winds of Lhasa: Human Rights, Cultural Difference, and Humanism. *Tibet Medical Anthropology Quarterly* 11 (2): 1–28.
　2000　　　Particularizing Modernity: Tibetan Medical Theorizing of Women's Health in Lhasa Tibet. In *Healing Powers and Modernity,* edited by Linda Connor and Geoffrey Samuel, pp. 222–46. Gordon and Breach, Science Publishers.
Adams, Vincanne, and Dashima Dovchin, M.D.
　2000　　　Women's Health in Tibetan Medicine and Tibet's "First" Female Doctor. In *Women's Buddhism, Buddhism's Women,* edited by Ellison Findly, pp. 433–50. Boston: Wisdom Publications.
Allione, Tsultrim
　1984　　　*Women of Wisdom.* London: Routledge & Kegan Paul.
Appadurai, Arjun
　1990　　　Disjuncture and Difference in the Global Cultural Economy. *Public Culture* 2 (2): 1–24.
Appadurai, Arjun, ed.
　1986　　　Globalization. *Public Culture,* vol. 12, no. 1. Durham: Duke University Press.
Appadurai, Arjun, Frank J. Korom, and Margaret A. Mills, eds.
　1991　　　*Gender, Genre, and Power in South Asian Expressive Traditions.* Philadelphia: University of Pennsylvania Press.

Associated Press
  1997   Dylan Plays for the Pope, the Crowd Goes Wild. *New York Times,* September 28.
Avedon, John
  1986   *In Exile from the Land of Snows.* New York: Vintage Books.
Aziz, Barbara Nimri
  1976   Ani Chodon, Portrait of a Buddhist Nun. *Loka 2, Journal of the Naropa Institute, Boulder,* pp. 43–46. New York: Doubleday.
  1989   Buddhist Nuns. *Natural History* 3: 40–48.
Aziz, Barbara Nimri, and Matthew Kapstein, eds.
  1985   *Soundings in Tibetan Civilization.* Delhi: Manohar.
Bakhtin, Mikhail M.
  1981   Discourse in the Novel. In M. Bakhtin, *The Dialogic Imagination: Four Essays,* edited by M. Holquist, pp. 259–422. Austin: University of Texas Press.
  1984   *Rabelais and His World.* Bloomington: Indiana University Press.
Barnett, Robert, ed.
  1994   *Resistance and Reform in Tibet.* London: Hurst.
Barth, Fredrik
  1969   *Ethnic Groups and Boundaries: The Social Organization of Culture Difference.* Boston: Little, Brown.
Basso, Keith
  1988   "Speaking with Names": Language and Landscape among the Western Apache. *Cultural Anthropology* 3 (2): 99–130.
Bell, Charles
  1928   *People of Tibet.* Oxford: Oxford University Press.
  1931 (1968) *The Religion of Tibet.* New Delhi: Oriental Books Reprint.
Berzin, Alexander
  1997   *Taking the Kalachakra Initiation.* Ithaca: Snow Lion Publications.
Bhabha, Homi K.
  1994   *The Location of Culture.* London and New York: Routledge.
Bhattacharya, Basu
  1984   Dreams and Forebodings. In *Indian Cinema: The Next Decade,* edited by G. Datt, pp. 5–7. Bombay: Indian Film Directors' Association.
Binford, Mira Reym
  1983   *Media Policy as a Catalyst to Creativity: The Role of Government in the Development of India's New Cinema.* Ph.D. dissertation, University of Wisconsin at Madison.
Bishop, Peter
  1989   *The Myth of Shangri-La: Tibet, Travel Writing, and the Western Creation of Sacred Landscape.* London: Athlone Press.
  1993   *Dreams of Power: Tibetan Buddhism and the Western Imagination.* London: Athlone Press.

Bottomley, Gil
1992   *From Another Place: Migration and the Politics of Culture.* Cambridge: Cambridge University Press.

Bourdieu, Pierre
1977   *Outline of a Theory of Practice.* Cambridge: Cambridge University Press.
1984   *Distinction: A Social Critique of the Judgement of Taste.* Cambridge: Harvard University Press.

Boyarin, Jonathan
1991   *Polish Jews in Paris: The Ethnography of Memory.* Bloomington: Indiana University Press.

Brace, Tim
1991   Popular Music in Contemporary Beijing: Modernism and Cultural Identity. *Asian Music* 21 (2): 43–66.

Brenneis, Don
1987   Performing Passions: Aesthetics and Politics in an Occasionally Egalitarian Society. *American Ethnologist* 14 (2): 236–50.

Briggs, Charles L.
1988   *Competence in Performance: The Creativity of Tradition in Mexicano Verbal Art.* Philadelphia: University of Pennsylvania Press.

Buchanan, Donna
1991   *The Bulgarian Folk Orchestra: Cultural Performance, Symbol, and the Construction of National Identity in Socialist Bulgaria.* Ph.D. dissertation, University of Texas at Austin.

Burns, John
1996   Where the Dalai Lama Muses, Sinful Intrudes. *New York Times,* March 21.
1998   Dalai Lama Is All Smiles over Debate. *New York Times,* June 29.

Calkowski, Marcia S.
1988   *Power, Charisma, and Ritual Curing in a Tibetan Community in India.* Ph.D. dissertation, University of British Columbia.
1991   A Day at the Tibetan Opera: Actualized Performance and Spectacular Discourse. *American Anthropologist* 18: 643–57.
1997   The Tibetan Diaspora and the Politics of Performance. In *Tibetan Culture in the Diaspora,* edited by F. J. Korom, pp. 51–58. Vienna: Austrian Academy of Science Press.

Cantwell, Catherine Mary
1989   *An Ethnographic Account of the Religious Practice in a Tibetan Buddhist Refugee Monastery in Northern India.* Ph.D. dissertation, University of Kent at Canterbury.

Canzio, Ricardo O.
1978   *Sakya Pandita's "Treatise on Music" and Its Relevance to Present-Day Tibetan Liturgy.* Ph.D. dissertation, School of Oriental and African Studies, University of London.

Cayley, Vyvyan
1994   *Children of Tibet: An Oral History of the First Tibetans to Grow Up in Exile.* Balmain, Australia: Pearlfisher Publications.
Cech, Krystyna
1987   *The Social and Religious Identity of the Tibetan Bonpos with Special Reference to North-West Himalayan Settlement.* Ph.D. dissertation, University of Oxford.
Chandavarkar, Bhaskar
1976   Film Music and the Classical Indian Tradition. In *Film Miscellany,* pp. 108–12. Pune: Film and Television Institute of India.
Chhetri, Ram Bahadur
1990   *Adaptation of Tibetan Refugees in Pokhara, Nepal: A Study of Persistence and Change.* Ph.D. dissertation, University of Hawaii.
Clifford, James
1986   Introduction. In *Writing Culture: The Poetics and Politics of Ethnography,* edited by J. Clifford and G. E. Marcus, pp. 1–26. Berkeley: University of California Press.
1994   Diasporas. *Cultural Anthropology* 9 (3): 302–38.
Cohen, Stanley
1980   *Folk Devils and Moral Panics: The Creation of the Mods and Rockers.* New York: St. Martin's Press.
Connerton, Paul
1989   *How Societies Remember.* Cambridge: Cambridge University Press.
Crossley-Holland, Peter
1967   Form and Style in Tibetan Folksong Melody. *Jahrbuch für Musikalishe Volks und Völkerkunde* 3: 9–69, 109–26.
1968   The Religious Music of Tibet and Its Cultural Background. In *Proceedings of the Centennial Workshop on Ethnomusicology,* edited by P. Crossley-Holland, pp. 79–91. Victoria: Aural History, Provincial Archives.
1986   The State of Research in Tibetan Folk Music. In *Zlos-Gar,* edited by J. Norbu, pp. 105–24. Dharamsala: Library of Tibetan Works and Archives.
Daniel, E. Valentine, and John C. Knudsen, eds.
1995   *Mistrusting Refugees.* Berkeley: University of California Press.
Das Gupta, Chidananda
1981   *Talking about Films.* New Delhi: Orient Longman Limited.
Davis, Fred
1979   *Yearning for Yesterday: A Sociology of Nostalgia.* New York: Free Press.
de Certeau, Michel
1980   On the Oppositional Practices of Everyday Life. *Social Text* 3: 3–43.

de Gerdes, Marta Lucia

1987 *Constructing Kuna Identity through Verbal Art in the Urban Context.* Ph.D. dissertation, University of Texas at Austin.

Derné, Steve

2000 *Movies, Masculinity, and Modernity: An Ethnography of Men's Filmgoing in India.* Westport, CT: Greenwood Press.

de Voe, Dorsh

1983 *Survival of a Refugee Culture: The Longterm Gift Exchange Between Tibetan Refugees and Donors in India.* Ph.D. dissertation, University of California at Berkeley.

1987 Keeping Refugee Status: A Tibetan Perspective. In *People in Upheaval,* edited by S. M. Morgan and E. Colson, pp. 54–65. New York: Center for Migration Studies.

Dhondup, Dhawa

1993 What Do the Lines Say? *Tibetan Review* 28 (5): 14–17.

Dickey, Sara

1993 *Cinema and the Urban Poor in South India.* Cambridge: Cambridge University Press.

Diehl, Keila

1992 *Tempered Steel: The Steel Drum as a Site for Social, Political, and Aesthetic Negotiation in Trinidad.* M.A. thesis, University of Texas at Austin.

1996 The Wedding Hostesses of Central Tibet. *Chö Yang* 7: 102–5. Dharamsala: Department of Religion and Cultural Affairs.

1997 When Tibetan Refugees Rock, Paradigms Roll. In *Constructing Tibetan Culture: Contemporary Perspectives,* edited by F. J. Korom. Quebec: World Heritage Press.

Dirlik, Arif

1997 *The Postcolonial Aura: Third World Criticism in the Age of Global Capitalism.* Boulder, CO: Westview Press.

Dodin, Thierry, and Heinz Räther, eds.

2001 *Imagining Tibet: Perceptions, Projections, and Fantasies.* Boston: Wisdom Publications.

Dorje, Rinjing, and Ter Ellingson

1979 Explanation of the Secret *Gcod da ma ru:* An Exploration of Musical Instrument Symbolism. *Asian Music* 10 (2): 63–91.

Dorjee, Lobsang

1984 Lhamo: The Folk Opera of Tibet. *Tibet Journal* 9 (2): 13–22.

Ellingson, Ter

1974 Music Flight in Tibet. *Asian Music* 2 (1): 3–43.

1979a *Don Rta Dbyangs Gsum:* Tibetan Chant and Melodic Categories. *Asian Music* 10 (2): 112–56.

1979b *Mandala of Sound.* Ph.D. dissertation, University of Wisconsin.

1979c The Mathematics of *Rol Mo. Ethnomusicology* 23 (2): 225–43.

Ellingson, Ter, and Mark Slobin

1979   Introduction. *Asian Music* 10 (2): 1.

Feld, Steven

1984   Communication, Music, and Speech about Music. *Yearbook for Traditional Music* 16: 1–18.

1990   *Sound and Sentiment: Birds, Weeping, Poetics, and Song in Kaluli Expression.* 2nd edition. Philadelphia: University of Pennsylvania Press.

1995   From Schizophonia to Schismogenesis: The Discourses and Practices of World Music and World Beat. In *The Traffic in Culture: Refiguring Art and Anthropology,* edited by G. E. Marcus and F. R. Myers, pp. 96–126. Berkeley: University of California Press.

1996   Waterfalls of Song: An Acoustemology of Place Resounding in Bosavi, Papua New Guinea. In *Senses of Place,* edited by S. Feld and K. H. Basso, pp. 91–135. Santa Fe: School of American Research Press.

Feld, Steven, and Aaron Fox

1994   Music and Language. *Annual Review of Anthropology* 23: 25–53.

Foley, Douglas E.

1990   *Learning Capitalist Culture: Deep in the Heart of Tejas.* Philadelphia: University of Pennsylvania Press.

1995   *The Heartland Chronicles.* Philadelphia: University of Pennsylvania Press.

Foley, Kathy, and M. Joshua Carter

1988   Tibetan Opera Music and Dance from Lhasa: An Interview with Dacidan Duoki and Xiaozhaxi. *The Drama Review: A Journal of Performance Studies* 32 (3): 131–40.

Forbes, Ann Armbrecht

1989   *Settlements of Hope: An Account of Tibetan Refugees in Nepal.* Cambridge, MA: Cultural Survival.

Forman, Harrison

1936   *Through Forbidden Tibet: An Adventure into the Unknown.* London: Jarrolds Publishers.

Forney, Matthew

2001   China Falls for Tibet Chic. *Asia Times,* January 29.

Frith, Simon

1981   *Sound Effects: Youth, Leisure, and the Politics of Rock 'n' Roll.* New York: Pantheon Books.

1987   Towards an Aesthetics of Popular Music. In *Music and Society: The Politics of Composition, Performance, and Reception,* edited by R. Leppert and S. McClary, pp. 133–50. Cambridge: Cambridge University Press.

1988   *Music for Pleasure: Essays in the Sociology of Pop.* Cambridge: Polity Press.

Fuss, Diana
1994   Interior Colonies: Frantz Fanon and the Politics of Identification. *diacritics* 24 (2–3): 20–42.
Geertz, Clifford
1983   Art as a Cultural System. In *Local Knowledge,* pp. 94–120. New York: Basic Books.
Ghatak, Ritwik
1987   *Cinema and I.* Calcutta: Ritwik Memorial Trust.
Giddens, Anthony
1979   *Central Problems in Social Theory.* Berkeley: University of California Press.
1984   *The Constitution of Society.* Berkeley: University of California Press.
Gilad, Lisa
1990   *The Northern Route: An Ethnography of Refugee Experiences.* St. John's, Newfoundland: Institute of Social and Economic Research, Memorial University of Newfoundland.
Gold, Ann Grodzins
1988   *Fruitful Journeys: The Ways of Rajasthani Pilgrims.* Berkeley: University of California Press.
Gold, Peter
1984   *Tibetan Reflections: Life in a Tibetan Refugee Community.* London: Wisdom Books.
1988   *Tibetan Pilgrimage.* Ithaca: Snow Lion Publications.
Goldstein, Melvyn C.
1978   Ethnogenesis and Resource Competition among Tibetan Refugees in South India: A New Face to the Indo-Tibetan Interface. In *Himalayan Anthropology: The Indo-Tibetan Interface,* edited by J. F. Fisher, pp. 395–420. Paris: Mouton.
1982   Lhasa Street Songs: Political and Social Satire in Traditional Tibet. *Tibet Journal* 7 (1–2): 56–66.
1991   China's Birth Control Policy in the Tibet Autonomous Region: Myths and Realities. *Asian Survey* 31 (3): 285–303.
1997   *The Snow Lion and the Dragon: China, Tibet, and the Dalai Lama.* Berkeley: University of California Press.
Goldstein, Melvyn, and Cynthia Beall
1990   *Nomads of Western Tibet: The Survival of a Way of Life.* Berkeley: University of California Press.
Goldstein, Melvyn, and Michael Kapstein, eds.
1998   *Buddhism in Contemporary Tibet: Religious Revival and Cultural Identity.* Berkeley: University of California Press.
Goodman, Michael
1986   *The Last Dalai Lama: A Biography.* Boston: Shambhala.
Gramsci, Antonio
1971   *Selections from the Prison Notebooks.* Edited and translated by Q. Hoare and G. Nowell-Smith. London: Lawrence and Wishart.

Grunfeld, A. Tom
1987   *The Making of Modern Tibet.* London: Zed Books.
Gupta, Akhil, and James Ferguson
1992   Beyond "Culture": Space, Identity, and the Politics of Differ-
            ence. *Cultural Anthropology* 7 (1): 6–23.
Gyatso, Tenzin (Dalai Lama XIV)
1980   *Universal Responsibility and the Good Heart.* Dharamsala: Li-
            brary of Tibetan Works and Archives.
1995   *Dialogues on Universal Responsibility and Education.* With S. K.
            Agrawala. Dharamsala: Library of Tibetan Works and Archives.
Hall, Stuart
1987   Minimal Selves. In *Identity: The Real Me.* ICA Documents 6:
            44–46. London: Institute of Contemporary Arts.
Handler, Richard
1988   *Nationalism and the Politics of Culture in Quebec.* Madison:
            University of Wisconsin Press.
Handler, Richard, and Jocelyn Linnekin
1984   Tradition, Genuine or Spurious. *Journal of American Folklore*
            97 (385): 273–90.
Hannerz, Ulf
1987   The World in Creolization. *Africa* 57 (4): 546–59.
Harrer, Heinrich
1953   *Seven Years in Tibet.* New York: Dutton.
Harris, Clare
1999   *In the Image of Tibet: Tibetan Painting after 1959.* London:
            Reaktion Books.
Havnevik, Hanna
1989   *Tibetan Buddhist Nuns: History, Cultural Norms, and Social
            Reality.* Oslo: Norwegian University Press.
Heath, Shirley Brice
1983   *Ways with Words.* New York: Cambridge University Press.
Hebdige, Dick
1987   *Cut 'n' Mix: Culture, Identity, and Caribbean Music.* New
            York: Methuen.
Helffer, Mireille
1979   Reflexions concernant le chant épique Tibétain. *Asian Music* 10
            (2): 92–111.
1983   Les instruments de musique liés à la practique des tantra,
            d'après un texte de *Kon grol grags pa, 'ja' mtshon snin po.* In
            Contributions on Tibetan Language, History and Culture. Vi-
            enna: Arbeitskreis für Tibetische & Buddhistische Studien,
            Universität Wien.
1985   A Typology of the Tibetan Bell. In *Soundings in Tibetan Civili-
            zation,* edited by B. Nimri and M. Kapstein, pp. 37–41. Delhi:
            Manohar.

1994   *Mchod-rol: Les Instruments de la Musique Tibétaine.* Paris: CNRS/ Editions.

Heruka, Gtsan-smyon, ed.

1983   *Mi lai mgur bum:* The Collected Songs of Spiritual Experience of *Rje-btsun Mi-la-ras-pa.* Gangtok: Sherab Gyaltsen.

Hilton, James

1933 (1990) *Lost Horizon.* Pleasantville, NY: Reader's Digest Association.

Hobsbawm, Eric, and Terence Ranger

1983   *The Invention of Tradition.* Cambridge: Cambridge University Press.

Hopkins, Jeffrey, ed.

1985   *The Kalachakra Tantra: Rite of Initiation for the Stage of Generation: A Commentary on the Text of* Kay-drup Ge-leg-bel-sang-po *by Tenzin Gyatso, the Fourteenth Dalai Lama, and the Text Itself.* Boston: Wisdom Publications.

Huber, Toni

1997   Green Tibetans: A Brief Social History. In *Tibetan Culture in Diaspora,* edited by F. J. Korom, pp. 103–19. Vienna: Austrian Academy of Science Press.

1999   *The Cult of Pure Crystal Mountain: Popular Pilgrimage and Visionary Landscape in Southeast Tibet.* New York: Oxford University Press.

Hymes, Dell

1981   *"In Vain I Tried to Tell You": Essays in Native American Ethnopoetics.* Philadelphia: University of Pennsylvania Press.

Irigaray, Luce

1985   *This Sex Which Is Not One.* Translated by C. Porter and C. Burke. Ithaca: Cornell University Press.

Iyer, Pico

1988   *Video Night in Kathmandu: And Other Reports from the Not-So-Far East.* New York: Alfred A. Knopf.

Jacobson, Calla

1994   Spirituality, Harmony, and Peace: Situating Contemporary Images of Tibet. Unpublished paper.

Jameson, Fredric

1981   *The Political Unconscious: Narrative as a Socially Symbolic Act.* Ithaca: Cornell University Press.

Jäschke, H.

1992 (1881) *A Tibetan English Dictionary.* Delhi: Motilal Benarsidas.

Johnson, Sandy

1996   *The Book of Tibetan Elders: Life Stories and Wisdom from the Great Spiritual Masters of Tibet.* New York: Riverhead Books.

Josayma, Cynthia B., trans.

1991   *Gyasa Belsa: The Story of the Marriage of King Songtsen Gampo of Tibet to the Princesses of China and Nepal.* Dharamsala: Library of Tibetan Works and Archives.

Kaplan, Caren

1987   Deterritorializations: The Rewriting of Home and Exile in Western Feminist Discourse. *Cultural Critique* 6:187–98.

Karanth, Prema

1984   New Cinema in Karnataka. In *Indian Cinema: The Next Decade,* edited by G. Datt, p. 45. Bombay: Indian Film Directors' Association.

Kaufman, Walter

1975   *Tibetan Buddhist Chant.* Bloomington: Indiana University Press.

Keil, Charles

1975   *Tiv Song.* Chicago: University of Chicago Press.

1985   People's Music Comparatively—Style and Stereotype, Class and Hegemony. *Dialectical Anthropology* 10 (1–2): 119–30.

Kirshenblatt-Gimblett, Barbara

1983   Studying Immigrant and Ethnic Folklore. In *Handbook of American Folklore,* edited by R. M. Dorson, pp. 39–47. Bloomington: Indiana University Press.

Klieger, P. Christiaan

1988   Tourism and Nationalism in Tibet. *Tibet Bulletin* 19 (2): 6–10.

1989   *Accomplishing Tibetan Identity: The Constitution of a National Consciousness.* Ph.D. dissertation, University of Hawaii.

1992   *Tibetan Nationalism: The Role of Patronage in the Accomplishment of a National Identity.* Meerut, India: Archana Publications.

1997   Shangri-La and Hyperreality: A Collision in Tibetan Refugee Expression. In *Tibetan Culture in the Diaspora,* edited by F. J. Korom, pp. 59–68. Vienna: Austrian Academy of Science Press.

Korom, Frank J., ed.

1997a   *Constructing Tibetan Culture: Contemporary Perspectives.* Quebec: World Heritage Press.

1997b   *Tibetan Culture in the Diaspora.* Vienna: Austrian Academy of Science Press.

Lavie, Smadar, Kirin Narayan, and Renato Rosaldo, eds.

1993   *Creativity/Anthropology.* Ithaca: Cornell University Press.

Leppert, Richard, and Susan McClary

1987   *Music and Society: The Politics of Composition, Performance, and Reception.* Cambridge: Cambridge University Press.

Lester, Robert C.

1987   *Buddhism.* San Francisco: Harper & Row.

Lhalungpa, Lobsang P.
    1969   Tibetan Music: Secular and Sacred. *Asian Music* 1 (2): 2–10.
Logotheti, Katerina, and Colwyn Trewarthen
    1989   Child in Society, and Society in Children: The Nature of Basic Trust. In *Societies at Peace: Anthropological Perspectives*, edited by S. Howell and R. Willis, pp. 165–86. London: Routledge.
Long, Lynelleyn D.
    1993   *Ban Vinai: The Refugee Camp*. New York: Columbia University Press.
Lopez, Donald
    1998   *Prisoners of Shangri-La: Tibetan Buddhism and the West*. Chicago: University of Chicago Press.
Lotman, J. M.
    1972   *Die Struktur Literatischer Texte*. Munchen: Fink.
Lutze, Lothar
    1985   From Bharata to Bombay: Change in Continuity in Hindi Film Aesthetics. In *The Hindi Film: Agent and Re-Agent of Cultural Change*, edited by Beatrix Pleiderer and Lothar Lutze, pp. 3–15. New Delhi: Manohar Publications.
Malkki, Liisa H.
    1992   National Geographic: The Rooting of Peoples and the Territorialization of National Identity among Scholars and Refugees. *Cultural Anthropology* 7 (1): 24–44.
    1995   *Purity and Exile: Violence, Memory, and National Cosmology among Hutu Refugees in Tanzania*. Chicago: University of Chicago Press.
Manuel, Peter
    1993   *Cassette Culture: Popular Music and Technology in North India*. Chicago and London: University of Chicago Press.
Marcus, George, and Michael Fischer
    1986   *Anthropology as Cultural Critique: An Experimental Moment in the Human Sciences*. Chicago: University of Chicago Press.
Martin, Bernice
    1979   The Sacralization of Disorder: Symbolism in Rock Music. *Sociological Analysis* 40 (2): 87–124.
McGranahan, Carole
    1996   Miss Tibet, or Tibet Misrepresented? The Trope of Woman-as-Nation in the Struggle for Tibet. In *Beauty Queens on the Global Stage: Gender, Contests, and Power*, edited by C. Cohen, R. Wilk, and B. Stoeltje, pp. 161–84. New York and London: Routledge.
McLagen, Meg
    1996a   Computing for Tibet: Virtual Politics in the Post–Cold War Era. In *Connected: Engagements with Media*, edited by George E. Marcus, pp. 159–94. Chicago: University of Chicago Press.

1996b   *Mobilizing for Tibet: Transnational Politics and Diaspora Culture in the Post–Cold War Era.* Ph.D. dissertation, New York University.

1997   Mystical Visions in Manhattan: Deploying Culture in the Year of Tibet. In *Tibetan Culture in the Diaspora,* edited by F. J. Korom, pp. 69–89. Vienna: Austrian Academy of Science Press. Forthcoming *Mobilizing for Tibet.* Princeton: Princeton University Press.

Michael, Franz

1985   Survival of a Culture: Tibetan Refugees in India. *Asian Survey* 35 (7): 737–44.

Mohan, Ram

1980   Stop the Action, Start the Song. *Cinema Vision* 1 (4): 30–36.

Murdock, Graham

1993   Cultural Studies at the Crossroads. In *Studying Culture: An Introductory Reader,* edited by A. Gray and J. McGuigan, pp. 80–90. London: Edward Arnold.

Nadkarni, Dnyaneshwar

1984   Marathi Cinema Finds Its Future. In *Indian Cinema: The Next Decade,* edited by G. Datt, pp. 40–41. Bombay: Indian Film Directors' Association.

Naficy, Hamid

1991   Exile Discourse and Televisual Fetishization. *Quarterly Review of Film and Video* 13 (1–3): 85–116.

1993   *The Making of Exile Cultures: Iranian Television in Los Angeles.* Minneapolis: University of Minnesota Press.

Nair, P. K.

1976   What Price Entertainment? In *Film Miscellany,* pp. 61–66. Pune: Film and Television Institute of India.

Norbu, Dawa

1997   *Tibet: The Road Ahead.* New Delhi: HarperCollins.

Norbu, Jamyang

1986   The Role of the Performing Arts in Old Tibetan Society. In *Zlos-Gar,* edited by Jamyang Norbu, pp. 1–6. Dharamsala: Library of Tibetan Works and Archives.

1992   Review of Nawang Khechog. *Tibetan Bulletin* (May/June).

Norbu, Jamyang, ed.

1986   *Zlos Gar.* Dharamsala: Library of Tibetan Works and Archives.

Nowak, Margaret

1980   Change and Differentiation in Tibetan Sex Roles: The New Adult Generation in India. In *Tibetan Studies in Honour of Hugh Richardson,* edited by M. Aris and A. S. S. Kyi, pp. 219–25. Warminster, U.K.: Aris and Phillips.

1984   *Tibetan Refugees: Youth and the New Generation of Meaning.* New Brunswick: Rutgers University Press.

Ortner, Sherry
1973 On Key Symbols. *American Anthropologist* 75: 1338–46.
Ott-Marti, Anna Elisabeth
1971 *Tibeter in der Schweiz: Kulturelle Verhaltensweisen im Wan-del.* Erlenbach-Zurich: Eugen Rentsch.
1976 Problems of Tibetan Integration in Switzerland. *Ethnologia Europaea* 9 (1): 43–52.
Palmieri, Richard P.
1970 *The Yak in Tibet and Adjoining Areas: Its Economic Uses, Social Inter-Relationships, and Religious Functions.* M.A. thesis, University of Texas at Austin.
Parsons, Talcott
1975 The Educational and Expressive Revolutions. Lectures given at the London School of Economics and Political Science (March).
Penny-Dimri, Sandra
1994 Conflict Amongst the Tibetans and Indians of North India: Communal Violence and Welfare Dollars. *Australian Journal of Anthropology* 5 (3): 280–93.
Pertl, Brian
1992 Some Observations on the *Dung Chen* of the Nechung Monastery. *Asian Music* 23 (2): 89–96.
Phuntsok, Chabpel Tseten
1990 A Historical Interpretation of the Songs of Tsangyang Gyatso. *Tibet Journal* 15 (3): 19–40.
Popular Memory Group
1980 Popular Memory: Theory, Politics, Method. In *Making Histories: Studies in History-Writing and Politics,* edited by R. Johnson et al., pp. 205–52. London: Hutchinson in association with the Centre for Contemporary Cultural Studies, University of Birmingham.
Powell, Andrew
1992 *Heirs to Tibet: Travels among the Exiles in India.* London: Heinemann.
Ramanujan, A. K.
1991 Toward a Counter-System: Women's Tales. In *Gender, Genre, and Power in South Asian Expressive Traditions,* edited by A. Appadurai, F. J. Korom, and M. A. Mills, pp. 33–55. Philadelphia: University of Pennsylvania Press.
Ramirez-Berg, Charles
1996 Stacking the Hybrid in Robert Rodriguez's *From Dusk to Dawn.* Paper delivered at Theorizing the Hybrid Conference, March 22–24, Austin, TX.
Ranade, Ashok
1980 The Extraordinary Importance of the Indian Film Song. *Cinema Vision* 1 (4): 4–11.

Ray, Satyajit
    1976   *Our Films, Our Lives.* New Delhi: Orient Longman.
Rinki
    1984   A Guessing Game. In *Indian Cinema: The Next Decade,* edited
            by G. Datt, pp. 15–16. Bombay: Indian Film Directors' Associa-
            tion.
Roberts, Donald F., and Peter G. Christenson
    1997   It's Not Only Rock and Roll. *Stanford Today* (November/De-
            cember), p. 43.
Rosaldo, Renato
    1988   Ideology, Place, and People Without Culture. *Cultural Anthro-
            pology* 3 (1): 77–87.
Roseman, Marina
    1991   *Healing Sounds from the Malaysian Rainforest: Temiar Music
            and Medicine.* Berkeley: University of California Press.
Saari, Anil
    1985   Concepts of Aesthetics and Anti-Aesthetics in the Contempo-
            rary Hindi Film. In *The Hindi Film: Agent and Re-Agent
            of Cultural Change,* edited by B. Pfleiderer and L. Lutze,
            pp. 16–28. New Delhi: Manohar Publications.
Sahlins, Marshall
    1985   *Islands of History.* Chicago: University of Chicago Press.
    1990   The Return of the Event, Again. In *Clio in Oceania: Toward a
            Historical Anthropology,* edited by A. Biersack, pp. 37–97.
            Washington, DC: Smithsonian Institute Press.
Said, Edward W.
    1984   The Mind of Winter: Reflections on Life in Exile. *Harper's* 264
            (1612): 49–55.
    1986   *After the Last Sky.* New York: Pantheon Books.
Saklani, Girija
    1984   *The Uprooted Tibetans in India: A Sociological Study of Conti-
            nuity and Change.* New Delhi: Cosmo Publications.
Samdup, Carole
    1992   Lessons of the Zaxi Luge Tibetan Dance Group. *Canada Tibet
            Committee Newsletter* 18 (2).
Samuel, Geoffrey
    1976   Songs of Lhasa. *Ethnomusicology* 20 (3): 407–49.
Sanjek, David
    1996   Book Review of *Rhythm and Resistance: The Political Uses of
            American Popular Music* by Ray Pratt. *Journal of American
            Folklore* 433: 347–49.
Schafer, R. Murray
    1977   *The Tuning of the World.* New York: Alfred A. Knopf.
Scheidegger, David A.
    1988   *Tibetan Ritual Music: A General Survey with Special Refer-
            ence to the Mindroling Tradition.* Rikon: Tibet Institute.

Schell, Orville
    2000   *Virtual Tibet: Searching for Shangri-La from the Himalayas to Hollywood.* New York: Henry Holt.

Schieffelin, Bambi
    1990   *The Give and Take of Everyday Life: Language Socialization of Kaluli Children.* Cambridge: Cambridge University Press.

Schieffelin, B. B., and E. Ochs, eds.
    1986   *Language Socialization Across Cultures.* New York: Cambridge University Press.

Schieffelin, Edward L.
    1993   Performance and the Cultural Construction of Reality: A New Guinea Example. In *Creativity/Anthropology,* edited by S. Lavie et al., pp. 270–95. Ithaca: Cornell University Press.

Schramm, Adelaida Reyes
    1986   Tradition in the Guise of Innovation: Music among a Refugee Population. *Yearbook for Traditional Music* 18: 91–102.
    1989   Music and Tradition: From Native to Adopted Land through the Refugee Experience. *Yearbook for Traditional Music* 32: 25–35.

Schrempf, Mona
    1997   From "Devil Dance" to "World Healing": Some Representations, Perspectives, and Innovations of Contemporary Tibetan Ritual Dances. In *Tibetan Culture in the Diaspora,* edited by F. J. Korom, pp. 90–102. Vienna: Austrian Academy of Science Press.

Seeger, Anthony
    1987   *Why Suya Sing: A Musical Anthropology of an Amazonian People.* New York: Cambridge University Press.

Seidel, Michael
    1986   *Exile and the Narrative Imagination.* New Haven and London: Yale University Press.

Shakya, Tsering
    1996   Exile Creativity Wasted by Tibetan Youth. *Tibetan Bulletin* (January/February).

Sharma, Narendra
    1980   Half a Century of Song. *Cinema Vision* 1 (4): 57–61.

Shils, Edward
    1971   Tradition. *Comparative Studies in Society and History* 13: 122–59.
    1981   *Tradition.* Chicago: University of Chicago Press.

Slobin, Mark
    1993   *Subcultural Sounds: Micromusics of the West.* Hanover and London: Wesleyan University Press.

Snellgrove, David, and Hugh E. Richardson
    1968   *A Cultural History of Tibet.* New York: Praeger.

Snyder, Jeanette
    1979   A Preliminary Study of the *Lha Mo. Asian Music* 10 (2): 23–62.

Sorenson, Per K.

1988   Tibetan Love Lyrics: The Songs of the Sixth Dalai Lama. *Indo-Iranian Journal* 31 (4): 253–98.

1990   *Divinity Secularized: An Inquiry into the Nature and Form of the Songs Ascribed to the Sixth Dalai Lama.* Vienna: Universität Wien.

Sperling, Elliot

1992   Book Review of *The Myth of Shangri-La: Tibet, Travel Writing, and the Western Creation of Sacred Landscape* by Peter Bishop. *Journal of the American Oriental Society* 112 (2): 350–51.

Stein, Rolf A.

1972   *Tibetan Civilization.* London: Faber and Faber.

Stephens, Sharon, ed.

1995   *Children and the Politics of Culture.* Princeton: Princeton University Press.

Ström, Axel Kristian

1997   Between Tibet and the West: On Traditionality, Modernity, and the Development of Monastic Institutions in the Tibetan Diaspora. In *Tibetan Culture in the Diaspora,* edited by F. J. Korom, pp. 33–50. Vienna: Austrian Academy of Science Press.

Taussig, Michael

1993   *Mimesis and Alterity: A Particular History of the Senses.* New York: Routledge.

Tethong, Rakra

1979   Conversations on Tibetan Musical Tradtions. *Asian Music* 10 (2): 3–22.

Tibet Information Network

1997   Two Children Die in Mountain Escape Bid. Internet News Update (ISSN 1355–3313), February 3.

Todorov, Tzvetan

1990   *Genres in Discourse.* Cambridge: Cambridge University Press.

Tuan, Yi-Fu

1977   *Space and Place: The Perspective of Experience.* Minneapolis: University of Minnesota Press.

Turino, Thomas

1984   The Urban-Mestizo Charango Tradition in Southern Peru: A Statement of Shifting Identity. *Ethnomusicology* 28 (2): 253–69.

1987   *Power Relations, Identity, and Musical Choice: Music in a Peruvian Altiplano Village and among Its Migrants in the Metropolis.* Ph.D. dissertation, University of Texas at Austin.

Turner, Victor

1967   Betwixt and Between: The Liminal Period in Rites of Passage. In *The Forest of Symbols,* pp. 93–111. Ithaca: Cornell University Press.

1969   *The Ritual Process: Structure and Anti-Structure.* Chicago: Aldine Publishing.

1974   *Dramas, Fields, and Metaphors: Symbolic Action in Human Society.* Ithaca and London: Cornell University Press.

van Gennep, Arnold

1908 (1960) *The Rites of Passage.* Translated by M. B. Vizedom and G. L. Caffee. Chicago: University of Chicago Press.

Vandor, Ivan

1976a   *Bouddhisme Tibétain.* Paris: Buchet/Chastel.

1976b   *La Musique du Bouddhisme Tibétain.* Traditions Musicales VII. Paris: Buchet/Chastel.

Venturino, Steven

1995   Translating Tibet's Cultural Dispersion: Solzenitsyn, Paine, and Orwell in Dharamsala. *Diaspora* 4 (2): 153–80.

1997   Reading Negotiations in the Tibetan Diaspora. In *Constructing Tibetan Culture: Contemporary Perspectives,* edited by Frank J. Korom, pp. 98–121. Quebec: World Heritage Press.

von Fürer-Haimendorf, Christoph

1990   *The Renaissance of Tibetan Civilization.* Oracle, AZ: Synergetic Press.

Waddell, L. Austine

1895 (1972) *Tibetan Buddhism with Its Mystic Cults, Symbolism, and Mythology.* New York: Dover Publications.

Wagner, Roy

1981   *The Invention of Culture.* Chicago: University of Chicago Press.

Wallis, Roger, and Krister Malm

1984   *Big Sounds from Small Peoples: The Music Industry in Small Countries.* New York: Pendragon Press.

Wangyal, Tsering

1982   Are Monks Permitted to Let It All Hang Out? *Tibetan Review* 17: 11–12.

Waterman, Christopher

1990   *Jùjú: A Social History and Ethnography of an African Popular Music.* Chicago: University of Chicago Press.

White, Hayden

1980   The Value of Narrativity in the Representation of Reality. In *On Narrative,* edited by W. J. T. Mitchell, pp. 1–23. Chicago: University of Chicago Press.

Whiting, Sam

1996   Concert for Tibet Burns through the Fog. *San Francisco Chronicle,* June 17.

Wicke, Peter

1987   *Rock Music: Culture, Aesthetics and Sociology.* Cambridge: Cambridge University Press.

Williams, Paul
    1993   *Rock and Roll: The 100 Best Singles.* New York: Carroll and Graf Publishers.

Williams, Raymond
    1977   *Marxism and Literature.* Oxford: Oxford University Press.

Willis, Janice D., ed.
    1987   *Feminine Ground: Essays on Women and Tibet.* Ithaca: Snow Lion Publications.

Willis, Paul
    1993   Symbolic Creativity. In *Studying Culture: An Introductory Reader,* edited by A. Gray and J. McGuigan, pp. 206–16. London: Edward Arnold.

Wulff, Helena
    1995   Introducing Youth Culture in Its Own Right: The State of the Art and New Possibilities. In *Youth Culture: A Cross-Cultural Perspective,* edited by V. Amit-Talal and H. Wulff, pp. 1–18. London: Routledge.

Yamada, Kazuyoshi
    1993   Exile on Music Street: An Examination of Modern Tibetan Music in Dharamsala, India. Unpublished Independent Study Project for Students in Training (SIT) program.

Yao, Wang
    1985   Tibetan Operatic Themes. In *Soundings in Tibetan Civilization,* edited by B. N. Aziz and M. Kapstein, pp. 86–96. Delhi: Manohar.

Index

Compositor:	Impressions Book and Journal Services, Inc.
Text:	10/13 Aldus
Display:	Aldus
Printer and Binder:	Friesens Corporation